The People and the Bay

The Nature | History | Society series is devoted to the publication of high-quality scholarship in environmental history and allied fields. Its broad compass is signalled by its title: *nature* because it takes the natural world seriously; *history* because it aims to foster work that has temporal depth; and *society* because its essential concern is with the interface between nature and society, broadly conceived. The series is avowedly interdisciplinary and is open to the work of anthropologists, ecologists, historians, geographers, literary scholars, political scientists, sociologists, and others whose interests resonate with its mandate. It offers a timely outlet for lively, innovative, and well-written work on the interaction of people and nature through time in North America.

General Editor: Graeme Wynn, University of British Columbia

A list of titles in the series appears at the end of the book.

NATURE | HISTORY | SOCIETY
GENERAL EDITOR: GRAEME WYNN

The People and the Bay

A Social and Environmental History of Hamilton Harbour

NANCY B. BOUCHIER AND
KEN CRUIKSHANK

FOREWORD BY GRAEME WYNN

UBC Press • Vancouver • Toronto

23 22 21 20 19 18 17 16 15   5 4 3 2 1

Printed in Canada on FSC-certified ancient-forest-free paper
(100% post-consumer recycled) that is processed chlorine- and acid-free.

___

Library and Archives Canada Cataloguing in Publication

Bouchier, Nancy Barbara, author
    The people and the bay : a social and environmental history of Hamilton
Harbour / Nancy B. Bouchier and Ken Cruikshank ; foreword by Graeme Wynn.

(Nature, history, society)
Includes bibliographical references and index.
Issued in print and electronic formats.
ISBN 978-0-7748-3041-6 (bound). – ISBN 978-0-7748-3042-3 (pbk.). –
ISBN 978-0-7748-3043-0 (pdf). – ISBN 978-0-7748-3044-7 (epub). –
ISBN 978-0-7748-3045-4 (mobi)

    1. Hamilton Harbour (Ont.) – Environmental conditions – History. 2. Hamilton
Harbour (Ont.) – Social conditions. I. Cruikshank, Ken, author II. Wynn, Graeme,
writer of foreword III. Title. IV. Series: Nature, history, society

FC3098.55.B69 2015   971.3'52   C2015-906146-6
                                                                   C2015-906147-4

___

Canada

UBC Press gratefully acknowledges the financial support for our publishing program
of the Government of Canada (through the Canada Book Fund), the Canada Council
for the Arts, and the British Columbia Arts Council.

This book has been published with the help of a grant from the Canadian Federation
for the Humanities and Social Sciences, through the Awards to Scholarly Publications
Program, using funds provided by the Social Sciences and Humanities Research
Council of Canada.

UBC Press
The University of British Columbia
2029 West Mall
Vancouver, BC V6T 1Z2
www.ubcpress.ca

Contents

List of Figures and Tables / vii

Foreword: Down by the Bay / xi
Graeme Wynn

Acknowledgments / xxii

Introduction: Whose Harbour? / 3

1 Civilizing Nature: Community Property Transformed, 1823–95 / 11

2 Conserving Nature: The Education of John William Kerr, 1864–88 / 36

3 Boosting Nature: The Contradictions of Industrial Promotion, 1892–1932 / 55

4 Organizing Nature: The Search for Recreational Order, 1900–30 / 86

5 Planning Nature: The Waterfront Legacy of T.B. McQuesten, 1917–40 / 114

6 Confining Nature: The Bay as Harbour, 1931–59 / 138

7 Unchaining Nature: Gillian Simmons's Backyard, 1958–85 / 171

8 Remediating Nature: Hamilton Harbour as an Area of Concern,
1981–2015 / 197

Conclusion: Choosing Nature / 221

Notes / 230

Note on Sources / 299

Index / 303

Figures and Tables

FIGURES

1 Hamilton Harbour/Burlington Bay, 1909–96 / 14

2 Town of Hamilton, 1842 / 17

3 T.C. Keefer's map detailing Hamilton's water supply, 1856 / 21

4 The opening of the new waterworks, 1860 / 22

5 Horse races on the frozen harbour in celebration of the royal wedding, 1863 / 25

6 Great Western Railway workshops, 1863 / 42

7 A fisherman in repose at Cootes Paradise, n.d. / 44

8 Aerial view of Sherman Inlet, ca. 1919 / 49

9 Men setting up an ice hut for spear fishing, 1909 / 53

10 Factories celebrated in 1892 promotional material / 56

11 Map of Burlington Bay, 1909 / 58

12 Promotional material for Hamilton, 1919 / 59

13 Factories in Hamilton's new industrial district, n.d. / 62

14 National Steel Car plant during the First World War / 67

15 Map of waterfront areas / 80

16 Brightside development amidst busy waterfront industry, 1912 / 82

17 Children swimming in dangerous waters, 1924 / 90

18 Children at the beach, 1892 / 93

19 Souvenir calendar featuring the Royal Hamilton Yacht Club, 1907 / 94

20 Kids in the water along the north shore of the bay at LaSalle Park, 1929 / 96

21 North End kids at the bay, ca. 1930s / 99

22 Kids swimming at the Bay Street Beach, n.d. / 100

23 Noulan Cauchon's infilling plan for Hamilton Harbour, 1917 / 115

24 Jack Miner and Calvin McQuesten, 1926 / 119

25 Pothunters at the Desjardins Canal basin, Dundas, n.d. / 120

26 Colony of boathouses at the Desjardins Canal, 1928 / 124

27 The boathouses of Cootes Paradise, n.d. / 125

28 A smoke-filled sky over Hamilton's old port, 1946 / 126

29 Plan for Hamilton's northwestern entrance, 1929 / 132

30 Advertising the Port of Hamilton's location / 140

31 Annual tonnages for the Port of Hamilton, 1922–50 / 141

32 Stelco's shoreline, 1959 / 142

33 Map showing changes to the harbour's shoreline, 1909– 96 / 144

34 Infilling at Pier 14, 1957 / 146

35 Traffic congestion on Beach Road, 1950s / 158

36 Construction of the Burlington Bay Skyway, 1958 / 159

37 Pier 8, the HMCS Star, and Eastwood Park, 1959 / 161

38 "Give Hamilton's Youth the Swimming Pools They Need!" 1944 / 165

39 West Harbour infill, 1970 / 175

40 "Our Polluted Bay," 1969 / 177

41 "Clear Up Pollution Chop-Chop," 1969 / 179

42a "The Dirt Excavated Here ..." / 181

42b "... Is Dumped in the Middle of This Bay," 1969 / 181

43 "No Trespassing on Hamilton Harbour," n.d. / 183

44 CHOP's "Clean Up Cootes Paradise" Day, 1974 / 189

45 Cleaning Up Cootes Paradise, 1978 / 190

46 Flooding on the Beach Strip, 1973 / 193

47 Pamphlet for Hamilton Harbour Remedial Action Plan, 2002 / 205

48 *The Maple Tree vs the Battery Cases*, 1992 / 207

49 Harbourfront park concept plan, 1992 / 209

50 The Waterfront Trail, 2007 / 210

51 Artificial islands along the Waterfront Trail, 2007 / 211

52 Windermere Basin, 2012 / 217

53 Cormorants and gulls on a human-made island, n.d. / 223

TABLES

1 Occupational profile, selected areas, 1921 / 81

2 Ethnic profile, selected areas, 1921 / 84

3 Stelco waste in Hamilton Harbour, estimated tons per year,
   1912–57 / 148

4 Occupational profile, selected areas, 1945 / 154

5 Ethnic profile, selected areas, 1945 / 155

6 Occupational and family earnings profiles, selected census
   districts, 1971 / 281

7 Ethnic profiles, selected residential areas, 1971 / 281

8 Occupational and family earnings profiles, 1991 / 282

9 Ethnic profiles, selected residential areas, 1991 / 282

Down by the Bay

Graeme Wynn

O NE OF THE FINEST, and yet most unusual, pieces of historical-geographical writing that I know is by poet, writer, and cabinetmaker John Terpstra.[1] It is a wonderfully thoughtful, evocative, and sensitive rumination on "what happens when one person becomes completely enamoured of the landscape, and a particular feature of the landscape, in the city where he lives." That city is Hamilton, Ontario, and the particular landscape feature for which Terpstra declares his love is the "superannuated" sandbar that divides Hamilton Harbour (2,150 hectares) from the marshy 250-hectare extent of Cootes Paradise – a locale that helps to define the western end of Lake Ontario to which historians Nancy Bouchier and Ken Cruikshank direct their own clear-eyed attention in *The People and the Bay.*

When John Graves, the lieutenant-governor of Upper Canada, and Elizabeth Simcoe, his lady, journeyed, in June 1796, across a quiet patch of water (soon to be known as Burlington Bay) sheltered from larger Lake Ontario by a ribbon of sand, they happened upon a prospect that pleased them mightily. By Elizabeth's account, the bay was "full of canoes; the Indians were fishing; we bought some fine salmon of them."[2] The Simcoes' destination, the log home of Henrietta and Richard Beasley, Loyalists from New York and the first settlers at the head of the lake, seemed a "very pretty object" to the lady diarist as she and her husband landed and "walked up the hill from whence is a beautiful view of the lake, with wooded points breaking the line of shore." In her estimation, the hill was "quite like a park, fine turf with large Oak trees dispersed but no underwood." The Beasleys' home was nestled between the bay and the Iroquois Bar, a gravel deposit – once the beach of glacial lake Iroquois – that rises a hundred feet or so above the present level of Lake Ontario. Here the Simcoes stayed overnight, to dine and to enjoy walks in the "park" and along the shore.

Today, most of those contemplating Hamilton Harbour do so more fleetingly than did the Simcoes. Whether they view it from one of the 150,000 vehicles a day crossing the Burlington Bay James N. Allan Skyway, which carries the Queen Elizabeth Way high across the man-made channel that now cuts through the sand bar to link lake and bay, or from the trains and automobiles that follow the six sets of tracks, the six lanes of highway, and the four lanes of secondary road that run the length of the Iroquois Bar, the scenes they behold are vastly different from those the Beasleys knew. Half a century after the Simcoes' visit, the City of Hamilton was incorporated. By 1914, one hundred thousand people lived there, twice as many as at the turn of the century. By 1950, the population had doubled again, and in the 1970s it reached three hundred thousand. When the city was amalgamated with five neighbouring municipalities in 2001, it counted approximately half a million residents.[3]

Commerce, manufacturing, and general economic expansion drove early growth. Then the railway boom of the 1850s spawned new industries. In the late nineteenth century this was known as a go-ahead place, with the first commercial telephone service in Canada and the first telephone exchange in the British Empire. Early in the twentieth century, Hamilton attracted major steel mills and other manufacturing. In the boom years after the Second World War, the city prospered from the production of automobiles, appliances, elevators, and farm equipment. Although the major steel works cut jobs by half late in the twentieth century, manufacturing, service, and other activities helped ameliorate the downturn that reduced much of the heavy-industrial heartland south of the Great Lakes to rustbelt status during these years.[4] In the new millennium, however, manufacturing jobs accounted for a shrinking proportion of Hamilton's labour force (down from 22 to 12 percent in the decade after 2003), and one of the steel plants shuttered its facilities in 2013.[5]

Bald as it is, this simple summary of population growth and economic activity captures a sense of Hamilton's transformation – a transformation that also had dramatic effects, over the course of two centuries, upon the landscape of this region nestled below the Niagara Escarpment. "Clearings in the trees, rail fencing, farms, orchards," these, Terpstra imagines, were what George Hamilton saw after the War of 1812, "when he first thought to arrange this marriage of place and people" that carries his name into the present.[6] First, a few buildings "at a fork in the path materializing into a town." Then the opening of a canal through the outer sandbar, bringing schooners and steamers into the bay and stimulating trade in the new administrative centre of the Gore District. At mid-century, the railway came steaming into town on the bayside of the Iroquois Bar, attracting manufacturers of stoves and farm implements and serving the clothing and sewing machine industries that grew during the American Civil War.

Later in the century, after decades of effort in the cause of progress, that great mantra of the Victorian age, some Ontarians began to count the costs of their devotion by venerating pioneer cemeteries, admiring abandoned farmsteads, and revering watermills silenced by steam power. George Washington Johnson, a Hamilton schoolteacher, tapped into this vein early, and in deeply personal tones, in "When you and I were young, Maggie," a melancholic poem for his ailing love that became a musical hall standard: "The green grove is gone from the hill, Maggie, / Where first the daisies sprung; / The creaking old mill is still, Maggie / Since you and I were young."[7] But though its effects might be lamented, the juggernaut of industrial growth continued its transformation of Hamilton. Steel mills and other industrial plants clustered along the bay, which became a major port. Squeezed between "the Mountain" escarpment and the water, the city spread more or less east-west along the southern edge of the bay and created new space for development by filling inlets and extending the shoreline. Before long, Hamilton became known as Steeltown or Steel Town.[8] Either way, it was a gritty city, its "life, economy and physical environment" – its geography, character, and politics – defined according to a retrospective article in the local newspaper, *The Hamilton Spectator,* by the two steel manufacturing giants that formed the backbone of its industrial economy.[9]

Of course, there was more to Hamilton than this. Communities and societies are complex multifaceted entities; human-environment relations are intricate ever-shifting engagements; and though simple nomenclatures (Steeltown; "gritty city") may identify a telling or essential element of a place, they rarely capture the full diversity of land and life as they are intertwined and understood in situ each and every day. Both John Terpstra's *Falling into Place* and Nancy Bouchier and Ken Cruikshank's *The People and the Bay* help to complicate and advance our appreciation of these convoluted realities, but they do so in remarkably different ways that, taken together, serve to illuminate variant forms of scholarly practice, heighten appreciation of the ways in which people know and shape places, offer important insights into various modes of human engagement with nature, and convey a good deal of information about that particular corner of

Ontario known to its first European settlers as Head-of-the-Lake. In all of this, Terpstra's work provides a revealing counterpoint to that developed in the pages that follow.

Falling into Place is a marvellous meditation on meaning in the landscape. It ranges more widely across time than does *The People and the Bay* (which focuses on the last 150 years) to hint at the Indigenous Attiwandaron presence at the head of the lake before the arrival of Europeans and to discuss, in detail, the scene at the turn of the third millennium; spatially, its focus is rather narrower than that of *The People and the Bay,* on the six kilometres of the Iroquois Bar and the areas immediately adjacent to it (although there are excursions up the escarpment to Niagara Falls and to the author's ancestral home in Friesland). *Falling into Place* is richly historical but it eschews chronology; it is profoundly geographical but (despite its four maps) it responds to, rather than charts, the landscape. To turn Terpstra's pages is to be carried on a deeply personal exploration in the company of a writer reflexive enough to wonder whether the immigrant experience impels one to understand the landscape in order to explain one's presence within it, and sensitive enough to know that he is part of the story.

In Terpstra's eloquent and imaginative prose, the very landscape is personalized, even occasionally anthropomorphized. He encourages readers to imagine the Niagara Escarpment as a giant asleep on his left arm, "which reaches out diagonally across a beach. The upper half of the arm rests on the sand, where much smaller figures have constructed houses and buildings, a city, tying down this Gulliver with bands of asphalt. From elbow to hand the arm lies half-submerged in water." This is that section of the Iroquois Bar dividing Cootes Paradise from the bay. Initially, the imagined fist is clenched as the outlet of the marsh curves between its knuckles and the far shore of the lake. But then railway builders see this arm as a useful route into town. They bridge the narrow channel with thirty metres of fill, and it is "as though the clenched fist of the sleeping giant had released his little finger, which now reached to the opposite shore." A few years later, there was another railway and another earth bridge: "this time the attachment was an index finger." And so the outlet channel was cut off and reduced to a pond between two earthen dams.[10]

Terpstra early declares his love for the Iroquois Bar, and his courtship of its history is deeply sensuous. He caresses and probes his chosen landscape, fondly marking each rise and declivity. Glacial landscapes, he says, "have a low-key, inviting energy that draws you into their features, folds and cleavages, their rolling roundnesses, into their meetings of land and water."[11] After two hundred years of settlement and city growth, the contours of nature are no longer as obvious as they once were. But to those who know this body of land, an approach to the top of the bar is signalled by an incline sufficient to raise "the body temperatures of walkers and cyclists" though barely steep enough to require drivers cocooned in automobiles to exert extra pressure on the accelerator.[12]

Elsewhere, as he contemplated the configuration of the Iroquois Bar beneath the property lines and infrastructure of modern-day development, Terpstra realized that the topography "still curved and climbed." Its lines "remained as true as they could to where they were first drawn."[13] There was a process at work here. The landscape is modelled and remodelled through time; it is a palimpsest, an object made for one purpose and then used for another, and another, so that earlier forms are variously obscured and obliterated as new (land)marks are etched over and upon those of preceding generations. In describing this process, Terpstra comes close to understanding landscape change as "sequent occupance," a phrase coined by geographer Derwent Whittlesey, who insisted that human settlement carried within itself the seeds of its own transformation, and that successive stages of occupation could be identified in the landscape.[14] In Terpstra's formulation, as change is layered upon change, "the changes that occur in one generation overlap the changes of the preceding generation in a kind of civic sedimentary layering. Together these layers become part of the "natural" landscape for the next generation, while the original lay of the land is secreted away underneath."[15]

Coupling this insight with his memory of the way his grandmother embodied generations of life in Friesland, Terpstra concludes that "the earth remembers." His book is, in one important sense, a concerted attempt to recover that memory. Forced to grapple with the challenge of understanding change in space and time together, he adopts what historical geographers once formalized as the retrospective method, by working backwards from the present as one might peel back the layers of an onion to discover the origins of current patterns in the landscape.[16] But *Falling into Place* is neither a study in sequent occupance nor an exemplar of that retrospective method. It achieves more than most work in these disciplinary veins precisely because Terpstra proceeds unencumbered by the baggage of formal methodology and seeks personal meaning in his quest to know the landscape. His is a poetic rumination:

> The earth remembers. What a thought. The battered earth remembers; on top of which, I shared that memory. By virtue of birth … and choice of residence, I was inextricably part of the land-filling, refuse-dumping,

train-riding, steel-making, car-driving family of earthlings who dwelt here, but by virtue of what a few old maps in the library downtown had shown me, and what I had pieced together driving around, awake to the shapes surrounding me, I was also part of this other relation.[17]

Years ago, geographer Phil Wagner pointed to the difficulties involved in understanding places and landscapes, difficulties that he attributed to the fact that "place, person, time and act form an indivisible unity."[18] Terpstra comes close to weaving this whole cloth as he tells of the ways in which his loved landscape "reveals itself to me over time in a kind of slow, affectionate undressing."[19]

The People and the Bay is a markedly different book – and its achievement is clarified by comparing it with *Falling into Place*. Where Terpstra essays "a kind of bioregional love story," Bouchier and Cruikshank shape their work to the more orthodox scholarly lasts of environmental and social history.[20] Largely eschewing the imaginative detours and sensuous engagement with the earth that distinguish Terpstra's pages, they focus on the people of Hamilton and their use of the bay to gain perspective on "the environmental changes associated with the modern processes of urbanization and modernization." Their story begins in the middle decades of the nineteenth century and unfolds in tight chronological lockstep as the nature of the bay is civilized and conserved (to 1893), boosted, organized, and planned (1893–1940), confined (1931–59), unchained (1958–85), and remediated (1981–2015). With clear thematic emphases, these eight chapters focus both the social and the environmental history of Hamilton through the prism of its residents' connections with the adjacent water. Resembling the numerous, charming bird's-eye views of the city sketched from the escarpment during the nineteenth century, this book offers a panoramic view of Hamilton and its harbour, although each chapter is drawn from a slightly different vantage point to emphasize and illuminate Hamiltonians' shifting recreational, residential, commercial, industrial, medical, and ecological interests in the aquatic/lacustrine environment.

To elaborate: *The People and the Bay* is, clearly, an environmental history, in that it pays close attention to the ways that people have defined "what a resource is, which sorts of behavior may be environmentally degrading and ought to be prohibited," and the ways in which they generally chose "the ends to which nature is put."[21] The first parts of the book trace the establishment of the city beside the bay and the attitudes and practices that shaped early interactions between people and the harbour environment; the second set of chapters examines the intensifying exploitation of the bay and shoreline, and efforts to manage these developments and their consequences through the late nineteenth and early twentieth centuries, as the city pursued a vision of orderly industrial modernity. The final three chapters reckon with the environmental legacies of this vision between the Second World War and the present, from the apex of Hamilton's industrial prosperity to postindustrial concerns with bay pollution and environmental amenities.

In tracing this arc, Bouchier and Cruikshank also ask a fundamental question that imparts a strong social dimension to their analysis: Whose harbour is this? In teasing out their answers, and by revealing how social inequality and power relations helped shape the landscape, the authors provide rich accounts of the diverse neighbourhoods and environments surrounding the bay, from the Burlington Heights and Cootes Paradise districts, upon which Terpstra heaps attention, to the Beach Strip and neighbouring areas of land reclaimed for industrial purposes that largely escape his concern. Ever sensitive to the ways in which race, class, and gender shape perceptions and understandings, Bouchier and Cruikshank illustrate how various individuals and groups rallied round or contested particular uses of (and visions for) the harbour, as change impinged (or was anticipated to impinge) differently, and unevenly, upon material circumstances.[22]

Translating these general claims into "real world substance" through the pages of their book, Bouchier and Cruikshank mount an extended argument demonstrating that the "power-brokers" of Hamilton worked, generation by generation, with and against the inertia of earlier decisions about and investments in the landscape to shape natural and social worlds according to their own particular visions of order (to be sought after) and disorder (to be reduced). In the middle years of the nineteenth century, these influential members of society aspired to discipline human conduct and to tame and tidy nature: "stability" and "improvement" were their watchwords. Early in the twentieth century, economic growth and livability were the overarching goals; these it seemed could be achieved by the efficient organization of society and space: public investment was turned to sorting out a seemingly anarchic waterfront, to creating better beaches here and pleasant parks there, and to sponsoring opportunities for healthy play intended "to fit the younger generation ... for the great work that lies ahead."

Through economic depression and war, the commitment to public investment in recreation and beautification waned; Hamilton became a "lunch bucket" city in which environmental degradation was accepted as the necessary price of progress and prosperity. Come the 1960s, however, civic leaders began to believe that degraded nature was "a source and symbol of urban disorder" even as they and the public lost faith in the capacity of governments to deal with such problems and embraced more democratic decision making and greater community engagement to address their concerns. Through all of this, unruly (or imperfectly understood) nature foiled or undid the intentions of civic leaders, and some less-than-docile citizens refused to bend to the will of authorities. The city was neither a simple artifact of human invention nor an expression of the collective ambitions of its inhabitants: "those in power ... had to contend with a social world in which the less powerful could have conflicting objectives and exert some influence, and with a natural world that did not always bend to their designs or respond as expected."

Read along a slightly different grain, *The People and the Bay* impresses for the scope of topics and literatures with which it engages. Historians of sport will find much of interest in discussions (in Chapter 4 and elsewhere) of recreation in the city (including swimming, angling, sailing rowing, and running); there are insights as well as local details here for those interested in sewage and sanitation in the city (and they are, perhaps, surprisingly numerous). The Canadian literature on civic boosterism and town planning is enriched by discussions within these pages. Those fascinated by the rise of widespread environmental concern in the 1960s and 1970s, as well as its local expressions (on which we have too little good scholarship in Canada), will find new nuggets in "Gillian Simmons's Backyard" (a chapter centred on the activist who led the charge to "save our bay" from further development). More broadly, this book is a significant addition to the still thin literature on the environmental history of Canadian cities. Its close focus on Hamilton, notwithstanding, *The People and the Bay* offers important perspectives on the challenges involved in trying to grasp and mark the significance of environmental and social change in Canada and beyond.

Among the many accomplishments of this book, one must number its treatment of complexity and constraint. Deeply rooted in all the standard sources of historical research, the rich tapestry woven through the pages of *The People and the Bay* is intricate and complicated. In working its way towards an understanding of what happened when, why, and how around Burlington Bay, this book trades in careful argument rather than sweeping claim. Its important contentions and timely strictures are the more robust for that – but the form of their delivery also poses a question, in this age of the sound bite, instant messaging, and unequivo-

cal pronouncements, about whether Bouchier and Cruikshank's thoughtful intervention will have the influence it ought among those concerned
with human (mis)treatment of Earth.

Consider. Late in the twentieth century, Carol Ann Sokoloff wrote a
poem in response to developments along the Toronto waterfront during
her childhood and later years. In the late 1950s and 1960s, the viability of
her father's motel on Lakeshore Boulevard had been undermined by construction of the Gardiner Expressway, and the parents of friends had
protested the continued infilling of Toronto Harbour; two decades later,
those friends had opposed efforts to evict residents of Toronto Island.[23]
Sokoloff's poem is called "Denial."[24] It reads, in part:

> Our cities have turned their backs
>   upon their source,
>   like a sated child that
>   pushes away the breast,
>
>   ...
>
> At water's edge men
> erected railyards and speedways
>   the modern medieval walls,
>   to keep from consciousness
>   all that is mysterious, vast and deep,
>   that cannot be understood;
>
>   ....
>
> ... as if to assert their own omnipotence [city fathers]
>   defiled the living spirit of the waves
>   pouring the wastes of commerce,
>   the poisons of greed,
> relentlessly into the clear pools,
> the well into which we still dip
>   for sustenance.
> In ancient days cities built walls
>   to keep invaders out,
>   and invaders sought first to take
>   the water source,
>   without which the city must fall.
> The cancer of our age
>   is that we have become the invaders
>   of our own self,
>   and have built

the wall
to keep us
from our source

There are lessons to learn in juxtaposing this poem with Bouchier and
Cruikshank's scholarship and Terpstra's rumination. Not least among them
is that there are horses for courses. Any number of stories can be told about
essentially the same people, places, and events, and the what and the how
of their telling reflect their purpose, even as they do much to determine
their audience, their reach, and their impact. The imagery of Sokoloff's
poem is vivid, its message clear and arresting. These few verses might be
taken to refer to Hamilton – or Melbourne, Australia, or Portland, Oregon,
for that matter – in the third quarter of the twentieth century. The poem
speaks, surely, to opposition, to protest, to the propensities of urban developers and the environmental anxieties of that period – and to some
degree our own. Just as surely (as any reader of Terpstra, or Bouchier and
Cruikshank, or the substantial historical literature on the Toronto waterfront will recognize), however, it simplifies for effect.[25] That is its strength
(as an evocation of sentiment) and its weakness (as an account of events).

Working the borderlands between memoir and creative nonfiction,
Terpstra is free to engage in what has been termed "instant archaeology,"
exploring the question "How much past is past?" (posed, according to
W.J. Keith, by Hugh Hood in *A New Athens*).[26] Much of his book rests
on painstaking research, but he makes no pretense at "objectivity" in the
"dry, pseudo-scientific sense" of that term. His collection of closely inter-
related but in other ways disparate essays includes (among other things)
personal reminiscences, careful accounts of local history and geology, the
testimonies of longtime residents, and meditations on the ways in which
people think of themselves, the world, and the future.[27] In sum, it speaks
in intelligent but accessible tones to those who seek to build a proper
relationship between the earth and humankind.

Engaged in serious academic, historical scholarship, Bouchier and
Cruikshank seek much the same audience, but they are necessarily more
constrained in framing and delivering their message. Not for them the
imaginative Terpstra-like riff ("Imagine Cootes Paradise-Hamilton
Harbour as an Aboriginal arrowhead, its tip still piercing the ribs of the
giant escarpment, though the finely serrated edge created by the careful
chiseling of flakes, that once formed the inlets of the southern bay, has
been lopped off by land reclamation and buried by the behemoth structures
of heavy industry." Perchance?). Nor do Bouchier and Cruikshank declare

abiding love for this place (apart from a quiet confession, tucked into the acknowledgments, to being hooked on its history). Few historians these days pretend to objectivity in any absolute sense, but they remain tied to sources and committed to showing that their interpretations are supported by evidence. The results may take longer to digest than striking poetic lines or musings in lyrical prose, but they are the "meat and potatoes" upon which so much else rests.

Yet for all their differences, "Denial," *Falling into Place,* and *The People and the Bay* reflect, in essence, upon the human transformation of land- and waterscapes. The two books deal with a tiny expanse at the western end of Lake Ontario (though the latter encompasses more of this territory than the former, and the former ranges more deeply through time than the latter). "Denial" speaks to proximate and parallel circumstances. The poem offers a firm indictment of actions but attributes responsibility for these only to broad, faceless groups ("men," "city fathers," "we"). Both *Falling into Place* and *The People and the Bay* include an extended dramatis personae, and a comparison of the two books reveals that they are peopled by many of the same individuals, although they play different roles and their characters are developed in dissimilar ways. In the end, all three works ask readers to reflect upon similar basic questions, and the books' authors reach hauntingly parallel, arresting conclusions. Here are Bouchier and Cruikshank: "There are no spaces ... that we should not care about ... if history teaches us anything, it is that the choices we have to make are not easy and that their consequences are hard to predict or control." Here is Terpstra: "Just who is guest and who is host in this relationship to the earth we share with others of our regenerative species? I am so pleased with this place, despite the hurt and history."[28] Blending, borrowing, and paraphrasing the insights of our authors leaves little doubt that love, of place or person, is a complex, contradictory, and embattled business in which mistakes will be made along the way but that we should not be deterred – as the unfolding story of *The People and the Bay* makes plain – in our efforts both to build a better relationship with the earth and to do right by humankind.

Acknowledgments

NEITHER OF US HAD ANY sustained encounter with Hamilton or its
harbour until 1993, the year that we both joined the community of
scholars at McMaster University. A few years later, we were asked to do a
little historical research for Ecowise, a project focused on the Hamilton
Harbour Remedial Action Plan. We thank the biologists, economists,
political scientists, psychologists, and other researchers in the project – and
most particularly Mark Sproule-Jones – for welcoming us to their group,
which had received funding from Canada's three research councils. We
also thank the many members of the Bay Area Restoration Council and
Bay Area Implementation Team – and most particularly John Hall – for
making us feel that we had something to contribute to their valuable work.
Our initial research led to an invitation to curate an exhibition at what
was then a new and innovative type of museum in Hamilton, the Workers
Arts and Heritage Centre. Mary Breen, Craig Heron, Franca Iacovetta,
and Renee Wetselaar encouraged us to undertake an exhibit and generously
tolerated two novice curators working at the centre.

We were by then hooked on the history of the city, its waterfront, and
its harbour. Various colleagues at McMaster (including Gordon Beck,
Cathy Moulder, Richard Harris, and John Weaver) and in the city (including Brian Henley, Margaret Houghton, and Ian Kerr-Wilson) made sure
that we at least knew how to learn about Hamilton's history. The research
that we undertook was generously funded by the Social Sciences and
Humanities Research Council of Canada and McMaster University's Arts

Research Board. That funding made it possible to involve others in the project. Andrew Bone and Matt Sendbuehler provided critical research assistance in its initial stages and set the bar high for all of the graduate students who followed them, including Jessa Chupik, Karen Dearlove, Michael McAllister, Heather Nelson, Heather Read, Peigi Rockwell, and Gregory Stott, as well as many (then) undergraduate students and a few community researchers, including Michael Boucher, Deborah Carr, Robert Fick, Christine Goldsack, Anna Krahotin, Jesstina McFadden, Daniel Pacella, Danielle Robinson, Laura Sanderson, Robert Sargant, Todd Stubbs, Angela Van Lanen, Caitlyn Watson, and Jelica Zdero. Ian Anderson undertook critical research into public health in Hamilton, with the support of an AMS/Hannah Summer Studentship, and Rahima Visram conducted her own interviews in the course of her arts and science undergraduate thesis. Andrew Stevenson from Niagara College generously worked with us and shared some interviews, as part of his own film project. This book is the better for our having scripted some of our ideas for a film, *The People and the Bay.* Our colleague Viv Nelles encouraged us to take this risk, and as director of the Wilson Institute for Canadian History matched us up with two great young filmmakers, Zach Melnick and Yvonne Drebert, and together helped make it happen.

Over the years we have received many constructive comments and words of encouragement from our professional colleagues at various scholarly conferences, and from those peer reviewers who read our early articles and this manuscript. They listened to or read our stories of Hamilton and encouraged us to articulate the broader significance of those stories. Aspects of this book have appeared in "Abandoning Nature: Swimming Pools and Clean, Healthy Recreation in Hamilton, Ontario, c. 1930s–1950s," *Canadian Bulletin of Medical History* 28, 2 (2011): 315-37; "Remembering the Struggle for the Environment: Hamilton's Lax Lands/Bayfront Park, 1950s–2008," special issue on environmental politics, *Left History* 13, 1 (Spring-Summer 2008): 106–28; "Blighted Areas and Obnoxious Industries: Constructing Environmental Inequality on an Industrial Waterfront, Hamilton, Ontario, 1890-1960," *Environmental History* 9, 3 (July 2004): 464–96; "'The War on the Squatters': Hamilton's Boathouse Community and the Re-Creation of Recreation on Burlington Bay, 1920-1940," *Labour/ Le travail* 51 (2003): 9–46; "'The Heritage of the People Closed against Them': Class, Environment, and the Shaping of Burlington Beach, 1870s– 1980s," *Urban History Review* 30, 1 (October 2001): 40-55; "Dirty Spaces: Environment, the State and Recreational Swimming in Hamilton Harbour,

1870–1946," *Sport History Review* 29, 1 (1998): 59–76; and "'Sportsmen and Pothunters': Class, Conservation and the Fishery of Hamilton Harbour, 1850–1914," *Sport History Review* 28, 1 (1997): 1–18.

We thank Graeme Wynn and Randy Schmidt of UBC Press for their patience and for thinking that this book could belong in the Nature | History | Society series. Lesley Erickson kept the final manuscript preparation on track; Deborah Kerr tried to fix our mistakes, grammatical and otherwise; and Stephen Ullstrom provided an index to help our readers. Their work has made this a much better book. Rajiv Rawat generously took time out of his busy schedule to prepare a few maps for us. Thanks also to Cees van Gemerden for letting us use his photographs yet again, and to Laura Lamb, Debbie Lord, and Jenny McFadden of the Hamilton Public Library, who responded to many last-minute queries. We are also thankful for our colleagues and students in the History Department at McMaster; we are fortunate to work with such a great group of people.

Neither of us had co-authored any major work before we started on this project, but we thoroughly enjoyed the experience. Readers who are looking to associate a particular chapter with one or the other of us will be disappointed; each chapter is the product of a collective effort, from conception to final revision. We learned a lot from working with each other and even managed to stay friends. It helped that we each enjoyed support and welcome distractions on the home front. Nancy comes from a line of people who have plied the waters of these parts for generations. She has inherited a real love of our Great Lakes, especially Cootes Paradise, an urban canoeist and kayaker's dream. She has learnt much about the city, its people, and culture from Pauline Kajiura, a proud and civically engaged Hamiltonian, beloved partner, and friend. In Ken's case, Peggy Sample has continued to be a good friend and helped him raise two young men – Gregory and Harrison Cruikshank – who constantly make their father proud. His father, Ross Cruikshank, has supported Ken from the moment he decided to pursue an academic career and has been a role model as a parent and an engaged citizen all of his long life. Ken is especially grateful for the thoughtful provocations, distraction, companionship, and loving support of art historian Alison McQueen, who has welcomed him (and the Cruikshank boys and cats) into her life.

The People and the Bay

Whose Harbour?

O N A COLD AND WINTRY SUNDAY in 1865, John Smoke, the son of a
local farmer, sat huddled in a fishing hut on Burlington Bay as he
speared black bass fish through a hole in the ice. Along came the newly
appointed fishery inspector for the Province of Canada West, John Kerr,
who caught him red-handed breaking the Fisheries Act. Wanting to make
Smoke an example to others in his campaign to uphold the law and conserve Lake Ontario's declining fish stocks, Inspector Kerr charged him
with three infractions – fishing with a spear, possessing bass caught with
a spear, and fishing on a Sunday. Later that week, the two men appeared
before Hamilton's Police Court. Magistrate James Cahill, having seen the
inspector's evidence and jurisdiction challenged in his courtroom on other
occasions, advised Kerr to drop the first two charges, which he did. The
magistrate then found Smoke guilty of fishing on the Sabbath, remarking
as he passed his sentence that all too often men like Smoke seemed to
think "that they were at liberty to do as they pleased with Her Majesty's
property."[1]

Many citizens of Hamilton and the nearby area struggled against nature,
and against each other, to determine the appropriate uses of "Her Majesty's
property." All three men in this story – the farmer's son John Smoke, the
fishery inspector John Kerr, and the police magistrate James Cahill – may
have agreed that Burlington Bay belonged to the community, but their
behaviours reveal that they disagreed about what that actually meant. Like
others in Hamilton, John Smoke fished in the bay, seeing it as a community property and resource that was accessible to anyone. In the winter, he

fished with a spear, a method that efficiently caught fresh, firm, and flavourful fish. Spearing put easily gotten food on his wintertime dinner table and a bit of off-season income in his pocket, from local dealers who bought his surplus catch. Fishery Inspector John Kerr held a different view of the bay. He policed this specially designated area on behalf of the Government of Canada West, aiming to protect black bass and other fish in order to sustain the fishery at the western end of Lake Ontario. Formerly the secretary of a local conservation-minded angling club, Kerr saw spearing as an unsportsmanlike threat to the province's fish populations. Police Magistrate James Cahill doubted that Her Majesty had granted Kerr or he himself the kind of authority that Kerr wanted. He had little doubt, however, of the state's authority to enforce the law against Sunday fishing, to ensure that the bay was a place where public morality and respect for the Crown were at all times preserved. As Cahill's comment suggests, he viewed the natural setting of the bay, with its city-lined shore, as being dangerously liberating, encouraging people "to do as they pleased."

The material world – the frozen bay and its fish – provided the setting for very human conflicts on Burlington Bay (later renamed Hamilton Harbour). Her Majesty's property was not just the stage setting for Her Majesty's subjects, however. It acted and reacted to human activities in ways that often were – and still are – poorly understood. The courtroom drama would not have taken place at all were it not for a change in the non-human world – the decline of certain fish populations in the bay. Of course, the courtroom drama represented a very human response to this decline, dependent on cultural ideas of what particular fish were to be valued and ideas about how best to account for the loss of a resource that once seemed so abundant. The behaviour of humans like John Smoke and James Cahill complicated Kerr's attempts to protect the fishery. So too did the habits and behaviours of the fish.

This small courtroom encounter in 1865, therefore, offers an introduction to our environmental and social history of Hamilton's bay. These three men, with their differing social positions and relationships to the natural world, encountered and envisioned the bay as community property in very different ways. Over the next century or so, as the city of Hamilton grew and emerged as a major Canadian industrial town and a significant Great Lakes port, others would see the bay in their own way too. Some saw it as a recreational playground – a place of fun for anglers, swimmers, and sailors. Others saw it as a practical source of sustenance – for its fish, game, ice, and water – key ingredients for supporting an urban population and fuelling local businesses. Some saw the bay as a beauty spot – an attractive site for gardens, cottages, parks, beaches, and philanthropic enterprises, making it a public place to see and be seen. Still others saw it as a convenient dump for residential and industrial wastes. As the work of Fishery Inspector John Kerr suggests, it did not take long to determine that this triangular, thirty-square-kilometre body of water and its adjoining marshlands and creeks might not be able to sustain all of those diverse activities.[2] As Hamilton grew, a bay that once seemed large and abundant enough to accommodate many uses and many different peoples appeared much less so. Human actors struggled to understand, control, and manage nature – and each other – to ensure that the bay would continue to be, or would become, the kind of place that they wanted it to be.

In the pages that follow, we offer an environmental history of Burlington Bay and Hamilton Harbour. We think of our history as environmental because it seeks to respond to Donald Worster's 1990 plea that historians pay more attention to the ways that people in the past have defined "what a resource is, which sorts of behavior may be environmentally degrading and ought to be prohibited" and the ways in which they generally chose "the ends to which nature is put."[3] Worster was most interested in encouraging his colleagues to consider these issues in relation to agricultural practices – capitalist agricultural practices in particular – and was criticized for being less interested in industrialization and urbanization, two other processes associated with the emergence of modern North America. So, like many environmental historians then and since, we are interested in Worster's questions, but in the ends to which nature is put in a setting that can seem so divorced from nature – the industrial city.

Hamilton is not an exceptional metropolitan giant such as New York, Chicago, Los Angeles, or Manchester, but the work of several historians has presented it as a good example of perhaps a more common type of North American city.[4] And it is a Canadian city, as our initial focus on Her Majesty's property clearly underlines. As Alan MacEachern recently noted, environmental historians have been slow to consider the city, being "often preoccupied by the Canada of the north and the Canada of the wild."[5] We join others such as Michèle Dagenais and co-authors Christopher Armstrong, Matthew Evenden, and H.V. Nelles in trying to ensure that Canadians better understand the environmental dynamics of urban industrial change in their country.[6] Like these authors, we are particularly interested in the fate of urban waters, and urban water.

Ours is also a social history of Burlington Bay and Hamilton Harbour. As scholars have turned to the examination of urban environments, they have focused on how the categories of interest to social historians, particularly class, race, and gender, shaped human conceptions of, and interactions with, the non-human world. We continue to see Andrew Hurley's pioneering work on the steel city of Gary, Indiana, as a model study, for he tried to understand how social groups conceived of their material environment – both for its problems and for its possibilities – in very different ways, while also showing that they experienced environmental change very differently.[7] Hurley's work also points to the important role that recreation could play in thinking about the urban environment. Conceptions of nature and the uses of the bay and the waterfront often incorporated some notion of the harbour as a site for sports and leisure. Recreational historians have for many years been interested in examining how sports and leisure activities were shaped by and could shape the social power of diverse groups in society. Although the harbour clearly differed from an urban park in important respects, our work is particularly informed by studies of urban parks. Historians such as Stephen Hardy, Robert A.J. McDonald, Sean Kheraj, and co-authors Roy Rosenzweig and Elizabeth Blackmar have all shown how in a potentially common urban space, various groups sought to produce and apply their own perspectives on nature.[8]

In writing a history of the harbour of another steel city, we have tried to recognize that not all ways of encountering, envisioning, and knowing the bay held equal social and political power. The contest over what the bay should be and how it should be used was shaped by inequalities in people's economic, social, and political power. It was, after all, the farmer's son and neither the government inspector nor the police magistrate who gave up almost two weeks' worth of earnings as a consequence of his behaviour. John Smoke learned whose harbour it was, and whose it wasn't. The bay might be community property, but the use of public authority clearly revealed who did, and who did not, have power over Her Majesty's property. There was no golden age when all members of the community shared in its abundant resources; from the outset, those with power struggled to shape nature to serve what they believed were their best interests.

Of course, the resulting material world did not necessarily correspond to what the most powerful members of the community wanted it to be. The power to remake the world was always restricted. Power was limited by the social world; the less dominant struggled to sustain their own conceptions of the non-human natural world, and the powerful did not always have the resources to overcome these other views. Power was also limited by the material world. The work of a generation of urban environmental historians makes us conscious that an environmental history must not lose track of the materiality of the non-human world, its potential to mould our behaviour and to act independently of our ideas about how it ought to respond to our efforts to manage it. As Swedish human ecology scholar Alf Hornborg rightly notes, attention to materiality does not mean, as it once might have, "believing that cultural patterns of consumption and production are determined by the physical environment, only that cultural behavior takes place within a material world whose properties constrain what is possible and determine the environmental consequences of that behavior."[9] To a considerable extent, we are interested in what certain groups of people did to and in nature. Nature did talk back, however, and we do our best to recognize that. How it talked back is often hard to tease out of the sources and, of course, is often mediated by either historical or current understandings of natural processes. Humans did not fully control fish populations, some of which declined while others thrived, but historical observations of fish populations are often episodic, and our current understanding of fish population dynamics is still not perfect. The natural environment of Hamilton Harbour played a role in the emergence of Hamilton as a major industrial city, but the precise role changed over time, in part because material and social processes complicated what needed to be done to achieve environmental and social goals.

OUR STORY BEGINS after Old World settlers began to arrive in the region, and after the almost enclosed waters of the bay were opened by a small canal to Lake Ontario in the 1820s and 1830s. John Smoke was part of a community of Hamilton-area fishers who had first learned winter spearing from observing or working with the Anishnaabe and Haudenosaunee peoples who regularly visited the shores of the bay. Long before them, and probably since the last ice age, North American peoples had migrated seasonally to use the resources of the bay and western marsh, which may have been full of wild rice – rather than cattails – before around 1100 CE. They modified it in various ways; some of the earliest maize growing in the region occurred near the marsh shoreline. If more settled farms and villages appeared, however, they were disrupted by the disease and warfare that followed in the wake of early contact with Europeans. Neutral Indian tribes settled in the bay area before the seventeenth century but dispersed during the Five Nations Iroquois invasions of that century. Neither the Iroquois nor the Mississauga peoples who had displaced them by the early eighteenth century seem to have settled at the bay, perhaps preferring locations with more direct access to the lake. By the time that Europeans from across the sea or from the colonies to the south began to seriously settle the region in the late seventeen hundreds, therefore, it had again been used for seasonal occupation.[10] We begin where we do, not because it was pristine and untouched by human hands, nor because its social and environmental history starts at this point, nor because there were no earlier conflicts over who ought to use the bay and who ought to access the resources. We do so largely because we are interested in the environmental changes associated with the modern processes of urbanization and industrialization.

We start our story, then, in the period from the 1820s to the 1890s, when Hamilton's social and political leaders struggled to construct an Old World city in the New World on the western end of Lake Ontario. To achieve this goal, the local government and residents had to civilize nature's wildness. Thus, Chapter 1, "Civilizing Nature," examines the efforts of Hamilton's social and economic leaders to create a working port for trade and commerce, and their attempts to counteract natural processes – such as fire and disease – that threatened the urban dwellers in their port city. It also considers several ways in which these individuals sought to secure their own position within the society and their efforts to create distinct social and geographical recreational spaces for those who would appreciate and use the bay's natural setting. The process of civilizing nature often meant excluding the rougher elements of a port society and cultivating "proper" social behaviour among the middle classes. Chapter 2, "Conserving Nature," returns to a more detailed accounting of the larger story of Inspector John Kerr, examining how he and others worked to conserve the fishery in Hamilton. We connect his story to broader movements that promoted civilized recreational behaviour in nature, while illustrating the limits of those efforts. We reveal the face of the Victorian state through John Kerr, exploring how both time and experience led him to change his views about the challenges facing the fishery that he was charged to protect.

The next three chapters cover the period from the 1890s through to the early 1940s generally, as Hamilton grew significantly and as large industrial employers came to dominate its physical and economic landscape. This era witnessed a much greater emphasis on the scientific management and organization of nature, recreation, and the city, and, in important distinction from earlier periods, ensuring that its rapidly growing population of immigrants and industrial workers had healthy living and wholesome leisure activities available to them. Chapter 3, "Boosting Nature," considers the phenomenon of urban boosterism as it occurred in Hamilton. It discusses the important consequences and frustrations associated with attracting industrialists to the port and explores the contradictions inherent in selling industrial Hamilton as a healthy place for workers. In Chapter 4, "Organizing Nature," we focus on the city's efforts to ensure that healthful waterfront recreation – including fishing and swimming – existed for Hamiltonians of all social classes, even as industrial growth limited these very activities. Chapter 5, "Planning Nature," explores the world of urban planning through the lens of one prominent social and political leader, Thomas B. McQuesten, who aimed to better organize Hamilton's planned development and create aesthetically pleasing publicly accessible green spaces for its citizens. In these three chapters, Hamilton's social leaders are shown to have used public power to reshape nature and people's experience of it, quite confident that they knew what was best for all residents. They believed that they could create a successful industrial city that was also livable and beautiful. Too often we assume that previous generations prioritized the smokestack over a healthy environment; together, these chapters suggest otherwise.

The final three chapters detail the environmental consequences of harbour development and the struggles and tensions that emerged. Chapter 6, "Confining Nature," considers the period between the 1930s and the late 1950s, when the smokestack did seem to prevail. Most civic leaders increasingly concentrated on promoting Hamilton Harbour as a heavy industrial port. Between the opening of the "Fourth" Welland Canal in 1932 and the St. Lawrence Seaway in 1959, Hamilton's steel industry and related enterprises colonized much of the eastern waterfront, with little regard for other uses of the harbour. Little was done to counteract the environmental damage of postwar growth, beyond ensuring that the waterworks produced water that was reasonably healthy for residents and useful for industry. For a time, the deterioration of the harbour seemed to have been accepted as a price of prosperity. But not for long. Chapter 7, "Unchaining Nature," turns to the late 1950s through the mid-1980s, when some local citizens – including a key figure in this chapter, Gillian Simmons – challenged the status quo. Her concerns over a waterfront development project in her North End neighbourhood were transformed into a larger crusade for a more balanced use of the harbour. She and others identified public accessibility as a critical issue for the health of the waterfront, asserting that people who knew and encountered the bay's shoreline would take better care of its waters. They also argued for the importance of working *with* communities affected by the environmentally poor state of the harbour, as opposed to planning *for* them.

These developments paved the way for a more collaborative approach to fixing the degraded and damaged harbour environment, which we consider in Chapter 8, "Remediating Nature." At the end of the twentieth century, Hamilton's social and political leaders sought once again to balance the uses of the harbour, but they aimed to involve more people in the decision-making process and to accommodate differing visions of the harbour. They also sought to ensure that non-human nature and natural processes – at least as they understood them – would be considered and respected. In 2015, no less than in 1865, human and non-human nature complicated outcomes.

In the pages that follow, then, we offer an environmental and social history of one city's harbour. We invite readers not to think of the past as an alien place where bad things were done to nature because it was not seen as an important part of the city. Instead, we hope readers might see the past as a familiar if different place where well-meaning social groups sought to build what they deemed a healthy and livable town, and believed that nature had a role to play in creating it. If at times we focus on the limits of their achievements, if we consider how they did not always understand or control the consequences of their actions, and if we seek to highlight the social and moral assumptions that shaped their efforts, we do so in the hope that we might more effectively reflect upon the present and future of our own urban societies and landscape. We invite readers to enter into and consider past worlds, but we do so that they might think about their own world differently. Cities are one of the places where human societies have dramatically transformed the non-human world, yet that world remains always present and active. We encourage readers to think about their own city as a vibrant place where the non-human world is always present and active, and where human actors seek to control the intended and unintended consequences of their encounters with both it and each other. We all have difficult moral and political choices to make about the social and natural world around us, just like those who came before us.[11]

I

Civilizing Nature

Community Property Transformed, 1823–95

IN 1846, A "LOVER OF NATURE" penned an ode to Hamilton, on the occasion of its incorporation as a city. Its author, "Camo," noted features of the local landscape – "the Mountain" ringed with a hazy mist, several church spires, the forest scenery, with "here and there a cultivated farm," the Desjardins Canal, and Dundurn Castle, the manor home of Sir Allan MacNab overlooking the western end of the bay. He mourned at the burial site of the recently departed Lady MacNab – "what bright visions of hope, benevolence and charity have vanished with her." He saved the most florid prose for the view of the bay, something "surpassing anything I have ever seen":

> The bay, smooth as a mirror, and blue as the heavens above it; there I have stood when the evening zephyrs, wafting the fragrance of wild flowers forth, could cause gentle ripples to beautify the scene; and wrapt in meditation, drank into my soul the poetic conceptions of grandeur and sublimity. It is there the lover of nature delights to muse on her variegated charms, and the maiden hears the song of her lover, as it comes in pleasing strains over the sleeping waters.[1]

In his ode, Camo imagined Hamilton and Burlington Bay to be part of a "romantic Canada" that could rival the greatest scenery of the Old World. He admired the bay and sang to his maiden, not amidst the wilds of Canada, but from the park-like grounds of MacNab's Dundurn Castle.

He imagined a picturesque rural landscape where civilization gently triumphed over nature, where forests served as "garniture" to the farm, the church, the canal, the manor house, and even the resting place of a virtuous lady. To do so, Camo erased significant features of the landscape. He ignored the docks, wharves, and substantial sailing ships just below his vantage point, which made it possible to imagine that a community of slightly more than six thousand people might actually be a city.

One wonders how Camo's imagination would have transformed the sight that would have greeted his poetic soul about seven months later, on a crisp wintery day. Would he have continued to dream of knights and ladies, as three horses galloped across the smooth but now frozen Burlington Bay? Would his maiden have heard his song, over the din of the "large assemblage of citizens" that had gathered to cheer on their favourite in a two-mile harness race? "A good deal of money changed hands on the occasion," we are told, "and after the horses started, bets of two to one were freely offered in favour of 'Jerry Snake.'"[2] Whereas Camo exercised his poetic licence in meditating upon the bay and its surroundings, many in the assembled crowd saw in those same surroundings a licence to escape, if only for an afternoon, from the normal social restrictions and the economic rigours of the slowed but still challenging pace of a commercial port in winter.

If Camo imagined a wilderness transformed into an idyllic rural world, by 1846 most residents of Victorian Hamilton saw nature as a resource to help them live, work, and play in a competitive, commercial city. The bay had a special role to play, and not just because Hamiltonians sought to create a major Great Lakes port. It might also serve as source of food, water, and ice, and as a place where the dirt and wastes of families and industries might be washed away. As the horse races suggest, the bay might also be a place of leisure, a space where the social and economic routines of the nearby city might be temporarily left behind. How these varied activities were to be organized, by whom, and in whose interest remained an open question. Camo's comparison of the bay's waters to the heavens suggested that its resources ought to be open and accessible to all, a viewpoint that seemed to be confirmed at community events such as the winter races. Such sentiments appeared to take legal form in the 1846 legislation that transformed Hamilton into a city: "All of the bay to the opposite shore thereof lying in front of the said City shall vest in the City Council of the said City."[3] Clearly, the bay was to be community property. Yet just what this meant would become increasingly contested as the city grew:

in time, the bay, which at first seemed large and abundant enough to accommodate many uses and many peoples, appeared much less so.

To BUILD A COMPETITIVE urban centre, Hamilton's community leaders needed to find ways to work with – and transform – nature's terrain surrounding the bay. The bay's triangular and almost fully enclosed thirty square kilometres were well situated for the British colony's early inland transportation networks that developed in the years following the Revolutionary War.[4] Yet long before that time, First Nations peoples had established a network of trails that connected the bay to the regions south of Lake Ontario to Niagara, north of Lake Ontario toward York (Toronto) and Montreal, and, thanks to a break in the ninety-metre-high limestone cliff face of the Niagara Escarpment, southwest toward London and Detroit. For ambitious European settlers, however, the bay posed several problems. Although its north shore lay on a direct route between York and London, steep shale bluffs and deep ravines limited the connections between inland transportation networks and the water (see Figure 1). At the west, a thirty-metre-high isthmus called the Burlington Heights separated the "long frog marsh" of Cootes Paradise from the bay proper. The series of streams that fed the marsh flowed over the escarpment, creating many mill sites that made the region well known. But the marsh's shallow depth made it hard to transport goods by boat from the mills through to the bay and Lake Ontario beyond. Although promising areas for a port could be found along the bay's southern shore, much of it was boggy and inundated by inlets, creeks, ravines, and ditches. Farther east, between the bay and Lake Ontario, a long, thin thirty-five- to ninety-metre sandbar ran north-south, known locally as the Beach Strip. It separated the bay from the lake, but not completely, even though some early European maps and observers actually termed it a lake. Few ships could pass through what one observer referred to as the Beach Strip's natural "shifting" channel, about forty-five metres wide and at most just over two metres deep, that ran between the lake and the bay.[5]

In the early nineteenth century, British military officers valued the natural barrier offered by the Beach Strip. It provided a strategic advantage. During wartime, American naval ships could not easily get into the bay to threaten the military encampments on the high ground at the Burlington Heights. By 1818, when treaties and agreements had created peaceful relations between Britain and the United States, what was once a strategic advantage now became an economic liability. To deal with the difficulties

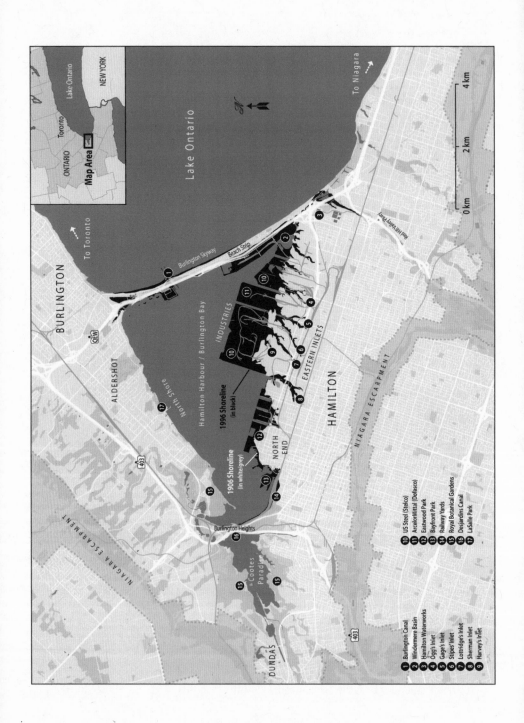

Map Area

ONTARIO
Toronto
Lake Ontario
NEW YORK

Lake Ontario

To Toronto

BURLINGTON

ALDERSHOT

GEW

To Toronto

Burlington Skyway

Beach Strip

Burlington Canal

Hamilton Harbour / Burlington Bay

North Shore

INDUSTRIES

1996 Shoreline
(in black)

1906 Shoreline
(in white/grey)

NORTH END

Burlington Heights

Cootes Paradise

DUNDAS

NIAGARA ESCARPMENT

403

403

HAMILTON

EASTERN INLETS

NIAGARA ESCARPMENT

Red Hill Valley Creek

To Niagara

N

0 km   2 km   4 km

1 Burlington Canal
2 Windermere Basin
3 Hamilton Waterworks
4 Ogg's Inlet
5 Gage's Inlet
6 Stipes' Inlet
7 Lottridge's Inlet
8 Sherman Inlet
9 Harvey's Inlet

10 US Steel (Stelco)
11 ArcelorMittal (Dofasco)
12 Bayfront Park
13 Railway Yards
14 Royal Botanical Gardens
15 Royal Botanical Gardens
16 Desjardins Canal
17 LaSalle Park

in passing between the lake and the bay, ambitious merchants in the inland village of Dundas promoted the idea of constructing two canals to make travel easier. One would run east from Dundas, going through the marshy Cootes Paradise to follow an existing channel at the northern tip of the Burlington Heights that connected Cootes with the bay while the other would go through the Beach Strip, connecting the bay with Lake Ontario. In 1823, supported by business leaders from other communities in the region, Dundas entrepreneurs convinced the colonial government to finance the construction of a hundred-metre cut through the Beach Strip. Great Lakes cargo ships began to pass through this new Burlington Canal in 1827, although it would not be officially open for another five years. However, creating the Desjardins Canal, through marshy Cootes Paradise, proved much more difficult. The private company that built it struggled to keep its shallow natural channel from filling up with silt, and it remained under construction until 1837. Ultimately, Hamilton's business and political leaders, in what was then a small struggling community on the south shore of the bay, benefitted much more than their counterparts in Dundas from the canals that transformed their "lake" into an enclosed harbour.

As families created inland farms to the south and west of the bay, they relied on their new port of Hamilton for imports and exports, and they began to purchase stoves and agricultural implements that were made in the city. Local merchants and manufacturers built wharves and warehouses for shipping and storage along the southwestern waterfront, three kilometres north of Hamilton's original townsite. During the 1840s, they garnered assistance from the government to finance the necessary dredging to combat the natural silting that constantly threatened to overwhelm the Burlington Canal.[6] Despite this challenge, what had once been a small village of several hundred people in the early 1820s grew tremendously. By the time that Hamilton achieved city status in 1846, its population exceeded six thousand. After that, the port and city both continued to grow, as community leaders sought to protect what they viewed as their natural

FIGURE I (FACING PAGE)   Orientation map of Hamilton Harbour/Burlington Bay, showing changes to the shoreline from 1909 to 1996. The Red Hill Valley Parkway *(bottom right)*, opened in 2007, is included to help orient contemporary viewers; it would have been a green space in 1996.

markets in the expanding settlements of southern Ontario. In 1854, Hamiltonians celebrated the completion of the Great Western Railway, a line that the city had been promoting since the 1830s. It linked Hamilton to a large agricultural hinterland, as well as to cities in the American northeast and Midwest. Local promoters worked hard to ensure that the railway would be connected to the North End port; they gave so generously to the railway company that they eventually bankrupted the city.[7]

Government financial aid in the 1840s and 1850s supported an expensive reconstruction of the bay's landscape to accommodate the growth of the port and its connection to the railway. Engineers from the Great Western Railway did not want to build a costly bridge across the channel at the tip of the Burlington Heights, so they created a bed for their tracks by filling it in. Yet frustrated railway contractors could not find anything solid enough for suitable bridge footings. They watched the marsh swallow whatever materials they dumped into it. That is, until someone thought to use tree trunks as fill, trunks that floated suspended in the muck, held fast by entangled roots.[8] The resulting bed and track blocked the Desjardins Canal between Cootes and the bay. To compensate the canal company for the loss of its waterway, the railway's engineers cut a new canal through the narrow centre of the Burlington Heights and built a railway bridge across it. In 1848, Hamilton City Council used its control of the bay to provide the railway with 15.6 hectares of waterlots along the southwestern shoreline to be filled in to locate its station and rail yards. "The spirit of improvement has made sad work of the old bathing ground," one observer noted in the *Canadian Illustrated News,* as railway contractors dumped material into the lots as they excavated and levelled the existing shoreline property, extending it into the bay some 222 metres.[9] The extension of the railway's property into the water continued when city council granted a further three hectares to accommodate the construction of the Great Western's main repair shops and rolling mill. A Detail Plan created in 1842 suggests that at that time little shoreline existed below the steep bluffs along much of the shoreline (see Figure 2).[10] Soon the Great Western's "made land" on the bay had a newly constructed shoreline that was ample enough for the railway, its station, yards, and shops.[11]

The extensive reconstruction of the waterfront and the coming of the Great Western Railway stimulated Hamilton's growth. Its population peaked at twenty-five thousand in 1857 but declined during the recession that started that year and did not reach that level again for another decade. Afterward, growth happened steadily, and by the mid-1890s, Hamilton

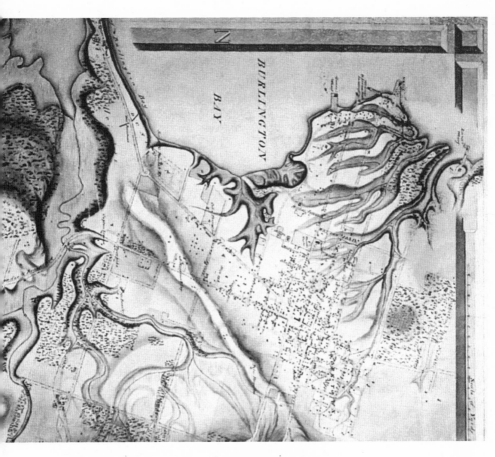

FIGURE 2 The Town of Hamilton, 1842. This image has been rotated ninety degrees so that north is at the top rather than on the left side of the picture. Small corners of Cootes Paradise and the southern part of the Burlington Heights are in the top left-hand corner, and the old North End is toward the right-hand corner. The darkened edge along the bay shows how little shoreline existed below the steep bluffs. The map also shows the many ravines that ran from the bay through the North End as well as reaching well into the original townsite *(the cluster of buildings centre right)*. *Plan of the Town of Hamilton, District of Gore, 1842. Courtesy of Local History and Archives Department, Hamilton Public Library.*

had become a city of fifty thousand. The railway altered its economy, although not quite as local promoters had expected. It gave customers in southwestern Ontario more reliable and direct access to goods coming from Toronto and Montreal, bringing in tough competition for Hamilton merchants. In 1865, they imported sixty-six dollars' worth of goods for every hundred dollars that their Toronto competitors imported. By 1885, and for the remainder of the century, Hamilton distributors handled about twenty-two dollars in imports for every hundred dollars of goods received at Toronto.[12] Hamilton business leaders could not maintain their competitive edge in distributing goods to the agricultural communities of southwestern Ontario, yet their city continued to prosper due to its rail and port connections. The railway and its waterfront workshops attracted marine supply, warehousing, and metalworking firms to the area. Although the Great Western didn't run along the shoreline, it passed along a number of inlets and ravines to the east of the port. There, it attracted oil refineries, soap factories, tanneries, and meat packers – industries whose owners preferred locations with ready access to rail transportation and water. Hamilton's manufacturing establishments more than doubled in number between 1861 and 1891, and by 1881, over 35 percent of its labour force was working in some form of manufacturing. Even closures in the railway repair shops in 1874 and 1888 did not seriously hinder Hamilton's industrial growth, which more than made up for its decline as a commercial centre.[13]

As craft shops and factories sprang up along the port, the most prosperous citizens avoided locating their homes, commercial offices, or administrative buildings there. To avoid the waterfront's marshy ravines and uneven terrain, Hamilton's city founders had situated their original townsite inland, near the escarpment and along a ridge that extended from there to the Burlington Heights. In a time when people associated "oozy" streams, stagnating waters, and putrefying vegetation with disease, the wealthier residents preferred the well-drained land near the higher and drier sector around the original town centre. With the opening of the canals and the coming of the railway, labourers and other workers, along with boarding house and hotel keepers, settled in and developed the port, in what became known as the North End. There they lived in the swampy waterfront area that wealthier residents perceived to be unhealthy, a zone largely separated from the main town by marshy inlets and ditches, and, after 1853, by the Great Western tracks. Some property owners thus benefitted from port activity while still avoiding the supposed environmental risks associated with the waterfront's low-lying and poorly drained areas.

HUMAN TRAGEDIES HIGHLIGHTED several kinds of environmental risk, such as fire and disease, "the twin scourges of urban life."[14] Hamilton's political and civic leaders, like other people in large mid-Victorian communities elsewhere, realized that a livable town required technological investments to deal with such risks. Hamilton needed systems to bring more water more quickly to fires, like the ones that burned down a major foundry in 1855 and destroyed St. Mary's Roman Catholic Cathedral in 1859. Those same systems could also prevent disease by providing water to clean the streets. Local outbreaks of cholera in 1849 (taking 98 lives) and 1854 (taking 522 lives in July and August alone) focused everyone's attention on the devastation that stagnant water could wreak on people's lives and their city's health.[15] The work of sanitarian reformers from other places, such as England's Edwin Chadwick, gave Hamilton's leaders new insight into their own situation. They began to see that their homes and businesses needed running water, which could dilute human and animal waste, and carry it away. They believed that running water would not putrefy or stagnate and that it could not propagate disease.[16] By the early 1850s, city council had begun to seriously investigate municipally run systems for both piped water and sewage. To do this, it needed to reflect on the role that the bay's waters could play in those systems.[17]

After several private ventures to supply water to residents faltered, council asked William Hodgins, the city engineer, to prepare a report on the construction of a public waterworks system. His report of 1853 considered several possible sources to provide clean drinking water, assessing both its quality and the expense of creating a pipeline system to transport it. He urged that the bay be crossed off the list, if possible. He cited the high cost of pumping its water to the more elevated parts of town, but he worried more about issues of quality. He contended that "no worse source could be selected," given "the nearness of the extensive marshes of Coote's [sic] Paradise, Ferguson's Inlet, and others, and their intimate connection with the bay, the masses of decayed and decaying vegetable matter, with which they are everywhere impregnated." He thus recommended that gravity be used to bring clean water from Ancaster Creek, which streamed down the escarpment into Cootes Paradise.[18]

Fearing the cost of this and other alternatives, city council ignored his advice and sponsored a competition in the fall of 1854 for the best plan to supply a population of forty thousand people with water from Burlington Bay. The well-known engineer Thomas C. Keefer, chief engineer of the Montreal Water Board, judged the submissions and awarded three prizes.[19] Before city councillors had time to consider the winning entry, the *Hamilton Spectator* generated a controversy by publishing Hodgins's 1853 report, prompting Keefer to continue his work as a consultant to review the problem. He concluded that though Hodgins was right about the bay, he was wrong about Ancaster Creek. Keefer thought that managing seasonal changes on the creek would prove complicated, particularly given the "individual interests" and "private rights" involved, doubtless referring to the difficulty of running the system without interfering in the operation of mills along the creek. Keefer also shifted the terms of the debate by arguing that council should invest in a system that could expand to serve a city of 100,000. What, then, was council to do?

Keefer introduced an expensive and audacious proposal to supply Hamilton with water from Lake Ontario, five to six kilometres from the city centre (Figure 3).[20] Although the lake's winds ensured that the water was not from a stagnant source, he proposed a further precaution – filtering it through the sand and gravel of the shoreline into basins. A large pump house would then draw out the filtered water and push it nearly five kilometres southwest and sixty metres up the escarpment into reservoirs. Gravity would then distribute it through pipes to the city. On behalf of a still wary city council, two experts from New York's Croton waterworks evaluated Keefer's proposal, confirmed its efficacy, and included some recommendations for reducing its cost.[21] Promoters of the expensive waterworks scheme seized upon this endorsement, taking advantage of an economic depression that began in 1857 to further their cause. They

FIGURE 3 (FACING PAGE)   T.C. Keefer's map detailing Hamilton's water supply, 1856. North lies at the bottom of this map, which shows the contours of the Niagara Escarpment as a dark triangular land formation pointing to the right and surrounding much of Burlington Bay, Cootes Paradise, and the City of Hamilton. The waterworks pipeline is shown as a thin line between the lake and the escarpment near the top left of the page, starting where the Beach Strip meets the south shore of the bay. The pipeline drew lake water to the Beach Strip pumping basin, then to the waterworks, and finally inland to the escarpment and the city's reservoir. *Thomas Keefer*, Report on Water Supply for the City of Hamilton *(Montreal: 1856). Courtesy of Brock University Map Collection, 21999.*

MAP to accompany
REPORT ON WATER SUPPLY
for the
CITY OF HAMILTON
Thos. C. Keefer,
Engineer.
1854

FIGURE 4   Rainbows and water fountains mark the opening of T.C.Keefer's Hamilton
Waterworks (built 1856–59) by the Prince of Wales during his visit to the city in 1860.
Now a national historic site, it houses Hamilton's Museum of Steam and Technology.
"View of the Hamilton Waterworks on the Occasion of the Prince of Wales's Visit,"
Illustrated London News, *17 November 1860.*

contended that constructing Keefer's system would both lower the
estimated cost and put a number of local businesses and labourers to work.
When completed, it would enhance depressed local property values.
Hamilton would also boast a modern water supply system by the time
the Prince of Wales came to visit during his widely anticipated tour.

The waterworks promoters won the day, and in September 1860 the
Prince of Wales officially opened the new waterworks as part of his much
publicized tour of the British North American provinces (Figure 4). An
aide-de-camp recorded the events of the tour, commenting, "Who living
in Canada has not heard of the Hamilton water-works – of the large
amount of money spent upon them, and of their final success as an engineering work?"[22] The new system connected over 150 fire hydrants to
protect the propertied interests of Hamiltonians and to reduce their fire
insurance premiums. However, only a hundred households were willing
or able to pay to have the water pumped into their homes. As a result,
hoping to recover costs, city council simply imposed a water rate on all
property owners. Even in a depressed economy, the city had spent almost
twice what the most expensive of the estimates from its 1854 competition
would have cost. Although all ratepayers did not benefit equally, they
each helped pay the $625,000 needed to ensure that wealthier residents
could avoid drinking the suspect water of the bay.[23]

Although the bay's suitability as a water supply was the subject of lengthy
controversy, few people questioned the idea that it was the appropriate

endpoint for a new sewer system. In the early 1850s, city council spent $195,000 to build underground brick sewers; situated beneath the main streets, they ran down to the bay. The project made the best use of gravity and enhanced the natural drainage of the slopes down from the escarpment toward the bay and its inlets. Sanitary reformers emphasized their belief that running water purified itself. Engineer William Hodgins, who had asserted that water from the bay was not fit to drink due to stagnant marshes such as the ones at Ferguson's Inlet, did not challenge the decision to use the bay as the outlet for the new sewer's main trunk line.[24] Perhaps he believed that the waste water would purify itself as it flowed through the system. Little further purification could be expected in Ferguson's Inlet, which, by Hodgins's own account, contained stagnant water and rotting vegetation. In his eyes, it probably did not matter, since the resulting unhealthy vapours would be far from existing wharves, and more significantly, from the commercial centre and the homes of wealthy Hamiltonians. The sewer system efficiently transferred the perceived environmental risks of the city to the working-class residents of the North End.

As the piped water system became available, a small but growing number of homeowners used relatively new fixtures, such as water closets, and connected their indoor plumbing to the sewer system. The domestic use of this system remained voluntary until 1910, and those who used it had to pay for the privilege. It thus expanded gradually and tended to be limited to wealthier neighbourhoods; about one in ten houses had access to sewers in 1876. Twenty years later, sewers served about half of Hamilton's residences. Despite the sewer system's slow development, its effects had become noticeable by the late 1880s. When a delegation from the Hamilton Board of Health visited the Ferguson sewer outlet in September 1886, it "found an accumulation of the most disgusting and filthy matter, which was being covered with earth."[25] Worried that owners of damaged property might bring "nuisance" lawsuits against the City, the board recommended that council purchase the adjoining property and instructed its chairman to increase the pay of the men working at the outlet![26]

As LONG AS SEWAGE was seen as a localized problem, it did not concern those who looked to the bay to be more than a sink or a transportation hub. As one lover of "pure air and wholesome exercise" declared, "Every nation that dwells on the water-side shows vigor and energy."[27] A successful city, in the view of such enthusiasts, featured spaces for athletics and entertainment that offered positive alternatives to the social and economic pressures – and the dirt – of urban life. The railway yards may have replaced an "old bathing ground," but it seems unlikely that anyone outside of the labouring families who lived in the North End cared very much.[28] There were plenty of other, less miasmatic places to bathe and play along the sheltered shores of the bay.

The construction of the port improved some of the swampy qualities of the southwestern corner of the bay and assisted those who sought recreational adventures on, in, and along the water. Local boatbuilders constructed yachts for those who could afford them and rented smaller rowing sculls and boats to those who could not. These and other local entrepreneurs soon recognized another potentially lucrative use for the improved port: there was money to be made in transporting residents on steamers and ferries to selected recreational areas in other parts of the bay, close enough, but not too close, to town. They quickly realized that those people who, like Camo, simply sought inspirational vistas were far outnumbered by those who, like the crowd that attended the winter horse races, sought places to actively play and be entertained. People found a liminal space at the water's edge, where social conventions and economic relations might be set aside for a few hours of fun. Whereas some embraced this liberating feature of the bay and its shoreline, it became a source of anxiety for others. Recreational pursuits offered one opportunity for middle-class residents to distinguish themselves from others while projecting an image to visitors of a civilized and cultivated city. They struggled to promote disciplined spectatorship at community events on the bay. At the same time, they sought to create distinct social and geographical spaces for those who would "properly" appreciate and use its natural setting.

The bay proved most accessible to a wide range of residents in winter, when it was frozen over and when the pace of economic life slowed down a bit. This very accessibility proved challenging for those who sought to cultivate respectability. By all accounts, trotting races on the frozen harbour remained a regular, popular February event between the 1840s and 1880s (Figure 5). Relatively informal races, first organized by a few private individuals with an interest in horses or gambling, or both, gradually became more formal events intended to promote a positive image of Hamilton. By 1870, organizers were seeking out business support for prizes, in order to attract "the best horses in the Province" to a series of races spread over several days. Whereas in 1847, newspaper coverage presented gambling in a lighthearted way, as a main feature of the event, by 1870 writers were noting approvingly that the local bookie had not taken in much money. They seemed concerned that whiskey stands were still "very numerous" at

CELEBRATION OF THE ROYAL WEDDING DAY ON THE ICE OF BURLINGTON BAY, LAKE ONTARIO, CANADA WEST.

FIGURE 5   Horse races on the frozen harbour in celebration of the royal wedding, 1863.
Mishaps on the ice did not mar the enjoyment of, and spirit of competition among,
well-dressed spectators as they watched horse races held to celebrate the wedding of the
Prince of Wales to Princess Alexandra of Denmark. *"Celebration of the Royal Wedding
Day on the Ice of Burlington Bay, Lake Ontario, Canada West,"* Illustrated London
News, *18 April 1863. Courtesy of Library and Archives Canada, C-111908.*

the races, and they condemned both those who brought their dogs along
and "certain young men" who threw snowballs at strangers.[29] Nevertheless,
informal horse racing continued to have a place in these events, including
special "butcher" and "cabmen" races.[30] In the 1880s, a special organizing
committee spent considerable time soliciting prize money from businessmen in the hopes of drawing large numbers to its two-day event. Later in
the decade, local business leaders incorporated the races into a larger, more
elaborate winter carnival to attract visitors to the city. To ensure local financial support, and to present Hamilton as a successful town, their event
needed to be "respectable."[31]

By 1881, well-heeled spectators no longer had to navigate mishaps on
the ice or mingle with the crowd: they could walk across planks on the ice
to a specially constructed grandstand. The character of the crowd also
changed as workers in North End factories and shops found it difficult to

slip away from work for a few hours to join in the fun when the races were held in the middle of the week, farther away from the shore. On the other hand, clerks in law offices and at wholesale grocers found that employer patronage and a half-day holiday gave them ample opportunity to attend. Those who did encountered a more subdued atmosphere than that of days gone by. Organizers arranged for local police to "keep good order" and to enforce regulations that outlawed gambling, liquor consumption, and other disruptive activities. Community leaders struggled to civilize a once boisterous winter affair.[32]

As the ice thawed each spring, horse racing gave way to other sports. Social leaders actively supported the creation of clubs devoted to the "manly" sports of sailing and rowing; one mayor praised boating for "training men for the defence of our lakes."[33] Boat clubs had little trouble finding room for their headquarters and vessels at the reconstructed port. A noted wharf owner, Captain Edward Zealand, became the president of the city's earliest yacht club, and the directors of the Great Western Railway helped found one of its first rowing clubs. Local bylaws prohibited swimming along the port not so much because of safety concerns, but because swimmers in various states of undress offended respectable boat enthusiasts – both participants and spectators.[34]

Sailing remained an exclusive sport, given the high cost of buying and maintaining a boat. It had trouble taking hold in the city, especially as a spectator sport. Doubtless, those Hamiltonians who could see the water as they conducted their daily business appreciated the distant glimpses of regattas, as the graceful boats tacked from buoy to buoy. They did not, however, flock to the shoreline as official spectators for events. A journalist for the local newspaper, which over the years praised every attempt to promote and revive "this manly sport," and which covered most races in considerable detail, admitted in 1870 that a race held by a new and short-lived yacht club attracted little attention beyond those who were involved in it; the newspaper lamented that Hamilton still had not sustained a yacht club for any length of time.[35] For those who saw clubs and regattas as symbols of a thriving city, this situation proved frustrating. Elite sportsmen welcomed the founding of the Royal Hamilton Yacht Club in 1888 as a portent of a better future for their pastime.

While the local press lamented the travails of sailing, rowing fared differently – Hamilton was home to three rowing clubs. Although it is tempting to attribute the success of rowing to the sheltered condition of the bay, which sometimes left yachts becalmed, success probably had more to do with access. Because of their membership requirements, club sports tended to be somewhat exclusive, but rowing attracted more socially diverse clubs and ranges of participants – and audiences – than did sailing. Rowing began as an exclusive affair in the 1850s, when, soon after the railway came to town, organizers from the Great Western Railway created the Burlington Bay Boat Club for company employees. This was more appealing to males working in the company's non-manual occupations, however, since annual dues and an initial membership cost nearly two weeks' wages for a railway labourer. Club rules required that its members wear, and could therefore afford, genteel boating costumes of white trousers, pink jerseys, straw hats, and little black neckties.[36] Here, it would seem, was a sport designed for the middle-class officers and senior clerks who worked in the railway's offices.

By the time Toronto's working-class hero Ned Hanlan had popularized rowing through his successful professional career in the mid-1870s, Hamilton workers had taken to the sport. For a small fee that was within reach of better-paid workers, boats of varying quality could be rented from Bastien's or other boatbuilders on the waterfront. Groups of workers generated excitement by creating their own challenge matches. Rowers raced from the waterfront north across the bay, east to one of the buoys marking the Burlington Canal, and then back again.[37] Boilermakers and machinists from the Great Western Railway shops challenged each other, as did workers from two local sewing machine factories.[38] In 1878, a number of skilled workers, including many glass-blowers from two North End factories, established their own rowing organization, the Nautilus Club. Another local club, the Leander, formed in 1877. In 1879, it followed the lead of the socially exclusive Montreal-based Canadian Association of Amateur Oarsmen and "decided to admit no mechanic to membership, nor such to take part in any of their competitive matches."[39]

Although the Leander rowers were good, their Nautilus counterparts were great, bringing Canadian Championship Cups to Hamilton for the Four Oars event in 1885, 1888, and 1889.[40] An 1891 survey of rowing clubs in Canada, written for *Outing* magazine, sought to explain the success of Nautilus, claiming that the club "has no social features to bear comparison with Leander, its members being chiefly of the artisan class, but it can turn out sturdy, muscular crews which take a lot of beating."[41] A Hamilton reporter suggested that the club's large membership was the by-product of the Nautilus organization's investment in a piano and billiards tables for its plain clubhouse, as if those who joined other rowing clubs did so only for the sport.[42] Such commentators were obviously discomfited by the social origins of Nautilus rowers, origins that nevertheless attracted a wide audience for the sport. Few could deny the working-class backgrounds of the rowers and the fact that Hamilton regattas in 1881 and 1885 drew very large and boisterous crowds; at least part of the attraction was the famed Nautilus rowers. Yachts carried bands that entertained the crowds, and boats of all sizes and conditions provided vantage points for the race. An estimated six thousand people made their way to the Beach Strip in 1885 to cheer on their crews. Organizers ensured a police presence to maintain order, yet they allowed beer and wine to be sold, and they did not restrict people from openly betting on the races.[43] Although the Leander ensured a separate social organization for middle-class rowing enthusiasts, the larger regattas in which the club and its members participated did not feature the emotional control or disciplined spectatorship that had become part of the middle-class ideal of civilized behaviour associated with the amateur movement of the day.

Races between rowing sculls in summer and between horses in winter produced tensions because they brought a variety of community members together, and at the same time they invited certain kinds of behaviour – gambling, drinking, and raucous spectatorship – that were at odds with emerging Victorian middle-class social values. Similar but more muted tensions arose over appropriate behaviour in some of the recreational areas that developed around the bay and offered various forms of escape from the city. For the most part, the creation of these resorts was left in the hands of local entrepreneurs – who saw that money could be made from charging for travel, meals, and other activities. The private nature of these ventures made some form of social exclusion and enforcement of respectable behaviour possible, but the profit motive also drove entrepreneurs to appeal to as wide a base as they could. In response, some of the social elite turned to public power to create spaces on the bay – ones more suitable to their tastes.

Before the 1870s, civic leaders left the earliest waterfront recreation to social clubs and private entrepreneurs. Between the 1840s and the 1880s, various individuals acquired properties around the bay and worked with steamer companies to attract Hamiltonians who were looking for leisure away from the busy and smelly waterfront. In 1860, the editor of the *Hamilton Spectator* reported with some satisfaction that "there is no lack of pleasure resorts this summer in the neighbourhood of the ambitious city."[44] By that date, at least three small steamers were travelling regularly throughout the summer season to docks at Rock Bay and Oaklands on the north shore, and at several points along the Beach Strip. For those who could not afford the steamers, enterprising individuals also ran smaller, more simple ferries to various locations.

Resort developers in each area competed to attract a broad audience of holidaygoers. The evolution of the resort area directly across the bay from the port suggests just what it took to remain competitive. The Rock Bay resort, situated at the peak of a north shore hill near Carroll's Point, featured an unusually good beach and a relatively gentle slope between its buildings and the water. Visitors could take in beautiful bay vistas from the resort buildings atop the hill. Those who wanted to bathe in the bay's warm waters could climb down a flight of stairs. In the early 1870s, a new owner expanded the resort, constructing a new ballroom and enlarging the dining hall. He also cleared the beach of weeds and undergrowth, and built better change rooms for swimmers. In the early 1880s, another new owner again transformed Rock Bay. Rechristened Bayview, it featured a new bar, billiards tables, an ice cream parlour, a merry-go-round, and a rink for the new craze of the day – roller skating. In 1886, its visitors could take an incline railway down to the water, a novelty that was available at a price. By the 1880s, other amusements could be found along the north shore at Oaklands and at the Beach Strip. Both places became popular excursion destinations for the annual picnics of many groups, including fraternal lodges, churches, labour unions, and the employees of industrial manufacturers.[45]

The Beach Strip had natural advantages that made it a particularly attractive resort area. Its narrow sandbar featured cooling breezes from Lake Ontario, fine swimming beaches on its warmer bay and cooler lakesides, and shady groves of oaks and willows, all of which provided a perfect environment for relaxation. As an important way station on the road from Toronto to Niagara, it had hotels and taverns that did a steady business. Travellers who passed through the Beach Strip could enjoy fresh food produced by the twenty-five to thirty fishing and market-gardening families that made up its small permanent community. In 1863, the *Canadian Illustrated News* published a sketch of the Beach Strip, showing the shoreline with its reels, nets, and fishing boats. The accompanying article described it as a place of "exceeding beauty." "A trip to the beach in Summer, either by land or water, will well repay the excursionist," it wrote. "A walk along the smooth sand, hard packed by the waves, will be found most agreeable – the beauty of the surrounding scenery, the broad blue expanse of the lake, stretching out into the invisible distance, its rippling waves breaking with a sound like shivering glass upon the shingle, all give the

Beach a rare combination of attractions."[46] By then a small steamer, the *Victoria,* regularly shuttled between the city and the beach, making more frequent trips on the 24 May holiday that celebrated the birth of its namesake. The *Victoria* took its passengers to Beach Strip resorts such as the Burlington Beach Garden Pleasure Grounds, where they could eat, dance, and be entertained. In 1865, between 1,500 and 2,000 people visited the strip during the August civic holiday weekend to seek out its sandy shores and cool picnic spots. By 1871, its five hotels and inns were offering visitors a rich variety of attractions.[47]

In the early 1870s, railway promoters and land speculators recognized the potential profitability of the Beach Strip. Its sandbar provided an alternative and more direct land route between Hamilton, the Niagara peninsula, and Georgian Bay, promising access to Great Lakes freight traffic from Canada's newly acquired prairie west. At the same time, it had potential as a railway tourist destination in its own right. A number of local civic leaders supported a railway that could boost their city's fortunes and also make travel to a favoured summer destination more convenient. City councillors granted the Hamilton and Northwestern Railway a $100,000 bonus to bring its train to the Beach Strip. At the same time, they shaped just what kind of resort the area would become.[48]

In 1871, prominent business leader James Williams, a local member of the Ontario Provincial Legislative Assembly, helped block the sale of Beach Strip Crown land to a private individual. He asked the provincial government to give the City of Hamilton control over all unclaimed land on the Beach Strip. The area lay far beyond Hamilton's jurisdiction, but Williams justified his suggestion on the grounds "that it is important for the health and welfare of the people to possess a place of this description where they may enjoy the fresh air from the lake breezes."[49] The government co-operated and permitted Hamilton to lease unclaimed land on the Beach Strip for a nominal annual payment of one dollar, "as a place of recreation for the whole people."[50] Hamilton's Parks Committee would determine what was done with the beach land, whereas Saltfleet Township Council would continue to collect taxes from area residents.[51] Hamilton City Council, which heretofore had created only a small public garden and exhibition grounds, was now to play an active role in waterfront recreation.

And so, in the late spring of 1874, the ever vigilant keeper of the Burlington Canal lighthouse, Captain George Thompson, observed the invasion of the Beach Strip by two groups of land surveyors.[52] One party plotted the line along the Beach Strip for a railway that would connect

Hamilton to the port of Collingwood on Georgian Bay. The completion of the Hamilton and Northwestern Railway two years later would provide an alternative to steamers for people who wished to travel from Hamilton to the beach. Within a decade, this railway's summer timetable sent seven trains to the Beach Strip six days a week, with two trains on the Sabbath.[53] The second surveying party represented the City of Hamilton, which had just acquired control of all vacant Crown land there in the name of public recreation. Just what that meant in practical terms soon became evident. The surveyed lots were auctioned to individuals, who then paid the City ten dollars a year. This arrangement ensured that the City would have money to spend on the area, since it didn't collect taxes from the residents. Captain Thomas Campbell, who succeeded Thompson as lighthouse keeper in 1875, later reflected sadly on the significance of this policy: "This was the first wall erected to keep out the public and confine the benefits of the beach and lake breezes to the favoured few, the pets of fortune, who were able to secure a lot. The very best of it was sold off and the public were deprived of the free use of the beach."[54]

Like Thompson, Captain Campbell kept a close watch on Beach Strip happenings, astutely identifying changes in the sandbar's social character. He recorded his own history of the place in a series of articles that he published in the 1899 *Burlington Gazette*. Indeed, the strip changed a lot. In 1892, some five hundred people could be found camping along the lakeside, north of the canal. The place "has within itself all the requisites of a jolly good time," mused a reporter from the *Hamilton Herald,* who described the arrangement of a number of families that were housed in sixty-five large tents, each of them accommodating six to eight people. Those who "roughed it" in wooden-framed canvas-covered structures were experiencing something akin to what would nowadays be called glamping (glamorous camping). Indeed, the description of the makeshift kitchens and cookstoves gotten up by the campers suggests that they had many amenities to make life in nature quite a bit easier.[55] Although the *Herald* remarked that "all sorts of citizens are indulging in the luxury of loafing around and lying in the sand," closer inspection of the article suggests that the campers were members of the more affluent elite. Their families were headed by men who held managerial and professional occupations in town.[56] A little steamer transported them back and forth between the beach and the city, ensuring that they got to their offices on time. By 6:00 p.m., they returned to the beach in time for a family supper. A few encampments, especially those toward the north end of the Beach Strip on the lakeside across from Brant Inlet, were described as "bachelor roosts." There, in a camp called Annie Roonie, young men such as Willie Southam and St. Clair Balfour Jr. could lead a devil-may-care existence away from the prying eyes of their wealthy and successful fathers – one the publisher of the *Spectator* and the other a prominent Hamilton grocer.[57]

Not all of the Hamiltonians who spent their summers on the Beach Strip, however, occupied such quarters or were inclined toward affectations of rustic life. Between 1875 and 1900, many members of the social elite constructed grand summer homes on the beach, a few of which still stand today. A land assessment roll from 1890 provides some sense of twenty-four of the summer vacation properties found south of the canal. Whereas the average permanent Beach Strip resident owned a fifth of a hectare valued at four hundred dollars, the average summer resident owned only half that amount, but it was worth nearly twice as much.[58] In 1900, about thirty-five households included in Hamilton's exclusive *Blue Book* social directory listed their Beach Strip homes as their summer residences – these homes represented more than half of the places listed for Hamiltonians who "summered" out of town.[59] In June 1895, the *Spectator* identified holders of summer homes on the Beach Strip, both north and south of the canal.[60] Some thirty of the properties belonged to members of Hamilton's entrepreneurial, managerial, and professional classes. The smaller community north of the canal, where the tent colony had existed, was more mixed in nature, including some clerks and craftsmen, although nearly half of those summer homes were also owned by members of the local elite.

By the close of the nineteenth century, Hamilton City Council's decision to auction Beach Strip land had thus helped create a recreational suburb that was available primarily to the upper classes. As in other British and North American towns, political, legal, medical, and business leaders sought refuge from the dirt, pollution, and disease of the city during the hot summer months, creating borderland communities along the water or out in the country. Hamilton's elite inherited a well-established tradition, one that historian John R. Stilgoe describes in his work on borderlands.[61] In the early nineteenth century, British and American tracts advocated summer residences for urban families outside of the industrial and commercial city, "beyond the effluvium of smoke and mud."[62] They hoped to counter the sedentary nature of middle- and upper-class work not through strenuous farm labour, but with pure air and places to ramble. Between the 1870s and 1890s, the Beach Strip provided an ideal "breathing place of tired citizens of Hamilton," since it was just a short train or steamboat ride from town. It enjoyed the "invigorating breezes" of Lake

Ontario, the protected, warmer waters of Burlington Bay, and soils suitable for "numerous garden plots of flowers and grass lawns."[63]

Unlike in many other suburban retreats elsewhere, Hamilton's municipal government played an active role in promoting this recreational area. Local politicians moved to prevent any individual from speculating on the beach land or developing it in ways that they might not approve. While providing the foundation for the creation of public recreational space, council also promptly privatized important segments of that space. Private individuals – the social peers of most city politicians and indeed sometimes the politicians themselves – acquired access to and control over the beach "for a song."[64] Bylaws, and the revenues derived from beach property owners, were used to ensure that the area would be a particular kind of summer resort. In the 1870s and 1880s, for example, the Parks Committee planted and maintained shade trees along the Beach Strip. In 1885, at the request of influential summer residents, the committee prevented the construction of boathouses that would "interfere materially with the enjoyment of the Beach promenading."[65] Summer residents also tried to stop the opening of a bar in the late 1880s; although unsuccessful, their opposition probably deterred some from even trying the same thing.

Apart from the many ornate summer residences on the Beach Strip, two buildings symbolized its social transformation between the 1870s and 1890s. In 1875, a luxurious resort hotel was built where the old Baldry tavern had once stood, a year after it and its hostelry burnt to the ground.[66] The new hotel was clearly more exclusive, borrowing its name from the American city of Newport's famous elite resort, the Ocean House. This elaborate three-storey structure near the south side of the canal piers on the bayside provided a social centre for high society. Those who could afford it enjoyed large, airy, and well-furnished rooms, excellent dining facilities, and impressive views from its second-storey wraparound balcony. Within a few years, the Ocean House added more amenities to offer the kinds of recreation typically found at a high-quality resort – a bowling alley, a billiards room, a ballroom, and a bar.[67]

In 1892, the opulence of the Ocean House was exceeded by the new clubhouse of the Royal Hamilton Yacht Club (RHYC), built next door after the RHYC relocated from the increasingly crowded North End port. Established in 1888, the RHYC promoted recreational sailing culture among Hamilton's elite.[68] To the general public, the new clubhouse was both conspicuous and inaccessible. Its "gem of a building" offered all the amenities of club life to its restricted membership. A roofed gangway covered its entrance to the canal pier. Wide galleries wrapped around its first two storeys, providing members with a magnificent view of both the lake and the bay. Inside, it had all the trappings of the good life: marble washstands; a banquet hall for fine dining, with an exquisite carved oak mantel and glazed tile hearth; and game rooms for whist, chess, and other such sedate entertainments. Like the Ocean House, the clubhouse was a place for the elite to see and be seen. Both helped set the tone of the Beach Strip as a fashionable resort community, bringing to it what Hamilton's populist newspaper, the *Herald,* dryly termed "sassiety."[69]

Hamilton politicians did much to pander to the recreational and aesthetic tastes of this group. In 1895, three city officials convinced the Canadian government to remove all unnecessary buildings on the land that it controlled around the Burlington Canal near the two magnificent buildings. This entailed the removal of a number of small venues for popular amusements – a photograph gallery, a candy shop, and an ice cream booth – along with a boathouse and an ice house.[70] The city officials also got swimming in the canal and camping on canal land outlawed, even though they were open for general public use. These actions represented efforts to define the type of recreational space the land would be. As a *Spectator* journalist noted approvingly of the clean-up efforts, "The beach is now beginning to be what it can and ought to be, a well-planned, well-laid out summer resort, in every way restful to the mind, body and eye."[71]

To make the beach community conform to their vision of an orderly recreational space, local politicians and officials worked with the provincial commissioner of Crown lands to firmly secure the City's claims to the area. Throughout the spring of 1895, the commissioner resolved a series of outstanding disputes over the exact claims of the original inhabitants of the beach. A newspaper headline captured the overall result: "More Land for the City: Squatters Compelled to Give Up Property on the Beach."[72] Although he recognized their property rights, the City's solicitor (himself a Beach Strip summer property owner) convinced the commissioner of Crown lands to restrict the extent of their claims.[73] By the summer of 1895, the City of Hamilton had acquired formal control over about a third of the Beach Strip. Of the land it controlled, about a fifth was already held by private individuals. Other parts of the City's land had been devoted to six short avenues running between the central Beach Road and the lake. These landscaped avenues would allow for further property development while ensuring that people who built summer residences could reach the lake. The Parks Committee also retained some of the property, to establish the kind of orderly and restful parks that it was working to create on the canal lands.

Despite the City's commitment to retaining accessible public space, some observers shared lighthouse keeper Campbell's sense that it had failed to seize the opportunity that public control of the beach had offered. In an angry letter to the *Spectator*, one writer with the pen name "Rustic" voiced some of this criticism:

> The beach was leased to the city in the interest of the public, but the city at once sold and shut the public out of the most desirable part. Those who remember the beach in the time of the Baldry hostelry, when the public were free to roam wherever they chose over that part of the beach, know that nothing can undo the mischief the city has done in ruining and closing forever what might have been one of the most desirable parks in Ontario. Talk of "great improvements made!" Talk rather of *the heritage of the people closed against them*.[74]

THE BAY MIGHT BE community property, but the use of public authority clearly revealed who did, and who did not, have power over that property. Plainly, there had been no golden age when all members of the community shared equally in its abundant resources; from the outset, those with power struggled to shape nature to serve their own interests, though conflicts regarding its use were often muted until the 1890s. Most Hamiltonians benefitted, if unequally, from measures to improve the competitive economic position of their city and its businesses. At least some of the advantages of the sanitation system gradually included the wider community, and only in the 1880s did some observers begin to worry about the consequences of the sewage system for some residents. In a bay that still contained wide-open spaces to play, efforts at regulation and exclusion did not appear particularly dramatic; its extensive shoreline and waters could still accommodate a range of activities and uses.

The fate of the Beach Strip, however, suggested what could happen when a resource was perceived to be in short supply. The narrow sandbar offered an ideal but limited area in which people could escape from the city, and civic leaders stepped in to ensure that the wealthier residents had access to it. But as early as the 1860s, another important resource was becoming increasingly scarce – fish. Efforts to conserve and revive fish stocks reveal the conflict regarding who ought to control that community property and how it was to be controlled.

2

Conserving Nature

The Education of John William Kerr,
1864–88

O N SUNDAY, 14 JANUARY 1866, Hamilton's fishery inspector, John William Kerr, observed two men spearing fish in an ice hut on Cootes Paradise, off Burlington Bay. Recently, and over Kerr's objections, the Province of Canada West had made winter spear fishing legal, but not on the Sabbath. Refusing to accept a bribe of "good whiskey," the energetic Kerr promptly confiscated the spear and set off with it. One of the men, Robert Barney, who lived in Hamilton's Irish Catholic working-class district of Corktown, decided not to let Kerr walk away. He chased him down and, perhaps inspired by some of the good whiskey, attempted to wrestle the spear away from him. He soon came to his senses. Kerr, a former member of the Irish Constabulary, broke free, drew his pistol, aimed, and threatened to shoot Barney dead in his tracks.[1]

The next day, in the quiet of his office, Kerr reported the incident to his superior, the commissioner of Crown lands, and requested to be furnished with a proper gun.[2] He then completed and submitted his first annual report as regional fishery inspector, in which he praised Burlington Bay as a "mine of wealth" and hoped that "every facility will be provided me for its proper protection."[3] The words recalled the views that Kerr had expressed in earlier correspondence, when he had promised that with good fishing legislation to protect Hamilton's enclosed harbour against all fishers except anglers, Lake Ontario would have "ten thousand more fish to one as compared with its present position."[4]

By the 1860s, the decline of fish stocks in Lake Ontario concerned provincial politicians, and as Kerr's comments suggest, Hamilton's civic leaders convinced them that Burlington Bay could play a crucial role in any conservation measures. They argued that for the sake of the lake fishery, the bay environment needed proper management. Although Kerr's jurisdiction extended throughout the western end of the lake, he paid special attention to Burlington Bay. According to one local source, from his home on the top of the escarpment overlooking the city and the bay, "he could see through a telescope for 20 miles in every direction and could usually reach offenders before damage had been done."[5]

Kerr took up his position with very clear ideas of what constituted "damage" to the fishery and began actively crusading to form and enforce the regulations governing fishing in the bay. It was no accident that he confiscated Barney's spear. In his view, spearing was unsportsmanlike and therefore both wasteful and the wrong way to fish. Class-based definitions of proper recreation shaped conservation initiatives such as Kerr's: fish and game would be protected if mid-Victorian ideas of cultivated and legitimate sporting behaviour were extended to fishing and hunting.[6] Faced with scarcity, Hamilton's social and political leaders thus once again sought to use the state to define for themselves and others the proper use of the bay's shared resources. Changes to the provincial fishery regulations in the 1850s and 1860s, and the appointment of Kerr, who was the secretary of the Wentworth Society for the Protection of Game and Fish, as one of the province's first fishery inspectors, testified to the power of elites to mould nature in their own image. The resistance of commercial fishers, local farmers, and urban workers to those regulations, the continued decline of fish stocks, and Kerr's re-evaluation of his own beliefs limited that power.

THE BAY'S EXTENSIVE WATERSHED – including the large western marsh known both as Cootes Paradise and Dundas Marsh, as well as the swampy inlets of the southern shore that some residents associated with disease – provided plenty of spawning and feeding grounds for a variety of fish. The early inhabitants were well acquainted with the abundance of this fishery. Elizabeth Simcoe, wife of the province's first lieutenant-governor, recorded in her diary on 11 September 1796 that "the River and Bay were full of canoes, the Indians were fishing, we bought some fine salmon of them."[7] Her account suggests that the fish were speared, a technique that fascinated European observers and was later adopted by early settlers in the region, much to the consternation of sportsmen who promoted the art and science of angling.[8]

By the mid-1840s, the fishing industry had contributed to the establishment of a small non-Native community along the Beach Strip. The sandbar provided an excellent base for fishing stations: its relatively shallow waters were good for dragging seine nets and (after 1853) for fixing gill nets. Although many settlers lacked formal legal title to their land, they worked out their own system of property rights.[9] Fishing stations gave fishers exclusive access to areas along the bay shoreline and in nearby Lake Ontario. As the market for fish grew in the 1850s, the price of a fishing station rose to around two hundred dollars. The beach community resisted efforts by the provincial government to formalize land and fishing titles, refusing to pay it more than ten dollars for twenty-one-year leases. Its members could not sustain this resistance, however, and by the mid-1860s, they were paying provincial authorities between thirty and five hundred dollars for the right to a station. Some squatters also negotiated legal land claim recognition, although some claims remained disputed for decades.[10] When the census-taker for the region arrived in 1871, he found over a dozen fishing families among the approximately twenty-five households that made up the small community.[11] Even as the Beach Strip attracted more summer recreational development in the last quarter of the nineteenth century, fishing and market gardening would continue to provide an important if declining economic basis for this core community.[12]

The construction of canals, the reconstruction of the bay's shoreline, and urban and industrial growth all affected the aquatic ecology of Burlington Bay, Cootes Paradise, and Lake Ontario. It is difficult to document the extent of these changes, however, since so little is known about the early fishery. In the 1820s and 1830s, the colonial legislature recognized the importance of the bay's fishery by creating laws to protect its herring.[13] During the 1840s, at least as fishers later remembered it, one could go into the bay and catch herring as well as pickerel, pike, and bass all in a day. However, fishermen most frequently caught the early mainstay of the Beach Strip fishery on Lake Ontario – whitefish, ciscoes, and salmon trout. As early as 1860, environmental changes and fishing practices threatened the most popular cold-water species such as trout and whitefish in the lake, and herring in both the lake and bay. Throughout the next two decades, these fish, as well as sturgeon and northern pike, adapted poorly to the changing environmental conditions. Fishers continued to catch herring through the late nineteenth century, but the bay also featured growing numbers of warmer-water and "rough" fish, including bullheads, freshwater drums, yellow perch, and carp. Some of these species began thriving at precisely the same time as some of their predators disappeared. Others proved better able to adapt to the conditions of an urban harbour.[14]

A series of related human developments altered the nature of the bay fishery. Hamilton's early settlement emerged around, and then over, a number of important marshes and wetlands. This transformed a significant component of the fish habitat. Sewage, garbage, and industrial pollutants such as acid from refineries and dyes from cotton mills changed the floor of the bay as well as the water's chemistry. Settlers also recognized the subsistence and commercial value of the fish. For a time, they ruthlessly exploited what appeared to be an inexhaustible resource. Overfishing doubtless contributed to the decline in some of the most valuable fish stocks. Nevertheless, as Joseph Taylor points out in connection with Pacific salmon, overfishing needs to be considered in its historical context; though the size of the catch could remain the same, it might nonetheless have a detrimental effect on fish populations because the quality of their environment has declined.[15]

In mid-Victorian Ontario, however, those who sought to counteract the decline of the fisheries in Lake Ontario focused on the problem of overfishing. Kevin Wamsley has shown that Upper Canadian game legislation before 1840 aimed to preserve stocks of animals, fish, and fowl by creating hunting seasons, ostensibly based on the natural breeding season for the species.[16] Although fishing laws penalized those who polluted the water, the state directed far more attention and administrative energy toward reforming the behaviour of those who caught the fish. In such a view, conservation required that fishing practices be civilized.[17]

By 1857, the United Province of Canada had adopted its first comprehensive fishery legislation, in an era in which the state increasingly legislated civilized methods of hunting and fishing.[18] The Fisheries Act created two superintendents, one each for Canada East and Canada West, to administer and enforce its regulations. It required that salmon, muskinonge, speckled trout, and black bass be caught by hook and line, and only during a predetermined six-month season.[19] To establish fair fishing methods, it also completely banned spearing of these species and forbade the use of torches or any form of artificial light to attract fish. These restrictions were clearly unpopular because within a year, a new Fisheries Act eliminated the closed season except for salmon. Nevertheless, the ban on unfair practices continued.[20] The 1858 legislation, however, introduced new restrictions that were specifically designed for Burlington Bay and Dundas Marsh. Earlier special legislation had already stopped fishers from taking advantage of the channel that connected the bay to Lake Ontario. It outlawed the setting of nets in any way that prevented the passage of fish to and from the bay.[21] The 1858 law incorporated these earlier provisions, completely banning the use of gill nets and seines in the bay and marsh.[22]

This legislation reflected the environmental concerns and social power of sport fishers. Although the regulations allowed angling at all times and in all places, they severely limited or simply outlawed other methods of catching fish. Even the proposed closed seasons, covering the late fall and winter months, suited anglers better than they did commercial fishers, who saw cold waters and weather as ideal for catching and marketing several types of fish. In Burlington Bay, legislators went beyond establishing closed seasons when they banned all fishing practices except angling year round. Yet the new legislation provided superintendents with few resources to enforce the regulations, which helped empower anglers since it left enforcement to local fish and game clubs.

In the summer of 1860, John William Kerr helped arrange a meeting of a small group of "gentlemen" in a Hamilton saloon to organize the Wentworth Society for the Protection of Game and Fish.[23] The powerful social and political leader Sir Allan MacNab lent his name and prestige to the society as its first president, yet the former prime minister of Canada West appears not to have played a significant role in its affairs.[24] Its active members better represented Hamilton's middle class than did MacNab. Of the twenty-one members whose names are recorded in the society's minutes and found in city directories, all but three worked in non-manual professional, business, government, or clerical positions.[25] They included a handful of politically active local leaders and men who served on the executives of other voluntary agencies such as the Militia and Hook and Ladder Companies, secret societies such as the Freemasons, and fraternal lodges such as the Oddfellows. As Christopher Anstead argues, the ritual, literature, and social practices of late-nineteenth-century Ontario fraternal organizations helped in the formulation of a middle-class culture and spread the ideology of middle-class respectability to a wider audience.[26] The Wentworth Society for the Protection of Game and Fish, a mid-Victorian middle-class sports club, had members who were interested in shaping the behaviour and activities of the larger community.[27]

The society aimed to "secure the observance of game and fish laws by information and by bringing to justice violations of the law."[28] During an era in which the state increasingly relied upon private fish and game clubs to protect wildlife resources, it lobbied for any changes in the legislation that it thought necessary.[29] The society was an exclusive affair; its members, who paid an annual fee of one dollar, were selected by club vote.[30] In keeping with its mandate to extend state authority in matters of fishery

conservation, this private voluntary organization offered a five-dollar re-
ward for anyone who got violators convicted for breaches of the game or
fish laws.[31]

The society quickly acted on matters that affected what it considered
to be its own sport fishery. In the spring of 1861, it held a series of special
meetings that focused member attention on the Fisheries Act.[32] While
praising the 1858 legislation that outlawed the use of nets in the bay, it
expressed concern about the difficulties of enforcing the law. Its members
petitioned the government to appoint officers who would have the time
and power to prosecute violators.[33] If necessary, they would pay the officers
themselves. But this turned out not to be required. The government responded to concerns about the act with a series of amendments, including
the appointment of local fishery inspectors. In 1865, it overhauled the
legislation further, leaving the precise details of many regulations to the
discretion of the commissioner of Crown lands and the government of
the day, presumably following consultation with local inspectors.[34]

It was in this context that John Kerr, a co-founder and secretary of the
Wentworth Society for the Protection of Game and Fish, was appointed
the first fishery inspector for western Lake Ontario in December 1864.
Born in County Fermanagh, Ireland, Kerr had served in the Irish Constabulary before migrating to Canada in 1844 at the age of thirty-three.
His uncle, an Anglican clergyman near St. Thomas, Ontario, probably
helped him secure employment as a schoolteacher and then as a clerk in
the London Post Office. By the late 1840s, Kerr had moved to Hamilton,
where he found work as a clerk, eventually chief clerk, in the engineer's
office of the Great Western Railway (Figure 6). He left the company in
1854, having obtained a sixty-eight-hectare land grant from the government. His land lay on the brow of Hamilton Mountain, the edge of the
escarpment overlooking the city and Burlington Bay. Politically conservative and socially active, Kerr had good social and political connections.
He sat on county council and was a long-time member of the St. John's
Masonic Lodge. After just fifteen years in Canada, he managed to become
the kind of middle-class landed gentleman farmer who could help organize
a game and fish society, a role that did not stop him from accepting a
government appointment.[35]

Indeed, Kerr eagerly took up his new position, thoroughly convinced
that angling in the bay and marsh was a "sufficient fair mode of fishing
for all." When the provincial commissioner of Crown lands expressed
concern that under the law the area's waters "seem to be kept for sportsmen" as a permanent reserve, Kerr clearly outlined the views that informed

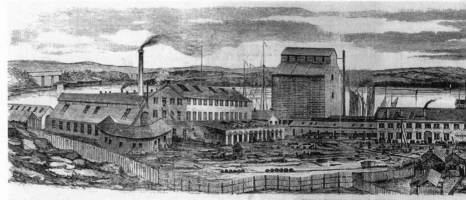

GREAT WESTERN RAILWAY WORK SHOPS, HAMILTON.

his vigorous enforcement of the law.[36] He rejected the claim that the conservationist project was elitist; he saw it as efficient and equitable, economic, and democratic.

Why did Kerr and others view angling as the only acceptable form of fishing in the bay? He contended that the use of nets and spears was ruining its fishery. The argument against nets, especially the gill nets that had been introduced to the region in the early 1850s, seemed more clear. The nets indiscriminately swept up large numbers of fish and held them for long periods, which proved particularly destructive; unwanted fish were often damaged by netting. People later told stories of the waste associated with gill nets and seines, claiming that, for example, fishers dumped hundreds of unwanted young whitefish on the beach, leaving them to rot or to become pig feed. Worse still, as one fisher recalled, the spawning season was the "best" time to net some of the most valuable fish, particularly herring.[37] Kerr saw establishing appropriate net sizes as a way to reduce waste in the lake fishery. He also saw the need for a special law to protect Burlington Bay and Dundas Marsh, since as spawning grounds for Lake Ontario, they "cannot be surpassed by any other water in the province for the propagating of [its] fish."[38] To preserve the bay for a healthy lake fishery, he maintained, the state needed to restrain a few greedy commercial fishers in the interests of the fishing industry as a whole, not just sport fishers.

Promoting a rational, respectable, and sporting approach to fishing, as well as conserving the sport fishery for sportsmen, also concerned Kerr.[39] As British historian Peter Bartrip concludes in his study of British fishery regulations, angling never acquired the same elite class connotations that

hunting held.[40] Indeed, resurrecting the idyllic pastoral image of fishing that was associated with the seventeenth-century writings of Izaak Walton, Victorian angling promoters emphasized the fact that anyone could – and did – engage in sport fishing.[41] Kerr believed that the 1858 Ontario fishing legislation had been designed to protect the sport of fishing on behalf of tradesmen, Great Western Railway mechanics, office and store clerks, merchants, and the "mixed multitude of all citizens," all of whom "repast there [on the bay] after the toils of the day for amusement."[42]

However, though the middle-class fishing clubs that held state-supported power projected angling as a classless activity, they also socially constructed it in class-based behavioural ways. They viewed it as a particularly worthy form of outdoors recreation for the working classes, to be preferred over the less respectable activities that took place in saloons, with their associated rough sports, swearing and drinking, gambling, and immorality. The emphasis on respectability in sport fishing itself is telling. Although the precise meaning of the word changed through time, its essence remained associated with industry, sobriety, and morality: respectable men took responsibility for their own welfare and that of their families.[43] They carried with them an innate sense of justice and honesty, and the highest regard for "fair play" in all aspects of life, but particularly in their leisure-time pursuits. Angling was thought to reflect and reinforce respectability, offering a healthy alternative to the temptations of the industrial city.[44] The *Hamilton Spectator,* whose editors actively supported this vision, told its readers to "go fishing" (Figure 7). Reprinting an article from *American Field and Stream,* it explained the larger social benefits of the sport for city dwellers:

FIGURE 7   With his canoe lying nearby, a man enjoys the lush marsh vegetation and peaceful solitude available along the shore in Cootes Paradise. *Courtesy of Local History and Archives Department, Hamilton Public Library.*

It is on the bosom of the sea or of the great lake, or along their shores, or by the breezy river, or willow skirted stream, or noisy brook, that the angler finds his natural rest and occupation, far enough from the busy haunts of his fellows to get rid of the foul atmosphere too often engendered, morally and physically, by their herding together.[45]

Because of the moral imperative associated with angling, sportsmen and legislators abhorred the use of jacklights, torchlights, guns, and spears. To them, such means were simply not sporting since they believed that angling was about skill and prowess, about "fairness" and "science," and about man's ability to conquer – not trick – nature.[46] Kerr believed that angling would preserve the fishery in the bay for the entire community and that it cultivated appropriate attitudes toward nature and society. The state would restrain a few greedy fishers in the interests of healthy and wholesome outdoor leisure for all.

KERR TOOK UP HIS NEW position as fishery inspector just as the annual ice fishing season commenced in January 1865. Within weeks, he began cracking down on spear fishing through the ice, a practice that he saw as damaging to the fish. He posted notices on all the ice huts he found on the bay and confiscated their spearing equipment. If the owners of the huts did not remove them, he destroyed them. The results, Kerr reported to the commissioner of Crown lands, were "most satisfactory ... Not a spearing box could be found," where more than a hundred had existed the previous winter.[47] His crusade to eliminate winter spearing had begun.

Fish spearing had a long tradition in the bay, passed on to European settlers by the Mississauga and Iroquois peoples. When the Reverend Patrick Bell visited Hamilton during the 1830s, he described winter spearing in his journal. The practice changed little throughout the century.[48] Using a wooden decoy fish to attract the fish to the hole, the fisher plunged a long-handled, multi-pronged spear into them as they surfaced. When they were plentiful, large numbers could be speared, something that commercial fishermen did throughout the winter. One man later recalled that he and others made a good living from winter spearing during the 1850s and 1860s, catching as many as six pike and an equal number of bass in a day. Winter-caught fish, he and others contended, stayed fresh longer at the market and tasted better than those caught by other means at other times.[49]

Not everyone agreed with winter spearing, however, and its nineteenth-century opponents developed a number of arguments to support their convictions. For example, they asserted that the hole broken in the ice had the same effect as torchlight, unfairly luring the target. They deemed this both unsporting and wasteful, since fishers could not distinguish between the types of fish being caught. Fish that managed to escape were often seriously injured, and caught fish were often damaged. Furthermore, indiscriminate spearing depleted important species. Spear fishers challenged these arguments, especially since the evidence against the practice never seemed to be fully proven; yet their opponents remained unmoved.[50] Perhaps the social prejudice against spearing had its roots in the types of people who used it for sustenance (such as Corktown's Robert Barney), and their presumed threat to respectability. The men who fished with spears, Kerr wrote, were transients who had no stake in the community, "intruders and trespassers – sailors in summer, poaching fishermen in winter."[51] Given this claim of transiency, it is ironic that many of the commercial fishers who had used nets in the bay also used spears during the winter. This troubled Kerr, who may have feared that any concessions on the issue of spearing would lead them to demand an end to the ban on netting.[52]

Indeed, Kerr and his crusade faced many challenges. Individual fishers resisted by threatening his life and setting up ice hut traps on thin ice, designed to "precipitate" him into the freezing waters of the bay.[53] The fishers who lived on the Beach Strip deeply resented government interference in their livelihood. They formally challenged Kerr's authority and subscribed money to obtain legal advice. They charged him with trespass and theft, sued him for the value of any property he confiscated, and argued that he could not bring them before a Hamilton magistrate if their alleged violations had occurred closer to the shores of other counties.[54] One fisher, the brother of a magistrate in a neighbouring county, declared that his family would "fish where they like, when they like and how they like."[55] Not surprisingly, Kerr pressed for legislative changes in 1865 to sanction his actions and provide him with a legal foundation that was less "open to challenge by crafty lawyers."[56]

Although Kerr managed to get his legal authority sustained and strengthened, and seemed unperturbed by several threats against his life, he eventually lost the political battle over winter spearing. Three prominent community leaders, including a local justice of the peace, had little trouble gathering signatures for a petition demanding people's right to spear. Kerr dismissed their appeals as the self-serving work of wealthy and greedy farmers, yet he couldn't stop his political masters from changing the fishing regulations.[57] In December 1865, the commissioner of Crown lands declared that people could spear pike, bass, and pickerel in the bay, both in daytime and by torchlight, if they bought a licence costing a dollar. Kerr had to limit his crusade to preventing people from spearing herring and stopping them from fishing on Sunday.[58]

A number of Hamiltonians who fished for a living or for survival had successfully challenged Kerr and his associates at the Wentworth Society for the Protection of Game and Fish. They contended that there was "something invidious" in their exclusion from the bay fishery, just because they chose to use spears instead of hooks and lines. Although the commercial fishers led the way in openly defying Kerr, local farmers and members of the working class, who fished to supplement their incomes and diet in winter, joined in their resistance at the time of year when other work was so hard to find.[59] Winter spearing became sanctioned as an exceptional activity, subject to constant regulation; each year, local fishers and residents had to petition for permission to to continue spearing fish. After 1866, however, in a surprising development, they could look to Kerr for support. He abandoned his crusade and regularly backed their petitions, even applying for permission on their behalf. He used his expertise and authority to assure other government authorities that spearing did not endanger fish populations.[60]

Why this about-turn? Perhaps recognizing that he was fighting a losing battle, Kerr might have supported winter spearing to get people on board with his larger efforts to regulate the bay fishery. More concessions were to come. In 1868, for example, local politicians supported a petition from nearly five hundred residents to allow fishers to spear herring through the ice, using torchlights during November and December. Kerr agreed to the expansion of the winter bay fishery but not during the critical time when herring were spawning there.[61] Yet only a year later, he reconsidered his position and argued that allowing the spearing of some of the "millions" of herring that entered the bay to spawn would "infuse a spirit of satisfaction amongst the community."[62] Like its winter equivalent, fall spearing remained a privilege, which the department, on Kerr's advice, controlled and granted annually. Since it occurred during the herring spawn, Kerr appeared much more alert to its impact on fish populations. Whenever his observations led him to conclude that herring were less abundant, in either the bay or the west end of the lake, he withdrew his support for fall spearing. For five seasons between 1874 and 1879, and again several times in the 1880s, he banned the practice and withstood complaints from various fishers and other members of the community. He faced less open resistance to these particular bans than in previous years, perhaps because people saw them as a temporary response to conditions, not an ideological aversion to spearing. Perhaps Kerr also succeeded because he linked respect for his bans to his continuing support of winter spearing.[63]

Kerr's concessions went far beyond the question of spearing. Just two years after taking up his post, he re-evaluated his opposition to the use of seine and gill nets in Burlington Bay. After "mature consideration" of the matter, including "several interviews" with members of the fishing community, he loosened some of the restrictions that he had so avidly defended in the past. He now believed that some net usage would not interfere with the fishery, confessing that "until very recently, I was not aware that our fishermen on Burlington Beach were so extremely poor and needy." He asked for the authority to permit nets in the bay but indicated that he needed to limit their use. He specified the time of year, the permitted area, the type of fish, and sometimes the names of fishers who were to be involved.[64] He began to allow the limited use of nets in 1867, and two years later he mapped out six Beach Strip bayside fishing grounds, equivalent to the fishing stations on its lakeside. He allocated them to six fishers for netting herring and rough fish such as pike, suckers, catfish, mullet, and eel. He allowed netting only from mid-April to mid-June, after the ice had thawed but before lake fishing started up. Kerr may have hoped that these moves would enhance his authority, which he apparently exercised even-handedly as he impartially recommended both fishers who had previously resisted his regulations and those who had assisted him.[65]

If commercial fishers welcomed the reintroduction of nets into the bay, even on a limited basis, other people did not. Hamilton factory owner and former mayor Ben Charlton led the way in opposing the policy change, arguing that the nets disrupted both spawning and the fishery more generally. Kerr now rejected a claim that he himself had once made. He pointed out that no seasonal restrictions existed for any of the fish enumerated for this special fishery, restrictions that usually applied to fish with clearly identified spawning seasons. He also emphasized that the licence represented only a minor exception to the rule against nets in the bay; it applied only to certain areas at the eastern end, to a season when fishing incomes were low, and to suckers and other coarse species, "the poor man's fish."

Opposition to the policy nevertheless delayed approval of the licences that Kerr had recommended in 1870, much to his dismay. After five years in his position, the former secretary of the game and fish society proclaimed in frustration that he hoped "never to see the Bay set apart again as a pleasure resort for rich fishermen, to the exclusion of the poor."[66] Throughout the remainder of his career, Kerr resisted efforts to ban the use of nets in the bay, although he faced considerable pressure from some local political leaders to do so. He saw the netting concession as relatively harmless to the fish – it was limited to about six weeks in the spring and to a specific part of the bay.[67] He continued to champion conservation measures that he saw as democratic and equitable, but after observing and working with the members of the community who relied on the bay fishery for subsistence, he no longer believed that angling was a "sufficient fair mode of fishing for all."

IN 1870, AS KERR BEGAN to defend the limited use of spears and nets, he took aim at another source of problems for fish in the bay – pollution. Section 18 of the Fisheries Act permitted prosecutions of those who allowed "ballast, coal ashes, stone or other prejudicial or deleterious substances" to be dumped into "any water where fishing is carried on."[68] In May 1870, Kerr noticed and promptly reported that a large number of oil-covered bass and sunfish were floating in the water. He believed that some of the oil might accidentally have entered the bay when a refinery near Dundas Marsh had burned to the ground. Yet he also suspected that it had come from a refinery at Sherman Inlet, one of the large eastern inlets. The ever-zealous Kerr apparently continued to monitor the refinery, which belonged

FIGURE 8 Aerial view of Sherman Inlet, ca. 1919. This is one of our earliest images of the inlet *(centre)*, taken long after much of it had been filled in. International Harvester *(immediately above inlet)* acquired Oliver Chilled Plow *(below inlet)* in 1919. The smoky industrial complex reaching out into the bay to the left of the Harvester Plant is Stelco. Note the series of narrow inlets *(top right)*, most of which stretched inland as far as Sherman would have back in the 1870s. *Courtesy of Archives of Ontario, McCarthy Aero Services Ltd. Fonds, C285-1-0-0-277.*

to James Williams, a prominent carriage and railway car manufacturer, a pioneer in the Canadian oil industry, and a provincial politician.[69] The following year, as Williams championed city council's effort to reserve recreational land on the Beach Strip, he found himself charged in Magistrates' Court with allowing chemicals and "other deleterious substances" to endanger fish in public waters.

Kerr took pains in preparing his case against Williams. He arranged for a local fisher who sometimes helped him in other matters to visit the oil refinery. The man testified that "black tar coloured stuff" flowed from the refinery into the inlet, where it covered the water's surface in a three-yard-wide streak. He added that vegetation on the banks of the inlet appeared to be burned and had stopped growing. Kerr had a local fish dealer give a customer some pike caught nearly five kilometres away from the inlet;

the customer testified that the fish was "impregnated with coal oil and unfit for food" (Figure 8). Kerr also had the refinery manager explain how a variety of chemicals, "all of which passed into the hole" under the building, made their way through pipes and drains to the inlet. The chemicals included 1,636 litres of sulphuric acid per week, used to remove impurities from the crude oil. Yet despite these efforts, the magistrate dismissed Kerr's case because he had not firmly proven that the company discharge harmed or tainted the fish. The results did not entirely disappoint Kerr. As a result of the case, Williams began to pass the chemicals through a large watertank before releasing them, which at least diluted their effect, though not, as he claimed, "neutralizing" it.[70]

John Kerr continued to keep an eye on factories along Sherman Inlet. In the spring of 1873, he again took Williams to court, along with the owners of another oil refinery and a slaughterhouse. Kerr withdrew the charges against the refinery when its owner agreed to construct tanks to dilute its discharge. When the magistrate levied a relatively hefty fine of fifty dollars and court costs against the slaughterhouse, Williams, whose oil refinery was again charged, took no chances. He pled guilty and paid a ten-dollar fine. Kerr persisted with this strategy. In 1876, he took a refinery to court after a year of operations. As before, he agreed to withdraw the charges when the company installed dilution tanks like the ones used by its nearby competitors.[71]

Emboldened by these small successes in Sherman Inlet, Kerr turned his sights on an industrial area along a creek that ran through the town of Dundas into Cootes Paradise.[72] In August 1877, he responded to reports of dead fish floating in the marsh, the Desjardins Canal, and the bay, and he soon connected them to a local gas works, which cleaned its tanks by pumping them into the creek. He quickly discovered that the problem involved more than the ammonia from the gas works, because other factories routinely disposed of their waste by pouring it into the creek. He identified sulphuric acid and dyestuffs from cotton and paper mills, as well as lime from the paper mill, a glue factory, and a tannery. "In one place," Kerr reported, "the lime was eight inches deep" at the bottom of the creek. He charged four of the owners of the factories, including the gas works, under the Fisheries Act. Once again, he hoped that the charges would convince the factories to alter their industrial practices, to either dilute – or divert – their waste products.[73]

He was wrong. Instead, what Kerr termed "influential parties," including the Dundas mayor and town council, objected to his crusade against these major industries. In September, they asked the minister of marine and fisheries to withdraw the charges, to forgo collecting the fines from the factories that were already convicted, and most importantly, to exempt the creek from the provisions of the Fisheries Act. Kerr pleaded with his political masters not to accede to their demands. He contended that the factories' waste disposal practices were careless, and citing the example of a Dundas tannery that had been given a warning a year earlier, he noted that they would not reform their practices unless pressed to do so. He refuted the argument that what happened in the creek did not affect the fishery in any substantial way and warned, "I cannot fine [refineries] for allowing coal oil to pass into Sherman's Inlet, which enters into [the] bay and destroys and kills fish, and allow all those Dundas people, who have done the same thing to a greater extent, with more deadly and poisonous substances, to escape – knowing as I do, that they can prevent it, if they try."[74] Claiming that this exemption would set a precedent that would weaken his authority elsewhere, Kerr may have overestimated the political support for his general campaign against industrial polluters. The minister promptly ordered him to suspend all proceedings against the Dundas factories and prevented any future action by exempting the creek from the Fisheries Act.[75] Significantly, when Kerr tried in 1882 to persuade the owner of a new North End cotton factory to treat its dyes before sending them directly into the bay, the man immediately applied for an exemption under the act, arguing that his competitor in Dundas had one.[76]

After this, Kerr rarely used his authority under section 18 of the Fisheries Act to combat pollution. Although some local business and political leaders may have been interested in recreational fishing, they would not jeopardize industrial development for the benefit of the fishery. As the 1880s wore on, an aging John Kerr grew more disillusioned with the increasingly contaminated bay because of the "filthy sewerage running into [it] from the city of Hamilton." As political leaders allowed more and more families to send their household and human waste through the sewers into the inlets of the bay, they seriously complicated Kerr's ability to link problems in the fishery to particular industrial practices.[77]

IN 1883, A SMALL GROUP of men, led by several local physicians and lawyers, including a former Hamilton mayor, gathered in a room at the St. George's Society to create the Wentworth Fish and Game Protection Association. It had the same aims and the same social background as the society that Kerr had helped to found nearly a quarter of a century earlier, seeking to ensure fish regulation enforcement and suggesting legislative changes. Kerr was invited to join. He declined. His defence of a regulated spear and net fishery, and his crusade against polluters, had alienated him from the city's social and political elite. Over the next few years, he feuded with the association. He attempted to prevent it from interfering with "legal, legitimate net fishing," while simultaneously alleging that its members used small gill nets in the bay and shot pike, all without even seeking permission.[78] When he was ordered in the winter of 1887 to prevent the spearing of bass, a species favoured by anglers, Kerr instantly suspected that the association was behind this "cruel" act. He complained to the deputy minister of fisheries that it was trying to take "the bit out of the poor man's mouth."[79] The association denied most of his charges and accused him of trying to link winter spearing with other practices such as open-water spearing and netting in the bay. These interfered with angling, which the association proclaimed the "true and legitimate sport."[80]

The feud revealed the education of John William Kerr. In 1860, when he had helped found a fish and game society, and in 1864 when he became fishery inspector, he, like the members of the new association, saw fishing as a sport. But his long career had widened his perspective, teaching him that fishing was also part of a livelihood for certain Hamiltonians. He supported open-water herring spearing in the late fall, winter spearing, and the use of nets in the spring, in an effort to sustain fishing as a means for some community members to feed themselves and their families, and, in particular, to maintain commercial fishing as a viable, if marginal, business. Kerr eventually concluded that the outlook of sports conservationists was more exclusive and elitist than he had originally thought. His experiences with prosecuting polluters simply reinforced this view. Some of the people who sought to end certain fishing practices appeared more than willing to condone using the bay as a convenient dump for industrial and household wastes. Kerr died in 1888, after passing on what he had learned to his sons, one of whom succeeded him as the local fishery inspector. Frederick Kerr continued to defend the same practices as his father.[81]

The feud also underlined the continuing community support for winter spearing. The new Fish and Game Protection Association carefully avoided being seen as opposed to the practice. In the early 1890s, when the Canadian government sought to ban winter spearing, it did so over the opposition of the Hamilton fishery inspector, and it prompted the creation of a new organization, the Hamilton Spearman's Association. This group had one purpose: to reinstate and sustain winter spearing in the bay. Fred Kerr and the new association countered arguments about the decline of fish stocks with a logic that was strongly rooted in historical and democratic terms. In 1891, Kerr explained that the fishery had been practised for over twenty-

FIGURE 9   Men efficiently set up a well-built and maintained hut for spear fishing, 1909. Note the spear lying on the ice at the far left. *Courtesy of Archives of Ontario, John Boyd Fonds, I0003387-OA.*

seven years and was conducted by "bricklayers, stonemasons and farmers who are out of employment in winter."[82] In even more colourful language, the Hamilton Spearman's Association stated, "For ages past, the poor and unemployed have, without restriction, enjoyed the privilege of spearing, and now, during this most unprecedented hard winter, with its numerous diseases and family bereavements, it seems more than cruel to deprive the honest citizen of even so meagre a means of living."[83] It succeeded in gathering four thousand names for a petition seeking to ensure that winter spearing, reinstated in 1895 on the eve of an election, would continue in 1896 and beyond. By 1910, more than 150 locals were paying a licence fee of one dollar for the right to spear fish through the ice.[84] Winter spearing remained controversial and still had to be defended but not within Hamilton and the nearby countryside. Despite continued opposition from a number of fishery officials outside the community, winter spear fishing would continue in Burlington Bay well into the twentieth century, actively supported by the members of John Kerr's family, who served as local fishery inspectors and who applied the lessons their father had learned (Figure 9).

IN 1893, CONSERVATIONIST Samuel Wilmot led an investigation into the Ontario fishery, reporting on the "almost complete destruction of the whitefish and salmon-trout fisheries in Lake Ontario and Lake Erie." Twenty-five to thirty years of regulation had not prevented their decline. Burlington Bay had not served as the great natural fish-spawning ground that John Kerr had envisioned. Even attempts at making it an artificial breeding zone, with the distribution of eggs and spawn from some of Wilmot's famous Ontario fish hatcheries, had failed. "Nature's balance," Wilmot concluded, had been "disturbed by the greed of man."[85] Wilmot continued to blame improper fishing practices, including what he called the "cruel and barbarous" sport of winter spearing and the ineffective regulation of the law. Others were not so sure. When Wilmot visited Hamilton in 1892, some spear fishers told him that the better class of fish could not be propagated in the bay, "owing to the marshy and seedy nature of its surroundings, and the fact that all or most of the city's sewage is being deposited in it." According to a *Hamilton Herald* reporter, Wilmot replied that that if they could "prove to him that the waters of the bay would in time kill off the fish by pollution, he would recommend that the fish be caught and eaten up." "The spearers," the reporter continued, "are of the opinion that they have fairly shown this will be the case before many years have passed."[86]

They probably would have said anything to lift the ban on winter spearing that Wilmot had helped impose for a few years. Nevertheless, by working in nature, they also had acquired local knowledge that sensitized them to the wider environmental changes that fishery conservationists like Wilmot needed to at least consider.[87] Some of these changes had concerned John Kerr in the 1870s and 1880s. He had learned that the civilized act of using the bay as a sink for waste posed a more serious threat to the fishery than the uncivilized behaviour of a few farmers, workers, and fishers.

3

Boosting Nature

The Contradictions of Industrial Promotion, 1892–1932

M ANY OF HAMILTON'S CIVIC leaders never imagined fishing as anything but a leisure pursuit because they were too busy envisioning their community as one whose fortunes rested on its other natural advantages, such as the ones that appealed to the interests of merchants and, increasingly, to industrialists. Yet economic and industrial development did not simply arise on its own: it had to be courted and shaped by human hands. Local urban boosters did just that in 1892, when they published a promotional book to advertise Hamilton to people who would be travelling through Niagara Falls en route to the World's Columbian Exposition (the Chicago World's Fair). Their large picture book sold Hamilton to travellers – and to potential investors – claiming that the bustling city of some fifty thousand people was "often called the Birmingham of Canada" and that it resembled the "larger and older hive of industry in her thrifty application of skill and capital to widely diversified industrial operations."[1]

To substantiate its claim of civic and industrial greatness, *Hamilton: The Birmingham of Canada* presented its readers with lots of evidence, especially photographs of local buildings and detailed descriptions of large and imposing factories (Figure 10). Readers could also see and learn about symbols of Hamilton's civic prosperity, such as its impressive banks, businesses, schools, and churches. They would discover that cutting-edge electrical and telephone wires ran down ordered, well-kept streets and that a large, attractive reservoir delivered clean water to homes and factories. An incline railway carried people up and down the escarpment, and a state-of-the-art electric street rail transported them around town. The many

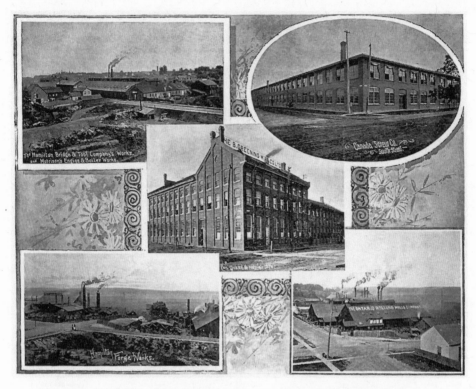

FIGURE 10   Some of the factories celebrated in 1892 promotional material. Ontario
Rolling Mills *(bottom right)* later merged with the Hamilton Blast Furnace Company
to become the Hamilton Steel Company, which, along with four other companies,
including the Canada Screw Company *(upper right),* became the Steel Company of
Canada in 1910 (commonly known as Stelco after 1915). Today, it is US Steel Canada.
From Hamilton: The Birmingham of Canada *(Hamilton: Times Printing, 1892).*

clubs made for a vibrant social and literary scene, and the many charitable
institutions showed that the place had a heart. The book paid particular
attention to the spacious elite homes at the foot of the escarpment – far
away from the factories – which bore impressive names such as Ravenscliffe,
Undercliffe, and Pinehurst. It also noted that though clearly an industrial
centre, Hamilton benefitted from the vineyards, fruit gardens, and orchards
that made the area "the garden of Canada."[2]

   In creating their book, promoters sought to distinguish the story of
Hamilton from that of other cities, especially those of the recently settled
American west. As they claimed, those towns seemingly appeared from

nowhere: "To boom [such a] town has become a perfect science in the hands of skilful land agents ... generally starting out with 'This City eight or ten years ago was a complete wilderness etc. etc. and now it has a population of etc. etc. and is etc. etc. and must become the etc. etc.'" By contrast, Hamilton was no frontier upstart. Its stately homes, banks, and factories had emerged as the logical products of years of "steady growth"; two decades of horse-drawn trolleys, for example, had preceded the new electric street rail. The book promised investors and immigrants the benefits of a mature but nevertheless modern city, one "with the most complete waterworks and sewer systems, both gas and electric lighting, and an excellent electric railway to all parts of town."[3]

Although the promotional book exuded confidence in Hamilton's industrial achievements and urban progress, its publication nevertheless reflected the anxious quest of late-nineteenth-century civic leaders to sustain and build their city in a highly competitive business atmosphere. Earlier initiatives had focused largely on building a strong regional town; by the 1890s, however, the development of a more tightly integrated North American economy spurred civic leaders to define a role for their town in national and transcontinental economies. Between 1888, when Hamilton began to benefit from the third reconstruction of the Welland Canal, and 1932, when further improvements reconfigured the canal for a fourth time and generated opportunities for new kinds of economic activity, the City confirmed its position as a significant Canadian industrial centre well connected by water, road, and rail (Figure 11). Whereas industrialists chose Hamilton for a variety of reasons related to access to markets, power, and productive materials, civic boosters certainly worked to fashion a city that would attract investment, particularly American investment. Initially, they "chased smokestacks," giving direct inducements to industrialists, such as cash bonuses, cheap land, low water rates, and tax incentives. They also promoted selective public investment in the harbour.[4] Significantly, Burlington Bay officially became Hamilton Harbour in 1919, taking a new name that emphasized its connections to commerce, industry, and the world beyond Hamilton's shore.[5]

Early Hamilton boosters took the natural beauty of the city, its bay, and the fertile land surrounding the Niagara Escarpment for granted, but they also understood that they were important features for selling their town to potential visitors and investors. "As the city falls away to the bay one realizes how Hamilton is blessed in its system of natural drainage," wrote Herbert Lister in 1913 (Figure 12). He explained,

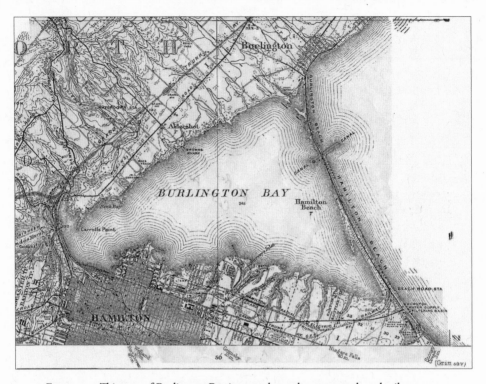

FIGURE 11   This map of Burlington Bay in 1909 shows the many roads and rail lines connecting the Beach Strip and Hamilton. *Department of Militia and Defence, Geographical Section, General Staff, No. 2197, Topographic Map, Hamilton, Ontario, Sheet 33, 1907–09, 1:63360. Courtesy of Library and Archives of Canada.*

The sewers gravitate, as naturally as could be wished, and these empty into a disposal plant that "treats" the matter and thereby ensures non-contamination of the waters of the bay. From a sanitary point of view Hamilton is right. Her water is drawn from the depths of Lake Ontario, six miles distant, is sand filtered and famous for its purity.[6]

Proclaiming the city "the prettiest and healthiest in America," Hamilton's new industrial commissioner had built on this theme a year earlier. In one booster publication, he listed twelve factors that made it "the Best Manufacturing City in Canada." They included its "Great Natural Beauty," "Cleanliness and Healthiness," and "Happy Home Surroundings."[7] Even as business and political leaders reconstructed and reimagined the water-front and harbour, they continued to believe that the bay could contribute

FIGURE 12 Projecting an image of Hamilton's industry and commerce. Vulcan, the Roman god of fire and metalworking, and Mercury, the god of commerce, adorn promotional material for the city in 1919. This image is a slightly modified version of the frontispiece in another booster publication from 1913. *From* Hamilton, Ontario, Canada *(Hamilton: Board of Trade, 1919).*

to the health and beauty of their industrial city. From the 1890s through the 1930s, civic leaders struggled to avoid the blight that they associated with other industrial towns, aiming to build a livable city in the face of challenges produced by the economic growth that they so anxiously promoted.

IF, AS PRIME MINISTER Wilfrid Laurier predicted in an oft-quoted speech, Canada was to fill the twentieth century just as the United States had filled the preceding century, Hamilton's political and business leaders actively and anxiously sought to ensure that their city would remain an important participant in the developing nation. Two Laurier government policies adopted on the eve of the new century – the imperial preference in the government's revised National Policy protective tariffs and the Crow's Nest Pass Agreement on freight rates – created new opportunities for Hamilton's ambitious boosters to attract new investment and industries. A number of business observers saw the 1897 tariff revisions, which contained preferential rates for free trading nations such as Great Britain, as an early step in the construction of an imperial trading zone and believed that Canadian-based companies would have favourable access to British markets. Ottawa also agreed to provide financial assistance to the Canadian Pacific Railway if it reduced freight rates from eastern to western Canada on a number of key commodities that a burgeoning settlement frontier would demand, such as agricultural implements, binder twine, wire, hardware, building and roofing paper, and furniture. Perhaps not surprisingly, Hamilton MP Andrew Trew Wood, whose hardware firm already had a salesman working in the west, enthusiastically supported the Crow's Nest Pass Agreement. Now the companies of Hamilton, including Wood's, potentially had preferential access to the established local market and to two distant markets bearing great promise – the west and the empire.[8]

By 1900, Hamilton was well positioned to benefit from visions of new imperial and transcontinental economies. In the 1890s, local business leaders undertook several initiatives to build on its manufacturing base.[9] When city council's Finance Committee expressed interest in attracting an iron-smelting works to Hamilton, two local foundry owners, John Tilden and John Milne, responded. In 1893, they began to work with several American manufacturing and financial interests, and negotiated to have the City provide their enterprise with $100,000 in cash bonuses and a thirty-hectare waterfront site free of charge. Although the Americans backed out, other local business leaders such as Andrew Trew Wood stepped in and ensured the completion of the blast furnace. The Hamilton Blast Furnace Company, located east of the city on a peninsula between Sherman and Harvey's Inlets, known locally as Huckleberry Point, began smelting pig iron in 1896. To finance its expansion into steel, it joined with another local firm, Ontario Rolling Mills, in 1899. City council arranged for it to acquire forty-two hectares of waterlots along the Huckleberry Point shoreline, presumably to allow for shipping facilities. The new company, Hamilton Steel and Iron Company, began producing steel the following year. During a merger boom, Canada's smallest steelmaker amalgamated with several finishing plants in Ontario and Quebec in 1910 to form the

Steel Company of Canada (soon referred to as Stelco). Supported by strong market demands for steel from local founders and moulders, the availability of waterfront land, and the financial aid of city council, local boosters established Hamilton as one of Canada's iron and steel centres.[10]

By 1900, a textile manufacturer and four men involved in real estate development and construction (known as the "Five Johns" because they shared the same first name) had transformed Hamilton into an "electrical" city through a daring bid. When, back in the 1850s, local civic leaders had sought a water supply for Hamilton, they turned to a Lake Ontario site several kilometres away; in the 1890s, the search for a waterway to generate the city's hydroelectricity drew business leaders to the east, over fifty kilometres away. Initially, the Cataract Power Company sought to tap into a large waterfall that tumbled down the escarpment, where its drop equalled the height of Niagara Falls. However, its flow proved unreliable, so contractors created their own. To do this, they diverted water from the old Welland Canal and directed it over the escarpment to power the electricity-generating turbines.[11]

The decision to use this power plant to supply electricity to Hamilton made the project particularly daring. In 1898, the company defied many skeptics and began to successfully operate the second-longest transmission line in the world. Reporting on its official opening, the *Hamilton Spectator* called Cataract's DeCew Plant "the finest and most up-to-date electrical plant in America," noting too that "the company seems to have struck a bonanza."[12] One writer for the *Canadian Electrical News and Steam Engineering Journal* pointed out the worldwide implications of the momentous occasion, claiming, "The successful completion of this undertaking marks an important point in the progress of electrical development, not only in Canada, but throughout the world, inasmuch as the generating plant is unique in many features."[13] Another observer, writing in the *Electrical World and Engineer,* commented on the booster spirit of this hydroelectric enterprise, observing that "by being able to furnish cheap electrical power Hamilton is leading the larger city of Toronto in securing industrial concerns."[14]

The establishment of the Hamilton Blast Furnace and Cataract Power Companies occurred during the heady days of local public initiatives that aimed to make Hamilton into a major industrial centre. In the 1890s, city council began to take advantage of the publicly owned water supply system to keep its rates low for factory owners. It also routinely offered interested manufacturers partial or full exemptions from municipal taxes for up to a decade. In 1891, civic leaders resolved a dispute with a neighbouring

FIGURE 13   The Graselli Chemical factory *(left)* and Hamilton By-Products (Coke Ovens) *(right)* along Gage's and Stipes Inlets in Hamilton's new industrial district. *Courtesy of Local History and Archives Department, Hamilton Public Library.*

county government by expanding the city's boundaries for the first time since 1846; the expanded area encompassed an industrial district and city sewage outlet at the base of Sherman Inlet but contained other land that could be used for factories and warehouses (Figure 13). In 1892, local politicians created the first of a series of special civic committees, whose mandate was to encourage new businesses to establish themselves in Hamilton. They worked to "keep the many advantages of the City prominently before the public" and to oversee the promotion of manufacturing and commercial enterprises.[15]

Yet attracting industry was a difficult venture, and neither financial incentives nor local entrepreneurship could guarantee its success. Generous public offers, for example, could not attract the Heinz Company of Pittsburgh in the late 1890s, despite its close proximity to the bountiful farms of the Niagara peninsula.[16] As well, the entrepreneurs who were involved in promoting iron and steel could not engineer the necessary economic or political conditions to establish a nickel refinery in the city. Nevertheless, favourable national policies, local supplies of electricity, iron, and steel, generous concessions from city council, and sustained Canadian economic growth all helped to make Hamilton an appealing site for industry. At the turn of the century, the decision of two major American-based companies to locate there fuelled the enthusiasm of boosters. The

Westinghouse Company arrived in 1896, with a promise from city council of a ten-year tax exemption and fixed water rates.[17] It began manufacturing railway air-brakes in a plant near the eastern industrial district at the foot of Sherman Inlet, close to the water but also, more significantly from the company's perspective, along the Grand Trunk Railway lines. In 1903, it expanded its factory and the range of products that it manufactured in Hamilton, receiving promises of a stable and fixed tax assessment for fifteen years.[18]

When International Harvester opened its large factory on the waterfront, between the steel company and Sherman Inlet, it did so after much courting from Hamilton's Industrial Committee.[19] One of its predecessor companies, Deering, had been approached before, but the deal had fallen through. In 1902, city councillors tried again, sending a spokesman to Chicago to sell Deering on the many advantages of Hamilton. After a company representative visited the area and judged it favourable, council awarded Deering a $50,000 cash bonus. Yet provincial legislation, which had outlawed such things in earlier years, now required that they be approved by two-thirds of the municipal electorate. Hamilton's voters defeated the measure, perhaps because they sympathized with union leaders who opposed giving money to a company with a questionable labour record or simply because they opposed giving money to any company. Since provincial legislation now required a similar vote for significant tax exemptions, Hamilton's civic leaders looked for a way to circumvent the electorate. In a neat move, city council annexed from neighbouring Barton Township the eastern waterfront land that International Harvester needed, but it retained the township's rural tax rates, which were about a third of those in the rest of Hamilton. It then created a larger "manufacturing district," annexing over 280 hectares from the township and retaining the low tax rates for those who located there.[20]

By the First World War, the development of Hamilton's industrial waterfront district was well on its way. The Westinghouse and International Harvester factories employed well over 5,000 people, and another 2,500 worked for Stelco. Hamilton boosters boasted that their "city of 400 varied industries" included almost forty American branch plants, "more than all other Ontario cities combined."[21] Praising the industrial commissioner William Mullis's efforts to snag a "great industry" such as the Canada Steel Company for the city, a *Hamilton Times* reporter observed, "He fishes with good bait, and he frequents the pools where the trout are large."[22] This industrial development both attracted and was fed by waves of immigration, creating the necessary pool of male labourers needed for most factory jobs. In the decade before the First World War, Hamilton's population doubled to 100,000 and grew steadily in the 1920s, reaching 155,000 by the 1930s. In 1931, more than a third of Hamiltonians were immigrants who had arrived in Canada after 1901. This population increase continued to depend on industrial development – in 1931, almost 30 percent of Hamilton's working men were engaged in the manufacturing sector, and another 20 percent worked in the building trades or as general labourers.[23]

Between 1890 and 1930, industrial expansion and the growing number of manufacturing jobs taken up by the new immigrants who settled in Hamilton thoroughly transformed what had once been a mostly rural area along the water's edge, east of the original North End port. The owners of many new factories, such as Westinghouse and Procter and Gamble, chose locations along the railway lines that crossed or were situated near the ends of the bay's eastern inlets. In 1917, the Grand Trunk Railway estimated that its 4.8 kilometre branch along the shoreline between the old downtown and the Beach Strip collected freight from twenty-one factories and privately owned industrial sidings.[24] Hamilton Steel and Iron and International Harvester really began the industrial expansion in the area, being the first major industries to establish themselves along the marshy peninsulas on the southeastern shore. When the implement manufacturer International Harvester received a portion of the steel company's waterlots, it built wharves and storage facilities out into the bay. Hamilton's publicity machine used these and other new waterfront industries as evidence that the city's position afforded "the best shipping facilities to the Northwest Provinces and European markets."[25] Local politicians and businessmen consistently pressed the national government to ensure that Hamilton had good port facilities that would appeal to shippers and manufacturers. In response to several campaigns, Ottawa agreed to eliminate the tolls on the Burlington Canal in 1886, and the following year it deepened the canal channel to 4.2 metres. These initiatives coincided with the completion of the reconstructed ("Third") Welland Canal between Lakes Erie and Ontario.[26]

Although Hamilton city leaders saw a 50 percent increase in the tonnage of goods passing in and out of the port during the 1880s and the 1890s, the experiences of new waterfront industries – particularly International Harvester and Stelco – suggest that problems were emerging. The most serious lay in the deficiencies of the reconstructed Welland Canal, which could not accommodate increasingly large Great Lakes ships. Some problems had more local origins. The Burlington Canal's fourteen-foot depth proved difficult to maintain because of silting and water-level changes. Ships delivering iron ore and coal from the upper Great Lakes to the Hamilton blast furnace often ran aground as they tried to enter the harbour.[27] After 1900, the steel company reverted to shipping most of its ore as far as Port Edward on Lake Huron and then bringing it to Hamilton by rail. Similarly, the general manager of International Harvester complained in 1910 that boats delivering goods to his plant often had to anchor for hours in the lake if the wind were blowing in the wrong direction, for fear of becoming grounded in the channel. His company had come to Hamilton, he claimed, "owing to the inducements offered in the way of water facilities," yet the canal had not been improved, and shippers weren't able to use the "better style of lake carriers."[28]

Local and business leaders understood that technological changes in shipping had outstripped the natural advantages of the bay. Considered "the only harbour of refuge" in the west end of Lake Ontario, it once again proved to be too well protected.[29] Hamilton's political representatives and Board of Trade pressed Ottawa for improvements but soon found that any alterations in the channel would have to await decisions about the Welland Canal. For a short time, some local enthusiasts worked with the city engineer to promote a dramatic alternative to modernizing the canal yet again. They proposed constructing a new canal between Lake Erie and Hamilton, with its terminus in Burlington Bay or Dundas Marsh. Once the impractical trial balloon quickly deflated, local leaders resigned themselves to supporting more improvements to the Welland Canal and to insisting that the Burlington Canal be enlarged at the same time. Although some dredging of the latter did occur, it was only in 1930, as the yet again modernized ("Fourth") Welland Canal neared completion, that serious work on the enlargement of the Burlington Canal began.[30]

Other challenges faced those who hoped to transform the bay into a competitive Great Lakes port. Its irregular shoreline and shallow inlets, which had once sheltered smaller vessels, could not accommodate the larger ships that supplied the new industrial sites on the eastern waterfront. Significant dredging and dock construction was required to remedy the problem. Whereas some of the new industries improved their sections of waterfront on their own, city politicians struggled to help others who sought financial aid. They looked to the Canadian government, which was responsible for shipping and navigation, to help them construct an attractive and up-to-date harbour.[31] Frustrated with the slow pace of improvements, challenged by the need to gather information for effective lobbying, and facing difficulties arising from the fact that several jurisdictions governed different activities on the bay, they embraced the idea of creating a special commission to manage the business of their harbour.

Thomas J. Stewart, Hamilton's popular MP and former mayor, fully supported by his fellow Conservative MP Samuel Barker, successfully championed a private member's bill in 1912 to create the Hamilton Harbour Commission, which was similar to the one established for Toronto a year earlier. It was to hold, take, develop, and administer the harbour "on behalf of the City of Hamilton." Its jurisdiction included the bay's waters, inlets, waterfront properties, waterlots, piers, harbour bed, shores, beaches, and Cootes Paradise, although not the Burlington Canal.[32] Its three members, one of whom was appointed by the City, enjoyed wide powers to control the waterfront, such as the ability to borrow money and raise their own revenues. Many visionaries hoped that the entrepreneurial energy and resources of the new agency would enable Hamilton politicians to work more closely with their federal government counterparts.[33] Soon after the appointment of the commission, Ottawa began infusing money for dock building, dredging, and reclamation work in the harbour. To prevent it from using its powers to collect fees from shippers who used the port, Hamilton City Council agreed to regularly allocate money to help finance harbour improvements. Although the commissioners initially moved cautiously, they financed the dredging of new and deeper channels for two agricultural implement manufacturers – one new and one already established – the Oliver Chilled Plow Company and International Harvester. They also helped complete a retaining wall already begun by the City along the eastern section of the old North End port, using some of the wall and the new land created behind it for wharves and warehouses. The outbreak of the First World War, however, disrupted this early push for development. At war's end, the official renaming of Burlington Bay as Hamilton Harbour in 1919 presaged a more aggressive policy of commercial and industrial development on the waterfront.[34] As the economy recovered by the mid-1920s, the commissioners began to use their borrowing and other powers more extensively to finance docks and warehouses, to dredge, and to create new land by filling in shoreline inlets. They hoped to have their port well prepared for the opening of the "Fourth" Welland Canal, and for the future as well, especially if discussions about the construction of a St. Lawrence Seaway were to prove successful. Their projects extended eastward, a process that the Great Western Railway had begun along the west harbour back in the 1850s – the creation of a hard, clean water's edge with no inlets or shallow areas, using infill and concrete retaining walls to replace the irregular vegetation-covered shoreline.[35]

FIGURE 14   National Steel Car plant during the First World War. Located at Kenilworth Avenue North, it lay alongside Ogg's Inlet. *Courtesy of Library and Archives Canada, PA-024625.*

Whether it was because of existing facilities or the promise of those yet to come, other industries joined International Harvester and Stelco on the waterfront, transforming the rural peninsulas along the eastern inlets into factory sites with hardened shorelines. Fire insurance maps of the era chart the course of this industrial development, meticulously detailing the environmental risks and hazards at the factory sites, such as the chemicals, oil, gas tanks, and acids stored at each property.[36] By the First World War, the area had two agricultural implement manufacturers, Oliver Chilled Plow and International Harvester, located across from each other on either side of an inlet, and the Cleveland-based Grasselli Chemical Company and a new local firm, National Steel Car, had new plants on two eastern peninsulas within the city's newly extended boundaries (Figure 14).[37] Within a decade, more waterfront land had been taken up. Hamilton By-Products constructed coke ovens on the small peninsula between Grasselli and Stelco, whereas Firestone built a plant beside National Steel Car and, immediately to the south, a subdivision to house its workers. These factories encouraged more changes to the waterfront as dredging continued and company pumps took in bay water for their manufacturing processes.[38]

Although Hamilton historian John Weaver rightly notes that the city's growth "did not flow as a simple consequence" of its industrial policies, it nevertheless fed the rhetoric of the boosters and confirmed the value of their efforts.[39] City councillors continued to make Hamilton competitive by creating tax incentives and low water rates. They supported the creation of the harbour commission in hopes of attracting more industry. But urban promoters throughout the province found it increasingly difficult to offer significant or particularly distinctive financial incentives to industry. Seeking to remain competitive, Hamilton city councillors thus turned away from "buying" industries to focus instead on "selling" their town. To do so, they developed and publicized the qualities and amenities that might entice industrialists, their managers, and workers to move to Hamilton. In 1910, city council consolidated various public and private initiatives by creating a permanent industrial commissioner whose department would "establish and maintain a bureau of publicity" to work with companies that were interested in coming to Hamilton.[40]

The appointment of the new industrial commissioner, William Mullis, "a clever newspaper man, a forceful writer, and a man of pleasing address," reinforced and institutionalized a particular component of the booster impulse – the need to advertise effectively. A former municipal reporter for the *Times* and, later, the *Spectator,* Mullis found an admirer in the *Hamilton Herald* for his "insight into municipal conditions" and his "understanding of the city's industrial needs."[41] His advertising schemes included a variety of inducements to get people to experience and think about Hamilton's industry. He sent out Christmas cards that highlighted the city's industrial growth. He offered free car rides so that people could tour forty-two of the most impressive factories. He threw banquets to celebrate local industry. He even handed out free tickets to the newly renovated Jockey Club, itself conveniently located along the industrial east end waterfront. There, people could make connections, eat, drink, talk shop, and maybe even win a few dollars while watching the races.[42] For boosters like Mullis, promoting Hamilton meant sustaining its image as "the prettiest and healthiest in America" – something they had claimed as early as 1892. A late 1920s brochure, *Hamilton, Canada: The City of Opportunity,* underlined the continuing importance of this self-image. Hamilton, it boasted, offered "an unusual combination": it had nearly five hundred industries but did not have the "atmosphere of a factory town."[43] In the face of continuing growth, this image proved challenging to sustain.

FOR CIVIC LEADERS WHO were anxious to construct an industrial city for the twentieth century, showing a concern for public health was just as essential a selling feature as possessing efficient water, fire, police, and educational services. Promotional brochures measured progress in terms of numbers of industries and the value of imports, and in miles of sewers and dollars invested in waterworks and sewage disposal systems. In 1905, James Roberts, a twenty-seven-year-old McGill medical school graduate, took up his new appointment as medical officer of health (MOH) for Hamilton. One of the first officers to see himself as a "full time guardian of public health," Roberts soon developed a reputation as a reformer, focusing on a variety of issues aimed at reducing the death rate, from improving the milk supply to eliminating poor housing. Many civic boosters, however, had a more limited view of public health – in the words of one city propagandist, "The most essential factors in the welfare and health of any community are *pure water* and *good drainage*."[44]

Roberts understood the importance of his role in using promotional literature to proclaim that the city had the first key to good health and welfare, a pure water supply. Generally, he was confident in doing so, expressing a certain "sense of pride" for his work with the city's publicity literature.[45] Shortly after becoming the MOH, he championed the more regular testing of drinking water and milk supplies, precise tests that accompanied the development of the new science of bacteriology. Although Roberts consistently defended the city's water quality, he used the ever-present threat of a typhoid epidemic – a potential economic disaster for Hamilton boosters – to acquire the necessary human and technical resources to carry out regular bacteriological testing of its supply.[46] He stated, "Show me a city's statistics of typhoid fever and I will tell you the character of its water supply," observing further that "pure water and high typhoid rates are quite incompatible."[47]

In 1908, Roberts convinced city council to appoint a bacteriologist for the city, and daily tests of drinking water began a few years later.[48] The tests appeared to vindicate Hamilton's mid-nineteenth-century decision to pump its water from the shore of Lake Ontario, which had been based on the miasmatic theory of disease. Before the First World War, Hamilton's water supply carried no *B. coli*, and Roberts emphasized that its negligible bacteria counts were as low as those in places that used extensive filtration systems. In a somewhat odd interpretation of the new science, the MOH, who had just been elected vice-president of the American Public Health Association, concluded that "there is not a germ in existence that could travel through the waters of the bay and into the lake and through the waterworks system and end up in a tumbler of drinking water with any life in it."[49]

Satisfied that the water supply was safe and being properly monitored, Roberts left other problems related to Hamilton's water to the city's water engineering staff. More people and industries used more water on a regular basis; this created a number of crises in an aging system, one that had been designed to meet the needs of the 1870s. The city engineer and manager of the waterworks responded quickly when problems arose in the water pressure, since the fire insurance rates of local manufacturers required guarantees of a reliable supply. They convinced city council to invest in new water mains, reservoirs, and pumping equipment, changes that also required a better flow of water from Lake Ontario. By constructing intake pipes from the lake, gradually clearing the pipes of obstructions, and keeping them open for longer periods, engineers and managers eliminated whatever filtering might once have been provided by letting the water seep through the sand.[50]

The crusading MOH worked to convince journalists and civic leaders that, from the perspective of the germ theory, the filtering basins represented the main weakness in the waterworks system, but not because they did not filter the water. Rather, they could actually be a source of its contamination. Roberts maintained that regularly cleaning the basins and reservoirs would fix the problem and that Hamilton need not concern itself with the modern filtration systems being installed by other cities throughout North America. He argued that unlike many other places, Hamilton was not located on "a stinking river of sewage" but drew its water "from the depths of that magnificent fountain" – Lake Ontario. Remarkably, by the First World War, the main water supply for a city of 100,000 remained relatively safe, without filtering or any other treatment.[51] Yet early-twentieth-century public health decisions and investments related to Roberts's second key to good health and welfare – *good drainage* – would eventually change all that.

As with the water supply, Roberts inherited what he saw as a good system for carrying waste away from homes and factories. "We are fortunate," he remarked in one of his earliest reports, "in possessing a natural land barrier to the contamination of our water supply by the sewage poured into the bay."[52] Yet he and the city engineer faced two immediate challenges in their effort to provide Hamiltonians with a sanitary city. Convinced that the water-carriage sewer system was far healthier than any other, they wanted to attack the "privy vault menace" and ensure that the ever-expanding city's homes and businesses were connected, and connected properly, to its sewer system.[53] At the same time, the two men had to deal with "end-of-pipe" controversies regarding the damage done by the sewage to parts of the shoreline along the bay. A 1905 meeting to discuss sewer issues in the annexed manufacturing district along the eastern waterfront underlined the importance of addressing the twin environmental hazards. Roberts reported that officials from various factories in the district supported the construction of a new sewer main there to end the need for privy vaults, but they also reminded both the doctor and the engineer that up-to-date facilities for hygienic recreation, such as bathing beaches, would help them secure and retain "a much better class of workmen."[54]

Although the sewage system took advantage of gravity and the contours of the landscape, controversies about its end-of-pipe discharge shaped its overall design. The germ theory of disease privileged scientific measurement over sensory reaction but did not supplant the view that what could be smelled and seen flowing from the sewers was "offensive as well as injurious to the health of the people."[55] "The average city or individual considers a sewage disposal plant a novelty or unnecessary expense," an American analyst remarked in the American journal *City Hall*, "and they only build them when a threat of a damage suit arises ... Then any sort of a plan or device prepared or proposed by an engineer or concern will do, so long as it is not too expensive."[56] These words might well have been written about Hamilton. Its property owners had sought relief for the problems created by the Ferguson Avenue sewer outlet since the 1880s, but city council did not act on them until 1895, when a resident won an injunction preventing the City from dumping any more sewage into another inlet, one popularly known as Coal Oil Inlet.[57]

Council quickly turned to the chief engineer for Rochester, New York, for advice. A well-known sanitary engineer, Emil Kuichling told a committee of councillors that Hamilton should redirect all of the storm and waste water from six of its seven outlets to one point and then pump the sewage through a steel pipe almost 1 metre wide and 1,219 metres long into the "deep waters of the bay," where it would be safely diluted. The only remaining concern, Kuichling noted, would be that some of the sewage might float to the surface of the bay. Only when he learned that the currents might move this floating matter to the vicinity of the water supply did he recommend the additional expense of adding chemicals to the sewage to quickly separate out the larger, potentially offensive sediments. This focus on large solids appeared to have more to do with miasmatic concerns about filth than the germ theory of disease.[58]

Hamilton's own city engineer convinced council to adopt a significantly modified version of Kuichling's plan. Surprisingly, and for reasons that were soon forgotten, it decided to construct *two* sewage disposal plants, one in the eastern industrial district at Coal Oil Inlet in 1896 and the other the next year in the old North End port, where Ferguson Avenue met the bay. The reasons may have been legal (since both locales had generated nuisance lawsuits), financial (because the City had already purchased considerable property at these sites, not at the one preferred by Kuichling), and political (since building two smaller plants would cost the same estimated price as a larger single one but would provide contracts and jobs in two different wards). Council authorized the construction of several intercepting sewers but only enough to redirect the flow of waste water from three of the other five main outlets. Raw sewage still flowed into the west end of the harbour at the railway yards and into marshy Cootes Paradise. A number of smaller outlets, which were situated low enough to meet the surface of the bay, remained open as well, presumably because water currents were believed to sweep the sewage away quickly, minimizing damage to the shoreline. Nevertheless, most sewage converged at one of the two disposal plants, which used sludge-drying presses and inexpensive chemicals such as lime and alum to remove larger sediments.[59]

By 1900, Hamilton's civic boosters could claim to have installed one of Canada's earliest sewage disposal systems. "Instead of the beautiful bay being polluted by the outpourings of sewers," one writer boasted, "all the solid matter is removed and retained, while the liquid residue is let escape into the bay, having been made as clear as filtered water."[60] Even at the time, many sanitary engineers agreed that chemical precipitation clarified the waste water but did not purify it.[61] They recommended it to help prepare the water for further filtering but not as the sole form of treatment. As one skeptical onlooker wryly concluded about Hamilton's system in 1912, these "sewage separators ... really make short work of all the chips and rats and straws they catch, and deliver the real extract, rich and brown, into the embrace of the charming bay."[62]

Nor did the new sewage plants dispose of complaints. In his capacity as medical officer of health, Roberts had inherited two ongoing controversies – the sewage problem at the Ferguson Avenue outlet and the heavily polluted Coal Oil Inlet. In the case of Ferguson Avenue, a scheme designed to fix the extant environmental degradation became a problem itself. In 1903, local newspaper editor and alderman John Morrison Eastwood pushed a city council committee to improve the waterfront in the old North End. He arranged for a photographer to document the sorry state of the shoreline immediately to the east and west of the Ferguson disposal works. The photographs were also intended to emphasize the need for its development, since the land had been acquired by the City for a much-needed park. Between 1904 and 1906, Eastwood convinced council to construct a revetment wall to cut off the inlet from the bay, a project that received Canadian government funding. To deal with the inlet – now reduced to a shallow triangular land-locked pool of water about four hectares in size – the City had its scavengers dump their collections of coal ash and other types of garbage there, but not rotting vegetables, which would attract rodents. Faced with complaints from the North End Improvement Society about a heavily damaged shoreline being replaced by an open garbage dump, Roberts denied that any real problem existed. He nevertheless agreed to have the garbage covered up as it was deposited there.[63]

He showed only slightly more concern for the issue at Coal Oil Inlet, a popular name variously applied to one or more of the southern fingers of Sherman Inlet and sometimes to the whole inlet itself.[64] Its upper end had become a real problem. A railway line had bisected it, disrupting the drainage of a sewer outlet that flowed from several "fragrant" businesses, including a cattle barn, a slaughterhouse, and a fertilizer plant. The construction of the sewage disposal works had satisfied the terms of a legal injunction to deal with problems in the area, but it had done little to resolve the upper inlet's environmental damage. As early as 1895, the Hamilton Board of Health reported on plans to connect the neighbourhood's industries to the city sewer system and to begin filling in the worst affected areas with garbage.[65] But ten years later, only some haphazard infilling had been completed, and the sewage plant did little except give the appearance of alleviating the environmental problems. It may have clarified the water pumped into the bay, but its managers simply disposed of the precipitated sludge on its surrounding property, where it gradually drained into the inlet.

In 1907, when two members of the Provincial Board of Health arrived in Hamilton to inspect Coal Oil Inlet, Roberts laconically reported on the handling of the complaints from local residents. He claimed that their reports and recommendations were "similar in intent and purport" to those of the Hamilton Board of Health, which had applied to city council for financial assistance to act on the recommendations though without success. "As a consequence the matter has come to a standstill. There it remains," Roberts wrote in his annual report.[66] He saw the case as typifying the general indifference of civic leaders to public health investments, but some residents and their political representatives viewed things differently. They saw little to celebrate in the Provincial Board of Health's recommendation that the upper inlet be filled with sewage sludge and topped off with lime.

Coal Oil Inlet continued to be viewed as "a pest hole," despite some improvements in disposal practices. Locals and nearby businesses, including International Harvester and Oliver Chilled Plow, pressed city politicians to find some way of following the Eastwood example and filling it in. During the war, the City paid companies to transfer land fill from their dredging and construction activities elsewhere and dump it into the bay's polluted coves. In the 1920s, garbage was still being used as fill, and it became obvious that the area could not be transformed into a park. Instead, Coal Oil Inlet would become the model for Hamilton's future waterfront development – infilling would be used to eliminate inlet nuisances while creating more land for industry. In 1930, Stelco began the process of filling in the damaged Lottridge's Inlet. Infilling seemed a perfect environmental solution for civic boosters, if not for those who lived and worked in the industrial districts.[67] Hamilton Board of Health reports and newspaper accounts reveal that Roberts simply did not see the problems created by sewage outlets as being significant risks to public health.[68]

Roberts always appeared to be much more interested in the other end of the drainage pipe and saw the homes of working-class neighbourhoods as breeding grounds for germs. There, he wrote, "overcrowding was very much in evidence, and the careless tendencies of the population were intensified by the lack of sewerage."[69] He sought to extend sewers to as many Hamilton homes as possible and supported the construction of new sewer lines and yet another sewage disposal facility east of the steel plant to accommodate the demands of city growth. In 1910, when a new Hamilton public health bylaw came into effect, landlords began to report that Roberts insisted they get rid of the privy vaults on their properties and, if necessary, pass on the costs of installing proper plumbing and sewer connections to their tenants.[70]

It is not clear whether Roberts had any authority beyond persuasion under the system of voluntary sewer connections, but in 1912 he found support in new provincial public health legislation.[71] It enabled him to order that households be connected to the system and, if necessary, to add the cost of the connection to people's tax bills. It also allowed city council to borrow money to finance the construction of new sewer lines without seeking ratepayer approval (or facing ratepayer resistance) if the Provincial Board of Health ordered that the work be done. By 1921, almost every household in the original city (some 98 percent) was connected to the sewer lines, up from slightly less than two-thirds (some 61 percent) in 1896.

Details on how many homes were connected are not available, although between 1911 and 1913, Roberts apparently ordered over 1,300 connections in older parts of town. In 1921, health inspectors found some 2,700 privies that were still creating problems, many of them in the newly annexed territories. But if privies could be found on the outskirts of Hamilton, they had become a rarity in its central area.[72]

Roberts's campaign ensured that an increasing number of households and industries flushed their waste water into the bay through an expanding and ever more efficient sewage system. It undoubtedly rid many neighbourhoods – and not just the wealthiest ones – of the health problems created by fetid backyards and alleyways. But it also destabilized the water system that residents depended on because it used the bay as a sink and the lake as a tap, but with little treatment at either end of the pipe that connected the two. Following the First World War, bacteriological tests began detecting *B. coli* in the city's water. In 1922, Roberts expressed concern that it was found nearly twice as often – some nineteen times – as had been the case a year earlier. Given his earlier expressions of confidence in the bay's purifying capacity, he probably supported the view of the city bacteriologist, blaming the high *B. coli* count on developments along the Beach Strip and the lakeshore near the intake pipe.[73] Other observers, however, had their doubts. Roberts's report came amidst a controversy over a much more visible form of pollution in the bay. Local sportsmen, the Chamber of Commerce, and the harbour commission complained of oil and gasoline floating on the water; it may have originated as runoff from the roads, but it might also have been poured directly into the sewers by mechanics and industrial factory workers. In 1921 and 1922, the city engineer reported to council that ten sewer outlets drained raw sewage directly into the bay. Civic leaders, therefore, had every reason to suspect that the pollution of the water supply was related to the poor state of the harbour.[74]

In July 1922, council accepted the city engineer's recommendation that it hire outside consultants to help assess the health of the sewage system. It turned to a relatively new consulting engineering firm, Gore, Nasmith and Storrie of Toronto, to do the work. This partnership of two civil engineers and a bacteriologist would become best known for its later work on Toronto's monumental R.C. Harris Filtration Plant. It worked with the Hamilton city engineer to conduct the first significant bacteriological tests of the bay's water and to review the sewage disposal systems. The consultants reached a conclusion that came as little surprise to many observers. The bay on the city side, they reported in April 1923, was "polluted and the areas in the immediate neighbourhood of the outfall sewers from these disposal works are very grossly polluted."[75] Although they observed that Cootes Paradise was "bacteriologically highly contaminated," the water that flowed from it into the bay was not, so sewage disposal into the bay was their focus of concern.

Their *Report on Sewage Disposal* showed that the sewage system had big problems. Whatever good the Ferguson Avenue and Coal Oil Inlet disposal plants might once have done, they had fallen behind in repairs as Hamilton grew and put increasing demands on the system. Although the sewage plant built in 1910 between Harvey's and Lottridge's Inlets, immediately east of the steel plant, used more modern disposal technology, the consultants found it to be the least effective, largely because too much sewage passed through it each day. They also showed that the three plants under-performed in dry weather and simply failed during storms, "when most of the sewage flows directly into the bay untreated and in this way a large proportion of the bacteria, dangerous and otherwise, passes into the Burlington Bay." When the wind blew, they warned, "masses of diluted sewage may travel almost unchanged" to other parts of the bay, or perhaps more ominously, into Lake Ontario, where it would become "the sport of winds" and reach the city's water intake pipe. As Hamilton grew in the future, the report predicted, conditions in the bay and at the intake would merely become worse. The bay would "be less able to take care of the sewage material being emptied into it."[76] While identifying the impact of pollution on the use of the bay, the consultants zeroed in on the one issue that they knew would get the attention of local civic leaders: if Hamilton were to grow in the way that urban boosters hoped, some things that made it attractive – its healthful and reliable drinking water, for example – would be in ever greater danger.

For the consultants, the solution seemed obvious and simple. They recommended replacing the three flawed disposal plants with one large, modern sewage treatment facility that was designed to expand and accommodate future population growth. They also made it clear that, unlike the system adopted in the 1890s, this time all sanitary sewer pipes needed to converge at one new central plant to be located at Gage's Inlet. They contended that of the three treatment plant designs, the city council could construct and operate the least expensive one, but only if it also upgraded the waterworks at the same time. Improvements would include the installation of chlorination equipment, the extension of a much longer intake pipe deep into Lake Ontario, and the elimination of the filtering basins, which the consultants saw as both useless and dangerous. Overall, then, they looked to a combination of sewage treatment and water purification to solve the pollution problem. They defined pollution in straightforward and measurable ways, based on bacterial contamination counts. They also raised the problem as a human health issue, since the city needed to protect against a typhoid epidemic.[77]

Medical Officer of Health James Roberts, who might have been expected to welcome the report's findings and recommendations, proved less than enthusiastic. Although couching his statements as supportive of the consultants, he reconfirmed his faith that Hamilton's "land locked harbor" was "capable of taking care of the sewage." To protect the water supply, he contended that city council needed only to close the filtering basins and to invest in a chlorinating system, which would be used solely on those occasions when bacteria were detected in the water. "If money is to be spent to safeguard the public," he emphasized, "I think it would be better to spend the bulk of it on a filtering plant, and when that is provided, then consider treating the sewage."[78] Roberts's comments anticipated the public debate that followed the release of the report. The consultants may have focused strategically on the impact of sewage on water supply quality, raising the spectre of an epidemic to generate support for their recommendations. Instead, concerns about the waterworks and the safety of the water supply completely overshadowed any discussion of improving the sewage treatment system. Even on this issue, in the absence of any serious health crisis, many local politicians, including Mayor Thomas Jutten, resisted spending money on chlorination, viewing it as likely to produce complaints "on the score of taste."[79]

Three years later, the consultants returned to a city council that had not yet followed any of their original recommendations. Predictably, council asked them to provide more detailed recommendations regarding water treatment, not sewage disposal. This time around, however, council did follow at least some of their suggestions.[80] In 1927, Hamilton ratepayers voted to support improvements to the water supply, and city workers duly laid a larger and longer intake pipe that extended 914 metres into Lake Ontario. They also closed the filtering basins and installed chlorination equipment at the waterworks. As Roberts reported with satisfaction, bacteriological tests showed that adding "a trifling amount of chlorine" to the water had eliminated the *B. coli*. The consultants' proposed $1 million water filtration plant won little support, least of all from Roberts, who considered it a completely unnecessary investment from a public health standpoint.[81]

By 1930, the system required more than a trifling amount of chlorine to keep the water pure for drinking and other uses. Local textile manufacturers began to complain that the heavily chlorinated water affected their operations, as did its "fairly large quantities" of phenols, an acidic by-product of several manufacturing processes, such as steel refining. Pollution from industrial wastes, including the oil and gasoline that had prompted concerns about the state of the bay in the early 1920s, became the subject of a Hamilton Board of Health investigation in 1930. Its discoveries would probably have mirrored those of a 1926 inquiry – that many individuals and firms violated city bylaws by simply dumping waste directly into the sewers. But as with the earlier debate, this investigation concerned itself most with what the pollution meant to water consumption. The Provincial Board of Health intervened and, contrary to the views of Roberts, declared that chlorination was not an adequate health protection. It subsequently ordered the City to install a rapid sand filtration system, and because this order came from the Province rather than the municipality, it bypassed the ratepayer approval that would otherwise be needed to finance the project. City council would comply but it could blame others for the expense incurred, and in the midst of the Great Depression, a public works project helped generate employment. The new plant began operating in 1933, addressing some of the health and manufacturing problems created by polluted water. With it, civic boosters could continue to brag that "the water supply of Hamilton is probably as good as any on the continent ... [Bacteriological] tests have for years been uniformly satisfactory."[82]

By 1933, the city had gotten the kind of water supply system that Gore, Nasmith and Storrie had recommended back in 1926; its sewer system, however, remained only slightly modified from the one that the environmental consultants had condemned a decade earlier. City council had closed the Ferguson and Coal Oil disposal plants, and moved the east end disposal plant, a measure that provided more space for the expanding Stelco. Residential and industrial wastes were redirected into the next inlet to the east, Stipes Inlet. Yet the new sewage works differed little from its predecessors because city money went into the construction of a more effective water filtration plant, rather than improved sewage treatment. Funds for further large-scale projects, such as a new sewage disposal facility, had simply become too scarce in a depressed economy. In 1934, the city engineer sadly reported that sections of the bay were "veritable cess pools." He concluded that the city was in no position to take action against any business that might be polluting the bay, as long as it continued to use the bay as a sink for its untreated sewage. As a consequence, the matter came to a standstill. And there it remained.[83]

BACK IN 1923, AS THE *Hamilton Spectator* was covering Gore, Nasmith and Storrie's *Report on Sewage Disposal,* it joined local civic boosters in promoting a general cleanup of the city. An anonymous reader, "One of the Many," wrote to its editor to remind people that there was another side to the story: What was being cleaned up from one part of town had to be put somewhere else. Much of the city's garbage, along with the twenty-five years of accumulated waste, ended up in a five-hectare dump alongside the letter-writer's neighbourhood. Since city council did not bother spending the money to regularly cover it up, garbage blew around the area, and the dump frequently burst into flames. The writer also noted that the neighbourhood in question – at Coal Oil Inlet – was at the wrong end of the city's other sanitary schemes. Despite legal injunctions and reports, council continued to allow sewage and other waste to be poured into the inlet. "I believe that many citizens of the south end of the city are ignorant of the conditions that exist in this section," the writer concluded. "They would not support ... the spending of large sums of money for beautiful mountain driveways and the paving of their alleyways with bricks if they were living in our vicinity."[84]

As civic leaders absorbed one of the first reports detailing the environmental consequences of the growth that they so keenly pursued and celebrated, the letter-writer stressed that not all Hamiltonians shared equally in either those consequences or their solutions. Like the promoters of civic beautification, however, people who sought to maintain the city's healthful reputation undoubtedly believed that they were serving the interests of everyone. Investments in chlorination and a waterworks filtering system helped prevent the contamination of the public water supply, which, as Roberts once noted, "unquestionably reaches a larger percentage of people than any other single disease vehicle."[85] His campaign to extend sewer services throughout town did benefit working-class families and compensated for the fact that they lived in poorly drained locales, although it should not be forgotten that they generally paid for those improvements themselves, either through their rent or a direct additional assessment on their property taxes. And those, like the letter-writer, who lived near the shoreline and shallow inlets of the waterfront encountered other environmental problems caused by sewer building and experienced less success in

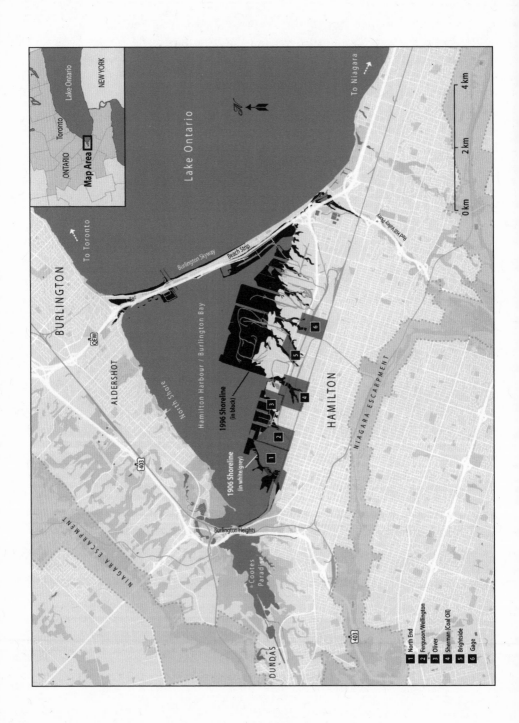

Map Area

ONTARIO

Toronto

Lake Ontario

NEW YORK

Lake Ontario

To Toronto

BURLINGTON

QEW

ALDERSHOT

North Shore

Hamilton Harbour / Burlington Bay

Burlington Skyway

Beach Strip

To Niagara

Red Hill Valley Parkway

403

Burlington Heights

Cootes Paradise

1906 Shoreline
(in white/grey)

1996 Shoreline
(in black)

403

DUNDAS

NIAGARA ESCARPMENT

NIAGARA ESCARPMENT

HAMILTON

1 North End
2 Ferguson/Wellington
3 Oliver
4 Sherman (Coal Oil)
5 Brightside
6 Gage

0 km   2 km   4 km

getting them addressed. Here Roberts proved to be less of a crusader, for he seemed unconcerned that the sewage disposal system created serious problems, except occasionally for the water supply.[86]

Who lived in the neighbourhoods that were most affected by the sewage system, those whose concerns seem to have been accorded the lowest priority when the city dealt with the consequences of urban and industrial growth? Figure 15 shows the various neighbourhoods that were adjacent to the shoreline and inlets: the old port with its railway yards and factories (North End), the area near the Ferguson Avenue sewage treatment plan (Ferguson/Wellington), the small waterfront community beside the Oliver Chilled Plow factory (Oliver),[87] the homes near the Coal Oil inlet with its factories and sewage treatment plant (Sherman/Coal Oil Inlet), and the relatively new housing development of Brightside, built between Lottridge's and Stipes Inlets. The social profiles of their inhabitants, given in Table 1, are based on information from the 1921 city directory, with total city information from the aggregate census of the same year.[88] In 1921, the

TABLE 1 Occupational profile, selected areas, 1921

	Total city	North End	Ferguson/ Wellington	Oliver	Sherman (Coal Oil) Inlet	Brightside
Proprietors, white collar	31%	*14%*	*16%*	*13%*	*12%*	*4%*
Skilled and semi-skilled workers	40%	42%	**49%**	**61%**	**52%**	**53%**
Labourers	29%	**44%**	**35%**	25%	**37%**	**42%**
N		450	131	122	200	201

NOTE: **Bold** indicates measure of overrepresentation, more than 5 percent above overall city total. *Italics* indicate measure of underrepresentation, more than 5 percent below overall city total. N differs between Tables 1 and 2 because ethnicity could be identified more often than occupations

SOURCES: *Vernon's City of Hamilton Annual Street, Alphabetical, General, Miscellaneous and Classified Business Directory 1921* (Hamilton: H. Vernon, 1921); for total city, Canada, *Census of Canada, 1921* (Ottawa: Dominion Bureau of Statistics, 1921).

FIGURE 15 (FACING PAGE) Map of waterfront areas.

Ferguson/Wellington and Coal Oil Inlet areas would have been most seriously affected by the polluted waters and shoreline. There were proportionately more skilled and semi-skilled workers and labourers in those neighbourhoods than in others. Unlike in other parts of town, few professionals or proprietors lived in these areas, and those who did ran small neighbourhood businesses, such as grocery stores or restaurants. These working-class districts faced exposure to significant environmental hazards.

All of the selected neighbourhoods, except in the Ferguson/Wellington area, had been affected by the arrival of a wave of immigration from southern and eastern Europe prior to the First World War. Most distinctive is the story of Brightside.[89] In 1910, real estate developer W.D. Flatt proposed to build Brightside on the tongue of land that lay between Lottridge's and Stipes Inlets, close to the Stelco, International Harvester, and Grasselli Chemical industrial complexes and just north of the railway tracks (Figure 16).[90] Flatt felt compelled to assure potential buyers that the land was not as marshy as other nearby areas and that their homes would enjoy the bracing winds of the harbour. Nevertheless, he was clear about the kind of neighbourhood that he aimed to create. The names selected for its streets – such as Sheffield, Birmingham, and Manchester – suggest its industrial character. Advertisements for Brightside emphasized the time and money that homeowners would save by living close to their factory workplaces.[91]

From its outset, Brightside attracted industrial workers, and, as Table 2 indicates, despite its British street names, proportionately more people of southern and eastern European descent lived there than in any other part of Hamilton. Its environment may have seemed superior to that of the more developed Ferguson/Wellington and Coal Oil Inlet neighbourhoods, but Brightside lay just south of a new sewage disposal plant and outlets where, in 1911, property owners sued the City because untreated sewage and sludge had flooded their land. A legal injunction against the

FIGURE 16 (FACING PAGE) The Brightside development *(centre)*, located directly below the city sewage treatment plant *(top centre)*, was located amidst busy waterfront industry. It was nestled between the Steel Company of Canada *(left)* and Grasseli Chemical *(right)* at the base of Lottridge's and Stipes Inlets, just above the Hamilton Street Rail and Grand Trunk railway lines. *J.B. Nicholson,* Map of the City of Hamilton *(Hamilton: Canadian Records Company, 1912), 1:3,600 ft., NMC 15354, H1/440/Hamilton/1912 (4 sections), Courtesy of Library and Archives Canada.*

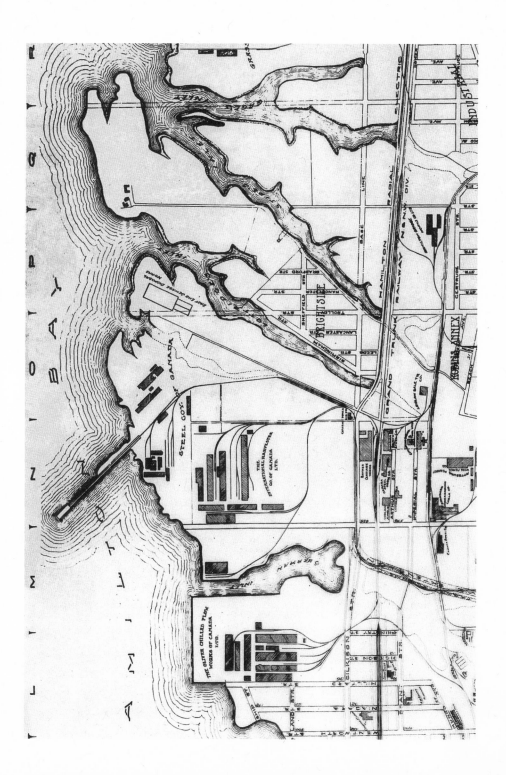

TABLE 2   Ethnic profile, selected areas, 1921

	Total city	North End	Ferguson/ Wellington	Oliver	Sherman (Coal Oil) Inlet	Brightside
British or western European	92%	*81%*	*92%*	*84%*	*82%*	23%
Italian	3%	10%	3%	4%	13%	20%
Eastern European	4%	5%	5%	10%	2%	**50%**
Other	1%	4%	0%	2%	2%	6%
N		543	131	120	202	235

NOTE: **Bold** indicates measure of overrepresentation, more than 5 percent above overall city total. *Italics* indicate measure of underrepresentation, more than 5 percent below overall city total. *N* differs between Tables 1 and 2 because ethnicity could be identified more often than occupations

SOURCES: *Vernon's City of Hamilton Annual Street, Alphabetical, General, Miscellaneous and Classified Business Directory 1921* (Hamilton: H. Vernon, 1921); for total city, Canada, *Census of Canada, 1921* (Ottawa: Dominion Bureau of Statistics, 1921).

plant, confirmed by a higher court and set to take effect in 1913, had little real impact since efforts were still being made to get it enforced in 1919. Flatt eventually acquired the affected land and then sold it to the City, which used it for sewage disposal purposes. In 1923, Gore, Nasmith and Storrie concluded that the plant was the least effective and most overtaxed in Hamilton's sewage system. By the end of the decade, the City had closed the plant, and local residents supported a plan to have Stelco dump slag into an already environmentally damaged inlet. They probably did not support the construction of the replacement disposal plant, which was to receive most of the city's waste, as it simply shifted the problem to the eastern side of their neighbourhood. In making decisions about cleaning up the environment, civic leaders overlooked neighbourhoods such as Brightside.[92]

IN SEEKING TO AVOID the atmosphere of a factory town, Hamilton's civic boosters struggled to construct a place that would attract investors and immigrants, a town where the waterfront could "afford Hamiltonians unlimited opportunities for aquatic sports" and where bathing, boating, and fishing could become "pastimes within the reach of the most humble."[93] The use of the bay for industries and port facilities, and as a sink for waste, clearly presented challenges to this idyllic vision and created tensions over who would define the best use of its limited and stressed resources.

4

Organizing Nature

The Search for Recreational Order,
1900–30

I N JULY 1924, A City-sponsored swimming program for Hamilton's inner-city children preoccupied the pages of the local press. For several weeks, a series of human-interest stories highlighted the free streetcar rides that took the children to the nearby shores of Lake Ontario. Because it simultaneously encouraged healthy play and removed the children from the dirty and dangerous streets and waters of the industrial districts, the program was hailed by the *Hamilton Herald* as a "humane act ... designed to fit the younger generation, both mentally and physically, for the great work that lies ahead."[1] The newspaper reports included photographs of boys wearing homemade bathing suits fashioned out of long sweaters sewn at the crotch and girls wearing old dresses to splash about in. And then there were the touching accounts of their experiences, including the streetcar ride – which in itself must have been a great treat for many working-class kids. Some five hundred children, voices raised happily in choruses of "Hail, Hail, the Gang's All Here," eagerly jammed themselves onto the radial cars to get to the lake. The ride ended at the Beach Strip, where they scrambled out of the streetcar, falling over each other in a mad dash to Lake Ontario. On the first day of the program, however, "there was a howl of disappointment ... The water was *cold*."[2] The kids then confounded the scheme by running west over the streetcar rails and across the Beach Strip. There they dove into the dirtier, yet warmer water of Hamilton Harbour!

The free rides represented a direct response to those who worried about how and where working-class children played in an industrializing city.

Early-twentieth-century reformers sought to protect them from what they saw as the medically and morally dirty spaces of their neighbourhoods. Working-class families and their political allies struggled to retain some access to the waterfront near their homes, as shipping and industrial interests claimed more of it. The ad hoc solution provided by Hamilton City Council, transporting children to swimming beaches on Lake Ontario, reflected concerns about the quality of the water in Hamilton Harbour. It illustrates the difficulties faced by civic boosters in creating the livable industrial city that their promotional brochures celebrated. Even as they offered swathes of waterfront property to industrial users, they promised potential workers, managers, and, particularly after the 1920s, tourists, a waterfront full of varied recreational opportunities.[3]

Ensuring such opportunities required a new level of public intervention in the planning and managing of recreation, paralleling the other interventions that were required to construct an efficient port and to safeguard water supplies. Civic leaders sought to protect the increasingly scarce recreational resources of the bay – whether they were fish for anglers or spaces for picnicking, swimming, or enjoying breezes. As they debated the best ways of doing so, older currents of thought – about proper behaviour and how nature ought to be enjoyed – remained pertinent. But they eddied and mingled with newer ideas, which placed greater emphasis on the scientific management and organization of both nature and recreation, and on the importance of making wholesome leisure activities available to as many people as possible. In Victorian Hamilton, civilizing nature often revolved around elite and middle-class residents who built comfortable structures in nature and modelled appropriate behaviour for themselves, often by excluding others. The approach of the early twentieth century, however, took more seriously the possibility that the natural world itself had value and could be properly constructed to reform behaviour. Of course, these currents did not run along the kind of neat and stable shoreline that planners and reformers would have liked – or that harbour engineers were in the process of constructing. The entanglement of social, political, and natural worlds greatly complicated the search for recreational order in Hamilton.[4]

BY THE 1920S, AS THE free streetcar rides suggest, swimming had emerged as an important form of recreation on the bay. As with other outdoor activities, such as horse racing and rowing, elite and middle-class residents saw an opportunity to civilize this sport. During the final quarter of the nineteenth century, swimming figured prominently in club and municipally sponsored community holiday events, such as the 24 May celebration of Queen Victoria's birthday and the 1 July Dominion Day celebration of Canada's birthday. On these occasions, the Royal Hamilton Yacht Club and other middle-class sporting clubs sponsored formally organized amateur swimming and fancy diving demonstrations. Appropriately dressed male athletes competed for ribbons and trophies before invited dignitaries and club members. Club rules prescribed proper behaviour for swimmers and spectators alike, banning gaming, gambling, intemperance, and "ungentlemanly" conduct.[5] Swimming events thus acquired respectability as a socially clean and beneficial sporting activity, and they soon became part of picnics that were sponsored by fraternal, benevolent, friendly, and church societies.[6]

By the turn of the twentieth century, a host of reform-minded organizations such as the Local Council of Women promoted waterfront leisure and the benefits of swimming to Hamiltonians who were excluded from private clubs and middle-class fraternal orders. Members of the Beach Girls Friendly Society Holiday Home, an Anglican charitable voluntary agency that was founded in 1905, aimed at affording working girls a clean space for respite, fresh air, and rational recreation. Like the Young Women's Christian Association, they attempted to "keep good girls good," believing that properly conducted leisure could keep them on the path of righteousness and away from the ills and vices that were thought to plague the industrial city. The Beach Strip Fresh Air Camp, created in 1921, worked with similar intent. It provided disadvantaged children with the "government of a Christian Home and Christian influences," using a rational, utilitarian approach to carry out this social agenda through recreation.[7] Both saw swimming as a way to create healthier citizens, especially healthier workers, given that factory jobs deprived them of much-need healthful physical activity in fresh air. Unlike other sports, swimming removed the grime of the city from those who participated in it. Although newspaper reports usually presented it in a light-hearted manner, many noted that it could ensure that young boys bathed with some regularity. Of course, swimming offered a positive alternative to the other attractions of the city. In the eyes of those who promoted them, respectable bathing beaches promised to offset the lure of saloons, dance halls, cockfights, and other popular rowdy entertainments.[8]

Charitable sponsorship of swimming and other outdoor activities reflected a concern that some members of society were excluded from, or avoided participating in, privately organized recreation. As industries increasingly located along the water, they threatened to crowd out other uses of the bay, privatizing what had previously been unclaimed and therefore open space along the waterfront or buying out the owners of recreational properties. The Otis-Fensom Elevator Company, for example, acquired what had once been a private waterfront recreational ground, Landsdowne Park, for its factory.[9] As waterfront space became scarce, a number of influential reform groups such as the Local Council of Women championed the creation of public, municipally run beaches on behalf of the "underprivileged classes" of Hamilton. They hoped to have the state rather than private institutions organize nature, creating clearly defined spaces that would be carefully designed to protect the physical and moral health of participants.

In establishing public beaches, community leaders hoped to restrict swimming in other parts of the bay. In 1924, when city council sponsored the streetcar trips to the Beach Strip, its members toured the North End waterfront and were dismayed by what they saw. Under the headline "Where Hamilton Children Swim," the reform-minded *Hamilton Herald* ran two striking photographs that showed "the unsightly condition of the water front" (Figure 17). Although working-class adults later recalled these swimming areas with considerable fondness, the dilapidated piers and wharves horrified the middle-class delegation. "Children of tender years," the paper noted, "were found swimming without any chance of protection in case of accident, in water varying from 8 to 20 feet in depth."[10]

Public beaches offered a solution to these problems. By selecting their location judiciously, planners could get swimmers away from the harbour's busy shipping and industrial activity. Nor would they be threatened by unexpected and dangerous drops in the water level. Beach designers sought carefully constructed "natural" environments, using fill and sand to create smooth and safe shallow areas for younger children and gentle slopes for those who ventured into deeper water. Designers and advocates of public beaches also pressed for safety measures, ideally in the form of a properly trained lifeguard who could resuscitate people via artificial respiration or a pulmotor, or, at the very least, make life buoys, ropes, and poles available at the water so that swimmers in difficulty could be pulled to safety. City beaches also served another safety function: groups such as the Young Men's Christian Association (YMCA) could offer swimming lessons for free while exposing kids to the lessons of rational recreation.

Supporters of public beaches hoped that they would serve moral objectives. As a member of the Local Council of Women explained, boathouses and piers along the waterfront were "well known to be a 'hangout' for crap shooting and other forms of gambling and vice." She reasoned

FIGURE 17   In 1924, a *Hamilton Herald* photographer captured the dangers associated with the busy North End waterfront, where neighbourhood children loved to swim. *"Where Hamilton Children Swim,"* Hamilton Herald, *9 July 1924.*

that swimming ought to be encouraged as a "healthy pastime" and warned that "when the young boys could not get healthy recreation, they turned to other things."[11] Those who advocated public beaches emphasized that they must be supervised by lifeguards and special police constables who could monitor "rowdies" that threatened the peaceful enjoyment of this public space.[12] The Local Council of Women also stressed that a properly constructed beach needed "enough buildings to assure privacy and respectability"; in other words, changing rooms were required to protect people's modesty and to clearly separate this space, where regular dress codes did not apply, from the eyes of the city. Of course, lifeguards and constables could also promote and enforce the bylaws that governed swimwear, such as the 1910 example in which all swimmers except boys under the age of fourteen were to be covered from the neck to the knees. "Many complaints have been made," reported the *Hamilton Times* in 1913, of "young men, and infinitely worse, young girls romping about … void of the regulation bathing dress." In a strategic move, planners for the official opening of a public beach featured a demonstration of the latest in appropriate bathing attire, which they deemed to be both modest and fashionable.[13]

Recreation advocates and their political allies hoping to create controlled and safe swimming environments for urban dwellers first looked to the sandy Beach Strip. Although city council had acquired control over a significant portion of the sandbar during the nineteenth century, it had kept very little for public use. Socially prominent and politically influential citizens had built themselves large summer homes and an exclusive resort. The City of Hamilton used the revenues that it received from them to finance improvements on the Beach Strip, whereas the rural township of Saltfleet continued to collect the property taxes that flowed from its development, but it was not interested in providing more urban services there, such as fire protection.

By the 1890s, some observers had begun to question whether this arrangement was working as expected. For Beach Strip property owners, a fire that destroyed the large Ocean House resort in 1895 highlighted the lack of fire-fighting facilities and other urban services. As they explored ways of addressing the problem, one city official emphasized that Hamilton's government already spent more on the Beach Strip than it garnered in revenues: in 1894–95, it had spent some $3,000 and had received only $600 from the property owners. Neither side could agree regarding what might have seemed the obvious solution – the city formally annexing the Beach Strip. In 1895, an annexation agreement got as far as the provincial legislature but collapsed in the face of sustained opposition from Saltfleet Township and most of the Beach Strip's permanent and summer residents, who feared rising taxes and losing control over future development. They decided to do without city services because they suspected that they would end up paying for public improvements – such as the establishment and maintenance of a public beach – "for the benefit of nonresidents or visitors from the city."[14]

The editor of the *Hamilton Spectator* responded critically to the failure of the annexation proposal, suspecting that Beach Strip property owners simply did not want to make the beach more accessible to the general public. He mocked their attitude in a satirical piece:

The summer residents desire to have a little aristocratic village all by themselves, and to that end try to make it appear that the soil is not fit for anything else. In the eyes of the exclusive people it is preposterous to imagine that the beautiful clean sandy bottom, or the shallow water along the shore, is at all adapted for wading purposes, and that John Smith's children from the city should be allowed to wade there; it is absurd to suppose that Peter Brown's children from the city could find any healthful pleasure in digging and rolling in the clean sand along the shore; it is utterly nonsensical to suppose that James Jones' wife and family from the city could find any amusement in a picnic on sandy soil in summer months; it is outrageous to imagine that companies of people from the city could discover any rational pleasure in sitting under the shade or walking about, by daylight or moon-light, in a locality where the soil is principally sand![15]

Clearly, the interests of private summer residents and the wider public did not, as the newspaper seemed previously to have assumed, necessarily coincide.[16] In 1900, the *Spectator* observed that summer residents were still determined to ignore the rights of Hamiltonians to enjoy a beach that the city had "acquired for the very purpose of affording citizens gener-ally enjoyment of a casual waterside outing ... and not merely for the lucky owners of lots who have their lawns and spreading verandas all to themselves."[17]

This and a number of other editorials reveal that the political influence of the beach property owners was limited. In the mid-1890s, they could not mobilize the necessary support to block the construction of the Hamilton and Toronto Radial Electric Railway across the Beach Strip.[18] The 1896 opening of the new line eroded what little hope they may have had of creating a socially exclusive beach resort (Figure 18). In 1897, the more prestigious method of travel, by steam railway, was unavailable to those who travelled to the Beach Strip. Soon the electric railway carried 2 million passengers to the sandbar every year, with its streetcars most crowded during the summer.[19] In 1912, an estimated twenty thousand people visited it on the Queen's birthday; five years later, a crowd of thirty thousand visited on Dominion Day.[20] Beyond enabling more Hamilton-ians to visit the Beach Strip on weekends, the relatively inexpensive street railway allowed those "of moderate means" to "go and live by the water." At the turn of the century, people began to acquire or rent modest "pretty bungalows and villas" to serve as summer cottages.[21]

Other changes in Beach Strip's built environment suggest its evolving social nature as a recreational space in the era of mass transit. No extensive resort hotel ever replaced the old Ocean House after it burnt to the ground in 1895, and its site remained vacant and untended for several years. The stately Royal Hamilton Yacht Clubhouse continued to provide an exclusive social centre for the elite, but when it also burned down in 1915, it was not

FIGURE 18 An 1892 promotional image of well-dressed children on the beach in the days before the Hamilton Street Railway made travel to the Beach Strip available to anyone who could afford the fare. *From* Hamilton: The Birmingham of Canada *(Hamilton: Times Printing, 1892).*

rebuilt (Figure 19). New attractions sprang up to replace them, such as the small amusement park running in 1903 under the Canada Amusement Company, which by the First World War operated a Ferris wheel and a merry-go-round.[22]

The interests of some beach property holders changed as well. In 1901, a merchandise broker from Hamilton, Alfred Powis, opened a community meeting by "regretting that a wrong impression had gone abroad that the beach residents were a very selfish lot." In fact, he suggested, they were "public spirited men, whose aim is to popularize the beach."[23] His investment in the area included a number of cottages, which he rented to Hamiltonians. He and other owners suspected that, following the rejection of the 1895 annexation proposal, the City of Hamilton devoted less money to the area, choosing instead to focus on the development of other parks for community recreation within city limits.[24] Powis suggested that some owners might reconsider some form of annexation, if it meant that the beach would be better managed.[25]

Powis, however, was wrong. Many permanent and summer residents sought a different means to get the services that they wanted. In 1907, they convinced the provincial government to appoint a beach commission consisting of two to five members, which would establish and administer

FIGURE 19   Hamilton Souvenir Calendar. This 1907 souvenir
features the pleasure craft of Hamilton's high society sailing near
the Royal Hamilton Yacht Clubhouse *(left)* on the Beach Strip.
Library and Archives Canada, Albertype Company Collection,
PA-032130.

policies for health, park development, policing, and public utilities. The
new Burlington Beach Commission, which gave Beach Strip residents
independence from both Saltfleet and Hamilton, took control of the
sandbar's property and permitted owners to lease or purchase properties.[26]
The provincial government did not completely abandon Hamilton's interests in the Beach Strip, however. It stipulated that the beach commission
must undertake a number of projects, including creating a public park for
Hamiltonians and people from nearby counties.[27] Still, some summer

residents continued to complain, and the commissioners assured them that monies spent on public parks would come from the sale of other properties – not from their property taxes.[28] They also assured Beach Strip residents that a carefully controlled approach to parks development would double their property values.[29]

The commission's development of parks land represented a significant recognition of the public's right to the benefits of the Beach Strip. Although its summer and permanent residents had acquired an agency that served their own particular interests, they also had to agree that its space for public recreation would be expanded. This, however, did not guarantee that a public swimming beach would be established, since the design of the new park conformed to an older vision. Thus, it did not provide facilities for informal and inclusive activities, such as a picnic grounds or a supervised swimming area where males and females could frolic. Instead, it featured a promenade and boardwalk, elaborately lined with little pagodas. Pedestrians could stroll along this genteel public space at a leisurely pace, with opportunities to stop, rest, and contemplate the bay in a sedate manner. It stood in stark contrast to other recreational spots on the Beach Strip, which were of a more popular nature. The unsupervised bathing beaches attracted masses of people on hot summer days, and the private amusement park near the canal had swings, slides, a crazy house, a Ferris wheel, and a carousel. Farther east, the Dynes Hotel was famous for its duck dinners and baseball matches.[30] However much the well-off Beach Strip property holders sought to control development, the fact that hordes of less well-to-do Hamiltonians could travel by street rail to places such as the Beach Amusement Park ensured that it would be a place of recreational diversity.[31]

THIS STRUGGLE OVER the Beach Strip left advocates of rational and organized recreation without properly organized swimming areas. During the First World War, they did make some progress in providing swimming facilities on the bay, at Landsdowne Park beach. In 1915, Thomas Jutten, a member of the Board of Control and a North End labour politician, convinced the Otis-Fensom Elevator Company to let the City use its Land's Inlet waterfront property for a bathing beach. Although city council appears to have initiated the process, the Hamilton Harbour Commission, with its access to the contractors who could help construct the site, played the lead role in its development. The harbour commission used sand from its dredging operations elsewhere on the bay to create a beach and a shallow, relatively level swimming area. When the new beach opened in 1916,

FIGURE 20   Kids in the water along the north shore of the bay at LaSalle Park
Pavilion. The City of Hamilton developed this park in Aldershot, across the water
on the bay's north shore, to create a safe and clean beach for Hamiltonians, but high
transportation costs and water pollution marred the success of the venture. *From
Hamilton Spectator, 23 May 1929. Courtesy of Hamilton Spectator.*

it featured change houses but little in the way of supervision or safety
devices.[32]

While the Landsdowne Park beach was being planned and constructed,
council acquired another former private recreational site that was situated
well beyond city limits, in Aldershot on the north shore of the bay. It saw
this site as particularly attractive because people already connected it with
recreation and because it lay so far away from the industrial waterfront
and residential sewage outlets. In its Master Plan of 1919, the harbour
commission had reserved the north shore for residential and recreational
development, viewing its shoreline as unsuited for port facilities and believing – as many did – that the harbour's currents prevented pollution
from reaching it.[33] Just after the First World War, Hamilton City Council
and its Board of Parks Management developed picnic and swimming facilities at Wabasso Park (renamed LaSalle Park in 1923) (Figure 20). It
featured a large, elaborately constructed waterfront bathhouse for people
to change into their swimming costumes or watch the fun from its expan-
sive second-floor balcony. Atop the hill lay an amusement park, with a
merry-go-round, roller coaster, and carnival games. It also had a pavilion
and a large picnic area with vast open spaces for people to play. Negotiating

with private steamboat companies, the City arranged for ongoing steamboat service to transport Hamiltonians to their new park across the bay, hoping that some day radial electric railway lines would eventually connect the two areas.[34]

Yet the two new beaches were not all that their promoters had desired. It took a double drowning in 1921 before city council installed safety equipment at both the Landsdowne and Wabasso beaches, and arranged for YMCA lifeguards to provide supervision and free swimming lessons. By the first week of July 1921, more than four thousand people had made use of the now well-supervised beaches.[35] Both, however, had their weaknesses. Given its location in the North End, Landsdowne attracted slightly more swimmers than Wabasso, which lay across the bay. But it was so shallow that it remained unpopular with older children and young adults, who continued to prefer the excitement of the wharves and piers of the North End waterfront. And it was dirty. In 1926, the medical officer of health warned that Landsdowne was "not fit for animals to bathe in," and he closed the beach shortly thereafter.[36] LaSalle Park offered cleaner water and superior swimming facilities, but it was much farther away. Getting there conveniently required an automobile or a boat. As a North Ender later recalled, "If we could have a big day on a Sunday morning, the family [would] go down and I think it cost 5 cents apiece to get on the ferry [to LaSalle Park] ... Man that was big money in those days ... It was a special treat if we went."[37] On such special days and on company-sponsored picnics, working-class families might have a chance to visit LaSalle Park. Otherwise, it was not very accessible to the "underprivileged classes." City council all but admitted the problem when for a few weeks one summer, it agreed to sponsor free ferry rides to the park in hopes of making its beach accessible to everyone, in the same way that it would provide free streetcar rides to the Beach Strip.[38]

As city council developed Landsdowne and Wabasso, it was also planning a third beach to solve the problem of poor access to safe and clean beaches. Located on the waterfront just below Dundurn Park, the new beach would have offered deeper and, many hoped, cleaner water than Landsdowne and be within easier reach than Wabasso. Dundurn Park, where the "castle" of former prime minister Sir Allan MacNab sat atop the Burlington Heights, had been the site of lodge- and club-sponsored picnics, baseball matches, and other recreations since at least the 1870s. In 1900, the City had acquired it for public parkland. The waterfront just below it, however, had not been used by the parks system because the railway yards (now owned by Grand Trunk Railway) lay between it and

the hill. Yet several city politicians doggedly pursued the idea of establishing a beach and got the city engineer to investigate a scheme for its creation.
It was no easy task. His plan involved leasing 716 metres of shoreline from
the railway company, constructing a pedestrian walkway under the train
tracks, and running a staircase up the escarpment so that people could
safely move between the park and the beach. In 1917, Hamilton ratepayers liked the project and voted to permit the issuing of a $25,000 deben-
ture to cover its cost. The Parks Board agreed to dip into its own funds to
pay for the bathhouses, lights, and the necessary "protection for the
bathers" on condition that it – not city council – would control the beach
when it opened. Yet by 1919, faced with federal government nationaliza-
tion schemes and preoccupied with its own struggle for survival, the Grand
Trunk refused to negotiate with the City. Thus, the promising and ambitious project collapsed.[39]

The wartime co-operative spirit among Hamilton's political leaders
in their search for suitable public swimming facilities also collapsed. Over
the next decade, city councillors and the Parks Board could not agree on
what to do with the taxpayer-approved money that had been committed
to the Dundurn project. A number of Parks Board members eyed the
$25,000 with a view to improving Hamilton's urban parks, measures that
would include the installation of a number of swimming and wading
pools. Some city councillors, including most members of the executive
Board of Control, found the proposal for swimming pools very attractive
but wanted to create a single indoor facility instead. Other politicians,
including two leading North End aldermen, Conservative "Boss" Alf
Wright and Independent Labour leader George Halcrow, continued to
advocate for a public beach along some other part of the southwestern
bayfront near the old port of the North End (Figure 21). Representatives
of the newer working-class suburbs in the East End championed beaches
or swimming facilities closer to their own neighbourhoods. One local
politician promoted free streetcar rides to the lake as being a less expensive and less divisive alternative to either beaches or swimming pools.
Wading into the debate, the head of the harbour commission urged city
council to get its act together and support any swimming beach that might
keep people away from the busy commercial and industrial areas of the
harbour. Few local leaders questioned the desirability of swimming facilities, but this did not ensure that they could reach consensus on how best
to provide them.[40]

Whereas city leaders agreed on the moral and physical value of swimming, they disagreed over questions of access to places to swim and water

FIGURE 21   In the 1930s, Canadian artist Leonard Hutchinson, now
famed for his work as a social realist of the Depression era, captured a
group of North End kids by the bay, some of them in their swimsuits.
Courtesy of McMaster University Labour Studies.

quality. Indeed, swimming pools emerged as a serious alternative to beaches
in the 1920s because they could serve many of the social purposes of a
beach, without subjecting participants to the dangers of pollution. By the
early 1920s, pollution had become more visible as oil and gas found their
way from streets and garages through the sewers and into the bay. By mid-
decade, the *Spectator* noted that people who celebrated the civic holiday
by taking a plunge in the bay "were coated in oil and had to [find somewhere to] wash it off."[41] Beach promoters countered this argument, warning that disease spread easily in swimming pools. They also feared that if
the City abandoned its commitment to public beaches, it would more
easily abandon its commitment to cleaning up the bay![42]

In 1925, and again in 1926, Hamilton City Council struck a committee
to determine what should be done with the $25,000 debenture formerly
earmarked for the Dundurn Park beach. Advocating a North End beach,
George Halcrow and other city politicians won key support from the Local
Council of Women, prominent waterfront businesses, the Parks Board,
and the chair of the harbour commission. Yet despite his labour connections, Halcrow had difficulty in getting the support of the local Trades
and Labour Council. Important city councillors and those who dominated
its Board of Control continued to resist and insisted on getting estimates
for a large indoor or outdoor pool. Ultimately, however, when a special

FIGURE 22   A throng of Hamilton kids swimming at the Bay Street Beach, which
opened in 1927. Note the smoke rising from the shore by the rail yards at the western
end of the harbour *(left)*. *Courtesy of Hamilton Port Authority.*

city council committee twice reported in favour of a beach along the
waterfront, the Board of Control finally conceded defeat and reversed its
position. When advocates of the beach located disused private waterfront
land and developed a proposal that was less expensive than the alternatives,
they won greater support. Even the medical officer of health agreed that
the water at the site was clean enough for swimming. In 1927, ten years
after the original vote on the Dundurn plan, a new beach at the foot of
Bay Street finally opened to the public (Figure 22).[43]

The Bay Street Beach was informed by the reformers' vision of organized nature. It featured change houses, a clearly designated and carefully
designed swimming zone, safety equipment, two lifeguards, and a special
police constable to monitor the area. Although several years would pass
before all the potential dangers were cleared from the water, it certainly
offered a level of safety that did not exist elsewhere on the waterfront.
Moreover, to make way for the beach, council authorized the destruction
of twelve "shacks," much to the satisfaction of some moral reformers who
saw the aging boathouses as suspicious "general gathering places."[44]

Nonetheless, the new beach continued to be a "gathering place," not
quite the orderly natural space that middle-class reformers envisioned. Its
lifeguard, "Pud" Murphy, was a familiar face in the neighbourhood, known
as a talented athlete and a man who wielded some political clout in the

working-class North End. His family's Modjeska House Hotel was a local institution, one with connections to the sorts of activities that reformers loved to frown upon. Referring to the cockfighting that was an open secret in the area, one resident jokingly recalled that people "could not walk near the bay without being chased by a stupid chicken." The Bay Street Beach also became a popular night-time hangout for young people. Another man recalled fondly, "They'd be there half the night. Down the foot of the bay – the old Civic Bathing Beach ... They'd be singing and playing guitars and swimming, cripes, 'till midnight. Hell, nobody'd give a damn then how long you stayed. There was no curfew, no cops, no nuthin."[45]

Although many children and young people used the Bay Street Beach for swimming, it was just one of several swimming areas on the harbour. The revetment wall at nearby Eastwood Park could still be used for diving, as could the boathouses of Thompson and Askew boatbuilders, which were a few blocks southwest of the official beach. Several former North End residents remembered that they and their friends learned to swim in the waters near those boathouses. Both as a swimming and a recreational area, the Bay Street Beach was simply incorporated into the larger community culture and did not become the carefully organized site of nature and recreation that some Hamiltonians imagined.[46]

REFORM IDEAS CONCERNING the value of recreation to the health of all urban residents shaped city efforts to create swimming beaches, as did a sense of urgency driven by scarcity – the loss of accessible waterfront spaces to industrial and port development. Similar motivations sustained continued efforts to maintain the harbour as a place where people could fish. The infilling of the shallow inlets and the revetment wall that hardened the shoreline undermined fish spawning and feeding habitats. Residential and industrial wastes threatened particular fish populations in both the harbour and Lake Ontario. So too did the oil and gasoline runoff from the roads that carried an increasing number of automobiles and trucks after the First World War. Between 1900 and the Great Depression, the degraded environment that had already created problems for the commercial fish – such as whitefish and herring – now affected a number of other species, including bass and pike. The carp, an exotic species that had been introduced into the Great Lakes during the 1880s, adapted best to ecological changes.[47]

The continuing decline of specific fish populations came at the same time as social reformers praised sport fishing as yet another of the "suitable open-air distractions and amusements" that should be made available to city dwellers who faced other less wholesome temptations. Kelly Evans, author of the provincial government's 1911 "Report of the Ontario Game and Fish Commission," elaborated on this view:

> Much of the physical deterioration prevailing in the more congested areas of great cities, and the vices and evils existing in cities and towns alike, are to be attributed in great part to lack of sufficient inducement to the people to seek health and wholesome exercise elsewhere than on the streets, and it must, therefore, be apparent that where an attraction does exist which is capable of drawing thousands daily, or at least weekly, out into the open air and providing them with both exercise and amusement, it must be morally and economically advantageous to foster and develop that attraction by every possible means. The potentialities of angling rank high in this regard. The sport is suitable to both sexes and to all ages, from the young child to the old man and woman. It is within the means of the poor as of the wealthy, for the most expensive equipment is but little guarantee of greater success than that which will be attained by the humblest tools.[48]

Evans, who also identified fish as an underused and cheap food source for poor city dwellers, argued that the sport fishery had to be maintained in every town. How? He began by recommending that only angling by hook and line should be permitted within an eight-kilometre radius of all cities and that the use of nets and other practices associated with the commercial fishery should be outlawed in urban waters. He then singled out one particular practice, winter spear fishing in Burlington Bay, as a factor in the decline of bass, a popular sport fish. Evans believed that while the provincial government more carefully and effectively regulated the urban fishery, it needed to invest further in its own fish hatcheries and focus on the propagation of two sport fish – speckled trout and black bass – whose populations had declined. Finally, he recommended the enforcement of the "excellent regulations" against the pollution that damaged fish populations.[49]

Evans's report reflects the provincial government's gradual displacement of Ottawa as the regulator of Ontario's inland fisheries. A jurisdictional dispute had complicated conservation efforts in the 1880s and 1890s, but an 1898 higher court decision strengthened the Province's authority by confirming its control of fishing licences and licensing conditions. Although elements of federal legislation still applied, effective enforcement and future initiatives rested with the Ontario government. Evans's report suggested that the Province would continue federal regulations regarding fisher behaviour, propagation, and pollution. Yet it would pay much greater attention to framing those issues in relation to the sport fishery, rather than its commercial counterpart. Officials continued to record routine statistics related to commercial fishing on the Great Lakes, but they showed a good deal more interest in demonstrating the value of sport fishing and tourist dollars to the provincial economy.[50]

Whereas the officials generally thought about the sport fishery in terms of central and northern Ontario, advocates of sport fishing in industrial cities such as Hamilton could take advantage of the provincial orientation away from the commercial fishery. In doing so, they sometimes spoke of tourism but often focused on the social benefits of fishing. As Ontario towns faced a growing number of unemployed workers during the winter of 1930, Hamilton angling devotee Thomas H. Barnes explained that his sport was the best one available to "the less fortunate city worker." He advocated fishing because it bred "happiness and contentment," not because it provided food or income to struggling workers. "Men," he enthused, "do not dream of trouble and sedition when they are beside a stream."[51]

As the president of the Hamilton Angling and Casting Club, Barnes championed the interests of local sport fishers. At its first meeting in 1921, the organization adopted the motto "Protect, propagate and preserve," words mirroring the three approaches to conservation espoused in Evans's report.[52] The Hamilton anglers both supported and complicated the work of Charles John Kerr, who had been the regional fishery official since 1905. He had resigned his job as a Grand Trunk Railway machinist to take up a post once held by his father and his younger brother Fred, which he would hold for more than twenty-five years. Kerr's situation differed from that of his predecessors, however, since although he sympathized with those who eked out a living from fishing, his provincial masters were much more interested in sport fishing, making commercial operations more marginal to the local economy.

Despite the enormous growth in the region's population after the turn of the century, the numbers engaged in some commercial fishing on Burlington Beach had stagnated. Between 1900 and 1914, their reported catches of whitefish, herring, and even rough fish in both the bay and Lake Ontario declined anywhere from 35 to 70 percent.[53] Retaining some kind of fishery for a growing number of sport and subsistence fishers thus took on even more importance for Kerr. The Hamilton Angling and Casting Club was created in 1921 after a local controversy erupted over commercial fishing. With few exceptions, Kerr enforced the regulations against net fishing in the bay and actively seized nets, most often from commercial fishers. He nevertheless saw an opportunity to help some of them by allowing them to net one particular and controversial species – carp. This fish had been introduced into North America during the 1880s in the belief that it could become a cheap food source for poorer families. It adapted exceptionally well to the altered ecology of the Great Lakes, particularly in shallow waters such as Burlington Bay and Cootes Paradise – so well, in fact, that many feared it was displacing more favoured fish. Critics accused the carp "of many villainies," including eating the young of other fish and destroying the aquatic vegetation needed for spawning grounds and duck nests.[54]

Kerr shared this negative view of carp, and in 1906 he requested and received permission to authorize local fishers to use seine nets on the bay to catch them. Six years later, he concluded that the nets harmed other fish populations more than they did the carp. He became concerned when fishers convinced his provincial masters to let them continue the practice. Even worse, they won the right to keep all their catch as a temporary wartime measure, and they applied to continue the practice after the war. One of Kerr's superiors from the provincial fishery visited Hamilton early in 1920 to consider their application in a meeting that, critics accused, was designed to be relatively private and limited. But local sport fishers mobilized to successfully oppose the application, and within a year they sought to more carefully entrench and protect their interests through their newly created association.[55] The Hamilton Angling and Casting Club remained committed to creating a sport fishery in the bay, even as its members discussed establishing a private game and fish reserve, and organized a lecture series that would appeal only to those who could take their fishing vacations in distant settings.[56] Like swimming promoters, angling enthusiasts saw a properly organized local fishery as benefitting society more widely.

To protect the fishery, the new club thus took aim at what it saw as two unsportsmanlike activities – netting fish and using spears in wintertime. Its members condemned even the limited use of nets to sweep the harbour clean of carp, arguing that the seines damaged other fish and that fishers could not be trusted to limit their catch. Kerr continued to permit carp netting, but the club's advocacy work ensured that he would monitor fishers more closely, making it less likely for him to extend this exception.[57] Club members also criticized winter spearing, but they avoided direct confrontation on the subject. They recognized that although Kelly Evans and other fishery officials had condemned spear fishing generally, Kerr had been authorized to allow it in the bay. Since the 1890s, commercial fishers had justified its use in an effort to make the most of a fishery that was in inevitable decline. About a hundred people, and sometimes more, continued to purchase licences to spear fish through the ice each winter.[58]

Whereas most local sport fishers sharply criticized the practice of spear fishing when they testified before provincial committees, they did not go as far as some provincial officials, or, after its formation in 1927, the Ontario Federation of Anglers, in calling for its abolition.[59] Instead, they sought to enlist allies by trying to make the practice part of a properly managed fishery, seeking to reduce the length of the season during which it would be permitted, regardless of ice conditions, and alerting people to the problem that springtime spearing endangered spawning fish. They also attempted to limit the types of fish that could be speared, arguing that spearing endangered some species that were preserved for the sport fishery. In the case of the seasonal limitation, they had some success. During the winter of 1922, the provincial department instructed Kerr to close the spearing season on 15 March. The club had less success in exempting certain species from the spear. Although the law excluded bass, the club failed to get a similar restriction for pike and pickerel.[60]

"The fish," as Kelly Evans had asserted in his 1911 report, "belong to the community."[61] By the end of the First World War, only six to eight families were engaged in commercial fishing on Burlington Beach; their ability to defend their interests or enlist the support of the fisheries inspector became increasingly limited, and therefore exceptions to net fishing became increasingly rare. In the case of winter spearing, however, a diverse group of community members mobilized local political leaders and a sympathetic Kerr to sustain their practice; the angling club succeeded only in restricting the season. Hamilton's sport fishers and provincial fishery officials learned – some of them to their dismay – that the fish did indeed belong to the community. Many Hamiltonians embraced and struggled to retain the right to engage in a type of fishing that offered an additional seasonal source of food and income in a working-class, industrial community. Throughout the Great Depression, they would continue to spear fish through the ice.

Hamilton anglers were not much more effective in their efforts to reduce pollution in the harbour, but a stronger crusade would have required them to directly confront the city's economic leaders. Although some club members called for more stringent government action against those who polluted fishing grounds, their leaders were ambivalent about challenging the industrial elite, preferring to rely on moral suasion. Citing the example of Stelco's decision to stop dumping hot slag into the harbour, one member explained that other manufacturers would co-operate if only they knew how much damage they caused.[62] Many club members, themselves small-business owners and white-collar workers, lacked the social and economic clout to have much influence, especially since so many of them depended upon the city's industrial prosperity. Nor could they anticipate receiving much support from fishery officials to strengthen the law or fully enforce it. A game fish commission observed in 1930 that when the Ontario Fish and Game Department published a summary of federal and provincial fishing regulations, it did not even list the existing anti-pollution laws. It noted that since only the federal fishery had such laws, provincial officials did not know who should enforce them, or even how to enforce them. A study of just four years later showed that pollution continued to undermine fishing in the bay; oil was more of a problem than it had ever been, and various "obnoxious substances" killed masses of fish.[63]

That should have been a serious concern for the Hamilton angling club. By the late 1930s, it had invested much time and money in restocking fish in the bay via an artificial propagation conservation program. Ottawa had long been involved in trying to sustain commercial fish populations this way, but early-twentieth-century provincial fishery officials pioneered hatcheries for sport fish – specifically, bass and trout. The angling club enthusiastically embraced intervention in the fishery and took credit for the 25,000 smallmouth bass fry that the provincial hatcheries deposited in Hamilton Harbour between 1921 and 1923, and the 180,000 speckled trout fry introduced to the region's creeks between 1921 and 1924. For the remainder of the decade, the region received just 40,000 more trout and 500 more bass. There is no evidence to suggest that the introduced populations became self-sustaining; the provincial hatcheries simply could not maintain the level of production necessary to continually restock Ontario waters.[64]

Indeed, although a provincial game commission warned against "accepting too readily that artificial handling improves on nature," the angling club embraced fish culture.[65] It promised that artificial propagation would bring the bay back to "its former status as a fisherman's paradise."[66] The club convinced city councillors that it could transform one of the old filtering basins along the Beach Strip – no longer needed for the water supply – into a bass-breeding pond. Adult male and female bass would be transferred to the basin from other parts of the province during the spawning season, and the resulting young fish would be introduced into the bay. Since the water of the basin was similar to that of the bay, and since more mature fish would be introduced into the bay, the club was confident that the plan would work. The club spent several years constructing the right pond environment – grading its shoreline, planting trees around it, and fencing it off to discontinue its use as a swimming hole. The plan to transfer mature fish did not materialize, but in the fall of 1932 the provincial government provided ten thousand largemouth bass fingerlings for the pond. The following spring, it released about two thousand young bass into the bay, not the ten thousand it had originally envisioned. It released more over the next two years and successfully raised some fish. In 1934, it announced that it would no longer be receiving fingerlings or fry. Whether the club could sustain the breeding pond without an infusion of new fry, let alone achieve its promise of creating one of the best fishing spots in the province by 1935 or 1936, remained to be seen.[67]

HAMILTON'S FISHING AND swimming enthusiasts won support for their recreational pursuits by emphasizing that all social classes could and should participate in their brand of wholesome activity. They promoted properly organized recreation in a carefully constructed natural world as a positive alternative to the disorderly attractions of the city. Local promoters of two other water-based sports – sailing and rowing – seemed less concerned about appealing to such democratic social impulses. The Royal Hamilton Yacht Club retained its commitment to social exclusivity, although it faced a rival that was more open to the wider community. The collapse of both local rowing clubs in the mid-1890s set the stage for a new organization that appeared more firmly committed to raising the social tone of the sport. The promoters of recreational boating tended to be less affected by the decline of water quality that shaped the behaviour of swimming and fishing enthusiasts. Yet they did share one concern – by the 1920s, the industrial harbour provided less shoreline for the kinds of marine facilities that were needed to sustain boat clubs.

The official historian of the Royal Hamilton Yacht Club, Harry Penny, describes the period from its founding until the First World War as its halcyon days – an era when photographs of the RHYC's magnificent Beach Strip clubhouse and yachts sailing on the bay became important symbols in the city's early promotional literature.[68] The images spoke to the prosperity of the city and the emergence of a class of people who could spend money on luxury sailing yachts and membership in a socially exclusive club. In the early years of the twentieth century, the club had little trouble attracting applicants for membership. The development of motorboats did little to change this dynamic; boat owners listed in 1911 included Samuel Beatty, a commission merchant, Kenneth Bethune, a car factory owner, and Harold Greening, the son of a prominent industrialist. The RHYC took pride in hosting the social elites of the Great Lakes area in the annual regattas of the Lake Yacht Racing Association. There, the biggest, most expensive, and fastest yachts raced with some of the region's most noted men at the helm.[69]

Although the RHYC retained a small building in the city, its members had both the time and money to operate its main clubhouse on the Beach Strip during the early 1890s. People who were attracted to yachting but felt excluded from this new location, or who simply wanted to set sail closer to home, formed the Victoria Yacht Club, which was anchored firmly in the North End. Among its founders were several original members of the RHYC, most notably Thomas Jutten, the former machinist turned boatbuilder and future North End politician. Key members of the Victoria Yacht Club included a machinist, a tinsmith, and other skilled workers, a leadership quite distinct from that of the RHYC. They located their docks and clubhouse in the heart of the North End waterfront, enabling skilled workers to sail during the limited leisure time at their disposal. Later accounts suggest that the club had as many as 350 members in the years before the war. It aimed for the same respectability as its rival, participating in many of the same regattas and sponsoring appropriately managed swimming contests in the first decade of the century.[70]

Although sailing proved popular enough to support two new clubs, Hamilton's rowing clubs struggled. To be competitive, rowers needed the financial resources to purchase and maintain the most up-to-date equipment, such as lightweight racing shells with sliding seats. The more socially exclusive of the clubs, the Leander, soon encountered difficulties. It amalgamated with a local canoeing club in 1888 in a failed effort to sustain itself and focus on a sport less tainted by "professionalism." The Nautilus Club had initially appeared more robust, but its limited financial resources proved its undoing. Neither club survived the financial depression that began in 1893. Not until 1901 could city promoters again boast that their town supported organized rowing. Robert T. Steele, a local wholesale grocer, founded the Hamilton Rowing Club in the image of the Leander, rather than the Nautilus. Few skilled workers found it welcoming, even though it was located on the North End waterfront, first in the old Leander clubhouse and then in a powerhouse. Nevertheless, both the club and the sport proved attractive to the cohort of young white-collar workers who sought to find fun, acceptable social activities, and spaces for their group. Its members included male office clerks, bookkeepers, bank tellers, insurance agents, and people involved in sales. Though they were wealthier than many Hamiltonians, club members sometimes struggled financially to keep their clubhouse going or to buy and maintain the state-of-the art equipment needed for them to be truly competitive. Shortly after the club failed in a bid to acquire used equipment from the Canadian Olympic team, the *Hamilton Spectator* warned that its young members could easily lose interest in the sport if they had to continue relying on old boats and outdated training facilities. To keep members amused and to provide off-season activities, the Hamilton Rowing Club, like clubs elsewhere, included other sports in its roster, such as snowshoeing, hockey, and, beginning in 1913, football.[71]

The war and the financial depression of the early 1920s undermined whatever successes the boating clubs had achieved. Fire destroyed the Beach Strip home of the RHYC in 1915; a plan to replace it with an equally elaborate building and recreational complex – including facilities for lawn bowling and tennis, as well as a parking lot – appeared in 1916. For a variety of reasons, the structure was never built. With its membership cut in half during the early 1920s, the RHYC made do with moving and renovating its modest city clubhouse, locating it in the heart of the North End. This move probably did not help the difficulties of the Victoria Yacht Club, which closed its doors for good in 1920.[72] According to the local press, the Hamilton Rowing Club was running "hand to mouth" by the early 1920s, supported in some years by fewer than a hundred members. An advisory board of prominent businessmen couldn't solve its problems, and it shut down in 1925. Several business leaders organized a new club in 1927. They called it the Leander Club, whether in reference to its Hamilton predecessor or the famous British rowing club of the same name is unclear. It remained a fairly small organization in the late 1920s and early 1930s, dependent on active, competitive racers for its leadership.[73]

Organized recreational boating thus remained a fragile presence in the harbour. The social structure of the industrial city did not align well with those who sought to create exclusive clubs; nor was it easy to sustain sports that, by the 1890s, required a significant financial investment for good equipment. More than changes to the harbour environment, economic downturns undermined the clubs; even the elite had difficulty keeping their RHYC afloat during the first half of the 1920s and then again in the first half of the 1930s. Local promoters of rowing and yachting saw these sports as a private good. They made little effort to present them as a social good that should be open to all and that therefore required the kind of public support that swimming and even fishing received. Civic boosters embraced images of the stately RHYC and its graceful sloops tacking across the harbour as symbols of private prosperity in a successful industrial centre. Yet the exceptions prove the rule. In 1928, city council helped the new Leander Club purchase a rowing shell from England so that it could be used in 1930, when Hamilton hosted its first British Empire Games. City councillors wanted to support this new international mega-sporting event and to help the local rowing team compete in its races. They also spent $150,000 of public debentures on the construction of a new indoor municipal swimming pool to be used during the games. Compared to this, the cost of the rowing shell was a minor investment, one that organizers capitalized upon when they advertised their event.[74]

A few years later, in 1934, the ever-hopeful editor of the *Hamilton Spectator* claimed a resurgence of interest in local sailing. The writer of a two-page feature article opined that Hamilton, "once the Mecca of sail," had "a magnificent opportunity to capture her former glory."[75] Yet he criticized it for failing to provide the necessary marine facilities to support sailing and suggested that yachtsmen were investing in other places such as nearby Oakville and Toronto. He outlined a proposal to exchange the RHYC North End waterfront property, which was adjacent to the Bay Street Beach, for almost 2.6 hectares of LaSalle Park, including its pavilion and wharf facilities. LaSalle Park was situated across the bay on the north shore, and many people had long criticized it as a white elephant because it lost money year after year. Day trippers from the city and the neighbouring lake ports no longer ventured there by steamboat.[76] Frederick Ker, vice president and managing director of the *Spectator*, who was himself an avid sailor and a member of the committee seeking to solve the RHYC's financial problems, doubtless had something to do with this trial balloon being floated in the local paper. Significantly, the *Spectator* framed the argument for public support of the RHYC scheme in terms of the financial investment that the wealthy yachtsmen could provide to the city, rather than invoking the wider public benefits of sailing. The promoters of the plan suggested that the city and its richest citizens could mutually benefit from the arrangement. Yet the idea of linking the RHYC to public space generated little interest, and the trial balloon deflated, leaving little trace.[77]

While elite and middle-class boating clubs looked for assistance in surviving the hard times of the Depression, workers sustained a flourishing boating culture. The shipwrights who profited from elite markets for sailboats and other vessels supplemented their incomes by hiring out simple rowboats to anyone who was in search of an afternoon excursion.[78] Bastien's boat works, established in 1865, for example, rented out sailing and rowing vessels for more than sixty years. One worker remembers getting together with friends to rent its "real good rowboats" for about seventy-five cents for the day. Renting two boats made the outing even more fun:

> We'd get way out into the middle of the bay and start chasing each other, and rowing and paddling. And one boat would catch up to the other boat and we'd all jump into the one and dump it over *[laughs]*. Out in the middle of the bay, over the boat would go. Of course, we'd all get underneath it and take one deep breath and heave, flip it over. And climb back in, start all over again.

The hilarity continued until "the harbour patrol come out – the police come out and tied us on the back of the police boat and towed us back in ... Next weekend we'd rent us another boat *[laughs]*."[79]

Some working men formed their own boating organizations, such as the Jolly Good Fellows Club, described by North End raconteurs as "a hard-drinking, fun-loving lot, who often found themselves in awkward circumstances and normally through their own fault."[80] Banding together and buying used boats from the area's wealthier folk, they created their own culturally rich boating milieu. Their excursions to Aldershot's north shore included picnics with fish fries, kegs of beer, baseball games, and quoits; dessert might take the form of melons pilfered from north shore market gardens. The Fellows were the same brotherhood who frequented the North End boathouses and parks for cockfights and crap games, and who had made the Bay Street Beach part of their cultural world. The bay's waters and boathouses were the site in which they acted out the rituals of their masculine culture, such as the game of cat and mouse they played with the police. Once, they reportedly responded to the strong arm of the law by stripping officer "Sneaky" Meyers and unceremoniously tossing him into the bay. Although they took advantage of public parks and beaches, they generally did not need orderly and organized forms of nature or recreation. They thrived in the North End waterfront, where many private and public spaces seemed equally open and accessible, despite efforts to manage and control them.[81]

MEMBERS OF THE Jolly Good Fellows may have been among the estimated thirty thousand people who lined the Beach Strip's western shoreline on the evening of 21 August 1930 to catch a glimpse of the Australian-born Olympic gold medallist Bobby Pearce in the premier rowing race of the first British Empire Games.[82] The much-anticipated event became the most troubled one of the games, for "Old King Neptune, or whoever guides the destinies of the water on the bay ... proved unkind."[83] Planners had attempted to organize nature to their advantage: the race course ran west from the open water in the bay through a lane that had been "mowed out of a weedshed" near the High-Level Bridge at the Burlington Heights. Rowers could anticipate a sheltered and calm course, protected from prevailing westerly winds. The best views of the race would come from a grandstand constructed for the paying customers, but it would be visible to folks crowding along the west harbour's embankments.

Organizers seemed unusually confident in their control of nature, as they appeared completely unprepared for the cool, wet northeasterly wind that churned the waters of the bay during the days before the race. Nor did they make any new plans, even as they delayed some early races because of the bad conditions on 19 August. On the afternoon of 20 August, twenty thousand Hamiltonians stood or sat along the heights, waiting for the great race to begin. And waited. And waited, until darkness fell. The race clearly wasn't going to happen. Unlike the spectators on the shore, the rowers at least had been told that it would be rescheduled for the next morning. Morning came and the bay "was a seething mass of cotton tops." Organizers once again attempted to postpone the event, until the evening. This time, however, the rowers protested: As one of them pointed out, the race "will not be fit to row to-night for anything except a whale boat." An exasperated Bobby Pearce exclaimed, "I don't believe we will ever have the race. It's blooming awful." "Only he did not say 'blooming,'" commented the *Toronto Star* reporter. "He used a more lurid word."[84]

Faced with the revolt of the rowers, officials hastily arranged to hold the race at the scheduled time, but on a course along the bayside of the Beach Strip, sheltered from the northeasterly winds that continued to blow. The postponements and change in venue did not deter the crowds; nor did they make much difference to the outcome of the race. As most people had predicted, Pearce easily triumphed. And when he accepted a job from the Distilleries Company of Canada, Hamilton secured a sporting hero, as the Olympic and now Empire champion made the city and its harbour his new home. Hamilton now had the perfect sporting champion for the imperfect social world of an industrial city. A carpenter and boatbuilder by trade, Pearce had been refused entry to the prestigious amateur Diamond Sculls event at England's Henley Regatta in 1928, and his career had been dogged by allegations of professionalism. Technically, he was no longer a manual worker engaged in a trade, so he might escape some questions about his amateur status. His new business position didn't help since it now floated him in the world of booze, which the strictest adherents of the amateur movement frowned upon.[85]

The rowing race and its outcome reveal the difficulties that sport promoters faced when trying to organize and control nature and society. In the end, their planning failed to contend with the unruliness of nature. And Bobby Pearce proved not quite the amateur sportsman of their ideal. Indeed, once he had gained admittance to and triumphed at the Henley races and one more Olympics, Pearce entered what amateur ideologues saw as the murkier world of professional rowing.[86]

Nevertheless, this hardly detracted from the pride that Hamilton's social and political leaders took in creating and hosting the first British Empire Games. They highlighted the ideal metropolis that civic boosters had imagined: a beautiful city that prospered – not suffered – from industrial expansion. This came at a moment when many local leaders believed they were taking the necessary steps to ensure that all Hamiltonians would continue to enjoy clean drinking water and morally appropriate recreational activities in socially acceptable spaces. Local swimming promoters must have been particularly happy that their events were among the most popular at the games. Although the swim meets were held indoors, in the impressive new municipal pool, the city had several bathing beaches where the sport could also be enjoyed outdoors. Plans were afoot to make the bay a paradise for anglers, and both rowing and sailing seemed to be gaining more support. Hamiltonians, a *Spectator* reporter enthused in 1934, were becoming "more water minded than they have been in some time."[87]

Whereas recreational supporters focused on organizing particular urban spaces, a group of self-styled planners was thinking more about the rational organization of the entire city. Like the recreational reformers, this group advocated the construction of natural and built environments that would shape the social and moral character of Hamilton. By the early 1930s, the local landscape bore the imprint of some of its ideas, owing in part to the influence of Thomas B. McQuesten. It is to the planners' vision and its consequences that we now turn.

5

Planning Nature

The Waterfront Legacy of T.B. McQuesten, 1917–40

IN 1917, NOULAN CAUCHON, one of Canada's pre-eminent town planners and a founder of the Town Planning Institute of Canada, created a grandiose urban design for Hamilton's Town Planning Board that was inspired by the City Beautiful movement. It featured garden suburbs, a high-speed electric commuter railway, and a grand boulevard from the bay to the escarpment that ended at a thirty-thousand-seat Greek amphitheatre to be built where a gravel pit had disfigured the face of Hamilton's "mountain shrines."[1] His plan also included an elaborate parks system that would provide "the lungs of the city" and would include "wilder and freer" parkland at the western end of the harbour and Cootes Paradise.[2] In a subsequent report, Cauchon proposed enhancing the industrial district that had been developing in the city's northeast end. He stated that all of the bay's eastern inlets should be reclaimed by the City and filled in to create even more room for industrial development (Figure 23). This would transform much of the waterfront, beginning in the old North End port and extending almost to the Beach Strip. Cauchon proposed that a narrow scenic lagoon should separate the waterfront industrial district from recreational sectors. He specified that only three areas – the western end of the harbour including Cootes Paradise, the north shore, and the Beach Strip – were to be kept for residential and recreational purposes. Even there, he argued, nature must be carefully planned to produce the appropriate aesthetic and recreational response. The rest of the waterfront would be left to development by Hamilton's growing industries.[3]

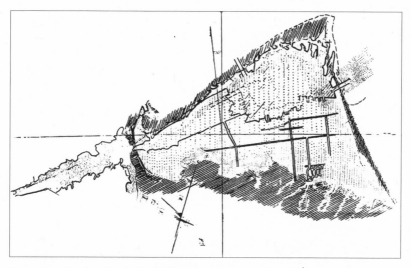

FIGURE 23 Noulan Cauchon's sketch marks the triangular bay's existing shoreline
and inlets with dark diagonal lines. Cauchon projected infilling roughly two-thirds of
the bay to bring its south shore as far north as the Burlington Canal (*marked as a cut
through the Beach Strip on the right*), which would cut off the west harbour rail yards
and the city's North End from the water. Note the shipping lanes planned to provide
access to existing eastern factories. The proposed lagoon is difficult to discern on this
rough sketch: there is a slight opening of white to the left of the existing Beach Strip,
where it narrows at its southern end. *Courtesy of Local History and Archives Department,
Hamilton Public Library.*

In 1919, the chief engineer for Toronto's harbour commission, E.L.
Cousins, produced a second planning report on the bay, this time for
the relatively new Hamilton Harbour Commission. Perhaps more surprisingly, given the commission's mandate to develop Hamilton's port
capacity, Cousins also emphasized the importance of balancing the harbour's recreational, residential, and economic uses. He maintained that
a large industrial city needed to set aside plenty of room for healthy outdoor
recreation. He declared that, "by their physiography," the Beach Strip and
the north shore "lend themselves admirably to aesthetic treatment," and
he determined that they should be saved for parks and outdoor amusement. Like Cauchon, Cousins sought a "clear cut line between the industrial area and beach development." But instead of creating a scenic
lagoon between the two, the port-oriented engineer favoured separating
them with a narrow ship canal and turning basin. His plan did not stop
at filling and extending the eastern inlets and shoreline for industry: he

proposed adding ninety-five hectares to the Beach Strip for recreational and residential purposes, and as much land as was necessary around the entire harbour shoreline – even at the foot of the bluffs on the north shore – to create a scenic parkway for automobiles.[4]

The audacity and expense of Cauchon's and Cousin's designs ensured that the City would never fully adopt either one. Nevertheless, the plans struck just the right notes, in harmony with what local civic boosters and recreational advocates wanted: an industrial city that still left room for handsome homes and healthful recreation. The plans also appealed to Thomas Baker McQuesten, a man who was a force of – and for – nature on the Hamilton Parks Board. Throughout the 1920s, McQuesten would champion one key part of the planners' visions – the creation of "wilder and freer" parkland at the west end of the harbour. But not too wild and free. He and others planned for the nature that they desired, a nature that would be aesthetically pleasing and morally uplifting. To achieve it, they needed to reshape the disorderly social and natural worlds at the edge of town.[5]

THOMAS BAKER MCQUESTEN was born into a once affluent Hamilton family that had hit hard financial times and struggled to maintain its high social status in local society. His grandfather, a medical doctor, founded the family's sizable fortune as a partner in Hamilton's earliest foundry, making agricultural implements and stoves. His father, a lawyer and mill owner, tried hard but nevertheless squandered the family fortune. He died an early death from an overdose of sleeping medicine just a few months before Tom's sixth birthday. A few investments survived and provided an income that might well have been the envy of many other Hamilton residents. But the size of the sum made it difficult for Tom's mother, Mary Baker McQuesten, to maintain her fine home, named Whitehern, and social standing, let alone guarantee the same for her six children. Mary managed her money and her children well. Her two oldest daughters stayed at home to help her, whereas her eldest son, Calvin, attended university. Her third daughter taught school in Ottawa, sending her earnings home to help finance Tom's education at the University of Toronto. Unlike Calvin, a sometime journalist and Presbyterian minister, Tom found a profession that paid well. His earnings as a lawyer and his activities as a politician sustained the family estate and reputation. Of all the children, Tom seems to have benefitted most and suffered least from Mary's determination to retain the family's social standing.[6]

Mary instilled in her family a social philosophy that, according to her biographer, Mary Anderson, was influenced by the Social Gospel and City Beautiful movements of her day, linking morality to "beautiful surroundings and to the quality of public spaces."[7] Tom McQuesten grew up surrounded by an inherited, elite-defined sense of beauty through works of art, fine furniture, a handsome library, and well-maintained gardens. Wilder nature could be encountered in Whitehern's walled garden, in a rowing scull, or through visits to the Muskoka summer homes of well-to-do family friends. True, Tom worked on a transatlantic cattle boat and as a lumberjack during his university summers, and he briefly practised law in a northern Ontario mining community, but these experiences merely appeared to confirm for him an association of disordered nature with low morals. He returned to Whitehern, with its mid-Victorian neo-classical design, in 1909, and would contribute to its upkeep for the rest of his life. It embodied his belief in the value of well-ordered and aesthetically pleasing environments. Over the next two decades, he would seek to extend that order and beauty to the unruly city that now surrounded its walls.[8]

McQuesten, a sometime vice-president of the Hamilton Liberal Club, first ran for city office in 1912 to defend his home and neighbourhood from the noise, dirt, and congestion created by the increasingly busy railway that ran behind Whitehern. His efforts to have the rail line relocated, or at least depressed below grade, proved futile, but they helped draw the new city councillor into the world of urban planning. In 1916, he joined Hamilton's advisory Town Planning Board, and in 1917 he helped convince city council to appoint a consulting engineer, William Tye, to advise on the routing of electric and steam railways through town. McQuesten publicly championed the resulting report and then arranged for Tye's assistant, the prominent Canadian town planner Noulan Cauchon, to "draw up plans for a new Hamilton." That new Hamilton would combine planned transportation routes and boulevards with a range of green spaces – from ornamental gardens to "wilder and freer" parkland. The latter would allow access to "the unsullied realm of nature for citizens bound up in the urban realm of culture."[9] Unsullied nature, however, was to be carefully cultivated and framed by the arches, colonnades, and balustrades of a proposed new northwestern entrance to town. Cauchon's new Hamilton aimed for social betterment through beauty.[10]

Cauchon presented town plans that, as McQuesten enthusiastically told the local press, represented "the ideal towards which we should work."

Support for this ideal appeared to build in 1919, when the work of the harbour commission consultant incorporated many of its important elements. Yet the Town Planning Board lacked the clout to convince city council to wholeheartedly adopt them. McQuesten soon discovered an agency that wielded real power, one to which he could turn for support – the Board of Parks Management, whose members held three-year appointments that could be renewed. After 1921 the Parks Board also enjoyed an independent and stable source of funding, receiving from the City a rate of one mill on the municipal tax levy. Within a year of his 1922 appointment to the Parks Board, McQuesten began working with its new chair, a lawyer and real estate developer named Cecil Vanroy Langs; together they planned and spent their budget wisely to expand the parks network and beautify the city.[11]

These two politically astute men quickly seized whatever opportunities came their way to further their plans to develop the parks system. This happened, for example, when some of McQuesten's siblings, along with other local bird lovers and nature enthusiasts, sought to protect Cootes Paradise, also known as Dundas Marsh, from development (Figure 24). In May 1919, they and about sixty bird lovers, including the naturalist Robert Owen Merriman, the wheelchair-bound son of a local wire manufacturer, met in the new public library to form a naturalists' club. By the time the Hamilton Bird Protection Society, later renamed the Hamilton Naturalists Club, sought incorporation in 1920, 147 members had joined the cause. They included people from socially prominent families like the McQuestens, as well as many individuals from the professional classes – physicians, lawyers, merchants, bank managers, accountants, and teachers. The teachers helped with public education outreach, so children could learn about the importance of conserving nature. Some nine thousand Hamilton schoolchildren became members of the society's Junior Bird Club, involved in birdhouse building and essay writing on conservation topics.[12] Including them helped naturalize the club's authority on matters of local conservation and land use.

The naturalist organization aimed to have Cootes Paradise designated as a bird sanctuary to protect its marshlands from development and hunting.[13] In a strategic move to garner support for their cause, club leaders sent copies of their plans to key players – the Board of Commerce, city council, the county council, and local MPs and MPPs and their respective governments. The hunting community responded quickly and decisively against what it saw as the effort to curtail hunting in the area (Figure 25). The Hamilton Gun Club, led by a small-scale entrepreneur named Nelson

FIGURE 24 Composite photograph of the famed naturalist Jack Miner *(left)* and Tom McQuesten's brother Calvin *(right)* with Canada geese at Cootes Paradise, perhaps taken when Miner came to Hamilton to deliver a public lecture in November 1926. *Courtesy of Whitehern Museum Archives, Hamilton, 977.6.1.1080003.*

Long, spearheaded a petition that bore a hundred signatures.[14] It presented a working-man's perspective of the marsh, contending that "hundreds of men went up at dawn to shoot ducks before going to work, and when they returned home at night they went out to try to get some more."[15] Local hunters argued that unlike wealthy sport hunters who had the time and money to travel north to hunt, Hamilton's working families needed access to marsh resources for their food; furthermore, with so little time for hunting, workers maintained that they couldn't possibly deplete the game stocks. Indeed, they contended that a sanctuary in Hamilton would simply fatten birds that would be slaughtered elsewhere, shot by wealthy American hunters at the unrestricted private game preserves of nearby Long Point, on the well-known migration route.[16]

The bird sanctuary debate proved contentious. At a meeting between city officials, naturalists, and hunters, a proponent of the sanctuary proposal underlined the connection between conservationists and moral reform. This prominent local doctor championed the value of birdwatching, suggesting that "the histories of many patients showed that no outside interests in childhood and youth had led them to center their thoughts too much

FIGURE 25   Pothunters at the Desjardins Canal basin, Dundas. Using shotguns and
homemade fishing poles to bag their catch, working men and the families of the
boathouse colony survived on the plentiful game in the area until Cootes Paradise
was designated a wildlife sanctuary in 1927. *Courtesy of Local History and Archives
Department, Hamilton Public Library.*

on themselves. If given healthful, natural interests ... many of these would
not drift into venereal clinics." An outraged gun club leader responded
heatedly to the implication that an "outside" interest in hunting was both
unhealthy and unnatural. "Do you mean," he asked, "that sportsmen are
depraved because they kill?"[17]

Advocates of the sanctuary generally sought to avoid direct confrontation
with local sportsmen and even looked for ways to win their support. From
an early date, the Hamilton naturalists cleverly enlisted the enormously
popular and populist bird conservationist Jack Miner to their cause. His
private bird sanctuary at Kingsville had been declared a provincial Crown
reserve in 1917. The celebrity conservationist believed that hunting was
acceptable in moderation, writing in his best-selling 1923 book that he
loved "to see wild ducks, both on the table and in the air."[18] Not surprisingly, then, he stated that a bird sanctuary at Cootes Paradise would be a
sound investment in Hamilton's hunting future. As he explained, "For a
very small sum of money ... you are only building up the sportsmen's
opportunities in other ways, because from a sanctuary like this, there would
always be an overflow of birds that are brought there. You cannot do wrong

by helping bird lovers, because we take nothing from the shooter, but we increase their opportunities tenfold."[19] He also framed opponents to the sanctuary as a vocal minority and appealed to the democratic manliness of the working class for support: "I don't see how any delegation of real men could object to it as there are only about 7 per cent of people who want to shoot. Why should these few deprive the other 93 per cent of their enjoyment?" Referring to the Long Point situation, he claimed, "What we Canadians want is the most good for the most people."[20] Miner thus helped reformers to frame their arguments in a manner that did not directly challenge sport hunters.

Buoyed by the publicity surrounding Jack Miner's involvement, and by the resulting donations of money and bird food from the Ontario Fish and Game Association, the naturalists sought to cultivate wider support for their proposal, including from the local Trades and Labour Congress.[21] In January 1922, after interviewing the property owners whose lands were in question, one member of the bird protection society confidently predicted that "the matter would soon be settled."[22] Proponents of the sanctuary, however, soon learned that settling the matter would not be so simple. Exactly who had jurisdiction over Cootes Paradise itself and some of its surrounding lands was unclear. Those with potential claims included several railway companies, the Hamilton Cemetery Board, various federal and provincial government departments, the harbour commission, and the local governments of two counties, three townships, the City of Hamilton, and the Town of Dundas.

Into this jurisdictional confusion stepped George Midford, a local entrepreneur who hoped to take advantage of the situation by developing tourism through a hunting business at the marsh. Just a year after the bird society lobbied the federal minister of the interior to create its sanctuary, Midford leased portions of Cootes Paradise from the federal Department of Marine and Fisheries, with the intent of establishing a private duck farm for hunters.[23] He had developed a similar operation in New Jersey, and his plan was supported by "an old-style politician who looked after his constituents," Hamilton Tory backbencher and former mayor Thomas J. Stewart.[24] With Stewart's assistance, Midford struck a deal with the Department of Marine and Fisheries, agreeing to spend $5,000 developing Cootes Paradise in exchange for leasing the property at the nominal cost of a dollar![25]

Incredibly, Midford and Stewart appear to have sidestepped city council, the Parks Board, and the harbour commission, all of which the local advocates of the bird sanctuary had carefully cultivated as allies. The Midford deal also alienated potential supporters among Hamilton hunters. Having already argued that a bird sanctuary would threaten the hunting rights of workers, gun club leader Nelson Long opposed the Midford plan for the same reason. Although Stewart claimed that no shooting would be allowed at the duck farm, Long worried that Midford was simply creating a private hunting preserve for rich sportsmen. From the perspective of working-class hunters, a commercial duck farm that outlawed hunting or, even worse, made it available only to those who could afford the admission fee, was no better than a bird sanctuary.[26]

The ensuing political controversy undid the Midford deal. Stewart distanced himself from the agreement, claiming that he had not fully understood the issue. "If I had known that anyone in Hamilton wanted the property, I would have not been in favour of it," he claimed, appealing to local sensibilities. "I did not know what the Parks Board wanted." When Stewart accused Long of threatening him over his support of the Midford agreement, emotions ran high. The *Hamilton Spectator* recorded their heated exchange at a lively Parks Board meeting in 1925: "Did I threaten you?" asked Long. Stewart replied, "You fight me and I will give it to you back." To this, Long tauntingly retorted, "I can take all you can give me." Whether the machismo expressed in the verbal sparring ever turned physical is not known. However, in response to the query of Tom McQuesten, "Now that your eyes are open Mr. Stewart, will you reconsider your position?" Stewart replied obliquely: "I don't want to make a double-shuffle. I will think the matter over." Then, in the next breath, he added, "But I won't support Capt. Midford."[27] Within a week, harbour commissioners were in Ottawa, getting the Midford lease laid over indefinitely.[28]

By quietly orchestrating a land deal to secure the bird sanctuary's creation, McQuesten and the Parks Board seized a tremendous opportunity to develop the city's system of public parks. They discovered that the financially distressed McKittrick Properties Company, developer of the Westdale suburb at the west end of Hamilton, needed cash to pay its large debt to the City. The ailing company owned property adjoining the south shore of the marsh, which an internal report had identified as having "no value from a residential standpoint," and thus the company had earmarked it as parkland.[29] Under McQuesten's direction, the Parks Board arranged a deal for the transfer of about 161 hectares of this property to the City of Hamilton, in lieu of the taxes owed. By the spring of 1927, local MPPs, supported by the Parks Board and city council, along with local conservationists, successfully petitioned to have this and other land designated as a wildlife sanctuary. In so doing, they carefully protected the hunting rights of other bona fide owners of the land adjoining the marsh, who could continue to hunt, although they needed "a special permit, free of charge, to trap on their own lands, in accordance with gun regulations."[30] They apparently gave no thought to protecting the rights of other Hamilton families, some of whom used the marsh as a commons in which to hunt.

WITHIN DAYS OF THE provincial decision, council gave control of the area to the Parks Board, which would supervise this newly minted "wilder and freer" part of the parks system.[31] As it contemplated how best to use the property, the board also needed to figure out what to do with the Hamilton families that had settled along the secluded edges of the marsh and the Burlington Heights. By 1928, nearly 120 contiguous buildings were running alongside and into the Desjardins Canal on both its bay and marsh sides (Figure 26).[32] For McQuesten and others, these improvised homes – converted boathouses and tarpaper and tin-roofed shelters – were just ugly shacks and shanties, susceptible to fire and dangerously beyond the reach of municipal services. Suspicious minds generally saw places on the waterfront as a source of disease, where gambling, prostitution, blood sports, and who knew what other crimes surely flourished.[33] In the eyes of its critics, this "shacktown" had no place in an idealized nature preserve. And worse, it obstructed McQuesten's plan to build a monumental western entrance to the city and a well-ordered parkland atop the Burlington Heights. If Noulan Cauchon's vision of a city beautiful were to be realized, the tarpaper shelters of working-class people would have to go.

But many would not go willingly. People had good reasons for being there and in a relatively short time had developed a real neighbourhood with a strong sense of community. Although some sources suggest that the community had earlier origins, the photographic record indicates that it emerged some time during or after the First World War and developed rapidly in the 1920s (Figure 27). Its impetus probably stemmed from Hamilton's shortage of good, clean, and affordable housing.[34] As early as 1909, the Board of Health regularly reported on and warned about the health consequences of this problem. In 1912, the medical officer of health reported that "every available four walls that under ordinary conditions of city growth would never be accused of being part of a home is eagerly seized upon and occupied, no matter how outrageous the rental."[35] Although Hamilton experienced a housing construction boom before the war, it did not keep pace with demand. Faced with high rents, crowding, and poor-quality accommodation, some residents chose to convert boathouses into homes or to build new shelters at the west end of the harbour

FIGURE 26   The little colony of boathouses at the Desjardins Canal, 1928. The houses sat alongside the mouths of the canal at the shores of the Burlington Heights between the bay *(very bottom)* and Cootes Paradise *(above)*. Note that the Desjardins Canal channel cut through the heights *(below)* and through the thick vegetation of the marsh *(above)*. *Jack V. Elliott Air Services. Courtesy of Royal Botanical Gardens Archives, Burlington.*

and along the Burlington Heights shoreline of Cootes Paradise. Some leased their land from farmers, the City, or railway companies for nominal rents of about $1.25 a month.[36] Others were squatters, whose legal claim to the land was tenuous at best.[37]

Given the community's proximity to the rail lines and yard, it is perhaps not surprising that railway yard workers, not necessarily the most skilled of that industry's workforce, were among those who lived there. One man was a Parks Board caretaker; another, of African Canadian descent, worked mortar in the local building industry. Other occupations included machinist, teamster, hydro worker, fire fighter, and painter. Not all of the boathouses were converted into permanent homes: the secretary of Hamilton's Works Department, who also sat on the Parks Board, owned and used his boathouse but lived in a well-to-do neighbourhood elsewhere.

Some boathouse dwellers were presumably financially better off than others; for example, one man who lived on the marsh side owned a large mahogany boat with an inboard motor, which, owing to its high cost would have been a rarity for any worker on the bay.[38]

Although middle-class Hamiltonians might have seen the outdoor privies, well water, and kerosene heat of the boathouses as too primitive for comfort, their occupants no doubt saw things very differently. Compared to the overcrowded and unsanitary conditions of the worst parts of the North End, the boathouses looked attractive in their natural setting, nestled between the water and grassy tree-lined hills, well upwind from the stench and grime of the factories (Figure 28). They offered easy access to fish, game, and green spaces for small gardens. Perhaps unsurprisingly, then, boathouse dwellers took considerable pride in their small community, which became large enough to support a little store. As one man recalled sentimentally of friends who lived there, "This marsh was not a marsh to them, this was truly paradise to them, these people. Believe me it was, because it had everything there. Out just beyond it, they had a

FIGURE 27 The boathouses of Cootes Paradise viewed from the top of the Burlington Heights, n.d. Note the wooden pilings of the canal jutting out of the water *(bottom right)*; they can still be seen when water levels are low. Today, the Royal Botanical Gardens Fishway runs across the mouth of the canal, near the telephone pole *(bottom right)*. *Courtesy of Osler Collection, McGill University.*

FIGURE 28   A smoke-filled sky over Hamilton's old port. The North End *(centre right)* and the new industrial waterfront *(centre left)* are pictured here from the Burlington Heights across the tree-lined Carroll's Point *(foreground)*. *Courtesy of Local History and Archives Department, Hamilton Public Library.*

couple of wells that they sank. Fresh water all of the time, you know. Outdoor toilets, but everything kept clean. Everyone took care of everybody's house."[39]

The boathouse residents reportedly developed a strong sense of community. They looked out for each other's children and participated in social events such as summer picnics and bonfire celebrations, as well as pickup hockey games in the winter.[40] Neighbours organized events that featured and took advantage of men's physical prowess. For example, they delighted in an unusual but hilarious entertainment called donkey baseball, which one observer described: "They'd have a little donkey, eh, and when you hit the ball, you had to pick the donkey up [over the shoulder] and carry him to the base. And these firemen were all big ... They didn't get them for their brains, they got them for their strength, eh, and that's what they did in donkey baseball."[41]

Boathouse children, like their parents, and like people in other Hamilton neighbourhoods, had a strong sense of community identity. Some classmates

at Strathcona School called them marsh rats, among other names, and clashes between them and North End kids were as inevitable as changes in the seasons. As one man reminisced, "Every early summer, we used to have our fight [against the North End kids] … and we used to meet each other at school in different days, and we'd get along just fine. But every bloody year we'd have a meeting. No one got hurt bad, you know."[42] Generally, the boathouse community offered more innocuous activities for its youth. "It seems to simply swarm with children," a *Herald* reporter noted approvingly in 1924, at a time when Hamilton, like many other urban places throughout the country, wrestled with the problem of determining what recreations were morally appropriate for youth. The marsh provided "a great natural playground" for them. The *Herald* argued that overall, the boathouse kids didn't do all that badly by their unsupervised surroundings. For example, they fared quite well when it came to nautical pursuits, swimming far away from the dangerous North End industrial waterfront and its busy wharves that so concerned officials. Clad in makeshift bathing suits (though sometimes going *au naturel*), they took to the water at a very young age. Many were said to be experts in swimming back and forth between the Desjardins Canal and Carroll's Point on the north shore. This helped certain boys to victory in Hamilton's annual Playground

Association swimming championships. Best of all, the canal's many bridges provided superb platforms for their well-executed dives and spectacular wave-crashing cannonballs.[43]

Most boathouse kids cut their teeth on outdoors pursuits at an early age – something that they would remember for a lifetime. Some used sticks for fishing poles and string for line that they pilfered from the wreaths left at the cemeteries on the Burlington Heights. They could fashion fishhooks from old nuts, bolts, and scraps of metal that lay along the tracks. Much could be learned about outdoors life simply by observing the sportsmen or pothunters who frequented the area. Since game was so abundant, achieving a good bag didn't require much prowess.[44] The marsh had everything – sunfish, catfish, shiners, bass, carp, ducks, partridges, wood-cock, snipe, muskrats, deer, and other plentiful game.

Reformers and planners like McQuesten, however, focused on what they saw as the darker side of the boathouse community. Given its proxim-ity to the waterfront and the tracks, it would be forever linked in the minds of Hamiltonians to rough culture. When, in 1920, the medical officer of health declared that "immorality was being practiced in boathouses and that this did much to spread venereal diseases," he made no distinction between the boathouses of the busy North End waterfront – where the prostitution trade was within easy reach of dock workers and sailors – and the boathouse colony far across the bay. Indeed, though the *Herald* pointed out that "there was no supervision of those places ... because undue supervision would be resented by the respectable owners of boathouses," it nonetheless became possible to see all boathouses as "retreats of those immorally inclined."[45]

Nor did it help that the Burlington Heights was a popular stop for the itinerant men known as tramps and hoboes, who rode the rails into town. They troubled reformers and other members of Hamilton's more stable population. The canal bridge, located just before the busy rail yards, was a convenient place for transients to jump off freight trains to avoid being picked up and perhaps beaten by vigilant railway police. Despite these harsh realities, workers who travelled in search of jobs would take their chances. One Hamiltonian, who spent much of his youth in and around the boathouses during the 1920s and 1930s, recalls that transient men would travel between Windsor and Kirkland Lake, shuttling between work in the auto factories and the northern mines. They gathered on the heights near the boathouse colony, used the resources of the bay, and lived off the land. They would camp in circles and "have tin cans that they heated their water in, and they washed in the streams and they stayed there for days and days and days and days, until all of a sudden, they heard something and they'd catch a freight train and move on."[46]

Readers of Hamilton newspapers were kept apprised of the presence of hoboes, which the press presented as dangerous and disruptive to society. Although they did not live in the boathouses, their presence in the area doubtless coloured how Hamiltonians perceived the community itself.[47] The boathouse dwellers and hoboes did share some common traits. Both took advantage of natural resources to hunt and fish, and males shared an interest in rough working-class recreations.[48] A man who knew many boathouse dwellers as a child commented on the prevalence of alcohol: "A lot of heavy drinking went on in the marsh. Because in them days, that's what they did. The men worked hard all day and then they drank. That's the way life was." But, as he quickly pointed out, "that's no different from what we were in the city neither, you know."[49] Drinking took place in homes, outdoors, or in inns and taverns on the top of the heights on York Street. Run by sportsmen of no mean repute, such establishments catered to travellers along the Toronto-to-Hamilton corridor and to the local hunting and fishing fraternity – sportsmen and pothunters alike.[50]

The boathouse community certainly had a rough side. One of its attractions was its distance from the gaze of harbour commission and police authorities, which was often felt by workers on street corners and in busy city taverns.[51] Cockpit Island in the marsh was a well-known landmark, one that was difficult to reach unless one had a boat, like men in the boathouse community.[52] Some marsh boathouses were home to other working-class diversions that offended middle-class reformers because they frequently included gambling and drinking. According to a sympathetic observer, gambling was mostly innocuous penny-ante stuff. It could be found everywhere: "Each and every one [of the boathouses] … probably had a card game going … nickel and dime, like that."[53] This may have raised some eyebrows, but it was an open secret, like the crap games that were mainstays of North End workers' Sunday afternoon entertainment.[54] As he recalled, boathouse dwellers were basically good, hardworking people: "I never heard of anyone doing any robbery, no rapes, no killings, no nothing like that; I never heard of nothing like that out there. Of course [there were] fights – lots of fights. But then nothing happened."[55]

"To the true artist's eye," a *Hamilton Herald* reporter mused poetically in 1924, those ramshackle dilapidated frame huts are a natural part of the varied and lovely scenery around the head of the bay and the foot of the marsh, however unlovely they may seem to eyes that can see no charm in anything save newness, brightness and order. On a city alley they would be an eyesore but not in their natural setting, on the water.[56]

Unfortunately for those who lived in the area, McQuesten, the Parks Board, and other urban reformers valued newness, brightness, and order. The rough elements of working-class leisure, the presence of transients, and what even this supposedly sympathetic reporter termed "the ramshackle dilapidated frame huts" were an affront to the moral and aesthetic vision of men like Tom McQuesten. Life in the borderlands of the city had provided working-class families with some real advantages, offering low-cost housing, ready access to fish and game, and for some, a means of escaping the surveillance of police and moral reformers. Now they were about to learn the disadvantages: they were in a weak position to defend their homes and community against planners and reformers who were eager to create morally and aesthetically pleasing natural spaces.

THE HARBOUR COMMISSION had already declared a "war upon the squatters" in the boathouses in 1926, but McQuesten's plans for the area were much more ambitious and in a way much more threatening.[57] The Parks Board sponsored a grand design competition for its new Burlington Heights property in 1928.[58] Three cash prizes, ranging from $500 to $2,000, were to be awarded, but the fact that the winner would carry out the construction of the design attracted the twelve meticulously crafted entries. Famous Canadian, American, and Swedish architects submitted their work to the competition, including former Hamiltonian John Lyle, a graduate of the famous Paris design school École des Beaux-Arts and a sometime member of the Toronto Civic Improvement Committee.[59] Among the designs were visions of fantastic proportions, with colonnades, obelisks, and a shoreline developed for aesthetic beauty and grace. Not surprisingly, none of them incorporated the boathouse community.

The Parks Board awarded first prize to a Toronto firm, led by the noted Swedish-trained architect and landscaper Carl Borgstrom. It estimated that his overall design would cost a staggering $1.3 million and take twenty years to complete. Always idealistic in planning but opportunistic in practice, Tom McQuesten and Cecil Vanroy Langs hoped to use Parks Board funds to enhance and beautify planning for a desperately needed new bridge that could carry automobiles over the Burlington Heights and across the Desjardins Canal. The City and the Province would pay for some of the work, but the two men successfully sought the approval of Hamilton ratepayers for a $50,000 debenture to support the beautification plan. Whether or not the ratepayers truly did approve of the plan is difficult to know, since the proposal had been cleverly included with a very popular recreational plan, the construction of a municipal indoor swimming pool in the east end of the city that would be used in the British Empire Games of 1930.[60]

In an effort to overcome continuing opposition to the northwestern entrance beautification project, McQuesten invited a Toronto journalist to tour the area and view the plans, hoping to appeal to the urban pride of Hamiltonians. In November 1929, *Toronto Star Weekly* columnist R.C. Reade extolled the vision of Hamilton's city beautifiers. In his article "Hamilton Shows Toronto How," the title of which must have piqued many a Torontonian, Reade outlined the parks plan as it had been presented to him by McQuesten (Figure 29). Clearly, he found it impressive:

> Hamiltonians have been long conspiring secretly to show Toronto how to construct stately portals and thresholds that will compel the speeding tourist to jam on his brakes and pause and look about him in awe and wonder. Toronto thinks it has done that in garish Sunnyside, which is only a bottle-neck entrance to a glorified midway. The soul of the city reveals itself at first glance as the soul of a merry-go-round and a hot dog stand. But far different is the soul of Hamilton, if one can judge from the introductory vistas it is in the process of developing.

Praising Hamilton for its approach to city beautification, Reade's comparison continued: "Toronto may desire to sell the tourist something as soon as he crosses the welcome sign. But you will go a half a mile into Hamilton without the least taint of commercialism, as the plush carpet that leads guests to a wedding at a fashionable church."[61]

The proposed scheme would offer a variety of sedate and morally acceptable recreational spaces, including a picnic park, model yacht pond, botanical and rock gardens, a zoo, and an art museum. Hamilton was to gain cultural mileage on its larger neighbour by eliminating those vestiges of working-class leisure that shaped "garish Sunnyside." "Do not think that Hamilton is going in for pure austere landscape, with no admixture of amusements," Reade was quick to note, however. "Hamilton … will

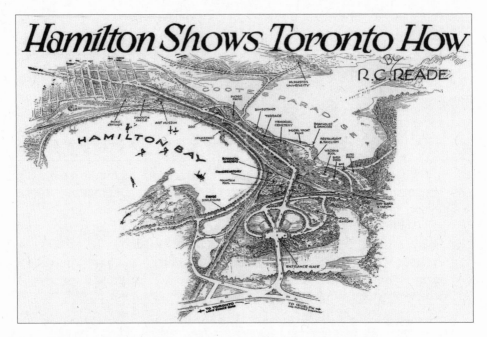

FIGURE 29. Plan for Hamilton's northwestern entrance. It included a variety of
amenities along the Cootes Paradise and bayside shores. Much of the plan – for instance,
the causeway between Princess Point and the Burlington Heights *(top centre)* – never
transpired; however, a version of the roundabout entrance to the city *(bottom right)* was
built, only to give way to the construction of the 403 Highway in 1963. *R.C. Reade,
"Hamilton Shows Toronto How,"* Toronto Star Weekly, *16 November 1929.*

have this advantage over Toronto. It will be able to make whoopee without
making a public exhibition of itself."[62] Its "whoopee" contrivances –
working-class pleasures that were considered unsightly and offensive to
middle-class moral sensibilities – were unsanctioned by the men who ran
the Parks Board. Their design left little room for either the boathouse
community or the culture that sustained it.[63]

The collapse of the international economy in 1929 and the ensuing
Great Depression complicated the working lives of the boathouse residents, but it also provided them with opportunities to resist the City of
Hamilton's plans. The early years of the Depression resulted in some funding
from the federal and provincial governments for public works projects,
but city councillors and the Parks Board had to scale back their construction plans significantly. The grand park scheme, once featured in the *Star
Weekly,* was reduced to a small rock garden constructed by relief workers

in an abandoned gravel pit. It would later form the basis of the Royal Botanical Gardens. And after a stormy debate that pitted city beautifiers against local politicians, council approved the construction of a bridge across the canal that was far more modest than any designed for the 1928 competition. Created by John Lyle, it featured four simple forty-foot limestone pylons, each of which was to house a statue.[64] Significantly, neither the rock garden nor the new bridge required the wholesale removal of the boathouses.

At the same time, the Depression generated greater public sympathy for the families who lived in the boathouses, as increasing numbers of Hamiltonians had trouble making ends meet. Although the local Trades and Labour Council appears to have remained silent on the subject, at least two city officials publicly supported the boathouse community.[65] Admitting that the boathouses were not beautiful, Alderman Sherring, who chaired the Public Works Committee, nonetheless stated, "We must remember that these are exceptionally hard times."[66] Similarly, Controller Nora-Frances Henderson, who a decade later would be publicly castigated by workers for crossing the picket line during the Stelco strike of 1946, declared that "it was going a little too far in beautification when we have to turn people out of their homes in these times. It isn't common sense."[67] Given the strain on the city's relief system as it stood, some sympathizers – who rightly or wrongly assumed that evicted boathouse dwellers meant a greater strain on the public purse – argued that, for the time being, leaving well enough alone was the best policy.[68]

Nevertheless, those who were still eager to wage war on the squatters looked for opportunities to turn public sympathy against them. In January 1931, a fire swept through six bayside boathouses, killing two children in homes that were closest to, and most visible to, the city. The tragedy attracted considerable public attention.[69] Although a coroner's jury deemed that their deaths were accidental, it noted that the boathouse community was not protected by the fire department. It recommended that "adequate fire protection be supplied or that these boathouses on the bay shore be condemned," a set of alternatives that the *Hamilton Spectator* conveniently reversed in its headline.[70] City officials were reluctant to extend fire services to people whose marginal status meant that they did not pay taxes and whose homes did not necessarily conform to building or fire safety standards. The use of kerosene for light and heat, and the presence of gasoline in some of the boathouses, increased the likelihood of fire. For those who were anxious to do so, this particular fire provided a reason to remove the boathouses, now in the name of protecting their occupants.[71]

Some boathouse dwellers – particularly those who had formally leased the land on which their homes sat – accepted their fate stoically. By the end of April 1931, about half of the occupants in the 107 boathouses officially counted by city council had agreed to leave, in return for compensation.[72] After the City paid them small sums in remuneration, they began their lives anew elsewhere. The amounts that they received, typically from $100 to $250, could pay for some form of housing and might even enable them to purchase one of the many homes held by the City for Depression-era back taxes. Using a strategy also employed by members of Vancouver's waterfront community of the day, some literally moved on, floating their makeshift homes to other parts of the bay, such as the relatively undeveloped north shore. A *Spectator* journalist joked about the futility of the situation for local authorities: "That game of squat tag – authorities *v* bayside – may be entering another phase ... 'Squat, you can't catch me!' say harried harbour dwellers from their new Flamborough fastness."[73]

Others resisted eviction by arguing their case in court under the Limitation Act, which stipulated that squatters who lived in a place for some ten years had certain legal rights.[74] Yet going to court provided little respite. It was a costly and time-consuming venture, one that did very little to alter the outcome. Workers and people who lived hand-to-mouth could ill afford court costs and lawyer fees if they were to lose their battle. One man who resisted eviction was fined thirty dollars for noncompliance; in fact, city authorities could strategically rely on the expense of litigation to wear down their opponents. This led many boathouse dwellers to their breaking point.[75]

After five years, the City served final eviction notices to those who remained, and its officials moved in to clean up the area. A *Spectator* reporter observed with some relief that four women from boathouse families had visited the sheriff's office to indicate that they would comply with their eviction order – one of them had already rented a place in town. "The belief was expressed," he wrote, "that a couple of men served with notices of eviction may be less easily handled."[76] As the newspaper implied, the expropriation was not always peaceful. One resident threatened to burn his boathouse rather than let anyone take it. An elderly resident who returned from a trip to town found that the bailiff had thrown out all his possessions and boarded up his home to prevent him from re-entering it. Dumbstruck, he didn't know which way to turn, claiming, "I've been there twenty-six years now ... I'm expecting the pension next December and I don't know where to go."[77] As a reporter commented, many of the tenants had been in their homes for ten to fifteen years and "felt rather bitter about the whole affair."[78]

Although most of the boathouses were destroyed by the late 1930s, some lingered for years – a few apparently as late as 1958.[79] A May 1940 letter to the editor of the *Spectator*, written by "A Boathouse Dweller," commented that the boathouse cleanup was like an annual sport for the Parks Board. It was a battle of wills and wits. The author stated with an air of righteous defiance, "We are not Germans, or Austrians, or Czechs, that we will stand for any of this concentration camp stuff. Through an attorney we have fought the city and the Parks Board for 15 years, and will do so for another 50 years."[80] A few days earlier, a local Girl Guides camp leader complained to the Parks Board about the few boathouses that remained at the marsh. She argued that "organizations ... would not countenance having young people spend their time in undesirable surroundings."[81] Clearly, like so many city planners and moral reformers before her, she assumed that the makeshift exteriors of the boathouses reflected the dubious morality of their owners. Such sentiments had justified and prompted the "war on the squatters," and largely eliminated a small working-class community that had developed on the margins of the industrial city.

On 17 June 1932, more than a thousand Hamiltonians gathered for the official dedication of a new boulevard entrance and high-level bridge along the Burlington Heights. Compared to the work of an earlier generation of transportation planners, in which a canal was carved through the centre of the thirty-metre-high isthmus, the ornamental bridge and landscaped boulevard celebrated by parks planners and civic boosters seemed a much more modest accomplishment. Just down the road lay the rock garden, planted with conifers and various flowers, though there was no sign of the picnic grounds, bandstand, restaurant, wading pool, model yacht pond, zoo, or art museum that Tom McQuesten had described to an impressed *Toronto Star Weekly* reporter. A number of boathouses and improvised shelters still marred the landscape design, the process of removing them, like the plans for a more elaborate park, slowed by the deepening of the international economic crisis. Even the bridge was incomplete: each of its forty-foot-high pylons featured an empty space, where statues might be erected when public monies were not being drained by relief payments.

None of this deterred a *Hamilton Herald* reporter from waxing enthusiastic about the bridge, which framed a "magnificent prospect":

> On the east, the Bay spread to its quiet water, dotted with boats and a
> steamer setting out on its voyage ... Southward, the smoke of industry
> blended with the haze and clouds of the skyline. On the west side Cootes
> Paradise lay still and shining in the setting sun ... Circling the whole scene,
> the rim of the escarpment deepened in the evening light with the varied
> green of the woods around a landscape as lovely as any in Canada.[82]

From his vantage point on the Burlington Heights, the reporter bore
witness to the hopefulness of planning nature in Hamilton. Although
Cootes Paradise and the escarpment had largely remained as marsh and
woods until the 1920s, in part because of the difficulties they posed to
developers, their subsequent development would be limited and defined
through the efforts of the Parks Board and local conservationists. They
would be preserved as "natural." No one would be permitted to live or
work there, and restrictions applied even to the types of play that could
occur there. If McQuesten had his way, the boisterous sounds of donkey
baseball or cockfights would be replaced by fine music, picnic food, and
acceptable hobbies, or the quiet contemplation of birds and flowers, in
cultivated gardens or even in some slightly wilder and freer settings.

Like other planners, McQuesten confidently believed that the real work
of the city – what the *Herald* reporter saw as the "smoke of industry" –
would continue to dominate the south shore of the bay. Planned nature
was a spatial solution to the problems of an industrializing city. Planners
believed that they could use public power to allocate urban space in a
rational manner for the benefit of all citizens; they envisioned that people
would work in one part of town and live and play in another part. Industry
and commerce thus could and should be restricted to the waterfront; elsewhere, beauty would flourish – in handsome homes and cultivated parks.
The boathouse "squatters" had learned, to their misfortune, that they were
living out of place; to planners, their behaviour simply confirmed the
moral dangers of disordered development.

In 1934, Tom McQuesten had an opportunity to more widely extend
his vision of social order and beauty. Appointed to the cabinet of Ontario's
Liberal premier Mitch Hepburn, he masterminded the creation of the
Niagara Parks System. He also sought to ensure that the Province would
construct beautiful parkways rather than utilitarian highways, and his
work can be seen in the earliest versions of the Queen Elizabeth Way,
which ran between Toronto and Niagara Falls.[83] McQuesten retained his
seat on the Hamilton Parks Board but did not play an active role in the
city until after the outbreak of the Second World War. In the early 1940s,

he used his provincial government position to help get the Royal Botanical Gardens incorporated and to transfer another 202 hectares – north of Cootes Paradise – to the new corporation, bringing the total property it controlled at the west end of the city to 688 hectares. He also commissioned Carl Borgstrom, whose entry had won the Parks Board competition in 1928, to draft a plan for the gardens. Borgstrom proposed a botanical garden on a small portion of the land, complemented by a zoo, a natural amphitheatre, and even athletic facilities. For McQuesten, the gardens represented the heart of the operation. There he hoped to train a new generation of landscape architects for the postwar era.[84]

Although much of McQuesten's vision was bound up with the fate of the Royal Botanical Gardens, he again became involved in Hamilton's city planning in 1944.[85] Once again, a world war provoked a reconsideration of the state of the city. Once again, a period of intensive industrial growth appeared to threaten its social and environmental order. In 1917, planners had looked forward to an era in which residential and recreational zones would be protected from industrial growth. When the bridge that would later bear McQuesten's name opened in 1932, there were good reasons to believe that Hamilton was on its way to building itself into a livable industrial city.[86] Only twelve years later, as Tom McQuesten joined others in planning for the new postwar reality, there were good reasons to believe that creating his ideal world would not be possible.

6

Confining Nature

The Bay as Harbour,
1931–59

I N 1960, THE *Hamilton Spectator* devoted a special issue to the relation-ship between the city and its harbour. In it, journalist Trevor Lautens wrote about the bright future that was anticipated for both. He asserted that over the next two decades everyone in town would "share in the benefits of Hamilton bay's natural harbour." He announced with confi-dence that if contemporary plans for the harbour were fulfilled, the waterfront would have "a place for everyone, and everyone in his place."[1] Thomas McQuesten and an earlier generation of planning enthusiasts would certainly have embraced and applauded the concept of a "place for everyone." Yet the "balanced bay" that Lautens wrote about in 1960 dif-fered significantly from that conceived by earlier planners, politicians, and journalists.

A Hamilton native, Lautens chronicled just how much the bay had changed as he grew up and how changes would persist in the years to come. "The bay's bathing beaches are no more and the boat liveries have all but disappeared," he noted, leaving recreation on the bay to "motorboat and sail enthusiasts ... seaplanes, iceboats, scullers and skaters." The bal-anced bay of the future would provide a relatively concentrated water-front space for the private Royal Hamilton Yacht Club, the Leander Rowing Club, and publicly built marinas. A wharf for the local naval reserve, which now separated the main North End park from the water-front, was "likely here to stay," he declared. Otherwise, the entire shoreline from the Desjardins Canal to the Beach Strip was to be a place for industrial and commercial wharves, with easy access to intermodal transportation such as trains and trucks. The bayshore of the Beach Strip would also house wharves, industrial sites, and a future four-lane highway bridge that would conveniently separate these places from the remaining residential homes on the lakefront. Lautens projected that by 1980, when he himself would be middle-aged, the harbour "will have lost much of its familiar shape" owing to the continued infilling of the inlets and the building of industrial sites out into the bay. The north shore would probably be spared this kind of development, so private homes could continue to be built there. As for public space on the north shore, LaSalle Park would remain "a permanent fixture," but Lautens noted that in 1959 the Hamilton Harbour Commission had again cancelled the ferry service that shuttled between the city and the park, little more than a decade after it had begun to offer it again.[2]

Although Lautens's 1960 article looked ahead, its vision of the future tells us a lot about how the bay had been transformed during the young reporter's lifetime and how ideas about balance had changed so much throughout the years. Trevor Lautens was born in Hamilton in 1934, just a few years after it hosted the British Empire Games. In less than three decades, the idea that the bay could or should be anything more than a dirty industrial port had become difficult for anyone to imagine. As a local observer put it, it had become the "largest and most beautiful septic tank in the world."[3] Although Lautens's piece articulated the value of balancing the bay's industrial, residential, and recreational uses, industry dominated the harbour. For many civic leaders, the recreational spaces of the future would be far from the city or in isolated places within it. Between the 1930s and 1960s, the changes in how the bay *was used* had significant environmental consequences, which, in turn, altered the ways in which Hamilton's social and political leaders imagined it *could be used* in the future. By the time that Lautens wrote, they had redefined the meaning of a balanced bay.

MANY ASPECTS OF THE harbour changed because of Hamilton's industrial expansion, its aggressive program of shoreline infilling, and the substantial modifications in the province's transportation industry and networks (Figure 30). Industrial factories had colonized the eastern shoreline since the nineteenth century, but the completion of the "Fourth" Welland Canal in 1932 significantly changed many of their operations. To accommodate the larger ships coming through the newly enlarged canal from Lake Erie and the upper Great Lakes, public and private investment funded the reshaping of the harbour during the late 1920s and early 1930s. Along with the Hamilton Harbour Commission, the Canadian government sponsored

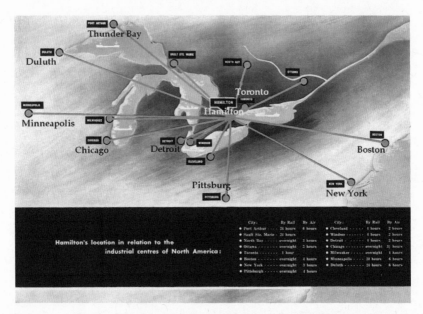

FIGURE 30 Hamilton's Harbour Commission advertised the Port of Hamilton's central location and close proximity to major industrial centres in the Greats Lakes region and the eastern United States. *Courtesy of Hamilton Port Authority Collection.*

doubling the width of the Burlington Canal – to ninety-one metres – and deepening harbour canal and shipping channels. Stelco built a large dock out into the water, equipping it with two bridges so that coal and iron ore from Great Lakes ships could be unloaded easily. The Hamilton By-Products Company and Canadian Industries Limited dredged and deepened an eastern inlet and built wharves along both of its sides. The By-Products Company spent millions to enable its coke ovens to process larger and more reliable deliveries of coal to fuel both its gasification plant and home furnaces throughout Ontario. Across the inlet, Canadian Industries Limited – successor to the Graselli Chemical Company and the Canadian face of the American and British chemical giants DuPont and Imperial Chemical Industries – shipped chemicals such as sulphur into its plant.[4]

The improved Welland Canal opened Hamilton to the Great Lakes system in ways that had only been dreamed of in the past. By 1934, even with Depression-era levels of production, its port outputs had doubled those of the prosperous late 1920s (Figure 31). Ships carrying twice as much

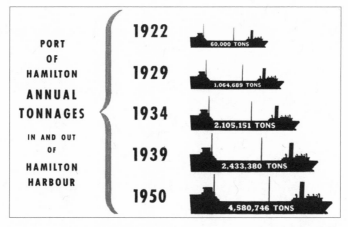

FIGURE 31   This image illustrates one of the many novel ways that the
Harbour Commission marked activities in the Port of Hamilton. The
graph shows increases in annual tonnage shipped in and out of Hamilton
Harbour from 1922 to 1950. *Hamilton Harbour Commissioners,* Annual
Report *(Hamilton: Hamilton Harbour Commission, 1951). Courtesy of
Hamilton Port Authority.*

freight replaced trains as a means for transporting coal and iron from ports
on Lake Erie and Lake Huron; one ship could hold as much iron ore as
five long freight trains. Although it may not have immediately changed
the overall level of economic activity in Depression-era Hamilton, the
new canal system reoriented the operations of the steel and other companies outward to the waterfront and carried the future promise of expanding
industrial capacity even more.[5]

That expansion took place during the Second World War and the early
decades of the Cold War. Yet not every industry in Hamilton thrived. Its
textile mills, which prospered and even expanded their operations during
and immediately after the war, struggled to meet intense international
competition in the 1950s. By the end of the decade, all but one had closed.
As the range of fuel sources used for heating homes expanded, demand
for coal gasification plants lessened, and by 1958 the By-Products Company had closed its coke ovens. Nevertheless, Hamilton continued to be
home to a wide range of manufacturers that employed thousands of
workers. International Harvester, Firestone Rubber and Tire, Canadian
Industries Limited, National Steel Car, and Procter and Gamble all
continued to operate plants along its waterfront. They imported coal

FIGURE 32   A work in progress – Stelco's shoreline, 1959. At this time, Stelco had both "hardened" shorelines of newly built ore docks *(the straight diagonal line on the right)* and "soft" shorelines of newly reclaimed land from the peninsula *(bottom centre)*. *Photo by Phil Aggus. Courtesy of Hamilton Port Authority Collection, 3601–7.*

and oil as a source of fuel, and they shipped in raw materials such as phosphates, sulphur, and other chemicals for their production processes. These manufacturers also used the harbour as a source of water and a sink for some of their wastes.[6]

Despite its industrial diversity, Hamilton became known as "Steeltown," with the iron and steel industry along Burlington Street in the northeastern waterfront leading the way in industrial and port development. In the 1940s and early 1950s, Stelco expanded its industrial complex (Figure 32). It acquired 38.8 hectares of waterlots from the harbour commission to create new land through infill and to construct a 305-metre-long shipping dock. Stelco's operations grew substantially to include 150 new coke ovens, two blast furnaces, and four 250-ton open hearth furnaces. By the mid-1950s, it had also secured a wire and nail mill.[7] During this time, Dominion Foundries (Dofasco) became an integrated steel company. It moved away from using scrap and pig iron supplied by other companies to make steel. As demand for Hamilton-made steel continued to grow, Dofasco acquired waterfront properties and 27.5 hectares of waterlots from the harbour commission, which it filled in to create sites for blast furnaces and shipping docks. Its first furnace opened in 1951, and two more were built during the mid-1950s. By 1957, 105 coke ovens were supporting Dofasco's operations. In 1960, its president, Frank Sherman, spoke about how important the port's development had become for his company. He observed that whereas Dofasco had not depended on water transportation at all in 1946, its docks now expected to receive over 2 million tons of coal and iron ore.[8]

The two steel companies boosted the fortunes of local foundries and other manufacturers by providing ready access to a variety of steel products. They also supported a number of ancillary companies that consumed sulphuric and other acids, and provided customers for Canadian Industries Limited. As steel production grew, both companies purchased more scrap metal, stimulating the rise of local recycling companies that opened yards along the harbour's southeastern shore. Other companies reused steel-making waste materials. After 1959, the Dominion Tar and Chemical Company moved its distillation of coal tars from its Toronto plant to the Hamilton waterfront. In the same year, American Cyanamid opened a branch plant to take Dofasco's waste gases and turn them into urea for fertilizer and other consumer products.[9]

Slag, the by-product of ore smelted for steelmaking, became a hot commodity.[10] In the early 1950s, Stelco and Dofasco worked with Buffalo Slag to create a new Canadian company, National Slag. It transformed the by-product into material to be used for construction and road building. Soon the company began using slag to reclaim areas of the harbour as Stelco pioneered a method of waterfront expansion that did away with using piling walls for the infill process. Instead, the company simply dredged the bottom silt and plowed slag forward into the water to create a base for new land along the shore. On this newly created land, Stelco built new furnaces and coke ovens. It also constructed new storage areas for the iron ore and coal supplies that it needed to remain in operation when the winter season interrupted Great Lakes shipping.[11]

The waterfront industries thus reshaped and hardened more and more of the bay's southeastern shoreline, building outward into the water and transforming marshy inlets into the straight channels of standardized depths that Great Lakes ships required (Figure 33). They found much support from the Hamilton Harbour Commission, which became more narrowly focused on the business of its port. From the 1920s until the

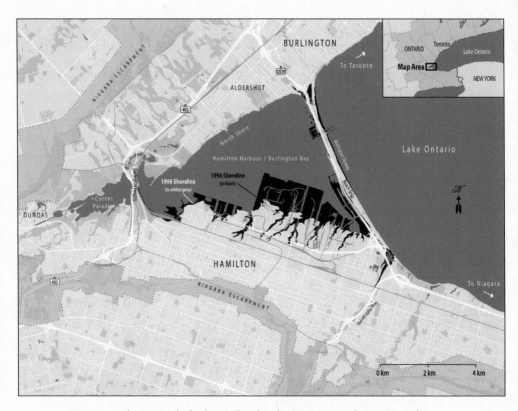

FIGURE 33   Changes to the harbour's shoreline between 1909 and 1996. Note the
creation of the industrial factory district along Hamilton's eastern waterfront, the
creation of the Windermere Basin adjacent to the Filtering Basins *(at the bottom right
corner of the bay)*, and new land at the Burlington Canal on the bay side, where the
Canada Centre for Inland Waters is now located.

opening of the Fourth Welland Canal, Hamilton City Council had given
the commission an annual $10,000 subsidy to help offset some costs of
port expansion and to avoid cargo and harbour fees being charged for
its use. This amount increased to $12,000 in 1932. But the commission,
which could earn much more money from charging harbour usage fees,
worried that the subsidy might give the City a claim to its surplus, and it
allowed the arrangement to lapse after five years. In 1938, the commission
began to rely on revenues collected from harbour usage to support its
various operations. Since its creation in 1912, it had always paid attention
to industrial and residential harbour pollution, co-operating with the City

on a number of parks projects. Although it continued to take some interest in such matters, after 1938 it had a strong financial incentive to focus more narrowly on developing the port's facilities.[12]

The expansion of shipping that accompanied the construction and opening of the St. Lawrence Seaway in the 1950s reinforced the harbour commission's move toward even more intense port development. The amount of material shipped in the harbour had grown through the 1930s to reach over 3.0 million tons during the Second World War and in 1950 to exceed 4.5 million tons. By 1955, it reached 7.5 million tons. Such rapid growth created high expectations for the opening of the St. Lawrence Seaway, which brought ocean-going vessels to Hamilton. The steel companies had a particular interest in the new Seaway route, since it brought in new supplies of iron ore from eastern Canada.[13]

Anticipating the creation of the Seaway, the waterfront industries invested heavily in wharves and handling facilities, relying on public monies to pay for harbour renovations. To help this industrial expansion, the harbour commission sold even more waterlots for infilling between 1957 and 1959, with 116 hectares going to Stelco, 58 to Dofasco, and 12 to National Steel Car (Figure 34). The federal government continued to bear most of the public expense for the port development, but the harbour commissioners now had greater resources to contribute and greater potential to share in the benefits from increased freight. Together, they invested at least $20 million to dredge channels and shoreline approaches throughout the harbour to Seaway depth. They moved the dredged material to build even more land along the shoreline and constructed wharves and warehouses there. They thus transformed the inlet-riddled less-developed southeastern shore of the harbour. They dredged a new channel and turning basin, and created a new dock at Strathearne Avenue. The governments of Ontario and Hamilton also did their part to support development, spending $16 million on a massive Beach Strip bridge that spanned the Burlington Canal. The 2,346-metre-long and 64-metre-high Burlington Bay Skyway (later Burlington Bay James N. Allan Skyway), a bridge that is part of the Queen Elizabeth Way, linked Toronto with the American border at Buffalo and Fort Erie. Towering high above the Beach Strip and the canal, it ensured that port traffic no longer interfered with the province's busiest highway.[14]

THE SAME INDUSTRIAL prosperity that enhanced Hamilton's status as a Great Lakes port after 1931 also generated growth in its urban and suburban

FIGURE 34 This photo of infilling in the Pier 14 area, between the northern ends of Wentworth and Hillyard Streets, in 1957, shows a factory, rows of parked cars (perhaps from the nearby Studebaker Plant), and residential homes. *Courtesy of Hamilton Port Authority Collection.*

residential areas. Over the next three decades, its population grew by 75 percent, from under 160,000 to almost 275,000, partly due to land annexations along its eastern and southern boundaries. The population outside the city also tripled during this time. Of the 120,000 new people who lived outside town, at least half resided in the bay's watershed. The characteristics of that growing population had also changed. Labour unions helped to ensure that more people shared in the benefits of postwar prosperity. Hamiltonians were now much more likely to own their homes, to possess an automobile, to enjoy shorter working hours, and to have paid holidays. Although local families participated in the new consumer society, much of their city's affluence rested on the heavy industries that supported it.[15]

The industrial and residential growth also transformed the aquatic environment of the bay. Industrial wastes continued to reach it, as did ever larger quantities of residential sewage, which completely overwhelmed the primitive sewage-screening facility. In 1931, a report on this situation pointed to acid and oil wastes, sometimes diluted with water, that entered the harbour from Stelco, the Hamilton By-Products' coke ovens, and two smaller metal-fabricating companies. It also recorded significant amounts of dyes, fats, and grease, presumably from textile mills and meat-packing companies, flowing through the sewers. Twelve years later, another investigation estimated that an average of 113 million litres of residential sewage and 318 million litres of industrial waste entered the bay every day, including phenols, acid, coal dust, and "appreciable" quantities of oil and gasoline.[16] By 1954, waste water flow estimates had reached 204 million litres per day, in dry weather. The city had combined storm and sewage facilities, and its sewage-filtering system could handle only 136 million litres a day. Imagine what would have happened during a rainstorm. Much of the waste water that entered the bay still remained a problem and sometimes contained even the larger solids when water bypassed sewage treatment altogether.[17]

The steel companies aimed to reduce waste while enhancing efficiency and minimizing their visible impact on the harbour, but increased production worked against their initiatives.[18] Table 3 provides an estimate of the changing load of waste that would have made its way into the harbour from Stelco alone, the city's largest steel company, either directly or after it had been diluted in site lagoons, between 1912 and 1957. It suggests that the expansion of Hamilton's industrial giant, especially during and after the Second World War, dramatically increased the tonnage of phenols, cyanide, ammonia, oils, and sulphuric acid emitted from the plant.[19] Of course, many other manufacturers also used the harbour as a sink. Dofasco also stood on the waterfront, and its production capacity had increased to 1 million tons by the end of the 1950s. By 1958, aside from the By-Products Company's coke ovens, plants producing acids, detergent soap, rubber tires, and other materials each had their own particular waste streams. They used both public and private sewers that flowed into the bay.

Not all of this waste entered the harbour unnoticed, as the record of repeated investigations suggests. Most complaints about water quality focused on the most visible pollution, such as the oil and fecal waste – the "turds" that floated by – and the large "fields" of heavy sewage, "thick and murky," that also sat on the water.[20] As automobiles and industries used

TABLE 3   Stelco waste in Hamilton Harbour, estimated tons per year, 1912–57

	Phenols	Cyanide	Ammonia	Oils	Sulphuric acid
1912	3	1	4	139	136
1917	12	5	14	518	509
1922	7	3	8	303	298
1927	13	5	15	568	559
1932	5	2	6	220	287
1937	16	7	21	715	931
1942	34	15	42	1,455	1,894
1947	35	15	43	1,483	1,930
1952	44	21	54	1,626	2,333
1957	70	34	85	2,581	3,703

SOURCES: Based on multipliers in US Federal Water Pollution Control Administration, *The Cost of Clean Water,* vol. 3, *Industrial Waste Profiles,* "Blast Furnaces and Steel Mills" (Washington: Federal Water Pollution Control Administration Publication, 1967), 9, 56. Steel production statistics from William Kilbourn, *The Elements Combined: A History of the Steel Company of Canada* (Toronto: Clarke Irwin, 1960); we adjusted for improvements in technology at the plant by using a different multiplier: 1912–27 inclusive, "old": 1932–47, "mixed"; 1952–57, "new," after Craig E. Colten, "Industrial Wastes in Southeast Chicago: Production and Disposal," *Environmental History Review* 10, 2 (1986): 97, 104n15.

increasing amounts of petroleum products, oil slicks coating the water also attracted a lot of attention. Many slicks resulted from relatively isolated dumping incidents, usually emanating from the combined sewer system. Investigators condemned the practice of dumping oil into the sewers and sought out particular culprits as each incident cropped up. Occasionally, they also commented on the general level of industrial pollutants in the harbour. Most investigations arrived at the same conclusion that Fishery Inspector John Kerr had reached way back in the late 1880s: until the City addressed the dumping of untreated residential sewage into the harbour, no concerted action could be taken against industrial polluters.[21]

To many people, pollution was still most easily understood when measured in terms of bacteria. Investigations in the late 1940s found that coliform bacteria counts in 1923 had averaged at three hundred per hundred millilitres along the eastern Beach Strip and at seventy-five per hundred millilitres in the west harbour; by 1947, the counts in the two areas had reached an average of two thousand and over nine thousand per hundred millilitres respectively. Bacterial contamination had clearly worsened.[22] But what civic leaders really wanted to know was whether Hamilton's "sink" was affecting its "taps." Was the drinking water still safe and healthy? The findings for 1947 did not cause much concern when the medical officer of health (MOH) assured local leaders that higher bacteria counts in the harbour hardly affected the water intake pipes in Lake Ontario.[23] Stelco shook this complacency a little in the early 1950s, when it hired a consulting engineer who warned that the city needed to replace its "obsolete and inadequate" sewage treatment plant. He recommended that the current site be abandoned and a new facility be built farther east. His suggestion convenienced the company, which coveted seven hectares of vacant waterfront that the City owned and had reserved for future sewage disposal plant expansion. That land, and the existing plant, stood in the way of Stelco's eastward expansion. The MOH responded to the report by, yet again, assuring city councillors that "it would be a long time before bay waters threatened the Lake Ontario intake of the city's water supply."[24]

Stelco did get the vacant land, but civic leaders immediately sought to dampen expectations that they would build a new sewage-screening plant. Without pressure from provincial and federal government officials, they would probably have continued to rely on the overburdened sewage plant for some time. Those governments, however, began to take a greater interest in water and waste water systems in response to the concerns raised by some American Great Lakes towns about sewage. Hamilton politicians baulked when they saw the estimated cost of even a basic primary treatment facility – at the very least $7.5 million – especially when other levels of government gave them no firm financial commitment. Thus, the same governments that together had spent nearly $60 million on port development during the 1950s appeared unable to find money for sewage treatment. City council postponed decision making by sponsoring yet another study of the sewage problem.[25]

For this new study, council turned to D.H. Matheson, the director of its municipal laboratories, perhaps worried that outside consultants such as those used by Stelco might be less sensitive to its budgetary priorities. Matheson's 1958 analysis of the harbour's waters used highly sophisticated testing procedures. His *Consolidated Report on Burlington Bay* went well beyond simply documenting levels of bacterial contamination: it recorded levels of phenols, nitrogen, phosphorous, synthetic detergents, radioactive fallout, and other substances. He also measured dissolved oxygen levels, paying more attention to industrial wastes than had earlier studies, and using an analysis of nutrients and dissolved oxygen that highlighted the impact of residential waste water on aquatic ecosystems.[26]

Still, Matheson knew that city councillors really wanted to hear about the quality of the drinking water. The scientist set out to measure and analyze levels of phenolic pollution. He measured phenol levels in the bay near the canal and in Lake Ontario near the water intake pipes. In part, he did this because phenols were known to interfere with water treatment processes. But he also did it because they served as an important marker regarding pollution – few people doubted their connection to coke ovens, such as those on the banks of the eastern industrial waterfront. The presence of phenols at both testing sites helped establish the movement of water from the bay into the lake and toward the source of the water supply. Anxious to prove that the harbour's bacterial contamination caused "the slow, irregular but very significant increase in coliform content of the raw water at the Filtration plant," Matheson noted that the amount of chlorine needed to properly treat the water should be doubled.

Although Matheson's report acknowledged that "the bay acts as a very efficient sewage disposal device," it suggested that this device was in danger of being overwhelmed. It noted that bacterial contamination in the harbour had increased steadily since the 1923 publication of Gore, Nasmith and Storrie's *Report on Sewage Disposal*. The installation of new intercepting storm sewers in the west harbour during the late 1940s had helped to improve readings in that area. Still, in 1958 the average count of 4,500 coliform organisms per 100 millilitres of bay water was quite high. The southeastern shoreline, around the sewage treatment plant, predictably showed the highest levels of contamination. The second-most polluted area lay along the eastern shoreline, by the Beach Strip. There, water sample readings rose dramatically between 1948 and 1958, from 2,300 coliform organisms to 11,500 per 100 millilitres of water. Given the prevailing winds and currents, the fact that pollution concentrated in this area was not particularly surprising. From there, however, it could pass through the Burlington Canal and into Lake Ontario – the source of Hamilton's drinking water.[27]

Matheson also pointed to the rising coliform counts near LaSalle Park to illustrate the widespread nature of pollution in the bay. For years, people held that the LaSalle Park area was safe from the effects of sewage, believing that the currents flowing through the centre of the harbour protected it from contamination. In 1923, the average coliform counts at LaSalle Park had been relatively low, only 1,200 and 1,800 per 100 millilitres of water. Yet by 1947, these numbers had risen to 6,600 per 100 millilitres. Matheson avoided being alarmist about the state of the water supply, but he aimed to show that the bay was becoming ever more contaminated; this contamination threatened to reach the water intake pipes. This trend, he argued, must not be allowed to continue.[28]

As it turned out, by the time Matheson completed his report, city council had already moved ahead on plans to construct a new $10 million primary sewage treatment plant. It had been given little choice in the matter: it needed permission from the provincial government to annex over 267 hectares to promote further industrial development, and inaction threatened its plan. One provincial agency, the Ontario Municipal Board, had strongly advised the provincial government to block the annexation without a firm commitment that Hamilton would improve its sewer system. Perhaps even more concerning, a second provincial agency, the Ontario Water Resources Commission, made it clear that, even if the City could get provincial approval, any extension of the sewer system to these newly annexed areas, or any other suburban area, would be delayed or even denied without a new treatment plant.

When in 1959 city council approved the call for tenders to build the new facility, a local politician and future mayor clearly outlined what was at stake: "The plant is the key to industrial development in the area annexed from Saltfleet. The sewers in this area all hinge on this plant being ready."[29] Of course, when the city engineer recommended that the plant adopt a relatively new and expensive system for dealing with sewer sludge, he found little support. A *Spectator* editorial reminded everyone that "the purpose of this huge project is not to purify bay water to the extent that it will be suitable for drinking or pleasant for swimming and boating (as it was in the 'good old days'), but to protect the Lake Ontario water supply intakes from contamination from the bay."[30] The new primary treatment plant, with a much less expensive system than the engineer had recommended, finally opened in October 1964. Five years later, an Ontario Water Resources Commission study concluded that the bay was little more than an "11 square mile sewer."[31] Hamilton's civic leaders had been forced to take action on a sewage treatment system, and responded by doing as little as possible.

How did the situation get so bad? Years earlier, back in 1927, a *Spectator* reporter anticipated sewage disposal improvements with considerable enthusiasm, proclaiming that "pollution will soon be a thing of the past." To him, the resulting cleaner water meant that people could swim at new bathing beaches in the North End and on the Beach Strip, row on a new course proposed for Cootes Paradise, and yacht on the bay. But in 1960, the paper's editor presented a less sanguine account of what a new disposal plant meant to Hamiltonians: its purpose was *not* to return the bay to the purity of the "good old days." Clearly, in the intervening decades, expectations for the bay's role in city life had changed substantially. In the 1940s and 1950s, popular perceptions of the bay as increasingly less attractive for outdoor pursuits both affected – and were affected by – public and private decisions. It became much less likely that many Hamilton residents would make the bay a part of their lives, while at the same time various organizations offered alternatives to outdoor recreation on the bay.[32]

SOME OF THESE CHANGES had already become apparent when civic leaders, for the second time in just over twenty-five years, embraced large-scale urban planning, this time near the end of the Second World War. Hamilton's Town Planning Committee wanted a Master Plan to inform postwar development, as had recently been done in nearby metropolitan Toronto. Prodded by planning enthusiasts such as Thomas B. McQuesten, and by the promise of funding under a new National Housing Act, city council appointed a new Toronto firm, Town Planning Consultants, to do the work. It was led by the man who had created Toronto's Master Plan, Eugenio G. Faludi. Trained at the University of Rome, Faludi fled Mussolini's increasingly intolerant regime for England, but he ended up in Canada, lecturing on town planning at McGill and the University of Toronto.[33] With his consulting firm, he turned his considerable expertise and experience to the Hamilton project.

To create his Master Plan, Faludi systematically studied Hamilton's neighbourhoods, assessing their condition to help him determine their future use. For this, he worked with the Town Planning Board and influential locals, interviewing representatives from businesses, professional and social welfare organizations, and labour unions to get a sense of their perspectives on the places under study.[34] He collected data on the neighbourhoods and recorded their population density; he also applied ten criteria to assess and determine the overall condition of physical structures. Faludi examined each building and the land that it occupied, noting its uses and flagging derelict properties. His assessment factored in things such as the quality of sanitation service in an area, and it documented whether or not residents benefitted from nearby recreational facilities. He also noted the amount of heavy traffic that flowed through a neighbourhood. On the basis of his data, Faludi concluded that roughly a quarter of the neighbourhoods were *sound*, almost half were *declining*, and another quarter were *blighted*.[35]

Faludi classified all neighbourhoods that lay closest to the harbour and all those on the newly filled inlets as blighted. Indeed, Faludi did not even study two of them – Brightside and Gage – because he did not perceive them as "recognizable neighbourhood communities." This assertion would have surprised Brightside's eastern European and Italian factory workers, who bought and cared for their homes, tended fruit and vegetable gardens, and patronized a local grocery store and tavern. They cared enough about Brightside to ask the City to deal with a heavily polluted inlet that bordered it, and they proposed what had become the standard solution – filling it in. Stelco complied, and in the process of solving the nuisance problem it created more land for expanding its manufacturing facilities. Back in 1911, when Brightside was built, its advertisements highlighted what its developers saw as a key selling feature – the ease with which the working men who lived there could get to their factory jobs. Yet by 1944, with Stelco's massive growth and encroachment into the area, Brightside's proximity to the factories prevented Faludi from even considering it a true neighbourhood.[36]

Not that the "real" neighbourhoods fared any better in Faludi's final report. In it, he recommended that regardless of how it was being used at the time, all the land between the harbour and the railway tracks, from the eastern edge of the old North End port, should be set aside for industry. In all, 131 hectares of residential districts would be zoned industrial. Another 404 hectares of nearby vacant land would also be set aside for industry, including the remaining inlets and waterlots along the shoreline. Faludi felt that only the old North End should be recognized as a residential area, and it should be redeveloped by razing old homes and constructing new ones. Although his work for the City considered places for people to play, Faludi tended to think of these in terms of small parks and playgrounds for every neighbourhood. He supported maintaining McQuesten's idea of a greenbelt as a large natural space for the city along Cootes Paradise, the escarpment face, and the Red Hill Valley Creek in the east end. He also believed that a waterfront park was needed but not on the bay. Instead, he recommended that a bathing beach facility, a swimming pool, and a restaurant be built on the shores of Lake Ontario.[37]

Like Noulan Cauchon's report of 1917, Faludi's Master Plan of 1947 did not challenge existing development. It reserved the northeastern area for industrial purposes and legitimated even more shoreline infilling. Also, like that of Cauchon, his plan sought to bring order to a disorderly town by carefully designating spaces for industry, homes, and recreation. Unlike its predecessor, however, Faludi's plan did not see the need to beautify the city with grand boulevards or extensive public gardens. Its most whimsical aspect was quite prosaic: it recommended setting aside landing fields

TABLE 4 Occupational profile, selected areas, 1945

	Total city (%)	Oliver	Sherman (Coal Oil) Inlet	Brightside	Gage
Proprietors, white collar	41	*17%*	*15%*	*10%*	*13%*
Skilled and semi-skilled workers	43	**65%**	**66%**	**77%**	*22%*
Labourers	16	18%	19%	13%	**65%**
N		147	275	211	24

NOTE: **Bold** indicates measure of overrepresentation, more than 5 percent above overall city total. *Italics* indicate measure of underrepresentation, more than 5 percent below overall city total. *N* differs between Tables 4 and 5 because ethnicity could be identified more often than occupations.

SOURCES: *Vernon's City of Hamilton Annual Street, Alphabetical, General, Miscellaneous and Classified Business Directory 1945* (Hamilton: H. Vernon, 1945); for total city, Canada, *Census of Canada, 1941* (Ottawa: Dominion Bureau of Statistics, 1941).

throughout town to accommodate what Faludi believed would be the preferred urban vehicle of the future – helicopters. Faludi's orderly city did not require large public projects, and that meant no large public investment. The exhibition of his Master Plan at Robinson's, a major downtown department store on James Street North, assured citizens that only 5 percent of it would require municipal financing.[38] New residential developments and redevelopment identified in the Master Plan would be funded by the private sector, with some assistance from the federal and provincial governments. Most of it, Faludi asserted, about 65 percent, did not involve money at all since legislation and land use regulation would keep the costs down. A reporter praised the Master Plan for its practicality: "Far from being a mere blueprint of utopia, it deals realistically with those problems which hinder the development of Hamilton and offers practical solutions."[39] For many local politicians, such practical solutions could be found in its assessment of neighbourhoods, which guided and legitimated what would be the city's first comprehensive zoning bylaws.[40]

Although public presentations of the Master Plan generally focused on the way that zoning would protect the residential character of neighbourhoods, zoning also helped to facilitate further industrial development elsewhere, and by so doing, it shaped the relationship of the city to its waterfront. Drawing on the recommendations of Faludi's report, the new

TABLE 5 Ethnic profile, selected areas, 1945

	Total city (%)	Oliver	Sherman (Coal Oil) Inlet	Brightside	Gage
British or western European	87	*74%*	*61%*	*27%*	*48%*
Italian	4	8%	23%	28%	4%
Eastern European	8	**15%**	14%	**40%**	**44%**
Other	1	3%	2%	5%	4%
N		169	323	254	27

NOTE: **Bold** indicates measure of overrepresentation, more than 5 percent above overall city total. *Italics* indicate measure of underrepresentation, more than 5 percent below overall city total. *N* differs between Tables 4 and 5 because ethnicity could be identified more often than occupations.

SOURCES: *Vernon's City of Hamilton Annual Street, Alphabetical, General, Miscellaneous and Classified Business Directory 1945* (Hamilton: H. Vernon, 1945); for total city, Canada, *Census of Canada, 1941* (Ottawa: Dominion Bureau of Statistics, 1941).

zoning regulations designated the entire area north of the railway tracks and east of Wellington Street as *light* and *heavy industrial*. The change had profound implications for this sector since it would prevent developers from building homes in neighbourhoods that were, or were becoming, environmentally degraded. But it did little to assist the people who *already* lived there. Tables 4 and 5 offer a glimpse of who these people were. Table 4 shows that the zoning designation affected working-class neighbourhoods. In each, the proportion of male household heads who held skilled, semi-skilled, and unskilled labouring jobs exceeded 80 percent of the area's workforce. Table 5 shows that whereas almost nine of every ten Hamiltonians came from a British or western European background, the inhabitants of Oliver, Sherman, Brightside, and Gage were less likely to share this heritage. Proportionately more southern and eastern Europeans settled in these neighbourhoods than in the city as a whole.

The working-class families who lived in Oliver, Sherman, Brightside, and Gage found that the zoning designations reduced the value of their homes and made it less likely that banks would give them loans for home improvements or maintenance. Because, according to the new designations, they did not live in a residential area, they had difficulties in getting even limited recreational facilities or other community improvements from the municipal government. It was inconsequential whether or not their neighbourhoods had been classified as blighted before the advent of the zoning; they were bound to become so once they were labelled as industrial. Hoping to cut their property losses while they could still afford to move elsewhere, some anxious homeowners would choose to sell to companies seeking to buy their land. Between 1945 and 1961, the number of homes in Brightside declined drastically. Zoning legitimated industrial encroachments on working-class neighbourhoods in northeast Hamilton.[41]

THE INDUSTRIAL ACTIVITY all around the harbour also encroached on the places where people had once played. The residents of the east end neighbourhoods, for example, found that leisure areas on the shoreline were becoming increasingly scarce. By the late 1920s, the Parks Board had sold the last waterfront park in the area, making it difficult, but not impossible, for people to enjoy recreation along the water. Informal access to the shoreline and inlets continued, but only while vacant or lightly used land existed. This opportunity ended as heavy industry expanded farther eastward along the shore, filling in the inlets or transforming them into slips for shipping. Of course, city councillors and local manufacturers had envisioned the southeastern shoreline as an industrial area since at least the 1890s. But not so the Beach Strip. After the First World War, planners continued to imagine that it would be a significant recreational locale for Hamiltonians. For example, when the Works Department widened the Burlington Canal it used the dredged material to create a new public beach on the bayside. This was done even though health concerns about swimming in the bay had existed since the 1920s, but people still preferred the bay's warm waters to the much colder lake. In the late 1950s, Ontario Hydro proposed to build a thermonuclear plant on the very same spot.[42] The changing perception of this bathing beach was part of a larger story in which the Beach Strip as a whole ceased to serve as a popular vacation spot.

Several natural and cultural changes also conspired to transform the Beach Strip. The city and its factories continued to pollute the bay, and prevailing winds blew industrial smoke and grime from the factories along the southeastern shoreline to the nearby beach community.[43] At the same time, automobile ownership, vacation time, and rising incomes allowed more Hamiltonians to go farther afield to escape the heat and soot of their city. They could go elsewhere to find bathing beaches with cleaner water than the bay and water warmer than Lake Ontario. As owners gave up their cottages on the Beach Strip, people of modest means saw an opportunity to rent or buy these relatively inexpensive places for homes, especially during the housing shortages that followed the two world wars.[44] As early as

1920, observers noted that an increasing number of cottages were being converted to year-round use. "Tax-harried citizens" were attracted to the fixed rate and low assessments that Beach Strip summer residents had secured many years earlier.[45] Although civic officials tried to regulate construction there, the Beach Strip's heritage as a place for summer cottages also meant that its building standards were less stringent than in town.[46] The permanent beach community, which probably never exceeded two hundred people during the nineteenth century, reached over a thousand immediately after the First World War. It doubled after the Second World War and had reached more than three thousand by the early 1950s.[47] The expansion of its local school reflected this growth. Whereas 45 children attended a one-room schoolhouse during the First World War, by the early 1950s a new school was accommodating 450 students.[48]

The rise of motor vehicles for commercial and personal use and the development of the province's road system also stimulated the growth of the permanent population on the beach. Automobiles altered the way in which people perceived the Beach Strip, and they helped stimulate new kinds of activity in the community (Figure 35). Although the electric street railway stopped running from Hamilton in the early 1930s, the completion of a bascule bridge across the Burlington Canal and the paving of the Beach Road during the early 1920s meant that increasing numbers of cars and trucks travelled through the strip en route between Toronto and Niagara.[49] By the early 1950s, some two thousand cars and transport trucks were driving along the narrow Beach Road every hour during the summer months. This caused tremendous traffic bottlenecks and delays, especially as the steadily increasing number of ships entering Hamilton Harbour required that the bridge over the canal be raised many times each day. Increased traffic made the Beach Strip less attractive as a residential area for some people, whereas others saw new opportunities created by the situation. The sandbar developed many amenities, including six grocery stores, four gas stations, and twelve licensed restaurants. Their clientele included local residents, vacationers, and people journeying between Toronto and Niagara.

The ever-growing community strained the limited resources of the special commission that was responsible for governing it. The Burlington Beach Commission was created in 1907 at the behest of cottage owners to oversee and administer its public health, park development, policing, public utilities, and other regular municipal matters.[50] Struggling to look after Beach Strip residents, it was unlikely to devote resources to developing beaches and parks for the people of Hamilton. In addition to the

FIGURE 35   A lane of cars, bumper to bumper, passing the Beach Strip Amusement
Park along Beach Road in the 1950s. *Photo by Lloyd Bloom, Gage Park Studios. Courtesy
of Local History and Archives Department, Hamilton Public Library.*

demands for modern city services that arose during the late 1940s and
early 1950s, it coped with the damage caused by a series of floods and
hurricanes that had battered the area. In 1957, after reconsidering the way
that the beach community was governed, Hamilton City Council finally
annexed the Beach Strip area southeast of the Burlington Canal. This was
hardly the same space that the city's politicians had been so anxious to
control in the nineteenth and early twentieth centuries, however; this
time around, recreation had little to do with the final annexation decision. Instead, with an eye on the opening of the St. Lawrence Seaway,
both the City of Hamilton and the harbour commission saw the annexation as a strategic way to assure their control over a bayshore that was
desired for port development in a new era of vastly improved shipping
communications.[51]

The opening of the Burlington Bay Skyway in 1958 further transformed
the Beach Strip community (Figure 36). This mammoth public works
project lay along its bayside, where a park had once been located. Its construction required the expropriation and razing of ninety-three residential

properties. Some bayside residents retained their homes but lost a portion of their lots, for which they were compensated financially. Worse still, they lived in the shadow of a bridge that now cut them off from the bay shoreline. Some demanded more money from the government for this lost access since they could no longer fish, trap, or hunt at the bay. And, despite their sacrifices, Beach Strip residents discovered that the new bridge did not reduce traffic at all. Rather than pay tolls to use the skyway, many drivers chose to travel down the Beach Road, taking advantage of a newly constructed lift bridge that was intended for local traffic. Beach community members had to mobilize and fight to get Beach Road truck traffic banned, and until they succeeded in 1964, heavy truck traffic further reduced the attractiveness of the Beach Strip as a place to visit.[52]

Although most of its cottages had been converted into homes, the Beach Strip retained some elements of its past. On very hot days, when people were willing to brave the cold waters of Lake Ontario, the lakeshore's sand beach still attracted crowds. The popular commercial amusement park that dated from early in the century remained open, and it even added more attractions in the 1950s.[53] Nevertheless, as a resort area the Beach Strip had

FIGURE 36 Construction of the Burlington Bay Skyway, 1958. The skyway spanned the bay side of the Beach Strip and was opened to traffic later that year. A second skyway was built for southbound traffic in 1985. *Photo by Broe's Studio. Courtesy of Library and Archives Canada, PA 138903.*

clearly declined. Elite and middle-class vacationers abandoned it as a place to stay, leaving behind a community somewhat on the margins, a locale full of industrial workers, truckers, and labourers. As one resident recalled, she and her husband moved to the Beach Strip in the late 1950s only as a last resort, when financial difficulties made it impossible for them to live anywhere else in the city.[54] Although the lake breezes continued to cool the Beach Strip, few people thought of it as a healthy or restorative area. Passersby increasingly saw it as an environmental disaster zone, not a "breathing place" where Hamilton residents could escape the heat and pollution of the city.

Just as the Beach Strip became less attractive as a waterfront recreational site, so did the old North End. Faludi's 1947 Master Plan had recommended that it maintain most of its residential character, largely through clearing old buildings and constructing new homes, something confirmed by Hamilton's new zoning regulations, which had designated the entire "blighted" North End a maximum-density residential district. This opened the way for the construction of apartment buildings, multiple-unit housing, and single homes on small lots.

Yet this planning did not view the bayshore as a major amenity, and both its formal and informal places to play became much more confined. Eastwood Park, for example, whose revetment wall along the bay had been used during the diving competitions in the British Empire Games of 1930, had been landlocked by the end of the Second World War. Naval docks and barracks built during wartime eliminated the last of its waterfront access, and what some thought was a temporary arrangement soon proved permanent. (Figure 37)[55] Most of the boatbuilders along the North End waterfront were no longer operating by the mid-1950s, and they had given up renting boats. As one member of a boat-building family later recalled, there were simply not enough people interested in spending a day on the bay.[56] Although some of their boathouses survived, they housed privately owned vessels and were off-limits for informal public recreational use. The City held on to its Bay Street Beach property, which remained a hangout for the local community, although it became increasingly unattractive as owners of adjoining properties built fences around their land. As waterfront space became scarce, the private boat clubs and marinas that remained took their right to privacy more seriously. These changes disrupted the sense that the North End waterfront was an open, public space.[57]

The fate of the Bay Street Beach stemmed partly from the problem of poor water quality. Although this had aroused some concern when the beach opened in 1927, as late as 1939 Medical Officer of Health James

FIGURE 37   Pier 8, the HMCS Star, and Eastwood Park, 1959. The open field in the upper right is Eastwood, a waterfront park created in 1908 from an infilled inlet. The park was cut off from the shore in 1943 with the building of the barracks and drill hall of the Canadian Naval Reserve, the HMCS Star *(the low-lying buildings just beyond the bow of the ship docked at Pier 8). Photo by Phil Aggus,1959. Courtesy of Hamilton Port Authority Collection, 3607–7.*

Roberts optimistically concluded that the water would be clean for at least ten more years.[58] He was wrong. Wartime city and industrial growth accelerated the rate of the pollution problem, causing his successor, Dr. J.E. Davey, to permanently close the beach in 1944. Just two years later, more alarm bells sounded when Davey closed another beach, at LaSalle Park on the north shore. He warned that pollution was "getting beyond the current which travels down the middle of the bay to the canal," which most people believed "acted as a barrier, keeping the polluted water confined to the Hamilton side of the current."[59] By then, city council had already begun to see LaSalle Park's waterfront differently. It let the harbour commission use it as a dock for construction materials, such as sand. Yet it retained LaSalle as parkland, installing a wading pool there to make it more attractive to locals and tourists.[60] Some civic leaders increasingly wondered why Hamilton invested any money in a park that seemed more likely to serve the community in neighbouring Burlington. After all, Hamilton had acquired the park to provide its citizens with a bathing beach, and it was no longer an attractive or healthy location.[61]

THE LOSS OF BATHING beaches posed a dilemma for those who still saw swimming as a healthy sport and positive recreational choice that was, above all, accessible to everyone. Bathing beaches had been promoted as places of orderly recreation, even if they had not always been as orderly as desired. Widespread automobile ownership offered part of the solution. As Ontario parks historian Gerald Killan demonstrates, after the Second World War provincial parks administrators struggled to manage the increasing numbers of people who visited parks, and they came under intense pressure to open more public parks near large urban centres.[62] More Hamiltonians turned to faraway places to swim, such as Wasaga Beach on Georgian Bay, a favourite and relatively affordable summertime haunt for industrial workers and their families. Of course, not everyone could afford the trip, and not everyone could spend much time away from home. Moreover, some people questioned whether families ought to spend their time in such places. Adopting a well-worn theme, a McMaster University professor warned recreation professionals that these beaches were morally dangerous hangouts for organized gangs (from other cities of course), such as "the Toronto Beanery and Junction groups."[63] He praised Hamilton's efforts to offer alternatives within its own borders, something sought by a new parks committee, because "persons wanting quiet recreation no longer wanted to go to the popular beaches, some of which were vulgar in tone."[64]

What were the alternatives facing Hamilton politicians and recreational leaders? Having closed the beach at LaSalle Park, the medical officer of health made two recommendations to city council in his 1946 *Annual Report*. He suggested that the problem of pollution at the bathing beaches be addressed by creating a more adequate sewage disposal system. He also proposed two ways of providing alternative places to swim: create a public bathing beach on Lake Ontario, and construct swimming pools "in the areas of the city where the need is greatest."[65] For the next fifteen years, councillors did little to improve the sewage system, but once again they searched for clean and orderly spaces to swim, shifting their focus away from beaches to the construction of municipal swimming pools.

Swimming pools, of course, were nothing new. For many years, Hamilton's supporters of the playgrounds movement had promoted wading pools because they provided a safe and well-supervised place for very young children. In fact, the City had installed a wading pool in Eastwood Park at a time when many people were still swimming in the bay.[66] It had also built an indoor pool in 1928, Hamilton's Municipal Swimming Baths, which was used for the swimming races of the British Empire Games. Yet the creators of this impressive state-of-the-art facility did not intend it to replace the waters of the bay, since it opened in the same year as the Bay Street Beach. Even the plain and fancy high diving competitions of the British Empire Games used the bay's waters at the Eastwood Park revetment wall. The new municipal pool provided the kind of controlled, enclosed aquatic environment that swimmers and water polo players would come to expect at major world competitions. This impressive new indoors venue garnered international recognition for the city and was just the kind of ambitious public project that Parks Board chair Cecil Vanroy Langs and Thomas McQuesten sought out and supported.[67]

The municipal pool proved very popular after 1930, especially as the water quality of the bay became more suspect and its shore harder to reach. Yet local recreational leaders knew that just one pool could not serve the needs of the entire city. They wanted to capitalize on wartime interest in physical fitness promotion and on the momentum generated by Hamilton's provisional Wartime Recreation Council to encourage local people to become more physically active and fit. The council hoped to make up for the Great Depression and the early war years when, in the words of Playground Superintendent J.J. Syme, city recreation had taken "an awful beating."[68] Hamilton's recreational promoters, including the head of its Board of Education, contended that children on the home front were "one of the serious casualties of the war."[69] Thus, the Wartime Recreation Council hoped "to plan activities to occupy the time and minds of the younger folks during the summer vacation months."[70]

However, the council did not have the financial resources to provide the kinds of facilities that a growing city needed. In 1944, it allied with the much more powerful Parks Board, still helmed by Cecil Vanroy Langs and influenced by Thomas McQuesten. The board aimed to help the council finance the construction of neighbourhood recreational facilities, including swimming and wading pools, by making it part of an ambitious project that both Langs and McQuesten wanted. It proposed to issue $1.5 million in debentures; $0.5 million of this sum would go to the neighbourhood facilities, and the remaining $1 million would be spent on building a major sports arena and auditorium to serve as a war memorial for Hamilton. Such a large debenture issue, however, would need the support of taxpayers, who were also being asked to consider a $2 million issue to construct a new hospital. The recreational council doubtless believed that the memorial arena would capture the imagination of ratepayers in ways that local swimming pools might not.[71]

The arena idea indeed captured the attention of ratepayers, but not in the way that the council had hoped. Serious opposition to the debenture proposal developed very quickly among people who questioned the expense of a costly arena and its appropriateness as a memorial to those who had died in war. During the heated debate that ensued, supporters of the proposal strengthened their case by focusing on all of the facilities that the debentures would finance, rather than just the arena. They characterized their opponents as selfish and narrow-minded plutocrats who would condemn inner-city children to swimming in the dirty waters of the bay. "Give Hamilton's Youth the Swimming Pools They Need!" proclaimed a Parks Board advertisement, "Vote 'FOR' the Parks By-Law!" (Figure 38).[72] Adversaries of the plan denied that they opposed community facilities and suggested, among other things, that arenas catered to passive spectators, not physically active or fit citizens. Their advertising campaign questioned why the arena was being linked to what they viewed as more important and much more needed community facilities. Arguing that Hamiltonians shouldn't have to accede to the building of a huge arena just to be assured of funding for other recreational amenities, they asked voters, "Are you being forced to vote in order to get sports and swimming facilities in our parks?"[73]

The Parks Board's ambitious battle plan failed. Many ratepayers doubtless agreed with the mayor, the popular trade unionist Sam Lawrence, and Nora-Frances Henderson, an outspoken local politician, both of whom consistently argued that city coffers had only enough money to finance a hospital.[74] Despite its defeat, the recreational council could take heart from the debate since it indicated a growing local consensus in favour of swimming pools. Both supporters and opponents of the arena proposal agreed that Hamilton needed community pools as a necessary alternative to the polluted local waters. Back in the 1920s, some people had voiced concern that the construction of swimming pools would allow civic leaders and health officials to avoid investing in effective sewage treatment facilities.[75] By the 1940s, however, few expressed the belief that the harbour should – or could – be kept clean.

The installation of more swimming pools would have to wait a few more years. In 1946, city council created a permanent recreation council "to assist, encourage, and co-ordinate athletic, sports, recreational and cultural

FIGURE 38 The great recreational facilities debate, 1944. This editorial cartoon lays out two options facing city voters: vote yes and provide Hamilton's children with swimming pools filled with clean, filtered water, or ignore the medical officer of health's warning and vote no, relegating them (as does the well-dressed stony-faced plutocrat) to the dirty, polluted waters of the bay. *"Give Hamilton's Youth the Swimming Pools They Need!"* Hamilton Spectator, *29 November 1944. Courtesy of Hamilton Spectator.*

activities ... in a local program based on the Ontario provincial plan of fitness and recreation."[76] With financial support from the provincial government, it appointed a war veteran, A.G. Ley, as the new director of recreation.[77] From his office at City Hall, Ley supervised the training of athletic officials and coaches. He championed the creation of Neighbourhood Recreation Councils, and he cultivated a network of alliances for times when lobbying was needed for new facilities, such as swimming pools. By 1948, the recreation council and its director worked with twelve neighbourhood councils and controlled local community centres that had been established by the provincial and federal governments during the Second World War. Merging with the older Playgrounds Commission, they became responsible for all community fitness and recreation programs beyond local school offerings.[78] The smaller councils were mainly interested in the provision of local parks and facilities, including swimming pools. By 1953, together with Ley, they convinced the City that it needed to construct four outdoor swimming pools to serve diverse neighbourhoods: thus, pools were built in Inch Park for the growing residential community on the Mountain, at Coronation Park in the western suburb of Westdale, and at Parkdale in the southeast. Significantly, the first of these municipal pools would be situated in the old North End port, at Eastwood Park.[79]

Those who did not want to swim in a pool could still brave the waters of Lake Ontario. In the 1940s, both the town planner E.G. Faludi and the medical officer of health had recommended the further development of the bathing beach on the City-owned lakefront property adjacent to the old waterworks filtering basins at the Beach Strip. The City had previously provided some limited facilities for the beach, but as the recreation council lobbied for resources for community swimming pools, development stalled. After the war, city council considered proposals to transform a filtering basin into a swimming pool, which would be warmer than the lake and cleaner than the bay, but for one reason or another nothing happened.[80] Hoping to get the area developed, council conveyed the property to a local agency that seemed to have the resources to do the work – the Hamilton Harbour Commission. The commission once again worked with the City to provide a public bathing beach, but this time it would be on the lake, not the bay. In 1960, a new Olympic-sized swimming facility, the Lakeland Pool, was added to the lakeside bathing beach and amusement park, which now included an aerial tramway so that visitors could take in the sights from high above the park.[81]

In the late 1950s, the City of Hamilton prepared to use its new authority over more of the lakefront to expand the park. It focused on an area south of the filtering basins, rather than the Beach Strip itself. There, a small community of about eight hundred people had converted cottages to create inexpensive houses. City officials applied their zoning standards to this semi-rural community of improvised housing and not surprisingly determined that it was blighted.[82] Councillors were not eager to extend costly services to a neighbourhood whose properties could generate very little in the way of tax revenues, especially when expropriating them could make space for revenue-generating attractions. By establishing that the community was in bad repair, the City might be able to finance the waterfront project by tapping into newly available urban renewal funding from other levels of government.[83]

Between April 1958 and 1962, without waiting for the funding to be granted, the City expropriated and razed most of the "blighted" buildings; eventually all would be cleared. Like the construction of the northwestern entrance over the Desjardins Canal on the Burlington Heights decades earlier, the creation of the new parkland destroyed a community. As before, those whose lands were expropriated received some compensation, although often not enough to purchase a good home elsewhere. Some residents became tenants in public housing projects, whereas others found ways to transport their buildings to cheaper properties in outlying rural districts. Although the City cited health and safety concerns to justify the expropriations, public officials appear to have made little effort to ensure that evicted individuals were better off after their relocation. In some cases, they even assisted in moving blighted houses elsewhere. Still, a local reporter made it all sound for the best, describing the area as a "swampy, storm-battered huddle of cottages, some converted into year-round slum dwellings."[84] The City opened a fairly simple park in 1964, but it had grand plans to turn Confederation Park into an extensive tourist resort.

IN ITS FOCUS ON THE LAKEFRONT park and the construction of municipal swimming pools in the postwar period, Hamilton's government confirmed a significant shift in recreational culture: in future, swimming would not take place in the harbour, where earlier generations of locals had learned to swim. Some informal swimming inevitably continued there – in July 1953, Medical Officer of Health L.E. Clarke felt compelled to remind residents not to bathe in the bay, stating, "It is dangerous."[85] Even those who were willing to brave the waters, however, found their options for getting to the shoreline increasingly limited. No wonder, then, that the version of a "balanced bay," as laid out by Trevor Lautens in the 1960 special issue of the *Hamilton Spectator*, had no room for swimming or bathing beaches.

In 1946, a *Spectator* editorial had contemplated the tremendous changes that had occurred on the waterfront. Titled "Our Deceptive Bay," it noted that from a distance the bay looked attractive and inviting. This, however, was illusory: "Nearby it is seen to be dirty and flecked with foulness, the pollution of its waters being the price we pay for modern urban life. The price may easily be too high. Our beautiful bay's water is unfit to drink. It is death to wild life."[86] This editorial reflected similar comments made that year by the outgoing medical officer of health, J.E. Davey, who had devoted a portion of his final *Annual Report* to the issue of pollution in the bay:

There was a time, not so many years ago, when Hamilton Bay was a 'Thing of Beauty and a Joy Forever' for the citizens of Hamilton. Fishing, bathing, boating and other aquatic activities added to the leisure time enjoyment of her citizens. It was even considered safe to secure ice supplies from these same waters. That day has long since passed. Bathing has been prohibited, fishing is almost abandoned, newly-painted sailboats or other craft venturing on bay waters run the risk of defacement from oil or other polluting substances ... Unless more active measures are taken to prevent further pollution and to remedy so far as possible what has already taken place, future generations will rise up to condemn us for the way in which we have mishandled this natural heritage.[87]

These concerns went unheeded. When Davey's successor, L.E. Clarke, responded to similar complaints about pollution made by the local Trades and Labour Council, he suggested that the bay would never "be approved again as a swimming hole because of continued industrialization." In the early 1960s, he boldly informed a *Spectator* reporter that pollution was an unavoidable reality of modern city life. "You can't have a big, commercial city on a Muskoka lake," he proclaimed.[88] The newspaper had earlier expressed a similar assessment of the situation:

The cesspooling of the bay was part of Hamilton's growth and prosperity. We could have a veritable Walden Pond ... but we'd probably have a population of 25,000 instead of a quarter of a million ... Let's have an end to the nonsense about how tragic it was that the bay ever got that way. It got that way because Hamilton was – and is despite the handwringers – a great industrial city.[89]

Such comments suggest a growing resignation about the plight of the waterfront.

The transformation of the harbour environment most immediately affected bathing beaches, but as the medical officer of health had suggested, fishing and boating also suffered from its degradation. Fish populations continued to change, although the transformations were less dramatic than those of the late nineteenth century or what had taken place in the other Great Lakes immediately after the opening of the Fourth Welland Canal. Constant changes to shoreline habitats led to declines in bass, walleye, and perch, although two introduced species, trout and smelt, appeared to be adapting. Carp flourished in the changing environment and were blamed for the decline of other fish and for the destruction of aquatic plants, turning parts of Cootes Paradise into shallow, open water.[90] The Hamilton Angling and Fishing Club itself adapted to the new environment by abandoning its efforts to make the harbour into a sportsman's paradise through fish culture. In the early 1960s, it struggled to rebuild its dwindling membership and began constructing its own new "paradise" on sixteen hectares on the edge of the growing suburban village of Ancaster. There, some twenty kilometres from the harbour, club members enjoyed a large fishing pond.[91]

The harbour's environmental transformation affected the Royal Hamilton Yacht Club and the Leander Rowing Club as well, both of which had difficulties attracting new members, particularly in the 1950s. Both groups had a clubhouse in the west end of the harbour – the yacht club opened a new one in 1938 just east of the Bay Street Beach, and the rowers retained an aging facility, just west of Eastwood Park. In the late 1950s, only about a fifth of the yacht club's thousand members actually owned a boat; far more people joined the club for its social events and restaurant.[92] Rowers tended to be more active on the water, perhaps because of local high school and university rowing competitions. In 1962, the Leander Club's healthy finances enabled it to construct a new clubhouse, just to the west of the old North End bathing beach. The rowers tended to be less socially exclusive during the postwar period, especially as the club sought new athletes to be competitively successful. At the time, some organizers thought that even more rowers might be attracted to the sport if both practices and races could take place in a more controlled environment than the harbour provided; they proposed dredging a course in the old Desjardins Canal in Cootes Paradise. This could be done, they promised, without marring the scenic qualities of the bird sanctuary.[93]

In the 1950s, the Cootes Paradise sanctuary and the northwestern shoreline along the Burlington Heights, now cleared of the remnants of the boathouse community, offered less confined natural spaces on the harbour and perhaps some of the best and most accessible places for informal recreation. Fishing was still permitted there, and although carp flourished, other more valued game fish could still be caught. When the Royal Botanical Gardens netted the marsh in 1954, it removed over 23,000 carp, but it also caught and released 111 pike and 84 bass into the marsh. Along the southeastern shore of Cootes Paradise, at Princess Point, those who sought recreation in nature enjoyed new facilities provided by the Westdale Kiwanis Club – barbecue pits and picnic tables for outings.[94] The botanical

gardens' extensive trails and gardens surrounding Cootes Paradise continued to give Hamiltonians and visitors access to nature throughout the
western harbour's watershed.

The yachting and rowing organizations provided another connection
to nature, even for those who used them primarily as dry-land social clubs.
Looking west from their clubhouses, members could appreciate the green
spaces on the harbour. They were not alone in enjoying this view. On the
ridge above the clubhouses, a housewife looked out from her Bay Street
home at the same vista. In the late 1960s, however, it started to change for
the worse, a development to which she did not take kindly. Launching a
crusade to stop the change, she was joined by others who were concerned
about the ongoing transformation of the bay into a dirty industrial port.
Developers were disrupting the "balance" that Trevor Lautens had optimistically sought after and alluded to in 1960, making significant incursions
into what was supposedly a "place for everyone."[95]

7

Unchaining Nature

Gillian Simmons's Backyard,
1958–85

GIL SIMMONS LIKED the view from her backyard window. That's what she told people when they asked why she and her husband were raising their family in a wood-shingled "cottage" in the old North End of Hamilton. And people would ask. After all, Robert Simmons was a former lieutenant commander in the Royal Navy and a mechanical engineer with expertise in the modern world of nuclear technology. He left England in 1956 to take up a good position with Westinghouse, so the couple could have afforded to live almost anywhere in the city. They started out in the Durand neighbourhood, where earlier generations of the most prosperous citizens lived far from the old port, in the higher and drier land near the escarpment. Yet the couple left the area and chose to rent a house, which they later bought, in the North End neighbourhood that planners had declared to be "blighted." Whatever the reason for their unconventional decision, they had a great view. Perched atop a ridge, their house overlooked the bay, with the remaining boathouses and the rowing club on the shore-line below. From her dining room window, Gil could gaze west across the water toward the Burlington Heights, where she could see McQuesten's bridge and, in the far distance, Cootes Paradise.[1]

And then, Gil Simmons stopped liking the view from her window. In 1969, trucks loaded with loose soil and rocks started making their way through the streets of her neighbourhood. The continuous procession drove down the ridge to waterlots at the shoreline, where they dumped their fill. This extended the shore and created a sizable peninsula in the western harbour.[2] The fill came from the escarpment, where the Claremont

Access road was being carved out of its face to better connect Hamilton to its growing suburbs on "the Mountain." Late in 1970, Simmons discovered what this activity was about. Sam and Sheridan Lax, owners of a successful local scrap metal firm, unveiled plans for a new North End housing development, Bayshore Village, to be built on the peninsula of newly reclaimed land. On five artificial islands stretched across thirty hectares of the bay, the development would feature parks, restaurants, stacked townhouses, and condominiums – all for some fifteen thousand people. Hamilton, it seemed, was to have its own version of that wonder of Montreal's Expo 67 – Moshe Safdie's Habitat 67.[3] If that were to happen, the Simmons family – Gil, Robert, and their three growing boys – would have a very different view from their backyard window.

And then Gil Simmons decided, "Not in my backyard." The forty-seven-year-old housewife, who had previously been active in documenting and preserving Hamilton's architectural heritage, turned her attention to its natural heritage – the bay. "There was a little community organization," she later recalled, "and they got together and they started yelling and screaming so I got in touch with them and said can I come and yell and scream too, you know, and anyhow that sort of began to turn things around."[4] What for Simmons began as a defence of her home and neighbourhood soon became a much broader crusade, part of what one journalist termed a "battle to unchain Hamilton Bay." The small group that Simmons led – the Save Our Bay Committee (SOB) – acquired a surprising range of allies, people who were also willing to stir things up and "turn things around," to question the cost of sustained port development. "We were the S.O.B.s, I'm afraid," said Simmons years later.[5] Together, they sought a "balanced bay" that was very different from the one the harbour commissioners had proposed during the 1950s and 1960s, and that *Spectator* reporter Trevor Lautens described in 1960. SOB struggled to determine *what* the harbour should look like in the future and *who* would make that all-important decision.

WHEN THE LURIA BROTHERS Company purchased waterlots in the west end of Hamilton Harbour in 1959, neither the firm nor its local agents, Samuel and Sheridan Lax, had any reason to suspect that this would generate much controversy. The Philadelphia-based Luria Brothers already supplied Europe with scrap metal and looked to the opening of the St. Lawrence Seaway to expand trade in and out of Canada's Steeltown. The Lax brothers did not have a waterfront location, so the company acquired some of the last available space on the industrial shore from the harbour commission: waterlots north of the rail yards in the west harbour. Their proximity to railway and shipping lines made sense for a scrap metal import-export facility, especially since a number of metal-working companies already existed in the area, including a scrap metal yard at the Canadian Iron Works property.[6]

There was nothing very unusual about this waterlot purchase. In 1958 and 1959 alone, the harbour commission had sold nearly 202 hectares along the shoreline as it looked for cash to finance new port facilities that were required for the traffic brought in by the new St. Lawrence Seaway. Selling to Luria Brothers, whose plans for the property appeared to coincide with its own objectives, seemed to be mutually beneficial. In the late 1950s, the commission produced plans that envisioned making land for more wharves and warehouses out of the shallow shoreline north of the rail yards and as far west as the Desjardins Canal.[7]

The economic growth of Hamilton in the 1960s did little to dampen the commission's enthusiasm for increased port development. The opening of the Seaway lived up to at least some of its promise, and the subsequent signing of the 1965 Canada–United States Automotive Products Agreement (known as the Auto Pact) further boosted the steel industry. Between 1963 and 1975, Dofasco's production increased by 120 percent and that of the larger Stelco factory by 67 percent. The total cargo tonnage shipped at the port – still mostly incoming coal and iron ore – increased by 57 percent in the same period, and the harbour commissioners continued to expand their dock facilities. In the 1960s, their Centennial Docks project, northwest of Eastwood Park, took shape in stages, with hectares of waterlots filled in. The port had almost three and a half kilometres of newly constructed berths of Seaway depth and five new buildings. Increasingly, the commission focused only on industrial and commercial shipping, cancelling its passenger ferry service in 1959. Within a decade, it had largely gotten out of the recreation business when it gave the Lakeland beach and pool back to the City of Hamilton.[8]

Whereas the commissioners imagined the west harbour as an extension of their other facilities, city planners developed a different vision. In 1963, city council released a plan for the "blighted" neighbourhood in the old North End – its second urban renewal project – which involved demolishing more than five hundred buildings. These would be replaced by new homes, some additional green space, and, along much of the heights that overlooked the water's edge, office buildings and high-rise dwellings. Although the advocates of urban renewal faced some opposition to this plan, they encountered even more difficulty in paying for it, or, more to the point, in having the national and provincial governments pay for it. Still, by the late 1960s, bulldozers had levelled over four hundred buildings, replacing them with new schools, low-rise housing complexes, and open space. Some of the open space was deliberately set aside, but a good deal of it was simply reserved for future development, including a right-of-way for a limited access road. Much of the levelling took place away from the waterfront; no office buildings appeared, and only three apartment buildings were constructed near the shoreline.[9] Nevertheless, the Lax brothers – who retained the waterlots even after Luria abandoned its plans for them – sought to accommodate and perhaps even profit from the City's vision of a residential and commercial North End. In 1965, they announced their intention to fill in parts of the west harbour for a "high class industrial park," which would feature light manufacturers and warehouses (Figure 39). And then, five years later, shortly after they actually began transforming the waterlots into land, they unveiled their ultramodern Bayshore Village apartment and marina project.[10]

In announcing the project, the Lax brothers unwittingly stirred up trouble for both city council and the harbour commission. The commissioners had already opposed the City's decision to allow a two-tower apartment complex – Marina Towers – to be constructed on a former old-age home property immediately south of the Centennial Docks project. They had hoped to acquire the land for their own port purposes, fearing that such dense residential development – in the absence of a serious investment in the road network in the area – would generate problems for trucking companies and others who hoped to use the new port facilities. Not surprisingly then, the commissioners were equally unhappy when they learned that the Lax brothers were thinking about developing a new apartment building and marina complex.[11] Their proposal conflicted with the commission's own futuristic vision of the harbourfront: created in 1970, it prioritized wharves and other transportation facilities, albeit topped by high-rise commercial and residential properties. Whatever consensus had existed among civic leaders regarding the shape of waterfront development began to break down, raising troubling issues about governance over development. Disagreements arose over important questions, such as which institution had the final say in determining the use of the waterfront. And what were the limits of that decision-making power? As the Lax brothers dumped fill off the shoreline for their development complex, they muddied jurisdictional waters.

The brothers unwittingly touched off another debate when they trucked fill from other parts of town and dumped it into the harbour: Was their

FIGURE 39   West Harbour infill, 1970. This peninsula of land, made by infilling the
Lax Brothers' waterlots in the West Harbour's shore near the rail yards *(right foreground)*,
would become a critical site in the battle to unchain Hamilton Bay. The land would
eventually become Bayfront Park. Note the truck on the left arm of the peninsula
heading to dump its load of fill into the bay. *Photo by Phil Aggus and Son. Courtesy
of Hamilton Port Authority.*

project, and others like it, literally muddying the waters? To their misfortune, they were dumping fill just as concerns about the quality of
water in the Great Lakes reached a peak. In the late 1950s, resort and vacation property owners on Lakes Erie and Ontario had begun making a
stink to the Ontario Water Resources Commission (OWRC) about decaying, smelly algae along shorelines. The commission sought to find ways
to counteract this nuisance, even as it began to recognize that residential
sewage – particularly human waste and phosphate detergents – represented
a key source of the problem. Conditions grew worse. During the summer
of 1964, algal blooms covered 2,072 square kilometres of Lake Erie and
111 square kilometres of Lake Ontario between Toronto and Presqu'ile.
The decaying algae offended people's sensory experiences of the waters
and was now also understood to be sucking life-supporting oxygen from

the lakes. The Great Lakes, the media informed the North American public, were dying.[12]

Although no algal blooms could be found in Hamilton Harbour at the time – iron sulphate in the waste from the steel factories counteracted some effects of phosphorous-rich sewage – wider public attention to the problem of pollution in Great Lakes waters informed local concerns.[13] In 1964, the OWRC released its first report on industrial wastes in the harbour, warning that water quality was already "a matter of great concern" and that "rapid deterioration" could result from further industrial development.[14] Five years later, when it studied the municipal sewage system, the OWRC produced what the local press described as "a damning indictment of a system that turned Hamilton Bay into a 10 billion cubic foot bacteria-laden sewer in which no animal can survive."[15] Although the OWRC's *Water Pollution Survey* contained plenty of quantitative data measuring bacteria, chemicals, and biochemical oxygen demand, it recognized the important role that people's experiences of seeing and smelling the algae had played in raising awareness of water pollution as a social issue. It noted how the seventeen waterfront sewer outlets looked and smelled. At the Wellington Street shoreline, for example, the researchers observed, "Bad odours. Human excrement visible. Severe pollution from industrial and domestic sources. Buildup of faecal solids on bottom." Farther east, along the shore at Kenilworth Street, they noted, "Human excrement visible. Foul odours. Gas bubbles. Severe faecal pollution with some industrial." Photographs underlined this emphasis through captions such as "Oil accumulations shown along shoreline, bubbles and foul odours indicate septic conditions, thermal effects of industrial discharge create steam on the surface."[16] In 1969, OWRC scientists embraced the aesthetic and the sensory as a legitimate way to give meaning to the problem and to highlight the significance of their measurements. In covering the OWRC report, the *Hamilton Spectator* also used vivid language and added its own images, including an editorial cartoon of a giant overflowing outhouse filling the bay (Figure 40).[17]

In this context, the trucks dumping dirt, rocks, and other construction debris into the harbour clearly invoked all the wrong images. Infilling had become associated with declining water quality. In its 1964 report, the OWRC had warned that three factors could contribute to the deterioration of the harbour: further industrial development, a change in the character of the discharged wastes, and the reduction of the bay's surface area due to the infilling of waterlots.[18] Its scientists helped make a critical connection

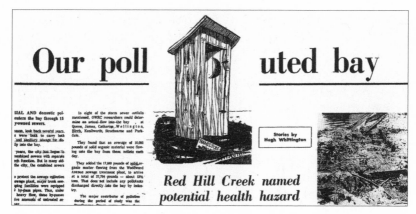

FIGURE 40 This cartoon of an outhouse atop Hamilton Bay and a photograph of a muck-filled and garbage-strewn shore accompanied Hugh Whittington's expose of the residential and industrial pollution flowing through sewer lines into the bay. *"Our Polluted Bay,"* Hamilton Spectator, *24 May 1969. Courtesy of Hamilton* Spectator.

between the people who were anxious about the Lax project and those who were concerned about water pollution. A *Spectator* reporter explained the situation in a 1970 feature article subtitled "Swimming in or Walking on the Water Is the Costly Choice We Have to Make." He observed,

> The bay is shrinking as the harbor commission fills in more and more of it and sells the lots. But the pollutants need every square inch of that water to have time to settle. The bay is a natural settling pond ... As the Ontario Water Resources Commission says, if you want to have a bay with a chance of survival, stop filling it in.[19]

The Lax brothers – and the harbour commission – *were* indeed muddying the waters.

Although the Lax project had the potential to raise these questions about the environment and to create a rift between city council and the harbour commission, it probably would not have done so in the absence of the contextual social and political ferment of the late 1960s. In cities across North America, new organizations engaged political authorities in innovative ways and challenged them over the construction of urban expressways, the redevelopment of neighbourhoods in the name of urban renewal, and the use of phosphate detergents and pesticides with the chemical dichlorodiphenyltrichloroethane (the insecticide popularly known as DDT). They linked their concerns to questions over the meaning of progress, democracy, and power.[20] Groups that formed around issues and neighbourhoods – some inspired by Saul Alinsky's call for community organizations to confront authority in creative ways – deliberately sought to muddy the political waters.[21]

In November 1969, young activists in Hamilton published *Ti Estin*, a special supplement edition of the McMaster University student newspaper, the *Silhouette*. The edition featured articles with titles such as "Who Will Save the Great Lakes?" and "Fighting Pollution: No Soap." Its photo essay, "The Photogenesis of Filth," captured images of ecological damage in Hamilton. *Ti Estin* clearly struck a chord and was revised and republished in June 1970, "to serve as an illustrated handbook through which people can learn the fundamentals of pollution, ecology, and conservation; that is, to help people become reasonably well-informed on environmental questions."[22] It had a ready audience since in the spring of 1969 some twenty-five concerned Hamiltonians – including a number of students and faculty from the university – banded together to form Clear Hamilton of Pollution (CHOP) (Figure 41). This new citizen action group aimed to increase public awareness about pollution, to pressure for political action, and to track down and sue environmental offenders.[23] The "cacophony of voices" that filled CHOP meetings was joined in the spring of 1971 with twelve other local organizations, which created Hamilton's new Federation of Anti-Pollution Groups. The federation attempted to work harmoniously to address environmental issues and to engage with city council's newly formed Pollution Committee.[24]

CHOP took a multi-pronged approach to fulfill its strategic goals. "Environmental groups such as ours," opined an early CHOP leader, "have a very important role to play in combatting public apathy and promoting the idea that it is 'people' who ultimately determine what is best for them – not some 'big brother' in Hamilton City Hall, Queen's Park, or Parliament Hill."[25] Throughout 1970, Hamilton motorists encountered young men and women carrying placards that protested air pollution, and high school students handed pamphlets to shoppers that asked them to think about phosphates as a social and environmental issue. CHOP approached local industries about specific pollution issues and asked residents to participate in trial recycling programs.[26] In early 1970, two CHOP representatives testified in Hamilton at hearings held by the International Joint Commission, the independent American-Canadian organization

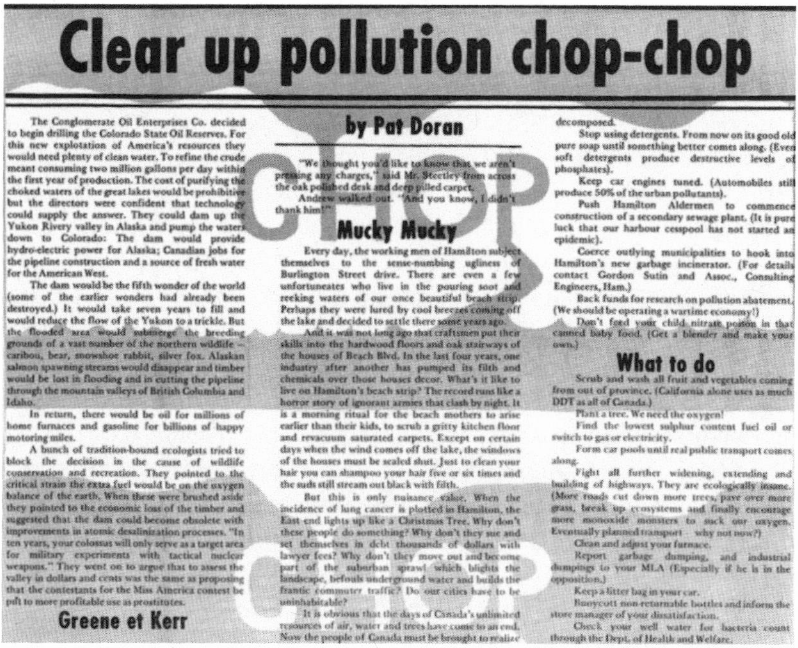

Clear up pollution chop-chop

by Pat Doran

Greene et Kerr

The Conglomerate Oil Enterprises Co. decided to begin drilling the Colorado State Oil Reserves. For this new exploitation of America's resources they would need plenty of clean water. To refine the crude meant consuming two million gallons per day within the first year of production. The cost of purifying the choked waters of the great lakes would be prohibitive but the directors were confident that technology could supply the answer. They could dam up the Yukon Rivery valley in Alaska and pump the waters down to Colorado: The dam would provide hydro-electric power for Alaska; Canadian jobs for the pipeline construction and a source of fresh water for the American West.

The dam would be the fifth wonder of the world (some of the earlier wonders had already been destroyed.) It would take seven years to fill and would reduce the flow of the Yukon to a trickle. But the flooded area would submerge the breeding grounds of a vast number of the northern wildlife - caribou, bear, mowshor rabbit, silver fox. Alaskan salmon spawning streams would disappear and timber would be lost in flooding and in cutting the pipeline through the mountain valleys of British Columbia and Idaho.

In return, there would be oil for millions of home furnaces and gasoline for billions of happy motoring miles.

A bunch of tradition-bound ecologists tried to block the decision in the cause of wildlife conservation and recreation. They pointed to the critical strain the extra fuel would be on the oxygen balance of the earth. When these were brushed aside they pointed to the economic loss of the timber and suggested that the dam could become obsolete with improvements in atomic desalination processes. "In ten years, your colossus will only serve as a target area for military experiments with tactical nuclear weapons." They went on to argue that to assert the valley in dollars and cents was the same as proposing that the contestants for the Miss America contest be put to more profitable use as prostitutes.

"We thought you'd like to know that we aren't pressing any charges," said Mr. Steetley from across the oak polished desk and deep pilled carpet.

Andrew walked out. "And you know, I didn't thank him!

Mucky Mucky

Every day, the working men of Hamilton subject themselves to the sense-numbing ugliness of Burlington Street drive. There are even a few unfortunates who live in the pouring soot and reeking waters of our once beautiful beach strip. Perhaps they were lured by cool breezes coming off the lake and decided to settle there some years ago.

And it was not long ago that craftsmen put their skills into the hardwood floors and oak stairways of the houses of Beach Blvd. In the last four years, one industry after another has pumped its filth and chemicals over those houses decor. What's it like to live on Hamilton's beach strip? The record runs like a horror story of ignorant armies that clash by night. It is a morning ritual for the beach mothers to arise earlier than their kids, to scrub a gritty kitchen floor and revacuum saturated carpets. Except on certain days when the wind comes off the lake, the windows of the houses must be sealed shut. Just to clean your hair you can shampoo your hair five or six times and the suds still stream out black with filth.

But this is only nuisance value. When the incidence of lung cancer is plotted in Hamilton, the East end lights up like a Christmas Tree. Why don't these people do something? Why don't they sue and set themselves in debt thousands of dollars with lawyer fees? Why don't they move out and become part of the suburban sprawl which blights the landscape, befouls underground water and builds the frantic commuter traffic? Do our cities have to be uninhabitable?

It is obvious that the days of Canada's unlimited resources of air, water and trees have come to an end. Now the people of Canada must be brought to realize

decomposed.

Stop using detergents. From now on its good old pure soap until something better comes along. (Even soft detergents produce destructive levels of phosphates).

Keep car engines tuned. (Automobiles still produce 50% of the urban pollutants).

Push Hamilton Aldermen to commence construction of a secondary sewage plant. (It is pure luck that our harbour cesspool has not started an epidemic).

Coerce outlying municipalities to hook into Hamilton's new garbage incinerator. (For details contact Gordon Sutin and Assoc., Consulting Engineers, Ham.)

Back funds for research on pollution abatement. (We should be operating a wartime economy!)

Don't feed your child nitrate poison in that canned baby food. (Get a blender and make your own.)

What to do

Scrub and wash all fruit and vegetables coming from out of province. (California alone uses as much DDT as all of Canada.)

Plant a tree. We need the oxygen!

Find the lowest sulphur content fuel oil or switch to gas or electricity.

Form car pools until real public transport comes along.

Fight all further widening, extending and building of highways. They are ecologically insane. (More roads cut down more trees; pave over more grass, break up ecosystems and finally encourage more monoxide monsters to suck our oxygen. Eventually planned transport — why not now?)

Clean and adjust your furnace.

Report garbage dumping, and industrial dumpings to your MLA (Especially if he is in the opposition.)

Keep a litter bag in your car.

Buoycott non-returnable bottles and inform the store manager of your dissatisfaction.

Check your well water for bacteria count through the Dept. of Health and Welfare.

FIGURE 41 McMaster University students called for Hamilton to clear up pollution in 1969. The Clear Hamilton of Pollution (CHOP) logo appears in the background of this article by Pat Doran. Note that the "H" becomes a smokestack and the "P" a sewer drain, expressing the organization's concerns about air and water pollution. *Pat Doran, "Clear Up Pollution Chop-Chop," Ti Estin, 28 November 1969. Courtesy of McMaster University Silhouette.*

that oversaw the two nations' boundary waters. Like Toronto's Pollution Probe, formed a year earlier, CHOP offered a general philosophical critique of water pollution. It also deconstructed the technical aspects of presentations made by detergent industry representatives at the hearings.[27] Drawing on the rhetoric of Pierre Elliott Trudeau, the charismatic prime minister whom Canadians elected in 1968, CHOP's leader explained, "Participatory Democracy, that fine sounding phrase, can only become a reality if our representatives listen to what we have to say."[28]

To those who were paying attention, the publication of *Ti Estin* and the growing environmental awareness of Hamiltonians signalled that the development project slated for the newly infilled land in the west harbour would be affected by the ferment. Three members of McMaster University's biology department co-wrote a piece for *Ti Estin*, titled "Pollution

As a Road to Nowhere: The Important Question Is Not: Can Man Progress? But, Can We Survive at All?" Two striking photographs accompanied the article and drove its point home. The first shot looked toward the escarpment, showing the construction of a new access road that cut upward and into its side. The second shot looked downward, focusing on the shoreline of the west harbour, where a newly created peninsula jutted into the bay. As Figures 42a and 42b show, the type that accompanies the photos implies a connection between the infill and pollution. The unknown photographer cleverly framed a second shot to sandwich the peninsula between a foreground of trees and a background of the lush green spaces along the Burlington Heights, Cootes Paradise, and the Niagara Escarpment; the photo revealed no sign of the area's railway yards and factories, which a different camera angle would certainly have caught. The paired images connected harbour infilling with road building at a time when expressway plans were generating considerable controversy in other cities.[29]

The group that directly challenged the Lax project was not CHOP but the Victoria Park Community Organization, another neighbourhood association formed in 1969 with Alinsky-inspired style. In early June 1971, its leaders went to court to stop the project, on the grounds that the dumping of material into the harbour contravened the Ontario Water Resources Commission Act.[30] Although the court would not do anything unless the group could offer scientific evidence to support its claim, the case helped attract about a hundred people to a "Save Our Bay" community forum that the Victoria Park Community Organization hosted a few weeks later. In reporting on that meeting, the local media paid particular attention to Thomas Beckett, who had led a new government agency since 1966, the Hamilton Region Conservation Authority. Conservation authorities generally dealt with flood control measures in watersheds, but Beckett had emerged as an outspoken critic of the harbour commission and its infilling operations. The media paid much less attention to another person at the meeting, whom they would come to know a lot better. North End resident Gil Simmons left the meeting as the head of Save Our Bay (SOB), a special committee that was "full of life and rebelliousness" and would lead the fight to protect the bay.[31]

SOB tapped into local concerns and memories in its efforts to stop the Lax project. Some people, including Gil Simmons, may have been concerned about their own backyards. Other people's reasons varied, as one writer for the cause recorded: "Some were tired of the noise, some

The dirt excavated here ...

... is dumped in the middle of this bay

FIGURES 42A AND 42B   In these two photos, McMaster
University student activists, writing for *Ti Estin,* connect the dots
between development, harbour infilling, and Hamilton's pollution
problem. *From* Ti Estin, *28 November 1969. Courtesy of McMaster
University* Silhouette.

were against the value of their homes being lowered, others were fighting against the destruction of their community."[32] Some residents of the old North End neighbourhood saw the project as typifying the lack of respect that had been shown to them and their community throughout the urban renewal process. "We were the dumping ground," recalled a man who grew up in the area.[33] Simmons helped transform those local sentiments into a broader campaign by invoking the history of the western bayfront. In a July 1971 letter to the *Hamilton Spectator,* she wrote,

> Let us hope that the people's voices will be heard loud and clear: it was for the people not only of this area but for us all that T.B. McQuesten created the entrance to Hamilton by way of the Botanical Gardens, Cootes Paradise and Dundurn. This is one of the loveliest approaches to any city in the world, and there is room for beauty and utility in our Bay, but not mangled into a shapeless unintelligible mass.[34]

She thus linked the west harbour to McQuesten's garden, his vision of nature, and his devotion to urban planning, not to rail yards, urban renewal, or high-rise buildings. For some older residents, this connection made a lot of sense. They readily thought of the area where the Lax brothers were dumping fill as public recreational space. One man, who grew up in the North End and remembered hanging out and swimming in and around the boathouses during the 1950s, explained that the waterlots "never should have been sold to a private individual, they belonged to the citizens of this city."[35] He, Simmons, and others like them undertook the campaign to stop waterfront infilling, "not only to save one of our natural resources, but to demand its availability to the people, for their enjoyment."[36]

They believed that the bay would be saved, if, as Simmons noted, people's voices could be heard. Their campaign framed the issue as one of democratic decision making, and on this count, it made the unelected harbour commission particularly vulnerable. As a reporter astutely observed, "Although the Save Our Bay Committee has lined up the Lax island development as its number one target, its 'enemy' on the wider scale is the Hamilton Harbour Commission" (Figure 43).[37] The commissioners proved particularly defensive when dealing with the controversy. When a local reporter indicated that "Hamilton has fenced off its port," the commission chair insisted that his agency was not responsible for "providing facilities for the general use of the public." Although trying to show that the commission would willingly co-operate with any private company or

FIGURE 43 "No Trespassing on Hamilton Harbour," n.d. Gil Simmons
peers through a fence past one of the many "no trespassing" signs
posted around Hamilton's waterfront. *Courtesy of Hamilton Spectator.*

other public agency that wanted to offer public facilities, his comment
hardly reassured people who were concerned about its future plans for the
waterfront.[38] Worse, on another occasion the chair reportedly responded
to critics of infilling operations by saying that "pollution is no concern of
mine. I have no intention of consulting the conservation authorities to
discover if land fill will contribute to the pollution of Hamilton Bay."[39]

Elected politicians could not afford to dismiss public concerns so readily. When the Burlington MPP for Halton West, George Kerr, visited the
harbour commission building on 6 August 1971, just two weeks after
becoming Ontario's first minister of the environment, he encountered a
picket line of SOB supporters.[40] Confronting Kerr, they got him to sit
down with them at an impromptu meeting at Gil Simmons's house to
discuss infilling, water pollution, and the Lax development. There, he
could hear their comments and concerns, but perhaps more importantly,
he could hear for himself the roar of the trucks carrying fill through the
North End residential neighbourhood. From Gil's backyard window overlooking the bay, he could also see the mess being made on the shore as
the trucks dumped their loads into the water. At the meeting, Kerr sought
to address the protests and to show concern by announcing that the

provincial government would initiate a study of the waterfront's future. When pressed about stopping the current infilling operation, he agreed only to look into it.[41]

Led by Gil Simmons, SOB members confronted municipal politicians a week later. They demanded that infilling the bay must stop, that its western end be protected from further development, and that a public park be created on the Lax site. "We are concerned that our last chance to provide free access for the citizens will slip away without protest," Simmons explained.[42] The politicians sought to calm the waters a little by agreeing that no more fill from municipal projects would be dumped into the bay, unless they approved the project. The other demands assumed that the City actually controlled the use of the waterfront. Whereas some local politicians wanted to confront that issue head on, others, including Mayor Victor Copps, hoped to reach an agreement with the harbour commission or have Kerr's promised waterfront study resolve the issue.[43]

Mayor Copps and the harbour commissioners continued to misread and inflame the controversy. In November 1971, Copps welcomed an agreement arranged by the commission concerning waterlots in the eastern harbour. Stelco and Dofasco surrendered 127 hectares along the bayside of the Beach Strip in exchange for the waterlots in front of their industrial complexes, which they had not yet purchased from the commission. The official announcement indicated that the waterlots amounted to 41.6 hectares, although the companies later estimated the size at 132 hectares. As part of the deal, the harbour commission agreed to set aside 71 of the 127 surrendered Beach Strip hectares for the City, which it could use for a public park. The commission, as Copps and some councillors proclaimed, "had made a good deal for the city."[44]

But that was part of the problem: the commissioners made the deal *for* the city. By undertaking private negotiations and not even conferring with elected city councillors, they effectively asserted their right to make decisions about the future of the waterfront. This was hardly the participatory democracy that CHOP and SOB had been championing, and they, members of the Hamilton Region Conservation Authority, and some city councillors quickly condemned the secret deal.[45] It did not help that the agreement completely ignored the concerns of environmental critics: indeed, it was predicated upon infilling another 162 to 243 hectares of the harbour. "If this area is filled in," one city councillor warned his colleagues, "we are just going to be left with a cesspool of a shipping canal ... Think of it – a park with a stagnant cesspool in front!"[46]

By early 1972, the controversy over the harbour had extended well beyond the Lax project and engaged the time and energy of several key
political figures, including Herman Turkstra, a new city councillor and
prominent Hamilton lawyer, and William Powell, who took over from
Thomas Beckett as chair of the conservation authority. Beckett remained
an important voice at the conservation authority, and he and Powell scored
an important moral victory when they convinced the provincial government to let the agency review and issue permits for infilling. Yet the effectiveness of this action proved limited since the harbour commission
refused to acknowledge the agency's authority and, although Stelco and
Dofasco reluctantly submitted applications to it, they used their political
influence to overturn its decisions.[47] Meanwhile, Turkstra sought to use
what little power the City had by seeking to oust its one appointee to
the commission. In doing so, he unexpectedly received information in the
summer of 1972 that involved serious allegations of conflict of interest and
outright corruption in some of the harbour commission's business dealings, including its awarding of dredging contracts. The ensuing scandal
resulted in the removal of the City appointee and the federal government's decision not to reappoint its two members on the commission.
Ultimately, and after considerable delays, an RCMP investigation led to
the arrest and conviction of the City appointee as well as other major
players in what became known as Harbourgate (a reference to the Watergate
scandal, which was unfolding at the time). Harbourgate discredited and
undermined the authority of the harbour commission for years to come
and even affected those whose dealings with the commission were in no
way implicated in the scandal, such as the Lax brothers.[48]

Although these political figures took an essential role in the developing
controversies over the harbour, citizen participation remained important.
Early in January 1972, Gil Simmons helped form and agreed to lead the
Lakeshore Citizens Council, which was to serve as a "friendly watchdog"
over the provincial government's promised waterfront study. The group
included representatives from Hamilton, Burlington, and four other communities along the western end of Lake Ontario. Some 150 people attended
one of its first meetings. A participant noted that none were "what you
might call 'far out' or 'weirdo.' In fact, you would go a long way to find a
more middle-aged, middle-class, middle-of-the-road bunch of citizens."
Some things went well, especially when the Province authorized the Hamilton and Halton conservation authorities to work together on the waterfront
study, since the two agencies already shared much of the Lakeshore Citizens

Council's vision of the waterfront. They also promised to engage the public as deliberations proceeded.[49]

While the study was under way, Gil Simmons and SOB remained a thorn in the side of city officials. Their constant attendance at council meetings prompted an exasperated mayor to proclaim that Hamilton really needed a "Save Our Jobs" committee. Doubtless, the group's determination to freeze industrial expansion on the harbourfront at its 1971 limits and to set aside all the western shoreline for public use concerned him.[50] In the summer of 1972, SOB managed to force the City's Planning Board to hold a hearing on the zoning of the land created by the Lax brothers for their development project. It then rallied a strong attendance for the hearing, making a concerted effort to reach out to the sizable Italian-speaking community in the neighbourhood.[51] The hearing dealt with a seemingly small matter – whether the Lax site was automatically subject to the zoning that governed the adjacent shoreline – but still it generated controversy. Clearly, the Lax brothers would either have to face an even more heated hearing for the kind of zoning that their project would require or they could rely on the argument that the harbour commission, not the City, could determine the appropriate uses of the waterfront. Yet, as the commission became engulfed in its own scandal, the latter option appeared unwise. In 1973, the Lax brothers simply stopped filling in the west harbour and put their project on hold. They insisted, however, that the property was not for sale, to the City or anyone else.[52]

The future of the site became even more uncertain with the release of the conservation authorities' waterfront study in the spring of 1974. The report called for severe restrictions on where dense high-rise or low-rise residential complexes might be constructed and demanded that "stringent design controls" be applied to all projects, "to ensure that waterfront development will enrich the lives of all residents and visitors." The Lax property provided one of several opportunities for the City to reclaim some of the waterfront for Hamiltonians. The report recommended opening to the public almost half of the ninety-seven shoreline kilometres that it had studied, suggesting that a hundred new parks, beaches, and public recreational spaces be created to accomplish this. Whereas earlier planning documents had typically identified the Beach Strip as the source of public recreational space on the waterfront, this was the first time that the west harbour was envisioned as providing citizens with open parkland for active recreation.[53]

Like earlier planning documents, the 1974 study recommended allocating differing parts of the waterfront to industry, homes, and recreation.

Unlike those previous reports, it also recognized the limits of such spatial solutions. The consultants called upon governments and industry to work toward reducing pollution emissions into the water and air, making specific recommendations that might restore some natural functions to the harbour. Perhaps not surprisingly, given that they had been hired by the conservation authorities, they contended that infilling undermined the harbour's ability to deal with sewage and industrial waste pollution through natural organic processes. They offered a broad view of the potential harm done by water pollution: for example, they identified degraded water quality as a threat to swimming, boating, aquatic life, and the food chain. They pointed out that the resulting losses of fish and wildlife disrupted the local and regional ecosystem, which reduced natural recreational activities such as fishing and birdwatching. This, in turn, deprived people of much-needed connections to nature that would make them care about their environment. "Species close to urban centres are particularly important," wrote the consultants, "because urban man may feel divorced from the biological environment."[54] Industrial, residential, and recreational uses of waterfront land now needed to be balanced and to ensure public access; planners now also had to contend with a space in which everything was organically interconnected.

The postwar focus on the bay solely as an industrial port was at an end. The harbour commissioners went to court in 1976 to affirm their authority over waterfront development but found that neither the lower court nor the appeal court in 1978 would give them a blank cheque. The rulings confirmed that Hamilton City Council – and by extension agents of the provincial government, such as the conservation authorities – also had a role to play in determining the future of the waterfront, except in cases where their actions interfered with the harbour commission's right to regulate shipping and navigation. The courts disagreed on just one matter: the appeal court criticized the trial judge for even attempting to suggest what this legal ruling might actually mean in practice.[55] Nor could the courts do anything about the commission's lost political legitimacy. In the wake of the serious Harbourgate scandal and a waterfront study that clearly sided with the views of concerned citizen groups and their political allies on matters of pollution and public access, the commission struggled to regain some wider support for its activities. In the late 1970s and early 1980s, it incorporated some of the waterfront study's ideas into its own work. The commissioners paid attention to improving water quality while expanding the amount of waterfront space that was open to the public, moving away from postwar planning that had focused exclusively on industrial port development.[56]

The Lax project also ended. The 1974 study singled it out as an example of what not to do on the waterfront, and although the courts eschewed specific examples, a project that was so clearly unrelated to navigation or shipping would be subject to provincial and municipal control. The Lax brothers made one last effort to do something with their land in 1982 and 1983, asking the City's planning committee to zone it as industrial. They were probably not surprised when their proposal was rejected in the face of vocal opposition from concerned citizens such as Gil Simmons. It seems likely that the brothers were anxious to force the City or provincial politicians to decide what would happen to the infilled land. Within a year, the City paid $900,000 for the site, although the Lax brothers reserved the right to file a claim for more.[57] Now democratically elected city councillors would contend with concerned citizens and determine the fate of Gil Simmons's backyard.

THE 1974 WATERFRONT study inspired environmental activists at CHOP to campaign on behalf of another part of the harbour that Gil Simmons could glimpse far in the distance from her window – the Cootes Paradise marshland. The 1974 study argued that improvements in water quality depended on immediate action in closing small, often ineffective, sewage treatment plants and redirecting them to larger modern facilities that could provide tertiary treatment.[58] CHOP launched a campaign to improve or close the sewage treatment plant at the western end of the Cootes Paradise bird sanctuary. Operated by the town of Dundas, the plant had been upgraded in 1962, and the Dundas public works department claimed that its effluent was "purer than water that comes through the cold tap in many cases."[59] Research scientists from McMaster University countered that the effluent threatened the environmentally sensitive marsh.[60] CHOP struck a subcommittee to focus on the Cootes Paradise issue and used government grants to hire students "to organize public action aimed at bringing about an improvement in the water quality."[61]

Gil Simmons inherited the Cootes campaign when she was asked to serve as president of CHOP, but it was a cause that she readily embraced.[62] She worked with the students and CHOP members to focus public attention on the destruction of Cootes. Together, they convinced the mayor to declare a Cootes Paradise Day and staged a big picnic event at Princess Point, a popular park on its southeast shore (Figure 44). The live music and the chance to sit by the water and enjoy the area attracted many people and their families. They could go on an interpretive hike or look at environmental information provided by the Royal Botanical Gardens, the

FIGURE 44   People attending CHOP's "Clean Up Cootes Paradise" event at Princess
Point in 1974. The event focused public attention on problems with the Dundas Sewage
Treatment Plant. *Royal Botanical Gardens Archives, Burlington.*

conservation authority, and the Hamilton Naturalists Club. The event
organizers even ran a raffle, with some lucky person taking home a prize
that any Canadian naturalist would covet – a canoe. In this way, CHOP
built public support for its campaign to do something about the Dundas
treatment plant.[63]

In the end, dealing with the issue fell to a new form of local government.
Created in 1974, the Regional Municipality of Hamilton-Wentworth allowed the city of Hamilton and five suburban municipalities to deal with
issues that affected them all, including water policy. Its regional council
ignored the recommendations of the waterfront study and CHOP by
voting to double the capacity of the Dundas plant, rather than to improve
it or divert sewage to Hamilton's newly opened treatment facility.[64] However, the vote had been so close that the chair had to cast a contentious
tie-breaker, which heartened those who opposed the decision.[65] The
president of the Hamilton Naturalists Club fired off an angry letter to the
Spectator, incredulous that officials could so easily cast aside a place that
played such an important role in outdoor recreation. She wrote, "To visit

the area on a weekend and note the amazing numbers of people enjoying the nature paths with the resultant mental and physical refreshment makes one wonder *how* any human being could possibly *vote* to destroy an entity such as this!"[66] Two weeks later, CHOP members organized a mock funeral procession, complete with a horse-drawn carriage and a band playing dirges, to mark the death of Cootes. It must have been a sight to behold as it travelled from the centre of Dundas down to the water.[67]

Demonstrations, petitions, and letters to the editor apparently spooked some members of the regional council.[68] Its chair, who had dismissed the need for citizen participation in the decision, now seemed keen to hold public meetings.[69] The council also had to submit to the relatively new provincial Environmental Protection Act (1971), which required that due process be followed. In October 1975, an Environmental Hearing Board public meeting considered the proposed expansion of the Dundas treatment plant. For the hearing, the CHOP Cootes Paradise Committee hired its own lawyer to voice its arguments.[70] In the brief that he presented to the hearing, CHOP affirmed the positions of the Royal Botanical Gardens, the Hamilton Region Conservation Authority, and indeed the

FIGURE 45   Cleaning up Cootes Paradise, 1978. Citizens participating in a cleanup carry away boatloads of old tires, steel drums, and other garbage. Today, this effort continues in annual cleanup events run by groups like the Stewards of Cootes Watershed and the McMaster Outdoor Club in the fall. *Royal Botanical Gardens Archives, Burlington.*

City of Hamilton itself, that the "most socially beneficial uses of the Paradise are first, a sanctuary, and second, an area for passive recreation." Thus, it stated, the regional council ought to pursue only the best – not the most financially expedient – long-term solution.[71] Although the regional council did not close the Dundas plant, as some might have hoped, it did invest in a plant that differed markedly from the one it originally proposed, one with tertiary treatment. After its opening in 1978, the new facility began to significantly reduce phosphorous loadings in the effluent flowing into the marsh. CHOP expressed a "qualified happiness" over the final decision, which gave hope to the vision in which Cootes Paradise remained an important environmental and recreational resource.[72] True, it might have been a smaller step than the environmentalists would have liked, but it was nonetheless a step in the right direction. CHOP played a key role in raising public awareness about the sewage issue, and it offered expert advice that was an alternative to that provided by government officials (Figure 45). In doing so, it dramatically asserted and demonstrated the value of participatory democracy. It certainly helped that what CHOP was proposing to "save" was a nature sanctuary that was popular with local birders and fishers, bordered by a university and several relatively affluent neighbourhoods.[73]

THE HAMILTON REGION Conservation Authority sided with concerned citizens in efforts to clean up the bay and the harbour, but it ran afoul of citizens' groups in its enthusiasm to solve environmental problems and enhance public access by reclaiming the entire Beach Strip as a recreational space. The conservation authority, city planners, and civic politicians envisioned a northward extension of Confederation Park, which, the 1974 waterfront study blithely noted, would require the removal of a railway line and between eight and nine hundred houses.[74] Local residents insisted on their right to be included in the planning process. By engaging in it, they resisted efforts to define their neighbourhood as an environmental hazard, standing up against the creation of parkland that would displace them. Theirs was not a privileged community; its converted cottages and small houses were seen by some as undesirable and therefore inexpensive. However, unlike the residents of what was now Confederation Park, or those who had lived along the Desjardins Canal and at Cootes Paradise decades earlier, this working-class community won broader support from other citizens, such as Gil Simmons, who saw the issue as a question of democracy – of people having control over what happened to their neighbourhoods.

As city officials had developed a new Official Plan for Hamilton in the late 1960s, a separate report on the Beach Strip emphasized the neighbourhood's "deterioration." Its homes were winterized cottages, which local officials had long considered to have poor structural quality and bad septic systems. Using the housing assessment standards of the 1950s, planners concluded that half the buildings were beyond rehabilitation and that almost all the rest were substandard. The absence of a sewer service also threatened the health of the community, as did a relatively new consideration at the time – air pollution. Planners used "interpolations from a limited number of stations" to map concentrations of sulphur, smoke, and dust fall in the city. On the basis of this ambiguous evidence, they suggested that the ultimate fate of the area would be determined by the success of new air pollution control measures adopted by local industries. If these were not taken, they stated that the neighbourhood ought to be cleared and transformed into "an (air-polluted) open space."[75]

In 1973, flooding from Lake Ontario severely damaged homes in the neighbourhood, providing planners and Hamilton health authorities with an opportunity to further condemn it (Figure 46). When many owners of water-damaged homes sought financial help from the local government, municipal authorities encouraged them to sell them to the City.[76] The conservation authority joined in, calling for the general transformation of the area. It concluded that the Beach Strip could not support adequate year-round housing and declared its open space to be both poorly distributed and unattractive. It also argued that water-level fluctuations and the technical and economic infeasibility of installing a sanitary sewer system along the beach were problems that had "now reached critical proportions." It maintained that the area should be cleared and turned into a large public park for the enjoyment of Hamiltonians. After all, "The Beach strip is unique and strategically located, and is particularly suited for beach activities, boating, fishing and for viewing the steel plants and harbour activities."[77]

In June 1973, the waterfront study consultants visited the Beach Strip, giving residents their first chance to preview and respond to the recommendation that the area be transformed into a park. "And reaction was what they got," noted a *Spectator* reporter somewhat gleefully. The president of the Beach Community Council shouted at those presiding over the meeting and then stormed out. As he told waiting reporters, the claim that local residents had been consulted about the park idea was "nothing but a pack of lies." Although he agreed that the sandbar suffered from pollution problems of "epidemic proportion," he focused on water, sewage,

FIGURE 46 Workers unloading sandbags in an attempt to hold back Beach Strip flood waters in 1973. *From* Hamilton Spectator, *2 May 1973. Courtesy of Local History and Archives Department, Hamilton Public Library.*

and flooding problems, all of which he attributed to government neglect. Inside the meeting, one woman expressed similar frustrations: "This is a beautiful concept but we are the people you are talking about dispossessing ... Hamilton has destroyed the Beach. It has downgraded us and tried to make us look like nothing. Now you say it is a beautiful area after it has been destroyed."[78]

The consultants ignored the protests, and their 1974 waterfront study supported the park plan. The conservation authority and the City of Hamilton forged ahead, although neither could afford to expropriate all the residences, especially since the federal government had ceased to fund such urban renewal projects. Instead, they began to buy up the properties, quietly taking advantage of the flood damage to acquire them as their owners became willing to sell. Yet even this stealthy plan proved contentious, and the Beach Strip's largely working-class inhabitants, mostly of Canadian, British, and western European descent, proved well organized and resistant.[79] Back in 1907, wealthy summer residents had created a system of self-government, which the less well-off permanent residents had inherited and perpetuated until it disappeared during the late 1950s. After that, the Beach Community Council might not have the same amount of political control, but it sustained a tradition of local organizing: community members quickly set up the Beach Preservation Committee to stop the park plan. By the early 1980s, nearly two hundred homeowners had joined it.[80]

Beach Strip residents did not share the image of their neighbourhood that appeared in newspapers and planning reports. A 1983 research survey, published in the journal *Environment and Behavior,* examined how they dealt with living in an environmentally degraded area. It found that most residents simply did not see flooding or noise as significant problems. Only one in three worried about water pollution, and even then the concern was largely in terms of unsightly dead fish or inadequate sewer services. A very high number, about 84 percent of respondents, expressed some concern about air quality, but many thought it no worse than elsewhere in Hamilton. Many respondents told researchers that they valued the sense of community in their area and, more importantly, that they believed the Beach Strip offered them a chance to own a house or to own a much larger house than they could have elsewhere in the city. In short, they did not see their neighbourhood as degraded, and they concluded that the benefits of living there far outweighed whatever risk they faced from air pollution.[81]

Although the City had managed to acquire some 175 Beach Strip properties by 1983, the Beach Preservation Committee forced both it and the conservation authority to review their redevelopment plans with a new planning committee. This consisted of Beach Community Council members and the public at large, including one Gil Simmons.[82] The new committee sponsored a series of studies that challenged some of the conclusions regarding the neighbourhood. The air quality measurement station was just eighteen metres from the highway; by moving it closer to where most Beach Strip residents actually lived, one study supported the committee's view that air quality was not, as had so often been suggested, "the worst in the City." In another instance, a firm hired to assess the risks of flood damage produced a study that suggested that only one in three properties was regularly flooded, and even they experienced minimal damage. Finally, the planning committee studied and championed several alternatives for providing the neighbourhood with sewers, the environmental problem that most residents felt needed to be addressed.[83] The Beach Strip residents successfully challenged who got to define their neighbourhood as an environmental hazard and seriously undermined the foundation of a plan designed to clear it. The conservation authority and the City stopped buying up properties on the Beach Strip, whose population now included many more people from middle-class backgrounds, although it would take two more decades to convince them to start selling off the ones they had already acquired.[84] The City of Burlington, which controlled the Beach Strip north of the canal, never abandoned the plan and gradually cleared its portion. But in the much larger area south of the canal, Hamilton's political leaders were forced to think of ways to reconcile residential, transportation, and recreational uses of the Beach Strip.[85]

GEOGRAPHER DAVID HARVEY contends that the "violation of the integrity" of intimate, "place-based ecological relations ... often provokes local protests that can build outward to a more universal ecological politics."[86] When trucks started dumping their loads into the still waters below Gil Simmons's window, they violated her sense of place and provoked a protest that soon became something more than a complaint about her backyard. As one of her close friends and neighbours later recalled, Simmons learned "more than most about fish counts, phosphorous loading, and algae blooms," but she "always brought the conversation back to the big picture. People needed to be able to walk by the harbour, sit near it and have a drink there, if they were going to care about it."[87] Simmons could join in the diverse battles to "save" the bay, the marsh, and the Beach Strip community – sometimes as a key player and sometimes in the background – because they all involved efforts to sustain and restore the connections of people to their environment.

For Gil Simmons, as for others, ecological politics required that people have access to open, natural spaces so that they could better appreciate the importance of incorporating the processes of nature into urban planning. Ecological politics also required that people from all walks of life have access to the planning process, so that it would be responsive to the problems of ordinary citizens from the middle bracket, like Simmons herself, as well as those of the poor. Simmons and others actively engaged the working-class communities in the North End and on the Beach Strip, and took seriously their desire to have their opinions respected. "One of the most important strengths of living in cities," she told a reporter in 1973, "used to be the variety of choices offered ... but city life is becoming hateful for a great many people. Why? Because they do not feel they can make choices, because they do not know what their options are, they are constantly threatened by change yet they may not choose what change may be."[88] Simmons did not claim to represent all people, but she did see her role – and the role of other concerned citizens – as ensuring that people had a chance to make choices and to question the plans that often seemed to be made for them, not with them. The struggles she joined involved giving people a sense of control over their backyards, their neigh-bourhoods, and their city. "We build our own history," Simmons told a reporter in 2004. "A lot of people have a role to play in that."[89]

8

Remediating Nature

Hamilton Harbour as an Area of Concern, 1981–2015

I N THE "BATTLE TO Unchain the Bay," many concerned Hamiltonians, such as Gil Simmons, challenged the postwar vision of their bay as an industrial port.[1] They convinced their city council to purchase the 10.1 hectares of Lax land in 1984 and encouraged its transformation into a public open space for the west harbour. Yet some observers in the mid-1980s wondered aloud whether it was already too late. Was there a public waterfront worth having in Hamilton? Was there any bay worth unchaining? Early work on the Lax land had not been promising. Whereas the original infill may once have been clean, what had been dumped on the vacant land since the mid-1970s contained high levels of lead, cadmium, and chemical toxins. Cleanup costs escalated from several hundred thousand to 9 million dollars – far more than had been anticipated – as contractors followed provincial environmental guidelines and removed some twenty thousand tonnes of soil and industrial wastes, including batteries, from the area.[2]

But it wasn't just the soil that was toxic: So too were the waters off the infilled peninsula. "Canada's worst in-place pollutants problem – and one of the worst anywhere – is in Hamilton Harbour, at the west end of Lake Ontario," declared the American environmental writer William Ashworth in *The Late, Great Lakes,* his award-winning book of 1986.[3] Discussing the harbour in a chapter titled "Sludge," Ashworth cited water-quality reports that had concluded that its sediments "exceed the provincial guidelines for open-water disposal with respect to iron, lead, arsenic, zinc, copper, nickel, mercury, chromium, total phosphorous, total Kjeldahl nitrogen, ammonia, ether extractables, oil and grease ... PCB levels in sediment exceed provincial guidelines ... the highest concentrations being found in the southeast portion, close to industrial discharges, storm sewers, and Red Hill Creek."[4] True, Ashworth noted, the effluents from Stelco and Dofasco and the sewage treatment plant would soon meet provincial government standards, but, he argued, "the sludge is going nowhere ... For Hamiltonians, cyanide, ammonia and phenols – like diamonds – apparently are forever."[5]

In writing his book, Ashworth could rely on evidence from the Great Lakes Water Quality Board, a group of high-level officials from various government agencies that reported to the International Joint Commission. In its 1981 report, the board questioned whether, despite the efforts made since the 1960s, the goals of the recently signed Great Lakes Water Quality Agreement of 1978 were at all "practically attainable" for the harbour.[6] For over a century, Hamilton authorities had typically done the least possible to address problems of residential and industrial sewage. This, when combined with the intensive industrial development of the eastern waterfront during the mid-twentieth century, resulted in a severely damaged ecosystem.

Yet the identification of the harbour as one of the most polluted parts of the Great Lakes did not deter some people from trying to make things better; in fact, it prompted extraordinary efforts by all sorts of people to do what they could to redress and hopefully repair damages done.[7] In 1986, a diverse group – representing research scientists, government agencies, municipalities, environmental organizations, industry, recreational clubs, and ordinary citizens – began gathering in regular workshops and public meetings to discuss the environmental problems of the harbour and its watershed. They sought to more clearly define the problems and then to recommend and monitor practical programs to repair the natural processes of the harbour and to balance its "essential economic function" with recreational and other uses.[8] Envisioning the harbour's future as a vibrant centrepiece of community life, the men and women at these meetings aimed to do their work on behalf of "generations to come."[9] They hoped to introduce a new way of doing things.

This new way of doing things would not be restricted to Hamilton – it became part of the International Joint Commission's official approach to cleaning up its designated areas of concern on the Great Lakes. Groups of community stakeholders would collaborate to develop a remedial action plan (RAP) that addressed the distinctive challenges of their particular area.[10] Each RAP was expected to identify the source of the problems –

why, for example, were dredging operations restricted, beaches closed, and fish consumption advisories issued? Having achieved this goal, each plan would then outline the solutions and list the particular governments, industries, and community groups that needed to be involved in them. Each plan would create measurable objectives that, if reached, would lead the International Joint Commission to delist the site as an area of concern. This collaborative approach to environmental regulation has witnessed more failures than successes in the Great Lakes.

Clearly, local solutions and local collaborations were critical to the success or failure of the RAPs. So, too, was local history. In Hamilton, the RAP made sense in the context of previous struggles over the uses of the bay, whether anyone realized it or not. The participatory process, for example, made a lot of sense to Gil Simmons, who by that time had at least a decade's worth of citizen action experience under her belt. In fact, she was one of the early participants in these discussions, and she helped ensure that the general public, not just government officials and special interest groups, was actively engaged in the development of the Hamilton Harbour Remedial Action Plan (HHRAP).[11] Had he been alive, Thomas B. McQuesten might have been puzzled by this participatory process but would no doubt have recognized its effort to manage nature through comprehensive planning. He might not have realized it, but his own work helped facilitate that planning: representatives from the university, which he helped bring to the city, and from the Royal Botanical Gardens organization, which he helped to create, spoke the language of government scientists but ensured that a diversity of expert opinion was represented in the development of the RAP. McQuesten would have been especially heartened by the plan's emphasis on aesthetics and public access. That emphasis no doubt was inspired by his own work – the natural lands of Cootes Paradise demonstrated to many Hamiltonians the value of positive recreational experiences in nature close to home. The connection between the action plan and the work of Victorian fisheries inspector John Kerr may be more tenuous, but he certainly would have been both perturbed and pleased by it. He would have been disconcerted to find that both the city and its industries still needed to improve their waste disposal systems, especially given his many warnings about the problem of water pollution and its effect on the bay a hundred years earlier. He would have been pleased that government officials seemed prepared not to repeat his initial mistakes, choosing to engage those who were most affected as they developed environmental policies. And he would surely have been pleased and even a bit astonished by the key overall objective for Hamilton Harbour that emerged from community meetings: the creation of an edible, self-sustaining fishery.[12]

The RAP was just as intent as previous initiatives to control and impose order on unruly and unpredictable non-human and human nature. What made the initiatives of the late twentieth and early twenty-first centuries distinctive were the efforts to respect and incorporate diverse social perspectives and the processes of nature into urban environmental planning.

HAMILTON HARBOUR POSED a particular challenge for the groups that hoped to create new spaces for people and wildlife along its shores. Unlike many port cities around the world, Hamilton didn't have vast stretches of abandoned docklands and industrial sites that were ripe for redevelopment.[13] True, a significant number of waterfront branch plant manufacturers had wound down and then closed their operations, including Canadian Industries Limited in the early 1970s, Firestone Rubber and Tire in the late 1980s, and both Procter and Gamble and International Harvester (by then J.I. Case) in the late 1990s. National Steel Car struggled under the ownership of Dofasco for several decades, but it regained its independence in the mid-1990s and remained an important waterfront presence into the twenty-first century. The two integrated steel mills, Dofasco and Stelco, cut their workforces in half during the final three decades of the century but produced almost as much steel as ever before. Both were acquired by global corporations during the early twenty-first century, although their experiences differed: ArcelorMittal benefitted from and invested in Dofasco's competitive strengths in the North American market, but US Steel could not resolve Stelco's financial challenges and gradually limited its Hamilton operations. It shut down the blast furnaces but continued to use the coke ovens and some of the finishing mills as late as 2013.[14] Even so, the waterfront retained much of its industrial character.[15]

Hamilton Harbour also remained one of the busiest and most important ports on the Great Lakes.[16] The growing size of ocean vessels and containerization meant that the St. Lawrence Seaway never lived up to some of its promise but also meant that plans in the early 1970s to move most Hamilton port operations to Lake Ontario never materialized. Although the steel industry continued to be essential – iron ore, coal, coke, steel, and slag represented nearly 85 percent of the 12 million tons of cargo that passed through the harbour by the end of the twentieth century – another hundred businesses operated on the waterfront.[17] While ambitious developers included the railway yards at the western end of the

harbour in many of their new urban waterfront plans, a problem remained
– Canadian National Railway had little interest in giving them up.[18] A
frustrated director of Hamilton's office of economic development and
real estate had to remind those who sought to remake the waterfront and
other parts of town that if brownfield sites were "not on the market, there's
nothing we can do about it."[19]

At the same time, the impact of all this industrial and commercial activity on the environment came to be understood in new ways. In 1972, the
Canadian and American governments adopted the Great Lakes Water
Quality Agreement, which concentrated largely on sewage and phosphorous discharges. As environmental scientists inside and outside of governments sought to improve some water-quality problems, they drew attention
to others that could affect human health as well as fish and wildlife. When
the Great Lakes Water Quality Agreement was reviewed and renewed in
1978, it focused greater attention on a range of materials – mercury, lead,
pesticides, and other inorganic substances – that could affect human and
non-human health. The 1978 agreement, in turn, prompted the kinds of
water-quality studies that Ashworth could cite in his lament for the
Great Lakes. The agreement also called for an "ecosystem" approach that
aimed to consider "man and resources of the lakes and basins in a mean-
ingful social context," a development that placed humans as a part of – not
external to – nature. The ecosystem approach widened the scope of the
International Joint Commission's concerns to the entire Great Lakes
basin, well beyond the use of shared international waters that had been
its traditional purview. As never before, this bioregional focus brought
urban industrial centres that were not on boundary waters – such as
Hamilton Harbour – under much closer scrutiny.[20]

In response to these new ways of thinking about water quality in the
Great Lakes, the Ontario government sponsored a series of studies on
Hamilton Harbour, which were summarized in a 1985 report. It item-
ized technical data on oxygen depletion and nutrient problems in the
harbour and offered a number of recommendations, varying in cost and
consequence. The question was, what to do with these findings? The
provincial government decided to hire Sally Leppard and her consulting
firm to engage the wider Hamilton community in a discussion of the
report. It was a good choice: Leppard and her firm had worked with a
panel of experts who were studying the impact of land uses on Great Lakes
water quality, successfully facilitating public consultations both as the
panel developed its report and after it released its preliminary findings.
In Hamilton, Leppard's team began by interviewing a number of key

individuals who had an interest in the state of the harbour and, having established their trust, convinced them to organize a two-day workshop so that they could identify the many uses of the harbour and propose various actions to sustain them. A follow-up meeting combined public input and responses to the drafted proposals.[21] People's serious sense of stewardship reportedly marked these meetings, as diverse individuals – citizens, civil servants, industrial representatives, scientists, and others – all came together to discuss the problem.[22] Observers noted that in her approach to facilitating the meetings, Leppard maintained a process-oriented, broad-based, and inclusive style. During an interview, she reflected on this approach: "Half the issue is process, the other half is fixing. If you can get process right, and involve a larger number of individuals with different backgrounds, you have a much better chance of arriving at a good solution."[23] Yet consensus building among stakeholders proved challenging at times, as when conflicting opinions reportedly clashed over the issue of shoreline filling. McMaster University political scientist and sometime Bay Area Restoration Council president Mark Sproule-Jones recalled, "There was almost immediately a struggle that went on between what was then the official view of government and what the stakeholders wanted to do."[24] Even so, as John Hall and Kristin O'Connor note in their case study of the Hamilton planning process, most people stayed at the table to work through their various conflicts.[25]

As these meetings were taking place, the International Joint Commission called upon the Canadian and American governments to work with local interests to formulate RAPs for areas of concern under their jurisdiction. Hamilton had already begun this process, so that the initial results of the community meetings were submitted to both the provincial and the federal ministers of the environment in September 1986. The report focused on both general principles and specific goals. The ecosystem approach represented the main principle, but the community stakeholders also insisted that to win public acceptance and financial support, the initiatives needed to address concerns about human health and well-being. They also needed to include aesthetic improvements and increased public access, so that the general public would better appreciate the potential of the harbour and believe that its water quality could be improved.[26] The more specific goals outlined in the report reflected the diversity of the group's interests: improving water quality for recreational boating and water sports, continuing shipping navigation in certain parts of the harbour, supplying sufficient water for industrial use (but enforcing environmental guidelines for industrial effluent levels), and using the harbour for sewage waste but establishing loadings targets for point and non-point sources of pollution.[27] Future goals included working on reviving fish habitats to sustain a warm-water fishery by enhancing and rehabilitating wildlife habitats and environmentally sensitive areas for waterfowl, improving the water quality to permit swimming in the west end, and encouraging the use of the harbour as an educational resource for primary, secondary, and post-secondary schools.[28] Through its emphasis on boating, swimming, and other water sports, the community group ensured that recreation remained an important aspect of the harbour's desired uses.

A group of government-agency scientists used the general principles and some of the specific goals of the stakeholders to produce a more detailed and technical document, a draft of the Hamilton Harbour RAP. The Hamilton process benefitted greatly from the presence of scientists who lived in and were committed to the local community, including those who worked at the university, the Royal Botanical Gardens, and the Canada Centre for Inland Waters, a Great Lakes scientific research centre located at the Burlington Canal along the Beach Strip's harbour side. Whereas the shared professional background of the scientists allowed them to reach consensus on technical matters, the other stakeholders and general public provided the planning process with momentum. Over two hundred citizens, politicians, and government officials reportedly attended public consultations on the draft document. They made it clear that the process would not be left solely to the scientific experts.[29]

Several rounds of consultation and collaborative work resulted in the production of a series of reports required in the formal RAP process. An initial report pointed to water clarity, bacterial contamination, stresses from urbanization and land use, toxic substances and sediments, fish and wildlife stresses, and inadequate public access as the main problems that plagued the harbour's watershed.[30] A second report separated the work to be done into six problem areas and made fifty recommendations for remediation, taking care to identify the agencies or institutions that would be responsible for each proposed task.[31] Significantly, the report hailed itself as "a community based proposal ... not a government report."[32]

The Hamilton group made key decisions to sustain this level of community involvement. It maintained the scientific team to oversee the implementation of the recommendations, but it created a separate organization with representatives from the general community to monitor that work and also to ensure that the public remained informed and engaged in it. The Bay Area Restoration Council worked with the local conservation authorities on watershed stewardship programs.[33] It offered educational programming in the schools.[34] And it sponsored community-based volunteer events such as tree and cattail planting, and developed and issued a regular, easy-to-understand report card on the progress of the RAP.[35] The scientific team and public organization also created a RAP Forum in 1998, a group of forty stakeholders to undertake an extensive formal review of all the initiatives and to produce an updated report, which it completed in 2002 (Figure 47). The forum reconvened in 2012 for another review.[36]

Once again, members of the Hamilton community imagined a harbour that could have room for both industry and recreation, a vision that had almost disappeared during the intensive economic development of the 1940s and 1950s. The remedial action plan differed from earlier twentieth-century planning efforts in two essential respects. First, the adoption of the ecosystem approach meant that planners recognized that activities in the harbour could not be neatly separated – the relevant issues were "so interconnected that in order to achieve success in any one area all others must improve at the same time."[37] Second, planners perceived that the ferment of the 1960s and 1970s meant that their plans had to be developed *with,* not just *for,* the community. Their plan needed to engage and accommodate diverse viewpoints.

Throughout this process, Gil Simmons remained a force to be reckoned with. Representing the public, she was a very active stakeholder and a signatory to the incorporation of the Bay Area Restoration Council. Critics of the RAP process, such as sociologist Kenneth Gould, contend that though it was "ostensibly created to increase local 'public' empowerment," the inclusion of so many government agency and industrial representatives among the stakeholders "simply reinforced the dominance of government and industry in local natural resource decision-making."[38] Simmons worked hard to make sure that this did not happen. She drew on her experiences in the 1970s to champion citizen participation in the environmental policy-making process, ever watchful that the process and the plans would include public access, engagement, and education.[39] She and other community participants believed that government agencies and industry representatives had to be at the table to make progress but that ordinary citizens needed to be, as Simmons put it, ever mindful, vigilant, and active: "We should be proud of how far the harbour cleanup has come, while remaining on guard against complacency."[40]

FOR GIL SIMMONS, public access was critical to the success of the RAP. She sometimes invoked the name of Thomas B. McQuesten, who had

FIGURE 47 This is one of many pamphlets designed to convey information about the progress of the Hamilton Harbour Remedial Action Plan in an accessible and visually appealing way to a broad public audience. *Cover of* HHRAP Remedial Action Plan for Hamilton Harbour: Stage 2 Update, 2002 *(Hamilton: Hamilton Harbour Remedial Action Plan Office, 2003). Courtesy of Hamilton Harbour Remedial Action Plan Office.*

supported comprehensive planning, and emphasized the beautification of the waterfront.[41] Her motives differed somewhat from his, however. She undoubtedly valued environmental amenities and beautiful settings, but she also saw them as a means to an end, as a way to convince people that the harbour was worth preserving. She was not alone. When a communications consulting firm hired Hamilton-born actor and comedian Martin Short to convey serious messages about the harbour through humorous radio commercials and newspaper ads, the *Spectator* sympathized with Short's "challenging task." "It's not always easy to get people excited about cleaning up a polluted, heavily-industrialized harbour which they can hardly get to," observed the newspaper.[42] Only some 2 percent of the shoreline was even accessible by 1990, and much of that was heavily polluted, smelly, and generally unappealing.[43] Simmons and others believed

that a key way to win wide support for the necessary environmental work
was to transform people's relationships with the harbour. If it could be
improved aesthetically and made accessible for recreational activities
in, around, and on the water, the public might believe that the quality
of the water could be improved. Then people might be more willing to
see governments spend public money on environmental initiatives; they
might even change their own practices and lessen their impact on the
watershed.

The Lax land in the west harbour represented one of the few available
spaces on the waterfront and therefore played a major role in this strategy.
Ever since Simmons had helped mobilize the community to stop the Lax
development, she and others had urged governments to create a public
park on the site. Although two 1974 studies supported this recommendation, nothing was done.[44] In 1977, the Ontario government rejected
proposals to purchase the property for a provincial or regional park, con-
cluding that "the air, water and land quality were too poor for the site to
be considered for recreation ... [and] because the property is a landfill
site it has no natural attributes to be preserved or developed."[45] Suspecting
that provincial politicians feared the purchase would be a "political boon-
doggle," the *Spectator* reported that an unnamed official had admitted, "We
knew the whole Hamilton harbor was a can of worms."[46]

If only the Lax land had had more worms and less industrial waste,
efforts to get people back to the water's edge might well have been hastened
along. But that wasn't the case. The abandoned property became an informal, illegal dump: a wire fence did not discourage local businesses
from using it to get rid of waste materials such as foundry sand and even
battery cases (Figure 48).[47] With each passing year, the site became ever
more toxic, a mess that would need to be cleaned up before any attempt
could be made at park development. Here was the dilemma – it was
difficult to get people interested in doing something about a locale that
was increasingly seen as toxic, yet this area had the potential to reignite
their interest in the harbour.

Simmons and other community leaders took every opportunity to
advocate for a park, finally convincing city politicians in 1984 to at least
purchase the site. The Lax brothers walked away with $900,000, and
their abandoned property became public land. Two *Spectator* headlines
enthused over the purchase, hailing, "Lax Land: Paradise Regained" and
"Taking over Lax Property Is a First Step Back to the Water."[48] Planners
dreamed big. Informed by an advisory committee, and with input generated from public workshops, a consulting firm produced an ambitious

FIGURE 48 *The Maple Tree vs the Battery Cases*. This photo, part of an
exhibit titled *Trespassing – More Power Anyone?*, by Hamilton artist
Cees van Gemerden, captures a small maple tree springing from contaminated Lax land soil before the remediation of the site.
Surrounded by a pile of discarded battery cases, the tree thrived
against all odds. *Courtesy of Cees van Gemerden.*

plan in 1985. It echoed aspects of Toronto's popular Ontario Place amusement park, calling for the creation of a grand boulevard, boardwalks, cafes,
a plaza, a swimming and skating lagoon, a bandshell, carefully landscaped
gardens, and a Cine Crystal Imax/Omnimax Theatre. Its principal feature

involved removing the centre of the Lax peninsula to create Hamilton Island, a large lagoon, and a series of smaller islands with interconnecting bridges.[49] Its designers proclaimed, "Crossing the bridge to the Island will be an important symbolic action, representing the change from the normal world of the mainland to the new recreational landscape environment of the new Island."[50]

Despite the boldness of this vision (or perhaps because of it), people never got to cross that bridge. Hamilton City Council, approaching a municipal election in 1985, balked at the $32 million price tag, especially as it became clear that the cost just to clean up the site was increasing.[51] The city councillors, lamented a *Spectator* editorial, threw a "wet blanket on a project that would bring Hamilton into an exciting new era as a city proud of its waterfront."[52] Local politicians finally settled on a much simpler, more modest park design in the late 1980s.[53]

All the delays in transforming the Lax land meant that the waterfront park became part of, and would be designed and built in ways that supported, the broader goals of the remedial action plan. Importantly, parks planners worked *with* nature, designing a site that would attract people while at the same time restoring the quality of the water and waterfront environment for fish and wildlife.[54] After removing its industrial waste and contaminated soil, workers capped the area with clay, brought in clean topsoil, and used native plants and trees for landscaping. Although the park offered far fewer amenities than the 1985 design had suggested, it still accommodated a wide range of recreational activities, including readily accessible walking and cycling trails, a boat launch, a small beach, a grass amphitheatre suitable for outdoor concerts, and a large field for seasonal festivals such as Aquafest (Figure 49).[55] Carefully placed along the shoreline, armour stone provided informal seating and public access to the water's edge; it enhanced the park's natural theme but was also designed to emulate a natural shoreline, providing refuge and feeding grounds for fish. The adjoining public parking lot covered a large tank designed to hold twenty thousand cubic metres of runoff from Hamilton's combined sewers, preventing raw sewage from entering the bay during heavy rainfalls. Working with biologists and in consultation with community groups, as well as with Stelco and Dofasco, planners designed a park that would support fish, birds, *and* people.[56]

What would eventually be christened Bayfront Park opened in 1993 and was joined by a second smaller waterfront park, very near the location of the old Bay Street Beach. Pier 4 Park provided a simple sand play area for children and water access for wind surfers, a water-spray pad, slides, and

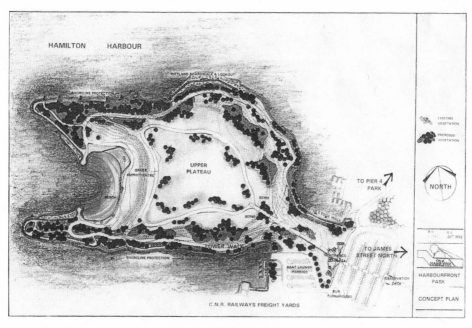

FIGURE 49 This 1992 concept plan proposed turning the remediated Lax land into a public park with lots of vegetation but only a few amenities – a grassy plateau, a beach, a wetland boardwalk and lookout, and a protected shore. *City of Hamilton, Pier 4 Park Master Plan Concept, October 1992, Plate 71F. Courtesy of the City of Hamilton.*

an old tugboat in dry dock for kids to play on.[57] The opening of both these parks generated public support for still more recreational space along the shoreline of the west harbour. On Canada Day 2000, the City opened a 3.4 kilometre multi-use waterfront trail (Figure 50). Consciously constructed to get Hamiltonians in touch with nature and to provide them with both visual and physical aesthetic experiences, the trail offered any number of ways to travel – on foot, on bicycles, in wheelchairs, on scooters, on roller blades, and after 2006 on a small trolley – an opportunity to progress from Bayfront Park to Princess Point in Cootes Paradise nature sanctuary. Its ingenious design also accommodated people and wildlife – the trail was built along the still active railway yards – and in doing so, it replaced the hardened shoreline with one that imitated a natural shore and was supplemented by several small artificial islands that could also provide refuge and feeding grounds for fish and birds (Figure 51).[58] To underline the public educative objective and value of the trail, the City invited citizens to help with the work of planting thirteen thousand native trees, plants, and shrubs along the trail in the spring before its official opening. For four days in late April and early May 2000, some 625 people showed up to help.[59]

Days after the waterfront trail's fanfare-filled Canada Day opening in 2000, a *Toronto Star* reporter hailed it as "Fantastic. Marvellous. Wonderful."[60] However, not everyone shared that view. A letter-writer complained to *Spectator* readers that his walk along the new trail was memorable indeed, but for all the wrong reasons. He recalled, "The smell of dead fish was beyond belief. And the dead fish along the shoreline easily outnumbered the anglers looking for a catch of the day."[61] His criticism, though pointed, nonetheless fell in line with ideas about access and aesthetics that informed the work of the remedial action plan: if real change were to happen, people needed to come face-to-face with the water's degradation, with its unpleasant sights and smells.

Change begins, this view holds, when people engage with their environment and see its horrible condition for themselves. Of course, restoration

FIGURE 50   Opened in 2000, the west harbour Waterfront Trail runs along the shore between Bayfront Park and Cootes Paradise. It has provided people with many opportunities to enjoy – and get to know – the city's bay. *From Zach Melnick, dir., The People and the Bay: The Story of Hamilton Harbour (Hamilton: Department of History, McMaster University, 2007). Courtesy of the L.R. Wilson Centre for Canadian History, McMaster University.*

FIGURE 51 Artificial islands along the Waterfront Trail. The remediated west harbour is designed to be a place for birds, fish, and people. Note the row of lights *(left to right, centre background)* used to illuminate the trail. Ducks, swans, and their cygnets *(centre and left)* can commonly be seen along the trail. *From Zach Melnick, director,* The People and the Bay: The Story of Hamilton Harbour *(Hamilton: Department of History, McMaster University, 2007). Courtesy of the L.R. Wilson Centre for Canadian History, McMaster University.*

work has the potential to erase certain features of a blighted area's past, so people could easily take improvements for granted and become complacent. In 2002, a local journalist worried, "How easy it was to sell the 'absolute horror' back in the 1970s and '80s. But if that horror is gone – no more oil slicks and floating human waste – how do you motivate people to go on?"[62] Gil Simmons and others had an answer: get them to experience and fall in love with the waterfront all over again. Had he been alive, Thomas B. McQuesten may or may not have comprehended the public engagement strategy, which differed so much from his elitist approach to giving people the beauty that they needed. He may or may not have comprehended projects that addressed multiple environmental goals, providing fish habitat, sewage control, and public space. But no doubt McQuesten would have smiled upon the efforts of so many people and organizations to beautify nature through comprehensive planning and civic effort.

DEAD FISH. THEY had been the bane of Fisheries Inspector John Kerr's existence, the subject of repeated observations and investigations during his tenure as inspector from the 1860s to the 1880s. Kerr had sought to protect all of the bay as a spawning and feeding ground for Lake Ontario fish and worried as the city's development undermined fish and wildlife habitat and wrecked water quality. He would have been immensely pleased that a century later, Hamilton stakeholders were determined to promote an edible, self-sustaining fishery in the harbour. Although he might have been astonished by some of the technology that made such initiatives possible, he would have appreciated the focus of late-twentieth-century environmental planners on two initiatives: the restoration of Cootes Paradise as a feeding and spawning area, and the construction of fish and wildlife habitat at various points in the harbour, to replace at least some of what had been lost.[63]

John Kerr was not alive to see Cootes Paradise designated as a nature sanctuary in 1927, although one of his sons was fisheries inspector at the time. By the late 1920s, broadleaf cattails and a range of visible and submerged aquatic plants dominated the marsh. In the 1930s and 1940s, around the time that boathouse dwellers were being evicted from their homes along the Desjardins Canal, only between 15 and 40 percent of the surface water was visible amidst the dense aquatic vegetation.[64] By the final decades of the twentieth century, however, Cootes Paradise more closely resembled a shallow lake – more than 85 percent of its surface was free of vegetation.[65] High-water levels at mid-century did some of the damage, but only because the marsh had lost its ability to rebound from such floods.[66] Poorly treated or untreated residential sewage affected water quality and supported the fish species that were most resistant to pollution, particularly carp.

Carp had been introduced into North American waters over a century before, in an effort to create a cheap food source for working-class families.[67] The species adapted exceptionally well to the changing ecology of the Great Lakes, especially to areas such as Hamilton's shallow bay and marsh. Early concerns that the "villainous" carp ate the young of other fish and the eggs of birds gradually gave way to criticisms that focused on how its spawning and feeding habits uprooted vegetation and created murky water that inhibited plant growth. In the 1950s and early 1960s, the Royal

Botanical Gardens, which was responsible for managing Cootes Paradise, tried various strategies to control the carp: it let commercial fishers use seine nets to catch them, while its scientists placed a pound net across the canal, and proposed to build a selective weir at the canal to stop them. They also simply replanted the receding marsh.[68] Any success was short-lived, however, as carp proved much more resilient than wetland plants. By the 1990s, an estimated fifty to seventy thousand adult carp thrashed about in Cootes each spawning season. Biologists contended that only forty kilograms of carp per hectare of wetland were required to damage a marsh ecology; Cootes had approximately five thousand kilograms of carp per hectare. When experimental replanting in fenced-off wetland confirmed that plants could thrive in the absence of carp, naturalists at the botanical gardens redoubled their efforts.[69]

Knowing that this fish migrated into the marsh in the spring to return to the bay later in the year, fisheries scientists and engineers took advantage of the narrow canal that separated the marsh from the harbour. They adapted the idea of a selective weir and constructed a fishway, which began operating in 1997. From March until November, this dam-like barrier prevents carp and other unwanted fish from entering Cootes Paradise.[70] Whereas fish that are smaller than thirty centimetres easily move through the fishway's grates, larger ones, including adult carp, cannot. Instead, they are channelled toward six large baskets and trapped inside them; the baskets are raised and lowered by a motorized, worker-operated overhead crane. Fishway technicians check them twice daily, sorting by hand as many as eight hundred fish per basket. They separate the carp from the others, diverting them into a release chute that sends them back into the bay. They monitor the other fish and record their species, size, weight, and condition before directing them into a chute that flows into the marsh. To track these large fish, they also monitor other baskets that trap them as they leave the marsh for the bay.[71]

This ingenious, labour-intensive operation is a very conspicuous one, and technicians use the opportunity to educate the public on the various fish that live in Hamilton's watershed and the challenges they face. It has also been very effective in keeping carp out of Cootes Paradise. Since 2004, their numbers have hovered around five thousand in the marsh, sometimes dropping as low as a thousand.[72] As a result, plants have begun to regrow in areas where aquatic vegetation previously existed. But challenges persist. Some people worry that too much of the new marsh growth consists of non-native plants. Others are concerned about the large amount of open water that still remains. Some are disappointed that neither removing the carp nor the regrowth of vegetation have produced more dramatic changes in other fish populations. The extent to which Cootes Paradise will rebound from its years of damage thus remains to be seen, since restoration always takes place in the context of a larger ecosystem. For example, sewage-induced oxygen depletions in the harbour continue to kill fish that might otherwise make their way into the marsh; new invasive species from else-where affect what plants, fish, and insects can thrive there; suburban de-velopments along the creeks that flow into Cootes Paradise generate new contaminants and sediments; and unexpected disasters that damage the watershed, such as the toxic runoff that entered Spencer Creek after a Dundas factory fire of 2007, set back painstakingly done remedial work.[73] These are constant reminders that the fishway may exclude the carp, but the carp represent just one factor that shapes the marsh ecology.[74]

Remediation workers have found few public and protected areas like Cootes Paradise in the main harbour save LaSalle Park, which the City of Hamilton still owned, a legacy of the early-twentieth-century search for clean swimming areas. After swimming had been banned there, the City permitted both the harbour commission and certain businesses, such as a concrete block plant, to use the docks for storing and transporting con-struction materials.[75] When postwar private homes replaced farmers' fields and amusement parks, the shoreline become increasingly hardened. People built private docks and retaining walls, sometimes using steel barrels, to store their pleasure craft and prevent their land from eroding. By the 1980s, the City of Burlington had leased the LaSalle land from Hamilton for a public park and subleased the waterfront to a marina association and a sailing and boating club, organizations that constructed new docks and a floating breakwater made of tires.[76] By this time, the shoal that had once paralleled the north shore no longer existed, depriving it of the fish spawn-ing ground, nursery, and shelter that it provided.[77] Still, the shore at LaSalle Park held much potential for fish habitat restoration. It remained the longest stretch of publicly accessible beach on the bay, and unlike the industrial docks of the southern shore, it could more easily be softened without interfering with economic activity. Its remnants of Carolinian forest could also provide wildlife habitat, and the gently sloping bottom offshore that had made it popular with swimmers could also once again make it popular with fish, reptiles, and shorebirds.[78]

As part of its effort to restore fish and wildlife habitat, the RAP team transformed the shoreline in the 1990s, constructing a diverse habitat for marine life.[79] The team dismantled the retaining walls and removed gravel that covered the sand beach, carefully bio-engineering the new shore to provide shelter and migratory paths to a forested wetland beneath the bluff. Community volunteers mucked through the mud to plant new stock, such as the soft-stem bulrushes that had been grown at the Royal Botanical Gardens aquatic nursery.[80] Seasonal flooding restores this wetland, now chock-full of cattails and other plant life.[81] Environmental scientists and engineers helped construct small islands, shoals, and spawning reefs off-shore, and embedded them with a variety of stumps, trees, and concrete pipes and culverts to provide safe shelter for plants and micro-organisms and to make this a good place for fish to feed and spawn. To protect this new environment from erosion, restoration workers built a promontory slightly to the west of the shore, which itself added another twelve hectares of spawning beds and marine habitat for young fish.

The LaSalle project also included 160 metres of boardwalk and a kilo-metre of new trail, giving people controlled access to the bay and the chance to admire the restoration work and its results.[82] Visitors may glimpse a few fish but are unlikely to fully appreciate that there are now twenty species in these waters, whereas in the 1980s scientists could find only six.[83] They are more likely to see the evidence of beavers, who have returned to leave their distinctive gnaw marks on the trees of LaSalle Park, and to catch a glimpse of a tern, bufflehead, or other shore-bird.[84] Even more obvious are the distinctive black-beaked trumpeter swans, whose rebounding population finds this new environment very attractive.[85] Like the parks in the west harbour, LaSalle was re-engineered to enhance public access and appreciation of the natural environment, and to promote natural processes that would support biodiversity.[86]

RAP planners took advantage of any opportunity to construct new fish and wildlife habitats, as in the small stretch of shoreline had been created and remained undeveloped along the northeastern corner of the harbour, following the construction of the second Skyway Bridge in the mid-1980s. There, some nearshore islands were constructed to accom-modate colony-nesting birds and to provide additional spawning beds for fish while some small islands built to hold hydrotowers were converted into fish and bird habitats. Perhaps the most remarkable of these projects took place at Windermere Basin, at the foot of the Beach Strip, a stone's throw from one of Ontario's busiest highways and in the shadow of Great Lakes freighters, factory complexes, and storage facilities. Although it was deemed so polluted in the 1980s as to be almost beyond repair, it remained "one of the country's most unlikely bird sanctuaries ... The presence of rare species draws naturalists from all over North America to what most people would view as an ugly cesspool."[87]

It was indeed an ugly and severely polluted cesspool. The harbour commission had begun constructing Windermere Basin in 1954, as part of a larger infilling project to create more industrial land and docks along the southeastern shore.[88] Engineers had designed the forty-hectare basin to catch silt from a creek and prevent it from clogging shipping lanes that had been dredged through the harbour's shallow waters. Because residential sewers discharged into the creek, the basin soon became heavily contaminated. Sometimes raw sewage, toilet paper, condoms, and tampon applicators bypassed the Woodward Avenue Wastewater Treatment Plant to float on its waters.[89] In the 1980s, sediment in Windermere Basin contained on average "three times as much lead, five times as much copper and 19 times as much PCBs (polychlorinated biphenyls)" as anywhere else on Lake Ontario.[90]

By 1988, toxic silt and sewage had filled the basin, and the harbour commission formulated a plan to dredge it. Naturalists and others involved with the RAP expressed concern that the plan did not incorporate habitat goals; they wanted a wetland shoreline that was suitable for birds and other wildlife.[91] They also worried about future contaminant discharges into the area, as one citizen stated in his comment form after viewing the commission's plan. "Unless steps are taken to restrict the flow of contaminants," he wrote, the "project at best should be considered an environmental bandaid-project providing a fat contract for a dredging company and employment for a few workers (hopefully made to wear masks and protective clothing)."[92] The harbour commission nevertheless pushed ahead with its project, creating a series of small lagoons behind dikes on the edge of Windermere Basin and filling them with contaminated sediments dredged from it. The lagoons were then capped, creating new land for industrial and port development, a good storage space for mountains of slag, and a new but smaller basin, now only 17.5 hectares.[93] Those who had hoped for fish and wildlife habitat turned to other projects.

Twenty years later, the bandaid was peeling off – the much smaller basin had simply filled more quickly than the original. Stronger environmental controls in place at the sewage treatment plant and local industries meant that the trapped sediments were much cleaner than before. When LaFarge, North America's Slag Plant (formerly National Slag), decided to remove the mountains of slag that once overshadowed Windermere Basin, members of the RAP, naturalists, and other citizens saw an opportunity to create

FIGURE 52   Windermere Basin, a thirteen-acre coastal wetland in the making, is located
in Hamilton's east harbour at the mouth of Red Hill Creek. It is populated by native
trees, migratory birds, and cold-water fish species. A fish way and fences keep out unwanted carp and beaver. In this photo, taken in 2012, you can see the creek *(left)* flowing
into the bay *(bottom)*, three islands providing fish habitat *(centre)*, and pump facilities
(white building and pipeline spanning the bottom of the basin). Although there is no
public access to the site, there is a walk to a viewing area across the creek *(middle,
left)*. Courtesy of City of Hamilton, #2U4Q9947.

another public space, and more fish and wildlife habitat on the harbour.[94]
Advocates were aided by the fact that bird enthusiasts had collectively
recorded more than four hundred species visiting this most unlikely bird
paradise despite its other uses. Hamilton City Council, which received
the lands from the Port Authority in October 2000, decided that dredging the basin every decade or so was a costly losing proposition and convinced other governments to help finance an environmental restoration
project.[95]

As a result, by 2012, Windermere Basin had become the site of a coastal
wetland in the making (Figure 52). Environmental engineers capped the
basin to trap any contaminated sediments that remained. Earthmoving

machines then carefully sculpted the cap, so that when the area was deliberately flooded, it mimicked a variety of marsh shorelines and bottoms.[96] Workers planted young trees on high land and aquatic vegetation in the marsh. The same dams and pumps that controlled the initial flooding are used to monitor and vary the basin's water levels. A fishway excludes carp that are already barred from Cootes Paradise, due to concern that they might enjoy this new wetland too much. Unlike many of the other initiatives, this wetland must be enjoyed from afar: there is no public access, and it is designed strictly to ensure that non-human nature will flourish in the harbour. Although it remains to be seen whether birds, flora, and fish will do well in this new habitat, the construction of this wholly artificial coastal wetland reflects the new ways in which Hamiltonians have begun to think about the connection between the built environment and the natural world.[97]

WHEN NATURE WRITER William Ashworth penned *The Late, Great Lakes* in 1986, Hamilton community leaders were just beginning to address the serious environmental challenges that faced their Great Lakes port. When he wrote his book, Windermere Basin represented what he thought was an almost irredeemably polluted site, probably one of the worst in the Great Lakes system. Just over twenty-five years later, its transformation into a carefully managed coastal wetland represented a remarkable achievement. It suggested how the community-engaged collaborative approach to environmental decision making had sponsored and inspired a number of important projects. Although this chapter focuses on built environments, equally important progress was made on improving sewage treatment and convincing industry to more effectively use harbour water and dispose of its wastes.

Unfortunately, it turned out that Windermere Basin was not the most polluted place in the harbour. In the late 1980s, scientists discovered a site far worse. And dealing with it has proved much more difficult, showing some of the limits of the collaborative approach that made Windermere Basin and other fish and wildlife projects possible. In 1988, a Canadian government research scientist identified a "black, oily, oozing sludge" in Randle Reef, a natural shoal some five to eight metres below the water's surface, just west of one of Stelco's docks.[98] It soon became apparent that Randle Reef contained a 630,000-cubic-metre blob, described by observers as a "toxic cocktail."[99] Its main ingredient, coal tar, is a by-product of coke making and other industrial activities, and it contains highly carcinogenic polycyclic aromatic hydrocarbons (PAHs). Randle Reef's "spill in slow motion" is the most toxic area in the harbour and the worst site of its kind in the Great Lakes.[100] Before 2013, it was the second-worst PAH-contaminated site in Canada, after the notorious Sydney Tar Ponds. Since then it has become the worst, owing to how much work was done in Sydney and how little was done in Hamilton.[101]

The discovery of Randle Reef just as stakeholders were developing the RAP ensured that it would be a priority. Unfortunately, this point was about all that could be agreed on. Although the Canadian government tried to follow the "polluter pays" principle at toxic sites, officials doubted that a court case against nearby Stelco would succeed, despite its proximity to the reef. Sherman Inlet also flowed into the harbour near the reef, and it would not have taken Stelco long to document other industries that might have contributed to the toxic blob over the years. Government officials hoped to take a page from the RAP process to encourage a more collaborative approach to solving the problem. Stelco officials were willing to collaborate but only as long as the company was not expected to pay very much of the cost. When they reportedly became concerned that some of the people who were involved in the RAP were pressuring for Stelco to pay a third of the cost, the company sought to undermine these efforts and even tried unsuccessfully at one point to convince other industries to withdraw from participation in and support of the RAP, which it claimed had "lost the confidence of the community."[102] Ottawa responded by creating a special Project Advisory Group in 2001 to deal with Randle Reef, a committee on which Stelco's interests were very well represented.[103] Some local environmentalists tried to force the Canadian government to move more swiftly, arguing that ships were stirring up the blob and causing it to spread more quickly.[104]

The process, however, remained painfully slow. The Port Authority simply prevented ships from disturbing the area, giving the committee plenty of time to reach a consensus on how best to handle the blob and secure the necessary funding for the expensive solution that it recommended. Instead of dredging and disposing of the toxic sediments elsewhere, the committee proposed to build a steel-walled container around them, adding other sediment before capping it. The result would create a 7.5 hectare peninsula, about two-thirds of which would be used for industrial and commercial shipping, with a third allocated to "green" or "light industrial space."[105] By 2013, the estimated cost of the project had escalated to $138.9 million. Most of this sum was to be paid by the federal, provincial, and municipal governments, whereas US Steel, the new owner of Stelco, was to cover about 10 percent.[106] Unfortunately, in 2014, no contractor who bid on the project felt that the estimated cost was in line with the actual cost of the work.[107]

And so, the toxic blob remains. Delay after delay in dealing with Randle Reef erased any hope that Hamilton Harbour might be delisted as an area of concern by the original target date of 2015. Although the federal government tried to ensure that the process of dealing with the site remained collaborative, it needed to accommodate and satisfy an industry partner that resisted certain outcomes. The proposed solution and Stelco's behaviour frustrated and alienated some Hamilton environmentalists, even as they were achieving so much elsewhere. Nevertheless, many advocates of the RAP remain optimistic and confident that an active and informed community will prevail. "This type of innovative project often entails a cycle of pencil sharpening and refunding before success," a former member of the implementation team assured critics in the *Spectator.* "What's needed now is people with vision and influence who want to get the job done for Hamilton and the success of the RAP. We need to let them know we want action!"[108]

CONCLUSION

Choosing Nature

I N 1865, INSPECTOR John Kerr tried to conserve Hamilton's fishery by arresting John Smoke and hauling him before a police magistrate for spearing fish on the Sabbath. In October 2010, some 145 years later, another Canadian court was seized by a case involving the protection of fish in Hamilton Harbour. This time, it was a government agency, the Hamilton Port Authority, that found itself in court, defending its proposal to sink Farr Island to create a shoal for fish spawning. The island had originally been constructed to support a hydroelectric tower, but now it served as one of several artificial islands that had been created to restore wildlife habitat to the harbour. AnnaMaria Valastro, whose Peaceful Parks Coalition championed the rights of "nuisance" wildlife, contended that the Port Authority's proposal to submerge the island had nothing to do with fish. Instead, its purpose was to destroy the habitat of some eight hundred nesting pairs of a troublesome waterbird, the double-crested cormorant (Figure 53). Although Justice Judith A. Snider of the Federal Court of Canada dismissed Valastro's injunction on technical grounds, she nevertheless sought to align her decision with substantive justice. She stated that Valastro failed to provide evidence that the cormorants were an endangered or at-risk species that was threatened by the loss of the island. On the contrary, Snider observed, the evidence showed that the cormorant population had grown rapidly, which had resulted in "public concerns regarding the impact to the environment." As she remarked, "Ms. Valastro is a very knowledgeable citizen, but not a scientist nor an expert."[1]

The scientists and experts – indeed, most locals who were familiar with the harbour – would have agreed that there were a lot more cormorants

FIGURE 53   Cormorants and gulls on one of the human-made islands across the bay
from the industrial waterfront. *Courtesy of Hamilton Spectator,* n.d.

than there had been several decades earlier. Whereas some estimates suggest there were fewer than 90 pairs in the entire Great Lakes in 1970, by
2004 an estimated 2,200 pairs nested in Hamilton Harbour alone. A variety
of environmental initiatives, including the ban on dichlorodiphenyltrichloroethane (DDT), assisted in their recovery throughout the Great
Lakes. In Hamilton, government agencies invested $2.5 million on shore-
line restoration and the construction of small islands in the mid-1990s
as part of the remedial action plan (RAP) for the harbour. They sought to
create, as a *Hamilton Spectator* reporter enthused, "a haven for Caspian
terns, common terns, black-crowned night herons and cormorants as well
as migratory birds and songbirds who may want to stop by."[2] The cormorants, then, were an intended consequence of the human bio-engineering
of the environment. The very dramatic increase in their numbers, however,
was not intended. What the designers of the islands could not and did
not predict were other changes in the ecosystem: Local cormorants
thrived on a brand-new diet of round gobies. This fish species originated
in the Caspian Sea and was inadvertently introduced into the Great Lakes
by ocean freighters; it started to colonize the harbour in the late 1990s. By
the early twenty-first century, a new ecological system had emerged in the
area, in which cormorants, whose population had been deliberately supported, helped control the accidentally introduced round gobies that had

made their way into the harbour. No one was entirely sure who or what would control the cormorants.[3]

Despite what Justice Snider implied, "public concerns regarding the impact to the environment" of the rising cormorant population had very little to do with science. True, scientists worried that the cormorants might be displacing other birds that they were trying to protect and even nurture, although a number of them still believed that with little to no human intervention, nature would work things out in this new ecological system.[4] Others panicked. Many local sport fishers were convinced that the cormorants were gobbling down game fish and therefore interfering with their sporting activity. As one fisher warned ominously, "Cormorants eat any fish they can catch which includes small bass, pike, sunfish, perch, trout and lots of them! The bird is a fish eating machine and if not controlled, will wipe out the Great Lakes fishery."[5] Recreational boaters hated the cormorants' guano, which stank and was so acidic that it quickly destroyed vegetation wherever the birds nested. So did wealthy homeowners, whose million-dollar homes were within a quarter of a kilometre of Farr Island. The RAP co-ordinator, fisheries scientist John Hall, also supported the sinking of the island, although not necessarily because science was on his side. He and other leaders of the restoration efforts were anxious to create more spawning beds in the harbour, and they saw the proposal as a golden opportunity, since the Port Authority and ArcelorMittal Dofasco were willing to pay for their creation. Moreover, getting rid of Farr Island would help appease the recreational users and wealthy residents who were concerned with a number of initiatives to construct wildlife habitat at the bay. The advice of the "scientists and local citizen experts," Hall pragmatically observed, "must be integrated with community interests."[6]

Justice Snider may have hoped that her decision represented the triumph in her courtroom of reason over passion, of scientific expertise over well-meaning but misguided activist knowledge. Instead, like John Hall, her decision was aligned with "community interests." Valastro and her supporters found themselves in the unenviable position of daring to speak up in court for a bird that working-class urban fishers, middle-class boaters, wealthy waterfront residents, and some scientists had decided was a nuisance. They spoke for a species that had long been associated with gluttony and destruction, one seen as a threat to the fishery in many parts of North America.[7] However much science might be invoked, ideas of moral and natural order were as present in the 2010 courthouse as in 1865, when John Smoke was charged with spear fishing on a Sunday.

Of course, the participants in the courtroom drama probably exaggerated the overall impact that sinking this one particular island would have on the cormorants, who had already shown considerable resilience in an urban setting and were likely to find other places to nest. It seems significant that the case revolved around Farr Island, the only one of the harbour's artificially constructed islands that was to be replaced by a shoal. After all, it was the island that lay closest to million-dollar waterfront homes. Significantly, the only formal public consultation about the proposed sinking of Farr Island involved a meeting with those homeowners and their immediate neighbours. The disappearance of the island was unlikely to seriously affect the cormorants, but it was very likely to displace them out of sight and smell of those wealthy property owners. However much science might be invoked, social power and aesthetic judgments were as present in the 2010 courthouse as in 1865.

Within weeks of the courtroom decision, construction workers excavated the island, replacing it with a fishing shoal. An island originally constructed to support a hydroelectric tower and then reconstructed to host colonial nesting birds thus disappeared from the urban landscape. The new shoal was no more or less natural than the island it replaced, and no more or less natural than the nearby canal that has connected Hamilton Harbour to Lake Ontario since the 1820s. Neither the canal, the island, nor the shoal could be considered natural, if we think of the natural as untouched by human hands. All were built by human actors who held a vision of the type of city they wished to create along the water's edge. All were shaped by the kind of negotiated political power that some actors could exercise in their society.

As political scientist and former Bay Area Restoration Council president Mark Sproule-Jones observes, Hamilton Harbour is "an artefact of human design."[8] The region's political and social leaders altered its ecological conditions as they sought to create what they hoped would be a livable, healthy, and prosperous city. Others who came to the area may not have had such ambitious plans, but many hoped that they and their families could secure healthy and economically secure places to live, work, and play. All believed that non-human nature had a role in creating that kind of place. Long before the age of ecology in the 1960s and 1970s, when urban residents thought about nature, they focused on what some scholars refer to as consumer amenities: they looked to nature as a source of recreation, health, and beauty, as well as the means of achieving material progress.[9] If they longed for the collective and individual prosperity that was associated with the industrial smokestack, most generations believed that the smokestack was not incompatible with the building of a livable town.

Every generation inevitably projected its own visions of order and disorder onto the natural world. Fearing forces that threatened the stability of the city they were attempting to build, mid-Victorian social and political leaders emphasized the control of nature and the control of the self. Nature had not quite created the perfect harbour; canals and dredging were needed to turn the isolated tip of Lake Ontario into a port. Shallow and stagnant water bred disease, and fire threatened life and property; running water promised to limit such environmental hazards. Wholesome recreational activities on the harbour, otherwise the scene of so much licentious behaviour, provided opportunities to model control of the self and to exclude those who were thought incapable of such control. The decline of some fish populations could be equally attributed to inappropriate behaviour, also to be solved through self-control or exclusion. Community leaders often saw nature as a potential source and inspiration of disorder; it could provide benefits, but only if it were approached and appreciated in the proper manner.

The next generation of social and political leaders shared some of the same anxieties. In the early decades of the twentieth century, it was more likely to see natural spaces as a source of order and stability, but only if they were properly arranged. The disorganization of the rapidly growing city became a particular source of concern. Urban boosters wanted to attract industry to Hamilton; monetary incentives helped, but so did investments that positioned the community as being socially stable – as a livable city for the families of industrialists *and* their workers. Those who sought to reform it attempted to harness public authority to allocate and organize separate spaces for various kinds of human relationships with nature. They turned to public investment to reorganize a chaotic waterfront, dredging and hardening the shoreline to make it more useful for industry in some places and creating beaches and attractive parks in other places. They sought to ensure that drinking water came from a safe locale, as their attention to bacteria replaced attention to stagnant water. Following the triumph of the British Empire Games and the construction of beaches, a new western entrance, and a new filtration plant, hopeful reformers believed they were on the verge of creating a prosperous and livable town.

From the 1930s to the 1960s, another generation might still believe that it had created a prosperous and livable city, but it gradually redefined the role of non-human nature in that city. Extensive infilling, regular dredging and hardening of the waterfront, and the continual use of the harbour as an industrial and residential septic tank had serious implications for all other ways of imagining nature. Now, encounters with nature and the recreational pursuits of earlier days would need to occur far from the industrial port, often distant from the boundaries of the city. Hamilton became, for residents and visitors alike, a "lunch-bucket" city, the gritty Steeltown, where some environmental degradation came to be expected as the price of progress and prosperity.

But not for long. By the late 1960s and early 1970s, the degraded space had become a source of anxiety for another generation of community leaders, who saw unbalanced nature as a source and symbol of urban disorder. Like early-twentieth-century environmental reformers, they believed in the positive role of natural spaces in the city, but they lacked faith in public authority. In their view, governments had betrayed the public they were intended to serve; solving environmental problems meant challenging government authorities, forcing them to listen to the communities that were affected by their decisions. And, in contrast to earlier generations, they were much more attuned – whether consciously or not – to Barry Commoner's first law of ecology: "Everything is connected to everything else."[10] What began in the 1970s and 1980s as a series of challenges to government decisions regarding infilling, sewage treatment, and displacing people for parks gradually became a concerted effort to engage the community in the remediation of the entire harbour environment. A healthy and orderly city needed properly functioning non-human nature, and that required democratic decision making and community engagement.

For every generation, the natural environment shaped some of the choices that could be made. More often, nature simply proved more unruly than anticipated, responding in unexpected ways. The canals filled with silt and their walls eroded; the canal that was intended to reach the small town of Dundas was gradually abandoned, whereas the other needed continuous maintenance and became a source of frustration to those who hoped to use it. Running water limited some environmental hazards, but it created new ones, moving the threat of sewage away from homes but into the shallow waters of the harbour and its inlets. Dredging, filling, and filtration helped address some concerns about sewage, but the use of the new land and improved waterfront for industry and commerce eliminated fish and wildlife habitat, and generated water-quality problems. Chlorine might offer a simple solution to improving drinking water, but when mixed with other materials in the water supply, it became a problem for some industries and residents. Preserving or restoring particular fish populations proved ineffective in a rapidly changing habitat. No matter how carefully designed, beaches could not overcome the threat to human health from poor water quality. Attempts to improve water quality and re-create fish and wildlife habitat have proven equally challenging. Even as sewage treatment plants have dramatically improved, human consumption of certain pharmaceuticals and personal care products poses new challenges for fish. The surge in the cormorant population, resulting from the unforeseen appearance of the round goby, suggests how much natural processes may complicate well-intended plans. These are just some of the unanticipated changes that nature may have in store for the careful plans of the current generation of environmental reformers.

For every generation, human nature could be equally unruly. Not everyone embraced costly plans for public investments in canals, recreational areas, or treatment plants. Those who wanted to play and relax on the waterfront did not always want to engage in the genteel activities defined for them. Nor did they always participate in recreational activities or respond to natural spaces as community leaders imagined. Public natural spaces – and even some private ones – provided opportunities for people to do what they liked. For their part, from the time that regulation began, local fishers challenged efforts to restrict their behaviour in the name of conservation. Indeed, the first public official who was appointed to enforce those rules soon became much more sympathetic to their arguments than to those of his social and political superiors. Families in working-class neighbourhoods insisted on the construction of more accessible beaches, even when others in the community doubted their healthfulness. Families that sought to survive in the city transformed boathouses and cottages into makeshift homes and community centres, and they tried to fish and hunt where and when they wanted. Alternative views of order and nature circulated in the society, and each generation of political and social leaders had to find ways to subjugate or incorporate those views while also attending to influential but tax-averse interests.

However imperfectly realized, the social and natural vision of those who held the most power in Hamilton had important consequences. The changes to the city were not experienced by all residents in the same way. Decades would pass before everyone enjoyed fresh water to drink, to wash away dirt, and to extinguish fire. When city councils refused to make significant investments in sewage treatment, their recalcitrance most seriously compromised the lives of working-class families. They were most likely to have few options but to swim in the seriously degraded water of the harbour or to play in the yards and vacant lots that were once polluted inlets but were now filled in with potentially hazardous materials. The decline of fish and wildlife habitat – and the banning of hunting and fishing – affected families who relied the most on subsistence activities to supplement low incomes and who had neither the time nor the money to travel farther afield in search of game and fish. The development and expansion of waterfront industries provided employment, but they also crowded homes, creating undesirable and degraded neighbourhoods. More often than not, the creation of public parks displaced people who had built makeshift homes in waterfront boathouses and cottages, who might move to even less healthful locales.

If we think of Hamilton Harbour as an artifact of human design, therefore, we must acknowledge that not all humans had the same social or political power to shape that artifact and that they experienced change in differing ways. We must also acknowledge that even the most dominant members of society could not simply impose their will on the urban landscape – they had to contend with a social world in which the less powerful could have conflicting objectives and exert some influence, and with a natural world that did not always bend to their designs or respond as expected. They also had to contend with history – an urban landscape and waterscape that had already been shaped and reshaped by the complex interaction of social and natural structures and processes.

Like recent scholarship on other cities, this history seeks to correct the impression that cities are simply artifacts of human design; it attempts to reintegrate nature and natural processes into our understanding of the development of the urban landscape and waterscape. Nevertheless, we see humans – and human choice – as central to the city-building process. Is a shoal that has been allowed to survive somewhere in the harbour since at least the early nineteenth century fundamentally different from a shoal constructed by sinking a former hydroelectric tower platform and cormorant nesting site? Is the preserved wetland in Cootes Paradise, protected from carp incursions by a fish barrier, different from the designer wetland in the east end of town? Do we value the bald eagles that have returned to Cootes Paradise more than the falcons that nest on a downtown hotel? All of these are now products of human choice, subject to our ambitious and imperfect management. What matters is not whether we deem a space natural or built, but the choices we make.

This is at once a liberating and humbling prospect. It is liberating and humbling, for it means that there are no places in the harbour or on the waterfront or in our cities that we should neglect because they have been "degraded" by the hand of human society. There are no spaces – whether perceived as natural or built – that we should not care about, and whose impact on human and non-human nature is not our collective concern. In making our choices, we can look back and reflect on both the achievements and limits of the visions that drove each generation, that motivated John Kerr, Thomas McQuesten, Gil Simmons, and many others. They all tried to create the city and society that they wanted. We can try to be as ambitious as they were. And we can try to do better. We can try to ensure that social power is better distributed, that our choices do not favour some residents over others. We can try to include a diversity of social visions and communities in our decision making. We can try to reflect on the impact of our choices on this and future generations, on diverse members of human society, and on non-human species. If history teaches us anything, it is that the choices we have to make are not easy and that their consequences are hard to predict or control. We will undoubtedly make mistakes. That should not stop us from trying to build a livable city. That should not stop us from trying to do what we think is right.

Notes

FOREWORD

1 John Terpstra, *Falling into Place* (Kentville, NS: Gaspereau Press, 2002), 11.
2 Quotes in this paragraph, drawn from Lady Simcoe's diary, are quoted in ibid., 28–29. See *The Diary of Mrs. John Graves Simcoe ...* (Toronto: Ontario Publishing Co., 1934).
3 The general history of Hamilton can be traced in John C. Weaver, *Hamilton: An Illustrated History* (Toronto: James Lorimer, 1982).
4 Barry Bluestone and Bennett Harrison, *The Deindustrialization of America* (New York: Basic Books, 1982); Steven High, *Industrial Sunset: The Making of North America's Rust Belt, 1969–1984* (Toronto: University of Toronto Press, 2003); Steven High and David W. Lewis, *Corporate Wasteland: The Landscape and Memory of Deindustrialization* (Toronto: Between the Lines Press, 2007).
5 "U.S. Steel Closing Steelmaking Operations at Hamilton Plant," *Toronto Star,* 29 October 2013, http://www.thestar.com/business/economy/2013/10/29/us_steel_to_close_hamilton_operations.html.
6 This and the following quote from Terpstra, *Falling into Place,* 217.
7 Gregory McIntosh, "Biography of George Washington Johnson," http://www.allmusic.com/artist/george-washington-johnson-mn0001674867/biography.
8 Michael J. Dear, John J. Drake, and Lloyd G. Reeds, eds., *Steel City: Hamilton and Region* (Toronto: University of Toronto Press, 1987).
9 Steve Arnold, "Hamilton's Steel Industry from Birth, to Boom and Beyond," *Hamilton Spectator,* 11 February 2012, http://www.thespec.com/news-story/2234571-hamilton-s-steel-industry-from-birth-to-boom-and-beyond/.
10 Terpstra, *Falling into Place,* 26–27, 30–31.
11 Ibid., 37.
12 Ibid., 16.
13 Ibid., 54.

14 Marvin Mikesell, "The Rise and Decline of 'Sequent Occupance': A Chapter in the History of American Geography," in *Geographies of the Mind: Essays in Historical Geography,* ed. David Lowenthal and Martyn J. Bowden (Oxford: Oxford University Press, 1976), 149–69; D. Whittlesey, "Sequent Occupance," *Annals of the Association of American Geographers* 19 (1929): 162–66.

15 Terpstra, *Falling into Place,* 52.

16 See "retrospective approach" (and also the somewhat allied "retrogressive approach") in Derek Gregory, Ron Johnston, Geraldine Pratt, Michael J. Watts, and Sarah Whatmore, eds., *Dictionary of Human Geography,* 5th ed. (Chichester: Wiley-Blackwell, 2009), 654.

17 Terpstra, *Falling into Place,* 53–54.

18 Philip L. Wagner, *Environments and Peoples* (Englewood Cliffs, NJ: Prentice-Hall, 1972), 49.

19 Terpstra, *Falling into Place,* 250.

20 Deborah Bowen, "Geographical Attachment," review of *Falling into Place,* by John Terpstra, *Canadian Literature* 183 (Winter 2004): 175–76.

21 Donald Worster, "Transformations of the Earth: Toward an Agroecological Perspective in History," *Journal of American History* 76, 4 (1990): 1091.

22 Here, their approach and emphases differ markedly from those reported in Michael B. Katz's *The People of Hamilton, Canada West: Family and Class in a Mid-19th-Century City* (Cambridge, MA: Harvard University Press, 1975), a much celebrated study in its time, which used multivariate quantitative analysis to explore issues of family and class, occupational differentiation and income levels, property holding and so on during the decade of the 1850s.

23 Carol Ann Sokoloff, email communication, 24 May 2015.

24 Carol Ann Sokoloff, "Denial," in Joe Blades, *Great Lakes Logia* (Fredericton, NB: Broken Jaw Press, 2001), 35–36.

25 For more on the Toronto waterfront, see Frances N. Mellen, "The Development of the Toronto Waterfront during the Railway Expansion Era: 1850–1912" (PhD diss., University of Toronto, 1976); Ted Wickson, *Reflections of Toronto Harbour* (Toronto: Toronto Port Authority, 2002); and Gene Desfor and Jennefer Laidley, eds., *Reshaping Toronto's Waterfront* (Toronto: University of Toronto Press, 2011). For the waterfront and other areas, see Richard White, *Urban Infrastructure and Urban Growth in the Toronto Region, 1950s to the 1990s* (Toronto: Neptis Foundation, 2003).

26 W.J. Keith, "A Sense of (Canadian) Place," review of *Falling into Place,* by John Terpstra, in *Books in Canada,* http://www.booksincanada.com/article_view.asp?id=3662. The quote that follows this superscript is also from this source. "Instant archaeology," as used here, might bear comparison with Michel Foucault's use of the term "archaeology" during the 1960s to describe his approach to examining the discursive traces and orders left by the past in order to write a history of the present.

27 Among the many observations worth more-than-passing attention in Terpstra's *Falling into Place,* I cannot skip by the following, knowing that it will resonate with all those who have a fascination for landscapes: *"What are your sources?* Mary asks, when my geo-sleuthing presents her with another find. She's a stickler. / A few books, some maps, I tell her. Looking. / When a landscape begins to inveigle itself into your consciousness, you assume it's you who's the initiator, coming and going, posing questions, nosing for answers. Later, as various pieces of its story have gathered and fallen into place, it can begin to seem as

though the place itself has been tipping its hand, playing prompter. Responding. The line that divides the two of you begins to waver" (101–2).

28 Terpstra, *Falling into Place*, 313.

INTRODUCTION

1 *Hamilton Spectator* (hereafter *Spectator*), 4 March 1865; Wendy Ratowski, "Kerr, John William," in *Dictionary of Hamilton Biography* (hereafter *DHB*), ed. T.M. Bailey (Hamilton: Dictionary of Hamilton Biography, 1991), 2:83–84; "Cahill, James," in *DHB*, ed. T.M. Bailey (Hamilton: Dictionary of Hamilton Biography, 1981), 1:41. Cahill's views regarding the waterfront persisted for many years. In 1920, John Taylor requested increased police protection for his building company's waterfront location, explaining, "It seems that anybody who wants to raise any kind of h – goes to the waterfront." "Waterfront of Hamilton No Man's Land," *Hamilton Times*, 1 October 1920.

2 This rough estimate of the bay's size in 1865, which aims to include its many inlets, is drawn from several historical maps and the historical records on infilling. Basing our calculations on recent topographic maps, we determined that the current area of the harbour is approximately 21.5 square kilometres, which means about 35 to 40 percent of what once was covered in water is now land. Natural Resources Canada, Centre for Topographic Information, *Hamilton-Burlington, Ontario,* 10th ed., Scale 1:50,000, Canada 1:50,000, 30M/5 (Ottawa: Canada Centre for Topographic Information, 1999). Gord Beck, map specialist in the Lloyd Reeds Map Collection, McMaster University, helped us in this and many other matters but should not be held responsible for our rough historical estimates.

3 Donald Worster, "Transformations of the Earth: Toward an Agroecological Perspective in History," *Journal of American History* 76, 4 (March 1990): 1091.

4 Most recently, Michael J. Doucet and John C. Weaver, *Housing the North American City* (Montreal and Kingston: McGill-Queen's University Press, 1991). Michael Katz's quantitative social history work focused on Hamilton as a window into the world of industrialization, family, and class formation in North America. Michael B. Katz, *The People of Hamilton, Canada West: Family and Class in a Mid-19th Century City* (Cambridge, MA: Harvard University Press, 1975); Michael Katz, Michael Doucet, and Mark J. Stern, *The Social Organization of Early Industrial Capitalism* (Cambridge, MA: Harvard University Press, 1982).

5 Alan MacEachern, "Foreword," in *Urban Explorations: Environmental Histories of the Toronto Region,* ed. L. Anders Sandberg et al. (Hamilton: Wilson Institute for Canadian History, 2013), vii.

6 Michèle Dagenais, *Montréal et l'eau: Une histoire environnementale* (Montreal: Boréal, 2011); Christopher Armstrong, Matthew Evenden, and H.V. Nelles, *The River Returns: An Environmental History of the Bow* (Montreal and Kingston: McGill-Queen's University Press, 2009). Stephen Bocking discusses some other Canadian work and introduces a special issue on urban environmental history in "The Nature of Cities: Perspectives in Canadian Urban Environmental History," *Urban History Review* 34, 1 (Autumn 2005): 3–8. A more recent collection and the first book on Canada in the University of Pittsburgh Press's urban environmental history series is Stéphane Castonguay and Michèle Dagenais, eds., *Metropolitan Natures: Environmental Histories of Montreal* (Pittsburgh: University of Pittsburgh Press, 2011).

7 Andrew Hurley, *Environmental Inequalities: Class, Race, and Industrial Pollution in Gary, Indiana, 1945–1980* (Chapel Hill: University of North Carolina Press, 1995); Michael Rawson

is attentive to the impact of class on ideas about nature, in *Eden on the Charles: The Making of Boston* (Cambridge, MA: Harvard University Press, 2010); and Harold Platt considers class, gender, and race, particularly in relation to "environmental" politics, in *Shock Cities: The Environmental Transformation and Reform of Manchester and Chicago* (Chicago: University of Chicago Press, 2005). Matthew Klingle offers an elegant environmental history and meditation on the urban environment that is consistently sensitive to class and race, in *Emerald City: An Environmental History of Seattle* (New Haven: Yale University Press, 2007).

8　Stephen Hardy, *How Boston Played: Sport, Recreation and Community* (Boston: Northeastern University Press, 1982); Robert A.J. McDonald, "'Holy Retreat' or 'Practical Breathing Spot'? Class Perceptions of Vancouver's Stanley Park, 1910–1913," *Canadian Historical Review* 65 (1984): 127–53; Sean Kheraj, *Inventing Stanley Park: An Environmental History* (Vancouver: UBC Press, 2013); Roy Rosenzweig and Elizabeth Blackmar, *The Park and the People: A History of Central Park* (Ithaca: Cornell University Press, 1992).

9　Alf Hornborg, "Introduction: Environmental History as Political Ecology," in *Rethinking Environmental History: World-System History and Global Environmental Change,* ed. Alf Hornborg, John R. McNeill, and Joan Martinez-Alier (Lanham: AltaMira Press, 2007), 3.

10　H.R. Haines et al., "The Point of Popularity: A Summary of 10,000 Years of Human Activity at the Princess Point Promontory, Cootes Paradise Marsh, Hamilton, Ontario," *Canadian Journal of Archaeology* 35, 2 (2011): 232–57; D.G. Smith and G. Crawford, "Recent Developments in the Archaeology of the Princess Point Complex in Southern Ontario," *Canadian Journal of Archaeology/Journal canadien d'archéologie* 21, 1 (1997): 9–32; Mary Jackes, "The Mid Seventeenth Century Collapse of Iroquoian Ontario: Examining the Last Burial Place of the Neutral Nation," in *9e: journées d'anthropologie de Valbonne: vers une anthropologie des catastrophes,* ed. Luc Buchet et al. (Valbonne: CEPAM, 2008), 347–73; John R. Triggs, "The Mississauga at the Head of the Lake: Examining Responses to Cultural Upheaval at the Close of the Fur Trade," *Northeast Historical Archaeology* 33, 1 (2004): 153–76; Michael F. McAllister, "A Very Pretty Object: The Socially Constructed Landscape of Burlington Heights, 1780–1815" (master's thesis, McMaster University, 2002), also discusses early European settlement.

11　To paraphrase historian and scholar James Green, *Taking History to Heart: The Power of the Past in Social Movements* (Amherst: University of Massachusetts Press, 2000), 11.

CHAPTER 1: CIVILIZING NATURE

1　"Sketches by Camo: City of Hamilton and Burlington Bay," *Hamilton Spectator* (hereafter *Spectator*), 20 July 1846, reprinted in *Spectator*, 5 June 1946.

2　"Winter Races," *Spectator*, 3 February 1847.

3　*An Act to Alter and Amend the Act Incorporating the Town of Hamilton, and to Erect the same into a City,* 1846, 9 Vic. c. 73, s. 3.

4　For an early analysis of winds and drift currents, as well as a geological description of the bay, including its barrier beach (Beach Strip), see A.W.G. Wilson, "Shoreline Studies on Lakes Ontario and Erie," *Bulletin of the Geological Society of America* 19 (1908): 471–500.

5　For example, a 1791 map referred to the bay as Lake Geneva, and *Plan of Burlington Bay on Lake Ontario* (1816) differentiates between Burlington Lake (the bay itself) and Burlington Bay, the area east of the Beach Strip. National Map Collection, 21678, Library and Archives Canada (LAC), Ottawa. Both maps, and others, show the narrow natural channel fairly close to the north shore. Robert Malcolmson discusses the channel in examining the myth of the Burlington Races during the War of 1812, in "What Really Happened? De-Bunking the Burlington Bay Sandbar Legend," 1999, http://www.warof1812. ca/burlingn.htm.

6 John C. Weaver, *Hamilton: An Illustrated History* (Toronto: James Lorimer, 1982), 42–45.

7 R. Louis Gentilcore, "The Beginnings: Hamilton in the Nineteenth Century," in *Steel City: Hamilton and Region*, ed. M.J. Dear, J.J. Drake, and L.G. Reeds (Toronto: University of Toronto Press, 1987), 106–7; "Hamilton's Railway Network: Rail Is Changing Our City," *Spectator*, 5 March 2013.

8 John Terpstra, *Falling into Place* (Kentville, NS: Gaspereau Press, 2002), 132–33.

9 "Workshops of the Great Western Railway, Hamilton," *Canadian Illustrated News*, 14 February 1863, 162.

10 *Plan of the Town of Hamilton, District of Gore, 1842*, Local History and Archives Department, Hamilton Public Library.

11 A map and descriptive history of waterlots can be found in "Map Submitted by Railways and Canals to Regional Land Surveyor, Canadian National Railways," 15 March 1928, Railways and Canals Series AI2, RG 43, vol. 235, file 1330, LAC. It is likely that, as Thomas McIlwraith shows in the case of Toronto, material from levelling the nearby shoreline property filled the waterlots. Thomas McIlwraith, "Digging Out and Filling In: Making Land on the Toronto Waterfront in the 1850s," *Urban History Review* 20, 1 (1991): 15–33.

12 Ken Cruikshank, *Close Ties: Railways, Government and the Board of Railway Commissioners, 1851–1933* (Montreal and Kingston: McGill-Queen's University Press, 1991), 22.

13 Weaver, *Hamilton*, 79–128; R.D. Roberts, "The Changing Patterns in Distribution and Composition of Manufacturing Activity in Hamilton between 1867 and 1921" (master's thesis, McMaster University, 1961); Gentilcore, "The Beginnings," 108–11; Bryan D. Palmer, *A Culture in Conflict: Skilled Workers and Industrial Capitalism in Hamilton, Ontario, 1860–1914* (Montreal and Kingston: McGill-Queen's University Press, 1979), 4–18.

14 H.V. Nelles, "Keefer, Thomas Coltrin," *Dictionary of Canadian Biography Online*, http://www.biographi.ca/en/bio/keefer_thomas_coltrin_14E.html.

15 "Report from the Board of Health on the Means of Preventing the Spread of Cholera Should It Reach the City," 11 June 1849; "Emigration Committee Report," 10 December 1849, 104; "Report of Cholera Being in the City," 4 September 1854; "Report of Fire and Water," 29 December 1854, 27, all in Hamilton City Council Minutes (hereafter HCCM), Local History and Archives Department, Hamilton Public Library, Hamilton; see also Geoffrey Bilson, *A Darkened House: Cholera in Nineteenth Century Canada* (Toronto: University of Toronto Press, 1980), 129, 134, 200; Charles M. Godfrey, *The Cholera Epidemics in Upper Canada, 1832–66* (Toronto: Seacombe House, 1968), 33, 47.

16 Edwin Chadwick, *Report on the Sanitary Condition of the Labouring Population of Great Britain*, ed. M.W. Flinn (Edinburgh: University Press, 1965); Martin Melosi, *The Sanitary City: Urban Infrastructure in America from Colonial Times to the Present* (Baltimore: Johns Hopkins University Press, 2000), 43–72; Christopher Hamlin, *A Science of Impurity: Water Analysis in Nineteenth-Century Britain* (Berkeley: University of California Press, 1990).

17 W. James and E.M. James, *A Sufficient Quantity of Pure and Wholesome Water: The Story of Hamilton's Old Pumphouse* (London: Phelps, 1978), 5–13.

18 W. Hodgins, "Report on Water Supply," *Spectator*, 19 August 1855; James and James, *A Sufficient Quantity*, 9–11.

19 *Specifications and Estimates of the Three Successful Competitors for Premiums Offered by the City Council, for the Best Mode of Supplying the City with Water* (Hamilton, 1855).

20 Thomas Keefer, *Report on the Supply of Water to the City of Hamilton* (Montreal, 1856), Canadian Institute for Historical Microreproductions (CIHM) 22575.

21 *Report of J.B. Jervis and Alfred W. Craven on a Supply of Water for the City of Hamilton* (Hamilton, 1857), CIHM 94671.

22 Robert Cellem, *Visit of His Royal Highness the Prince of Wales to the British North American Provinces and United States in the Year 1860* (Toronto: H. Rowsell, 1861), 324, CIHM 63688.

23 *Water Rates, Rules and Regulations* (Hamilton, 1859), CIHM 94683; James and James, *A Sufficient Quantity,* 14–25.

24 James and James, *A Sufficient Quantity,* 12–13.

25 Hamilton Board of Health Minutes (hereafter BOHM), 20 September 1886.

26 Ibid., 7 September 1886, 47. See, for example, BOHM, vol. 1: 20 September 1886, 48; 5 April 1887, 53; 5 October 1887, 54.

27 "Boating on the Bay," *Spectator,* 2 July 1888.

28 "Workshops of the Great Western Railway," 162–63.

29 "Races on the Bay," *Spectator,* 4 February 1870; "Hamilton Races," *Spectator,* 17 February 1870.

30 See, for example, "Racing on the Bay," *Spectator,* 16 January 1875; "Race on the Bay," *Spectator,* 13 February 1875.

31 On winter carnivals, sport, and respectability, see Gillian Poulter, "'Our Winter Sports': The Montreal Winter Carnivals," in Gillian Poulter, *Becoming Native in a Foreign Land: Sport, Visual Culture, and Identity in Montreal* (Vancouver: UBC Press, 2009), 143–206; Frank Abbott, "Cold Cash and Ice Palaces: The Quebec Winter Carnival of 1894," *Canadian Historical Review* 69, 2 (June 1988): 167–202; Don Morrow, "Frozen Festivals: Ceremony and the Carnival in Montreal Winter Carnivals, 1883–1889," *Sport History Review* 27, 2 (November 1996): 173–90.

32 "Trotting," *Spectator,* 23 February 1881, 9, 15; "Hamilton Winter Races," *Spectator,* 24 February 1881; "Our Winter Carnival," *Spectator,* 8 January 1887; "Sporting News: Winter Races," *Spectator,* 11 February 1888; "The Races on the Bay," *Spectator,* 9 February 1888.

33 "Burlington Boat Club," *Spectator,* 29 May 1865.

34 For the yacht club founded by Edward Zealand, see "Regatta," *Spectator,* 15 October 1857; "Zealand, Edward," in *Dictionary of Hamilton Biography* (hereafter *DHB*), ed. T.M. Bailey (Hamilton: Dictionary of Hamilton Biography, 1981), 1:218. On indecent bathing and regulations, see "Bathing in the Bay," *Spectator,* 16 July 1857; "City Council," *Spectator,* 21 July 1874.

35 "The Yacht Race," *Spectator,* 24 September 1870; "Regatta on the Bay," *Spectator,* 11 June 1870, speaks of sailing as a "manly pastime." See "Hamilton Regatta," *Spectator,* 13 October 1855; "Yacht Race," *Spectator,* 18 August 1865, which laments two entries for a race and notes that "yachting seems to be deplorably on the decline in Hamilton"; "The Yacht Races," *Spectator,* 13 July 1874, which notes with disappointment that only three yachts entered for a local race; "Inaugural Dinner," *Spectator,* 6 July 1875; "The Burlington Yacht Club," *Spectator,* 1 September 1875.

36 *Rules and Regulations of the Burlington Bay Boat Club* (Hamilton: Nicholas, McIntosh, 1854), sections 4, 5, 7, and 16, CIHM 51901; a different organization had this name by the 1860s, although a crew made up of Great Western employees was racing in 1865. "Rowing Match," *Spectator,* 26 July 1865.

37 "Hamilton Rowing Club," *Spectator,* 13 June 1870; "Rowing Club," *Spectator,* 17 June 1870; "Hamilton Rowing Club Regatta," advertisement, *Spectator,* 18 August 1870; "The Regatta," *Spectator,* 22 August 1870.

38 "Boat Race," *Spectator,* 1 May 1871; "Boat Race," *Spectator,* 8 May 1871.

39 *Spectator,* 23 September 1879, quoted in Palmer, *A Culture in Conflict,* 269n103; Robert S. Hunter, *Rowing in Canada since 1848* (Hamilton: Davis-Lisson, 1933); on amateurism, see Don Morrow, "A Case-Study in Amateur Conflict: The Athletic War in Canada, 1906–8," *British Journal of Sports History* 3, 2 (1986): 173–75; Alan Metcalfe, *Canada Learns to Play: The Emergence of Organized Sport, 1807–1914* (Toronto: McClelland and Stewart, 1987), 99–104.

40 *Constitution and Bylaws of the Canadian Association of Amateur Oarsmen* (Toronto: Dominions Best, 1890), 20, CIHM 00422.

41 Captain Thomas Blackwell, "The Rowing Clubs of Canada, Part II," *Outing,* June 1891, 246.

42 "Nautilus Rowing Club," *Spectator,* 8 June 1881.

43 "The Oar," *Spectator,* 15 July 1885; "Rowing," *Spectator,* 25 July 1885; "The Big Regatta," *Spectator,* 5 August 1885; "Unenterprising and Unwise," and "Battle of the Oars," *Spectator,* 6 August 1885; "The CAAO," *Spectator,* 1 August 1885.

44 "Pleasure Seeking," *Spectator,* 28 June 1860; "Burlington Beach Garden Pleasure Grounds," *Spectator,* 19 May 1858; "Recreation," *Spectator,* 18 July 1859. See many references to recreation on the bay in the Diaries of Captain Thompson (hereafter Thompson Diaries), 1854–86, 26 August 1858, 15 June 1859, 14 August 1861, 17 June 1864, 1 July and 10 August 1868, 25 August 1869, 29 July 1870, and 15 August 1871, Brant Museum, Burlington.

45 "The Bay," *Spectator,* 24 May 1870; "Pic-Nic's To-day," *Spectator,* 2 July 1870; "Rock Bay," *Spectator,* 1 August 1870; "The Battery Excursion," *Spectator,* 11 August 1870; "Typographical Excursion," *Spectator,* 14 September 1871; "Centenary Sabbath School Picnic," *Spectator,* 29 July 1871; "Excursion," *Spectator,* 28 August 1871; "The Ocean House," *Spectator,* 22 May 1880; "Oaklands," *Spectator,* 7 July 1880; "Yesterday's Excursion," *Spectator,* 24 August 1880; "Row at Rock Bay," *Spectator,* 30 August 1880; see also John James Halcrow, "Burlington Bay as I Remember It," *Wentworth Bygones* 9 (1971): 57–58; and Claire Emory Machan, *From Pathway to Skyway Revisited: The Story of Burlington* (Burlington: Burlington Historical Society, 1997), 132–33, 137.

46 "The Beach" and "The Beach" (sketch), *Canadian Illustrated News,* 12 December 1863, 37, 40.

47 "Burlington Beach Garden Pleasure Grounds," *Spectator,* 19 May 1858; "The Civic Holiday: The Beach and Oaklands," *Spectator,* 3 August 1865; "Pic-Nic," *Spectator,* 29 June 1870, 1 July 1870; "Excursion," *Spectator,* 16 October 1871. On the beginnings of the *Victoria,* see "Steam Ferry Boat for Burlington Bay," *Spectator,* 5 May 1857; "The Steam Ferry Boat," *Spectator,* 18 May 1857; "Untitled: *Victoria,*" *Spectator,* 15 October 1857, which speculated on the increased value of north shore properties; "Her Majesty's Birthday," *Spectator,* 25 May 1880; "Oaklands," *Spectator,* 7 July 1880.

48 See Ken Cruikshank and Nancy B. Bouchier, "'The Heritage of the People Closed against Them': Class, Environment, and the Shaping of Burlington Beach, 1870s–1980s," *Urban History Review* 30, 1 (October 2001): 40–55; and Dorothy Turcotte, *The Sand Strip: Burlington/Hamilton Beaches* (St. Catharines: Stonehouse, 1987).

49 "The Beach History: How Burlington Beach Became Tyrannical," *Burlington Gazette,* 13 April 1899.

50 Ibid.

51 On the leasing of the beach land, and the creation of a standing committee to oversee the planning and surveying of parks lots on the Beach Strip, see HCCM, 23 November 1874, 797; 12 April 1875, 777; and 7 June 1875, 805.

52 Thompson Diaries, 27 May and 1 June 1874.

53 "Beach Trains," *Spectator*, 11 July 1881.

54 "The Beach History," *Burlington Gazette*, 13 April 1899; Thompson Diaries, 2 July 1874.

55 "Campers at the Beach," *Hamilton Herald* (hereafter *Herald*), 10 August 1892. Perhaps this is the same group of tents that McCowell, Pikor, and Cain identified from an August 1888 *Spectator* article titled "Canvas City at the Beach: Camping at the Beach Has Attained Unprecedented Popularity This Season – Over 20 Large Wigwams Decorate the Waterfront." See Lewis D. McCowell, Joan L. Pikor, and Winsome M. Cain, *Hamilton Beach in Retrospect* (Hamilton: Hamilton Beach Alternate Community and History Project, 1981), 18; about elite camping culture, see Jessica Dunkin, "Canoes and Canvas: The Social and Spatial Politics of Sport/Leisure in Late Nineteenth-Century North America" (PhD diss.: Carleton University, 2012).

56 Thirty-one of the names listed in the paper have been record-linked to the *City of Hamilton Directory, 1893–4* (Hamilton: Griffin and Kinder, 1893). They include lawyers, the president of the local gas company and its foreman, grocers, merchants, the manager of a local newspaper, bookkeepers, accountants, and others engaged in non-manual occupations. Seven campers come from families listed in *The Toronto, Hamilton and London Society Blue Book: A Social Directory, Edition for 1900* (Toronto: William Tyrrell, 1900).

57 Colin Crozier, "Balfour, St. Clair," and William Newbigging, "Southam, William," in *DHB*, ed. T.M. Bailey (Hamilton: Dictionary of Hamilton Biography, 1991), 2:4–5, 2:146–51.

58 Saltfleet Township, *Assessment Rolls* (1890); "Who Is Over at the Beach," *Spectator*, 26 June 1895. Just south of the canal, the average value of a tenth of a hectare was seven hundred dollars.

59 *The Society Blue Book of Toronto, Hamilton and London Society* (Toronto: William Tyrrell, 1906).

60 "Who Is Over at the Beach?"; record linked to *The Society Blue Book*, city directories, and Census of Canada, 1881, District 149, and 1891, District 72, Hamilton (microfilm).

61 John R. Stilgoe, *Borderland: Origins of the American Suburb, 1820–1939* (New Haven: Yale University Press, 1988). This book devotes a number of chapters to the summer residence ideal. See also Roy I. Wolfe, "The Summer Resorts of Ontario in the Nineteenth Century," *Ontario History* 54 (1962): 149–60. In his useful overview of suburban Canada, Larry McCann briefly mentions the "seasonal migration of wealthy local residents" to outlying areas. Larry McCann, "Suburbs of Desire: The Suburban Landscape of Canadian Cities, c. 1900–1950," in *Changing Suburbs: Foundation, Form and Function*, ed. Richard Harris and Peter J. Larkham (London: E & FN Spon, 1999), 114.

62 Thomas Trotter, quoted in Stilgoe, *Borderland*, 42.

63 "Summer at the Beach," *Herald*, 26 June 1895.

64 "Concerning the Beach," *Herald*, 1 March 1895.

65 "The Local Legislators," *Spectator*, 4 August and 1 September 1885; "The Beach," *Spectator*, 17 June 1880; "Burlington Beach," *Spectator*, 7 May 1881.

66 This building was located on the south side of the canal reserve, an area where the Department of Interior prohibited development. See Staunton and Franks, *Plan of Burlington*

Beach Situate in the Counties of Halton and Wentworth in the Province of Ontario, 1877, Lloyd Reeds Map Collection, McMaster University.

67 "The Ocean House Is No More," *Spectator,* 20 July 1895; Turcotte, *The Sand Strip,* 21–22; Brian Henley, *The Grand Old Buildings of Hamilton* (Hamilton: Spectator, 1994), 47–49; Machan, *From Pathway to Skyway Revisited,* 44–45.

68 The prefix "Royal," granted to only three clubs in Canada, presented decided social advantages for members visiting distant places. On the history of the RHYC, see Harry L. Penny, *One Hundred Years and Still Sailing: A History of Hamilton Yachts, Yachtsmen, and Yachting, 1888 to 1988: Centennial Yearbook* (Hamilton: Royal Hamilton Yacht Club, 1988).

69 "Summer at the Beach," *Herald,* 26 June 1895. On the social tone of the area in this period, see Turcotte, *The Sand Strip,* 21–27; Brian Henley, "In 1883, the Beach Strip Was Widely Famous," *Spectator,* 26 July 1997; McCowell, Pikor, and Cain, *Hamilton Beach in Retrospect,* 16–20.

70 "Of Interest to Beach Residents: Old Buildings to Be Removed from the Canal Reserve," *Spectator,* 18 April 1895; "Improvements at the Beach: Buildings to Be Removed by the Interior Department," *Spectator,* 9 May 1895; "Clearing the Canal Reserve: Buildings Must Be Removed by May 18," *Spectator,* 10 May 1895. For a diagram of building locations around the southern canal piers, see Hamilton City Engineers Office, *Plan Showing Proposed Changes at Burlington Beach,* 2 April 1897; see also E. Barrow, *Map Showing Lots on North Side of Canal,* 5 September 1892, both in Lloyd Reeds Map Collection, McMaster University. The Barrow map identifies a tract of reserved land on the bayside just north of the canal piers, which was to be kept undeveloped by the city corporation.

71 "Bathing in the Canal: Saltfleet Council to Be Asked to Stop This Objectionable Practice," *Spectator,* 15 June 1895.

72 "More Land for the City: Squatters Compelled to Give Up Property on the Beach," *Spectator,* 26 April 1895.

73 "Settling the Beach Claims: The Williams Case before Hon. A.S. Hardy at Toronto," *Spectator,* 12 February 1895; "Another Beach Dispute," *Spectator,* 18 February 1895; "More Land for the City: Squatters Compelled"; "Other Cases Settled: More Beach Property Awarded to the City by Commissioner Hardy," *Spectator,* 3 May 1895; "Acreage of the Beach," *Spectator,* 7 August 1895.

74 "Rustic," letter to editor, "The City and the Beach," *Spectator,* 8 October 1895 (emphasis added).

CHAPTER 2: CONSERVING NATURE

1 Diaries of John William Kerr (hereafter KD), 14 January 1866, 2:1 (microfilm), Local History and Archives Department, Hamilton Public Library, Hamilton (originals are in the Queen's University Archives, John William Kerr fonds, F01041). Found guilty, Barney was charged five dollars and costs by the local police magistrate; his identity emerged at trial and has been linked to a city directory.

2 KD, Kerr to commissioner of Crown lands (hereafter CCL), 15 January 1866, 2:1.

3 KD, 19 January 1866, 2:1.

4 KD, Kerr to CCL, 13 February 1865, 1:1.

5 Wendy Ratowski, "Kerr, John William," in *Dictionary of Hamilton Biography* (hereafter *DHB*), ed. T.M. Bailey (Hamilton: Dictionary of Hamilton Biography, 1991), 2:83–84.

6 See Richard P. Manning, "Recreating Man: Hunting and Angling in Victorian Canada" (master's thesis, Carleton University, 1994); Thomas L. Altherr, "The American Hunter-Naturalist and the Development of the Code of Sportsmanship," *Journal of Sport History* 5, 1 (Spring 1978): 7–22; Tina Loo, *States of Nature: Conserving Canada's Wildlife in the Twentieth Century* (Vancouver: UBC Press, 2006).

7 Mary Quayle Innis, ed., *Mrs. Simcoe's Diary* (Toronto: Macmillan, 1983), 182.

8 Bill Parenteau, "Care, Control and Supervision: Native People in the Canadian Atlantic Salmon Fishery, 1867–1900," *Canadian Historical Review* 79, 1 (1998): 1–35. For descriptions of spear fishing in the writings of early European explorers, see Edwin C. Guillet, *Pioneer Days in Upper Canada* (Toronto: University of Toronto Press, 1979), 109–18. A nineteenth-century account of spear fishing in the region is found in Paul Kane, *Wanderings of an Artist among the Indians of North America* (Toronto: Radisson, 1925), 21–22.

9 "Beach Once Haven for Smugglers," *Hamilton Spectator* (hereafter *Spectator*), 15 July 1946, cites the 1844 observations of Peter Carroll, whose Rock Bay mansion on the north shore afforded a panoramic view of the Beach Strip. He had recommended very early on that some arrangement should be made to facilitate the surveying and formal development of the area. A land surveyor and road builder, Carroll would become a highly successful fruit farmer, director of the Great Western Railway, and board member of the Gore Bank. His name is memorialized in Carroll's Point, a landmark that lies across the water from the Desjardins Canal on the bayside. See "Carroll, Peter," in *DHB*, 2:42–43; also William F. Johns, "The Historical Evolution of Hamilton Beach," *Wentworth Bygones* 2 (1960): 34 (originally published 1945).

10 "The Fishery Act and the Fishermen at the Beach," *Spectator,* 15 November 1858; "Report of Superintendent of Fisheries," 31 December 1859, United Province of Canada, *Sessional Papers,* 1860, no. 12; Canada West Census, 1861, Hamilton (microfilm), and Canada Census, 1871, District 24, Hamilton (microfilm).

11 Kerr's diaries provide a good description of the Beach Strip households in this period, the location of fishing stations, and the existence of market gardens on the beach. KD, Kerr to Robert Chisholm, chairman of the Hamilton Finance Committee, 1 August 1874, 6:1. One early account of the community comments on this deeply rooted connection to fishing: "The pioneer story of the Beach is closely bound up with the story of fishing, for almost all of the early permanent residents were enthusiastic fishermen. Not all made fishing a source of revenue, but some of the most colourful figures of the Sandstrip were actively engaged in the selling of their catch." See *The History of Hamilton Beach* (Hamilton: Beach Bungalow School, 1943), 5.

12 "Hamilton Beach Scene of Extensive Fishing," *Spectator,* 5 September 1919. From 1871 to 1901, manuscript census data for the Beach Strip (Saltfleet Township) trace this decline: in 1871, 51 percent (forty-five people) of the Beach Strip community was employed in fishing and farming; by 1901, the proportion had dropped to 33 percent (ninety people).

13 *An Act for the better preservation of the Herring fishery at the Outlet of Burlington Bay,* Statutes of Upper Canada, 1823, 4 Geo. IV, c. 37; *An Act for the preservation of the fishery within Burlington Bay,* Statutes of Upper Canada, 1836, 6 Will. IV, c. 15. For a general overview of fishing regulations, see A.B. McCullough, *The Commercial Fishery of the Canadian Great Lakes* (Ottawa: Ministry of Supply and Services, 1989).

14 "Report of Ontario Fishery Commission, 1893," Ontario, *Sessional Papers* (hereafter *OSP*), 1893, no. 10c; see also T.H. Whillans, "Fish Community Transformation in Three Bays within the Lower Great Lakes" (master's thesis, University of Toronto, 1977); T.H. Whillans,

"Historic Transformations of Fish Communities in Three Great Lakes Bays," *Journal of Great Lakes Research* 5, 2 (1979): 195–215.

15 "Report of Ontario Fishery Commission, 1893"; Joseph E. Taylor, *Making Salmon: An Environmental History of the Northwest Fisheries Crisis* (Seattle: University of Washington Press, 1999). For the mid-twentieth-century scientific debate over the relative role of overfishing, pollution, and other environmental changes in the decline of Great Lakes fish stocks, see Frank N. Egerton et al., "Overfishing or Pollution: Case History of a Controversy on the Great Lakes," Great Lakes Fishery Commission Report 41 (Ann Arbor: Great Lakes Fishery Commission, 1985). On the Great Lakes fishery generally, see Margaret Beattie Bogue, *Fishing the Great Lakes: An Environmental History, 1783–1933* (Madison: University of Wisconsin Press, 2000).

16 Kevin Wamsley, "Legislation and Leisure in 19th Century Canada" (PhD diss., University of Alberta, 1992), 75–77. For example, the "proper" season for salmon fishing was established in 1810 by *An Act for the Preservation of Salmon,* Statutes of Upper Canada, 1807, 47 Geo. III, c. 12, and 1810, 50 Geo. III, c. 3. The prohibitions on Sunday hunting were set in *An Act to Amend ... An Act for the preservation of Deer within this Province and to extend the provisions of the same; and to prohibit Hunting and Shooting on the Lord's Day,* Statutes of Upper Canada, 1839, 2 Vic., c. 7.

17 On related developments, see McCullough, *The Commercial Fishery,* 19–21; Parenteau "Care, Control and Supervision"; Clare Brown, "Management of the New Brunswick Sport Fishery during the 19th Century," *Proceedings of the 5th Canadian Symposium on the History of Sport and Physical Education* (Toronto: School of Physical and Health Education, University of Toronto, 1982), 58–64; and Claire Guyer, "Game Protection in New Brunswick, 1889–1971," *Proceedings of the 5th Canadian Symposium on the History of Sport and Physical Education* (Toronto: School of Physical and Health Education, University of Toronto, 1982), 65–75.

18 Wamsley, "Legislation and Leisure," 129–31.

19 *Fisheries Act,* Statutes of the Province of Canada, 1857, 20 Vic., c. 21.

20 *Fisheries Act,* Statutes of the Province of Canada, 1858, 22 Vic., c. 86.

21 *Fisheries Act,* Statutes of Upper Canada, 1836, 6 Will. IV, c. 15.

22 *Fisheries Act,* 1858.

23 KD, Minutes of the Wentworth Society for the Protection of Game and Fish (hereafter MWSPGF), 19 June and 3 July 1860, 2:5; "Wentworth Society for the Protection of Game and Fish," *Spectator,* 28 June 1860.

24 D.R. Beer, "MacNab, Sir Allan Napier," in *DHB,* ed. T.M. Bailey (Hamilton: Dictionary of Hamilton Biography, 1981), 1:135–44.

25 The three included a shoemaker, a stone mason, and a prominent local builder – all members of labour's aristocracy. List of members sent notice of meeting, KD, 28 June 1862, 2:5; *City of Hamilton Directory* (Hamilton: W.A. Sheperd, 1853, 1856); *Hutchinson's Hamilton Directory* (Hamilton: J. Eastwood, 1862); *Sutherland's City of Hamilton and County of Wentworth Directory* (Hamilton: Sutherland, 1866–68); *DHB* 1 and 2. Professional occupations of society members included engineer and lawyer; business occupations included newspaper proprietor, railway entrepreneur, and bank manager; government employment included provincial surveyor and coroner; and clerical employment included Great Western Railway clerks, bank clerks, and store clerks.

26 Christopher J. Anstead, "Fraternalism in Victorian Ontario: Secret Societies and Cultural Hegemony" (PhD diss., University of Western Ontario, 1992).

27 More generally, see the arguments in Nancy B. Bouchier, *For the Love of the Game: Amateur Sport in Small-Town Ontario, 1838–1895* (Montreal and Kingston: McGill-Queen's University Press, 2003); Kevin B. Wamsley, "Good Clean Sport and a Deer Apiece: Game Legislation and State Formation in Nineteenth Century Canada," *Canadian Journal of History of Sport* 25, 2 (December 1994): 1–20; and Peter Bailey, *Leisure and Class in Victorian England* (Toronto: University of Toronto Press, 1978).

28 KD, MWSPGF, 3 July 1860, 2:5.

29 On state reliance on fish and game clubs, see Wamsley, "Legislation and Leisure," 229.

30 KD, MWSPGF, 19 and 27 June 1860; 3 July 1860, 2:5.

31 Ibid., 3 July 1860, 8 March 1861, 2:5.

32 Ibid., 8 and 9 March 1861, 2:5.

33 Ibid., 8 March 1861, 2:5.

34 *An Act to Amend ... For the better regulation of Fishing and protection of Fisheries*, Statutes of the Province of Canada, 1865, 29 Vic., c. 11.

35 KD, Robert B. Kerr, "Biographical Introduction."

36 KD, Kerr to CCL, 3 February 1865, 1:1.

37 "Report of Ontario Fishery Commission, 1893," testimony of Frederick Corey, 321–23.

38 KD, Kerr to CCL, 15 January 1866, 2:1, see KD, Kerr to CCL, 13 February 1865, 1:1, 1 July 1865, 1:4, 23 March 1866, 2:2.

39 For fishing-related literature on the phenomenon of rational recreation, see Manning, "Recreating Man"; John F. Reiger, *American Sportsmen and the Origins of Conservation* (Oklahoma: University of Oklahoma Press, 1986); and Altherr, "The American Hunter-Naturalist." On rational recreation generally, see Bailey, *Leisure and Class;* and Gerald Redmond, "Some Aspects of Organized Sport and Leisure in Nineteenth Century Canada," in *Sports in Canada: Historical Readings,* ed. Morris Mott (Toronto: Copp Clark Pitman, 1989), 81–106.

40 Peter Bartrip, "Food for the Body and Food for the Mind: The Regulation of Freshwater Fisheries in the 1870s," *Victorian Studies* 28, 2 (Winter 1985): 297–98.

41 John Lowerson, "Izaak Walton: Father of a Dream," *History Today,* December 1983, 28–32.

42 KD, Kerr to CCL, 3 February 1865, 1:1. For an analysis of the class dimensions of angling, see Manning, "Recreating Man," 117–30.

43 Anstead, "Fraternalism in Victorian Ontario."

44 On the use of sports and recreation to counter urban ills and moral disorder, see Steven A. Reiss, *City Games: The Evolution of American Urban Society and the Rise of Sports* (Champaign: University of Illinois Press, 1989); and Paul S. Boyer, *Urban Masses and Moral Order in America, 1820–1920* (Cambridge, MA: Harvard University Press, 1978).

45 "Go Fishing," *Spectator,* 18 August 1886.

46 Although the views of Kerr and others were decidedly middle class, they were not shared by all members of this class. For a fine discussion of intra-class differences in leisure consumption, see Lynne Marks, *Revivals and Roller Rinks: Religion, Leisure, and Identity in Late Nineteenth Century Small-Town Ontario* (Toronto: University of Toronto Press, 1996).

47 See, for example, KD, 5, 6, 9, 10, 13, 14, and 21 January 1865, 9, 13, 15, and 18 February 1865, 1:1; "Raiders on the Bay," *Spectator,* 11 January 1865; "Raid on Fisherman," *Spectator,* 18 January 1865; "Fish Case," *Spectator,* 20 February 1865; "Mr Inspector Kerr Seems to Be Busy among the Poachers," *Spectator,* 20 February 1865.

48 Journal of Reverend Patrick Bell, 1833–37, 2:48–60, MG 24 H 16, Library and Archives Canada, Ottawa.

49 "Report of the Ontario Fishery Commission, 1893," testimony of Jonathan Corey, 313–14. A local fish dealer told the Ontario Fishery Commission that winter was really the "only season fish is any good in the bay." Ibid., testimony of John David, 319.

50 "Report of the Ontario Game and Fish Commission," 74–76, *OSP,* 1912, no. 52. This two-year commission investigated all matters relating to fish in the province, including the condition of the fisheries, the advisability of establishing provincial fish hatcheries, issues related to public parks and tourist sportsmen, and the management of provincial government offices related to game and fish. Although most of the witnesses mentioned and expressed support for spearing during the earlier hearings of the 1893 Ontario Fishery Commission, the most extensive description of the fishery is the testimony of Jonathan Corey in the "Report of the Ontario Fishery Commission, 1893," 313–14, and several newspaper articles, which are striking in their condescension toward the fishers. "The Idle Spectator," *Spectator,* 18 February 1884; "Spearing through the Ice," *Spectator,* 14 February 1895.

51 KD, Kerr to CCL, 23 January 1865, 1:1.

52 KD, 3 February 1865, 1:1.

53 For examples of other threats, see KD, 4 December 1867, 3:5; KD, Kerr to minister of marine and fisheries (hereafter MMF), 19 April and 14 May 1870, 4:8, 29 May 1876, 7:1. Kerr also believed that the workshop of a man who assisted him in prosecutions was set on fire by a fisher. KD, Kerr to CCL, 5 May 1866, 2:3. Such sabotage over the issue of Sunday fishing may have been behind Kerr's experience of 22 January 1871, which he recorded in his diary: "On Bay having heard persons were out spearing fish, and breaking the Sabbath – did not find a single person out, got into the water at Harvey point, the ice was cracked, and the mare went down plunged out [sic] again."

54 KD, Kerr to CCL, 21 and 23 January 1865, 16 June 1865, 1:4 (Kerr fined $7.50 for demolishing spearing boxes), 8 September 1865, 1:5 (Kerr arrested and fined $28.95).

55 KD, Kerr to CCL, 21 January 1865, 1:1.

56 Ibid., 4 February 1865, 1:1. Section 22 of the Fisheries Act gave stipendiary magistrates the explicit power to issue search warrants and convict for infractions related to the legislation, permitted prosecutions in multiple counties, and relieved fishery officers of being liable for trespass. *Fisheries Act,* Statutes of the Province of Canada, 1865, 29 Vic., c. 86, s. 22.

57 KD, Kerr to CCL, 23 January and 13 February 1865, 1:1.

58 Ibid., 26 January and 8 February 1866, 1:3.

59 Widespread support is evident in the January 1868 petition for permission to continue winter spearing, signed by five hundred local residents, including both members of Parliament, the mayor, and several city councillors. KD, Kerr to MMF, 1 January 1868, 3:5.

60 See, for example, KD, Kerr to MMF, 26 August 1868, 4; 8 September 1868, 4:2; KD, Kerr to CCL, 28 January 1882, 1:1; KD, Kerr to S.P. Bauset, 31 November 1883, 11:40; KD, Kerr to deputy minister, 13 November 1886, 14:7.

61 KD, Kerr to MMF, 8 September 1868, 4:2; for an example of Kerr's earlier prosecution of fall spearing, see "Fishing with Spears Contrary to Act," *Spectator,* 7 December 1865; and "More Proceedings under the Fisheries Act," *Spectator,* 8 December 1865.

62 KD, Kerr to MMF, 2 November 1869, 4:6.

63 Ibid., 8 January 1874, 6:6, 7 November 1874, 6:13, 19 December 1874, 6:14, 21 November 1879, 8:9; KD, Kerr to Fisheries Overseers Office, 15 October 1881, 10:9; KD, Kerr to W.F. Whitaker, Commission of Fisheries, 16 October 1882, 10:34, 19 December 1882, 11:5; KD,

Kerr to deputy minister, 27 October 1884, 12:25; 3 November 1885, 13:20; 13 November 1886, 14:7.

64 KD, Kerr to CCL, 8 March 1867, 3:2.

65 KD, Kerr to MMF, 6 February 1868, 3:6, 4 April 1868, 3:7, 6 February 1869, 4:3, 12 February 1870, 4:7.

66 Ibid., 29 April 1870, 4:8; "Charlton, Benjamin Ernest," in *DHB*, 1:48.

67 See a summary of the conflict during the mid-1870s, in "Burlington Bay and Dundas Marsh," newspaper clipping, 1876, KD, 6:21.

68 Statutes of the Province of Canada, 1865, 29 Vic., c. 81, s. 18, "Injuries to Fishing Grounds and Pollution of Rivers."

69 "Williams, James Miller," in *DHB*, 1:211–12.

70 KD, Kerr to MMF, 17 May 1870, 4:8, 17 April and 14 June 1871, 5:4–5.

71 KD, 21 and 30 May 1873, 4 June 1873, 6:3, 7 July 1873, 6:4; KD, Kerr to MMF, 18 July 1873, 6:4, 26 October 1876, 7:3, 13 March 1877, 7:4.

72 This is now known as Spencer's Creek; Kerr called it both Dundas and Morden's Creek.

73 KD, Kerr to MMF, 14 September 1877 (overall summary of case and investigations), 17, 28, and 30 August 1877, 7:7–8.

74 Ibid., 14 September 1877, 7:8. For the earlier prosecution of tanneries in Dundas, see ibid., 26, and 29 September 1876, 7:2.

75 Ibid., 29 September 1877, 7:8.

76 KD, Kerr to W.F. Whitaker, Commission of Fisheries, 2 and 15 May 1882, 10:25; KD, Martin Elliott to Kerr, 18 May 1882, 10:25–26.

77 KD, Kerr to S.P. Bauset, 20 April 1886, 13:35; KD, Kerr to S.P. Bauset, 6 March 1888, 15:17.

78 KD, Kerr to W.F. Whitaker, 27 March 1883, 11:14; KD, Kerr to S.P. Bauset, 26 and 28 November 1883, 11:39; KD, Kerr to S.P. Bauset, 24 June 1885, 13:8; KD, Kerr to S.P. Bauset, 20 April 1886, 13:35. Various newspaper reports on association meetings mention twenty-five officers and others. Cross-referencing with city directories indicates that only two or three were skilled workers, the rest being composed of professionals, manufacturers, merchants, or clerks.

79 KD, Memo for S.P. Bauset, 19 December 1886, 14:9; KD, Kerr to deputy minister, 6 January 1887, 14:12.

80 "Fish and Game," *Spectator*, 26 March 1887.

81 Fred Kerr's stance on winter spearing is discussed below. For an example of his support for spring netting, see KD, Fred Kerr to deputy minister, 25 March 1889, 15:28; for his position on fall spearing of herring, see Fred Kerr to deputy minister, 4 November 1891, 16:19. Canada, Department of Marine, *Annual Report of the Department of Fisheries, 1889* (Ottawa: Brown Chamberlin, 1890), xxxix.

82 KD, Fred Kerr to deputy minister, 27 January 1891, 16:5.

83 Letter to the editor, *Hamilton Herald*, 22 January 1892; see also letter to editor, *Hamilton Herald*, 5 February 1892.

84 "Meeting of Spearmen," *Spectator*, 17 December 1896; "They May Spear in the Bay," *Spectator*, 26 January 1895, 1; "Fourth Annual Game and Fisheries Report," 1910, 43, *OSP*, 1911, no. 13.

85 "Report of Ontario Fishery Commission, 1893," vi–vii. In 1872, John Kerr asked Wilmot for a supply of salmon-trout to stock a number of creeks around the bay and marsh. After a few attempts to stock fish in the 1870s, he tried in 1881 to refuse a shipment of salmon-trout

fry, believing that they would be eaten by other fish in the bay. Wilmot sent them anyway. KD, Kerr to MMF, 3 June 1872, 5:9; KD, Kerr to Samuel Wilmot, 7 March 1881, 9:9; KD, Kerr to Samuel Wilmot, 9 May 1881, 9:10. On the complexities of fisheries administration in Wilmot's day, see William Knight, "Samuel Wilmot, Fish Culture, and Recreational Fisheries in Late 19th Century Ontario," *Scientia Canadensis: Canadian Journal of the History of Science, Technology and Medicine* 30, 1 (2007): 75–90.

86 "Want to Spear Fish," *Hamilton Herald,* 29 January 1892.

87 On working in nature, see Richard White, "Are You an Environmentalist or Do You Work for a Living? Work and Nature," in *Uncommon Ground,* ed. William Cronon (New York: Norton, 1996), 171–85.

CHAPTER 3: BOOSTING NATURE

1 *Hamilton: The Birmingham of Canada* (Hamilton: Times Printing, 1892), 1.

2 Ibid.

3 Ibid., 2.

4 Elizabeth Bloomfield, "Municipal Bonusing of Industry: The Legislative Framework in Ontario to 1930," *Urban History Review* 9, 3 (February 1981): 59–76; Diana J. Middleton and David F. Walker, "Manufacturers and Industrial Development Policy in Hamilton, 1890–1910," *Urban History Review* 8, 3 (February 1980): 20–46; Stephen V. Ward, *Selling Places: The Marketing and Promotion of Towns and Cities, 1850–2000* (New York: Routledge, 1998). In 1946, the McMaster University geographer (and later chief geographer for Canada) J.W. Watson identified "geographical opportunity and historical initiative" as keys to Hamilton's industrial success. J.W. Watson, "Industrial and Commercial Development," in *The Hamilton Centennial, 1846–1946,* ed. Alexander H. Wingfield (Hamilton: Hamilton Centennial Committee, 1946), 21.

5 Board of Control, Report (hereafter BOCR), 11 February and 12 August 1919, in Hamilton City Council Minutes (hereafter HCCM), 1919, 82, 603, Local History and Archives Department (hereafter LH&A), Hamilton Public Library (hereafter HPL), Hamilton; "New Name: Burlington Bay Changed to Hamilton Harbor," *Hamilton Times* (hereafter *Times*), 23 August 1919. On forms of boosterism, see Ward, *Selling Places,* 236.

6 Herbert Lister, *Hamilton Canada: Its History, Commerce, Industries and Resources* (Hamilton: Spectator Printing, 1913), 65.

7 Commissioner of Industries, *Hamilton, Canada: The City of 400 Varied Industries* (Hamilton: Commissioner of Industries, 1913), 9.

8 Richard Clippingdale, *Laurier: His Life and World* (Toronto and Montreal: McGraw-Hill Ryerson, 1979), 72 (Laurier's speech), 44 (imperial preference tariff); R. Craig Brown and Ramsay Cook, *Canada, 1896–1921* (Toronto: McClelland and Stewart, 1974); Ken Cruikshank, *Close Ties: Railways, Government and the Board of Railway Commissioners, 1851–1933* (Montreal and Kingston: McGill-Queen's University Press, 1991), 41, 232. Cruikshank downplays the importance of the freight rate concessions from the perspective of the Canadian Pacific Railway, but this does not mean that potential business investors perceived them as insignificant. The concessions suggested that the government was willing to keep eastern-manufactured goods competitive in the expanding settlement frontier. On Wood, see "Hon. A.T. Wood Dead," *Hamilton Spectator* (hereafter *Spectator*), 21 January 1903; "Senator Wood Borne to Grave," *Spectator,* 23 January 1903; "Wood, Andrew Trew," in *Dictionary of Hamilton Biography* (hereafter *DHB*), ed. T.M. Bailey (Hamilton:

Dictionary of Hamilton Biography, 1981), 1:215; Peter Hanlon, "Wood, Andrew Trew," *Dictionary of Canadian Biography Online* (hereafter *DCB Online*), http://www.biographi.ca/en/bio/wood_andrew_trew_13E.html.

9 For an overview, see Diana J. Middleton, "Industrial Entrepreneurship in Hamilton, 1871–1911" (bachelor's thesis, University of Waterloo, 1978); on steps taken to encourage iron smelting, see H.V. Nelles, *The Politics of Development: Forests, Mines and Hydro-Electric Power in Ontario, 1849–1941* (Toronto: Macmillan, 1974), 108–38.

10 "Huckleberry Point Once Worthless Land! Can't Say Same Now," *Hamilton Review*, 30 December 1953, Stelco Scrapbooks, vol. 1, 171–73, LH&A, HPL. On Stelco, see William Kilbourn, *The Elements Combined: A History of the Steel Company of Canada* (Toronto: Clarke, Irwin, 1960), 44–50, 63–78; Middleton, "Industrial Entrepreneurship," Appendix A, 90–94; Shelley Wall, "Tilden, John Henry," in *DHB*, ed. T.M. Bailey (Hamilton: Dictionary of Hamilton Biography, 1991), 2:172; "Milne, John C.," in *DHB*, 1:154–55.

11 Carolyn Gray, "Business Structures and Records: The Dominion Power and Transmission Company, 1896–1930," *Archivaria* 19 (1984): 152–61; William M. Cody, "Who Were the Five Johns?" *Wentworth Bygones* 5 (1964): 14–17.

12 "Power Turned On," *Spectator*, 26 August 1898; "The Cataract Power Company," *Spectator*, 14 November 1898; "Power Works at St. Catharines Opened: Means Much to Hamilton," *Globe*, 14 November 1898.

13 "The Long Distance Plant of the Cataract Power Company," and "The Cataract Power Company of Hamilton," *Canadian Electrical News and Steam Engineering Journal* 8, 12 (December 1898): 236–37.

14 Quoted in Thomas H. Ferns, "Patterson, John," *DCB Online*, http://www.biographi.ca/en/bio/patterson_john_14E.html.

15 HCCM, 25 February 1901, 6, Bylaw 138, "To amend Bylaw No. 1 and for the appointment of a Reception Committee." It evolved into the Industrial Committee to promote the establishment of new industries in Hamilton. HCCM, 27 January 1902, 51–52, Bylaw 186; HCCM, 14 April 1903, Bylaw 268; HCCM, 28 December 1904, Bylaw 328, "To Promote the Establishment of New Industries"; "Businessmen Boom Hamilton: The Preliminary Steps Taken to Form an Aggressive Association," *Hamilton Herald* (hereafter *Herald*), 16 March 1909; "Waking Up," editorial, *Herald*, 16 March 1909; "A Publicity Commissioner," *Herald*, 27 January 1910; Middleton and Walker, "Manufacturers and Industrial Development," 35–36.

16 Middleton and Walker, "Manufacturers and Industrial Development," 30; Kilbourn, *The Elements Combined*; Craig Heron, "Working Class Hamilton, 1896–1930" (PhD diss., Dalhousie University, 1981), 14–16; Nelles, *The Politics of Development*, 90–91.

17 HCCM, 1896, Bylaw 856; "To Locate in Canada," *Spectator*, 19 October 1896; "Consolidation of Westinghouse Plants," *Spectator*, 8 October 1903; "Westinghouse Plant to Be Enlarged," *Spectator*, 9 May 1903; "New Company Has Capital of $1,000,000," *Spectator*, 10 June 1903; "Westinghouse History: Thirty Years of Progress," and "New Foundry Most Modern Structure of Kind in Canada," *Spectator*, 11 December 1924.

18 HCCM, 1903, 551.

19 "When the Factories Began to Hunt a Location in Hamilton," n.d., and "Saturday Musings: A Bit of History Worth Remembering," 1 March 1919, 31–32, International Harvester Scrapbook, vol. 1, 1–2, clippings, LH&A, HPL; "Industrial Hamilton: A Trail to the Future: International Harvester Company of Canada, Limited," HPL, Canada's Digital Collections program, 2000, http://epe.lac-bac.gc.ca/100/205/301/ic/cdc/industrial/harvester.htm.

20 "[Proposed] Bylaw No. for Granting a Bonus of $50,000 to the Deering Harvester Co.,"
    Spectator, 28 April 1902; John C. Weaver, *Hamilton: An Illustrated History* (Toronto: James
    Lorimer, 1982), 88–89; Heron, "Working Class Hamilton," 20–21.

21 Commissioner of Industries, *Hamilton, Canada.* This book's subtitle is *Hamilton, Ontario
    Canada Cheapest Power in Canada: Unrivaled Shipping Facilities: The Home of Manufac-
    turers; Hamilton: The Electric City* (Hamilton: Seavey, 1900), 42; *Hamilton: The City Beautiful
    and Industrial Hub of Canada* (Hamilton: Department of Industry and Publicity, 1926).

22 "One More Great Industry," *Times,* 22 September 1910; this reference is to the Canada
    Steel Company (renamed Burlington Steel in 1914), which rolled bar products out of scrap
    rails. See Craig Heron, "Baillie, Sir Frank Wilton," *Dictionary of Canadian Biography* online,
    http://www.biographi.ca/en/bio/baillie_frank_wilton_15E.html.

23 Discussion and statistics on population and industry from Weaver, *Hamilton,* 92–96,
    137–41, Appendix Tables V, VII, X, and XI, 197–99; Heron, "Working Class Hamilton,"
    9–19.

24 Applications to the Board of Railway Commissioners for an order for the restoration of
    beach passenger service between Hamilton and Burlington via Burlington Beach by City
    of Hamilton, HCCM, 1917, 13 October 1917, 833. For a good discussion of the eastward
    movement of industry, see Heron, "Working Class Hamilton," 10–11.

25 Assessment Commissioner's Department, *Hamilton, Canada: The Visitors' Handbook*
    (Hamilton: Assessment Commissioner's Department, 1904), 15; Commissioner of Indus-
    tries, *Hamilton Canada,* claimed that it had "unrivaled shipping."

26 "The Burlington Canal," *Spectator,* 11 March 1885; see also Harold A. Wood, "Emergence
    of the Modern City: Hamilton, 1891–1950," in *Steel City: Hamilton and Region,* ed. M.J.
    Dear, J.J. Drake, and L.G. Reeds (Toronto: University of Toronto Press, 1987), 121, although
    we believe that he exaggerates the significance of this event to Hamilton's transformation.
    See Ivan S. Brookes, "Chapter 14," in *Hamilton Harbour, 1826–1901,* transcribed for the
    Maritime History of the Great Lakes by Walter Lewis (Halton Hills: Maritime History of
    the Great Lakes, 2001), http://www.maritimehistoryofthegreatlakes.ca/documents/
    Brookes/; John N. Jackson, *The Welland Canals and Their Communities: Engineering,
    Industrial, and Urban Transformation* (Toronto: University of Toronto Press, 1997).

27 For example, Brookes, *Hamilton Harbour, 1826–1901,* mentions the *W.J. Suffell* (April
    1895), the *Carlo* (June 1900), and the *Strathcona* (October 1900), all of which ran aground
    in the canal.

28 "To Urge Government to Widen the Canal," *Spectator,* 9 August 1910; on the complaints
    of International Harvester, see "A Larger and Deeper Beach Canal Needed," *Spectator,* 24
    August 1910. The 1897 decision by a coal importer to move his firm's warehouses from the
    waterfront closer to the rail lines had already suggested harbour problems. "Will Ship by
    Rail," *Spectator,* 17 May 1897; see also "To Deepen the Canal," *Spectator,* 12 February 1896;
    "Beach Canal Is Much Too Narrow," *Spectator,* 5 July 1910; Brookes provides a detailed
    chronology of the various ships carrying iron, coal, and other supplies to the steel mills,
    based on contemporary newspaper reports. Brookes, Chapter 16, "The Iron Age," in *Ham-
    ilton Harbour, 1826–1901.*

29 HCCM, 1899, 30–31, "Report of the Harbour Committee"; HCCM, 1903, 534–35, Memorial
    to Hon. James Sutherland, Minister of Public Works.

30 "Canal Deepening Will Start Soon," *Spectator,* 13 March 1930.

31 "The Dredging in the Harbor," *Spectator,* 20 June 1892; "Work at the Piers," *Spectator,* 25
    January 1900. In 1903, the city's Bay Front Improvement Committee led a deputation to

Toronto to meet with the federal engineer for public works, requesting support for harbour development projects, including sewer and recreation improvements, the construction of a break wall, piling, and dredging. HCCM, 1903, 534–35.

32 *An Act Respecting the Harbor of Hamilton,* Statutes of Canada, 1912, 2 Geo. V, c. 98; Mark Sproule-Jones, *Governments at Work: Canadian Parliamentary Federalism and Its Public Policy Effects* (Toronto: University of Toronto Press, 1993), 160–61; Hamilton Port Authority, *Spanning Two Centuries, 1912–2001: Commemorative History, the Hamilton Harbour Commissioners* (Hamilton: Hamilton Port Authority, 2001).

33 "Hamilton May Have a Harbor Commission," *Spectator,* 22 April 1911; "Hamilton Will Have a Harbor Commission," *Spectator,* 2 February 1912. The harbour had what Sproule-Jones terms an "exceptional constitutional status" since it was vested in the municipality rather than the province under *An Act to Alter and Amend the Act of Incorporating the Town of Hamilton, and to Erect the Same into a City,* Provincial Statutes of Canada, 1846, c. 73, s. 3. Sproule-Jones, *Governments at Work,* 157–58; Frank Bomben, "Stewart, Thomas Joseph," in *DHB,* ed. T.M. Bailey (Hamilton: Dictionary of Hamilton Biography, 1992), 3:199–200.

34 The name change came at the request of C.W. Kirkpatrick, Hamilton's commissioner of industries and publicity, acting on behalf of city council. He cites the name change and Hamilton's acquisition of a franchise in the Michigan-Ontario baseball league as great accomplishments of his department's publicity work. Despite this, according to the *Times,* certain local groups, such as the Wentworth Historical Society, opposed the name change. HCCM, 1920, 132–33; BOCR, 11 February and 12 August 1919, in HCCM, 1919, 82, 603; "New Name: Burlington Bay Changed to Hamilton Harbor"; Ted Wickerson, *Reflections of Toronto Harbour: 200 Years of Port Activity and Waterfront Development* (Toronto: Toronto Port Authority, 2002); "Kirkpatrick, Clarence Willoughby," in *DHB,* ed. T.M. Bailey (Hamilton: Dictionary of Hamilton Biography, 1999), 4:145–47; Hamilton Commissioner of Industries and Publicity, *Hamilton, Canada: The City of Opportunity* (Hamilton: Reid Press, 1900); Hamilton Commissioner of Industries and Publicity, *Hamilton, Canada: The City of Opportunity: 500 Diversified Industries* (Hamilton: Commission of Industries and Publicity, 1920).

35 "Splendid Donation for Hamilton's New Harbor Announced," *Spectator,* 25 March 1912; "Will Spend $250,000 on Harbor This Summer," *Spectator,* 20 May 1912; "Harbor Work of Last Year Reviewed," *Herald,* 6 January 1914; "A Free Harbour," editorial, *Herald,* 2 February 1914; "Harbor Work Done Last Year," *Herald,* 10 January 1916; "Improvements to the Harbor Are Numerous," *Times,* 14 July 1916; "Government Will Do Some Harbor Work," *Herald,* 21 January 1919; "Now It Is Time to Improve Our Harbour: Before Private Owners Get Control of Bay," *Times,* 22 January 1920; "Harbor Plans Are Extensive," *Spectator,* 1 February 1921; "Hamilton Harbor as It Was and as It Is," letter to editor, *Herald,* 2 June 1922; "Harbor Board Making Plans: Increase in Freight Business Expected," *Spectator,* 5 December 1924; "Hamilton's Harbor an Important Link," *Herald,* 13 November 1926; "Hamilton Harbor Great Asset," *Herald,* 17 December 1927; "Hamilton's Harbor Playing Big Part in City's Progress," *Spectator,* 15 December 1928.

36 *Key Plan of Hamilton, Ontario* (January 1898), 1 inch = 500 miles; *Insurance Plan of Hamilton Ontario,* vols. 1–3 (January 1898, revised to March 1911 up to c. 1916), 1 inch = 500 miles; see also maps: *Hamilton, Ontario* (1878), 1 inch = 50 miles, National Map Collection, 88304–5, 11617; Department of Militia and Defence, Geographical Section, General Staff, No. 2197, Topographic Map, Hamilton, Ontario, Sheet 33, 1907–09, 1:63360. The

revetment wall, Oliver Chilled Plow Works, and a section of Sherman Inlet to be filled in are visible on this map. "Plan Showing Portion of City of Hamilton," *Times,* 19 November 1910; Dianne L. Oswald, *Fire Insurance Maps: Their History and Applications* (College Station, TX: Lacewing Press, 1997).

37 *Insurance Plan of Hamilton,* 1916, s. 233, no. 1329, shows the Grasselli Chemical Company's intake pump and tanks.

38 *Insurance Plan of Hamilton Ontario,* 1898, s. 34, no. 227, shows the Canadian Coloured Cotton Mills pumping house; no. 117 shows the Gartshore-Thomson Pipe and Foundry private hydrant; Heron, "Working Class Hamilton," 12; on the various companies and their locations, see "Industrial Hamilton: A Trail to the Future," http://epe.lac-bac.gc.ca/100/205/301/ic/cdc/industrial/intro.htm.

39 Weaver, *Hamilton,* 89.

40 HCCM, 31 January 1910, Bylaw 931, "Respecting the Commissioner of Industries William Mullis"; "A Publicity Commissioner," *Herald,* 27 January 1910; Carolyn Gray, "Historical Records of the City of Hamilton, 1847–1973" (McMaster University, 1986), 84–85; Heron, "Working Class Hamilton," 21–22.

41 "A Publicity Commissioner," *Herald,* 27 January 1910; "Mullis, William," in *DHB,* 3:156.

42 "$4,000,000 Capital in New Industries," *Times,* 9 December 1910; "Publicity Commissioner Mullis," *Times,* 22 December 1910; "Industrial Day: Large List of Places Open to Inspection Tomorrow," *Times,* 1 May 1911; "Industrial Day Was a Success," *Times,* 4 May 1911; "Hamilton Has Mark of Destiny upon It," *Herald,* 21 June 1912. Mullis spent only eighteen months on the job, eventually returning to newspaper reporting to become the city news editor. "Has Returned to First Love," *Times,* 22 June 1911

43 *Hamilton: The Birmingham of Canada,* 1–2; Hamilton Commissioner of Industries, *Hamilton, Canada: The City of Opportunity* (Hamilton: Department of Industries and Publicity, 1928), 12, 17. On the changing nature of boosterism, see Ward, *Selling Places;* and D. Beeby, "Industrial Strategy and Manufacturing Growth in Toronto, 1880–1910," *Ontario History* 76, 3 (1984): 199–232.

44 Hamilton Commissioner of Industries, *Hamilton, Canada: The City of Opportunity,* 11 (emphasis added). On Roberts, see Rosemary Gagan, "Mortality Patterns and Public Health in Hamilton Canada, 1900–1914," *Urban History Review* 17, 3 (February 1989): 169–70; more broadly on his activities, see Rosemary Gagan, "Disease, Mortality, and Public Health: Hamilton, 1900–1914" (master's thesis, McMaster University, 1981); and Rosemary Gagan, "Roberts, James," in *DHB,* 3:175–78. On measuring progress through sewer and other investments, see Max Jesoley, *Hamilton, the Birmingham of Canada* (Toronto: J. Phillips, 1903), 3; Assessment Commissioner's Department, *Hamilton, Canada,* 7, 32; Commissioner of Industries, *Hamilton Canada,* 3; *Hamilton: The City Beautiful and Industrial Hub of Canada: The Ideal Canadian City in Which to Reside and Do Business* (Hamilton, 1924, with 1925 revisions: W.E. Stone and Co.); for comments on the role of boosterism in the development of sewage systems, see Douglas Baldwin, "Sewerage," in *Building Canada,* ed. Norman Ball (Toronto: University of Toronto Press, 1988), 225.

45 James Roberts, "Healthy Hamilton," in Assessment Commissioner's Department, *Hamilton, Canada: The Visitors' Handbook,* 61; James Roberts, "Healthy Hamilton," in Herbert Lister, *Hamilton, Canada: Its History, Commerce, Industries, Resources* (Hamilton, 1913), 125–35; James Roberts, "Annual Report to the Provincial Board of Health," Ontario, *Sessional Papers* (hereafter *OSP*), 1913, no. 452. On his contributions to booster publications, his ability to "prick the city's conscience on matters of civic well-being," and his reflections

on them, see Gagan, "Disease, Mortality, and Public Health," 157–58, 185–86, 197. On Toronto sewers and public health, see Catherine Brace, "Public Works in the Canadian City: The Provision of Sewers in Toronto, 1870–1913," *Urban History Review* 23, 2 (March 1995): 33–43.

46 This also preoccupied his predecessor, Dr. W.F. Langrill. On typhoid, see, for example, "Report to the Provincial Board of Health," *OSP,* 1901, no. 36, 92; Ian R.G.J. Anderson, "'Our Dead Sea': Environmental and Health Issues concerning Hamilton Harbour throughout the 20th Century" (Hannah Undergraduate Summer Studentship research paper, McMaster University, 2003), 3–4; Gagan, "Disease, Mortality, and Public Health."

47 In his first annual report as MOH, he recorded the lowest number of typhoid cases for the past six years, stating that "the decrease speaks volumes for our city water." James Roberts, *Annual Report of the Board of Health* (hereafter *ARBH*), 1904–05, 9.

48 *ARBH,* 1905–06, 15; "Citizens Must Boil All Drinking Water," *Spectator,* 19 September 1906; "City Must Have a Laboratory," *Spectator,* 2 October 1906; *ARBH,* 1909–10; "Bacteriological Reports," *ARBH,* 1911–12, 30–32. The discussion of Roberts in this chapter has been informed by our reading of Anderson, "'Our Dead Sea.'"

49 "Treatment of Sewage Needless," *Herald,* 3 October 1912; Gagan, "Disease, Mortality, and Public Health," 189.

50 "The Sluice Business," *Spectator,* 3 October 1906; "Filtering Basins May Cause Water Shortage," *Spectator,* 29 April 1910. Such changes dated to the 1870s. See Willis Chipman and Andrew F. Macallum, *Report No. 1 on Waterworks Improvements* (Hamilton: Board of Control, 1911), 5–6, Canadian Institute for Historical Microreproductions, 80720; W.L. McFaul (city engineer and manager of waterworks), "City Growth," *Spectator,* 29 December 1942.

51 "Water Filtration," *Spectator,* 10 August 1901; "Pure Water," *Herald,* 7 January 1914; "Water Supply," *Spectator,* 23 March 1923.

52 *ARBH,* 1905–06, 11.

53 See, for example, the report of Roberts's predecessor, W.F. Langrill. *OSP,* 1901, no. 36, 95–96. A dozen years later, unsanitary privy vaults were, in Roberts's estimation, a key aspect of the city's "housing problem." *OSP,* 1913, no. 20, 453.

54 "Sewerage of the Annex," *ARBH,* 1904–05, 15–16.

55 Hamilton Board of Health Minutes (hereafter BOHM), 4 October 1892, 157.

56 Chester A. Smith, "The Use and Abuse of Sewage Disposal Plants," *City Hall* 23 (July 1912): 167–71, quoted in Martin Melosi, *The Sanitary City: Urban Infrastructure in America from Colonial Times to the Present* (Baltimore: Johns Hopkins University Press, 2000), 165.

57 *Annual Report of the Medical Officer of Health,* 6 December 1892, 164, and 4 December 1893, 211; the City instructed local scavengers to dump their fill in Coal Oil Inlet three days a week. HCCM, 4 January 1895, 266–67; regarding potential lawsuits, HCCM, 1 April 1895, 277. The inlet's poor condition was well known in many circles. When Fred Kerr's successor, Charles Ogg, wrote his first annual report to the Department of Game and Fisheries, he remarked that "nothing has come under his notice excepting the foul condition and appearance of what is known as Coal Oil Inlet in Burlington Bay, but this is of long standing." *OSP,* 1899, no. 27, 51.

58 On the controversies surrounding Ferguson's and Sherman Inlets, see BOHM, 1884–93: 20 September 1886, 47; 19 January 1887, 52; 24 March 1887, 52; 5 April 1887, 53; 5 October 1887, 54; 5 July 1892, 150; "To Dispose of Sewage," *Herald,* 16 September 1895; on Kuichling, see William F. Peck, *Landmarks of Munroe County, N.Y. Part III* (Boston: Boston History,

1895), 152; Blake McElvey, "Turbulent but Constructive Deeds in Civic Affairs: 1867–1900," *Rochester History* 7 (1945): 16–17. Jamie Benedickson discusses the difficulties of using nuisance law with respect to public health, in "Ontario Water Quality, Public Health and the Law, 1880–1930," in *Essays in the History of Canadian Law*, vol. 8, *In Honour of R.C.B. Risk*, ed. G. Blaine Baker and Jim Phillips (Toronto: Osgoode Society and University of Toronto Press, 1999), 115–41.

59 The sewage system design and decisions are described at a later date, in E.R. Gray, *Report on Sanitary Intercepting Sewers, Pumping Stations and Drainage* (Hamilton, 1923), Appendix E, 5–8.

60 Jesoley, *Hamilton, the Birmingham of Canada*, 3; see also *Hamilton Spectator Carnival Souvenir, 1903* (Hamilton: Spectator Printing, 1903), 10–11; Assessment Commissioner's Department, *Hamilton, Canada: The Visitors' Handbook*, 7.

61 Gore, Nasmith and Storrie, *Report on Sewage Disposal* (Hamilton, 1923), 9; the limited effectiveness of chemical precipitation except as a treatment that preceded others is discussed in W.H. Maxwell, "Sewage Disposal," in *Encyclopedia of Municipal and Sanitary Engineering* (New York: D. Van Nostrand, 1910), 404–6. See also Melosi, *The Sanitary City*, 168; Sharon Beder, "From Sewage Farms to Septic Tanks: Trials and Tribulations in Sydney," *Journal of the Royal Australian Historical Society* 79 (1993): 74–76.

62 W.C., letter to editor, "That Bay Ice," *Spectator*, 15 January 1912.

63 "North End Men Again Protest," *Spectator*, 16 March 1901; "The North End of Hamilton Is Coming into Its Own at Last," *Times*, 17 November 1910; "Great Improvements Have Been Made in the North-End of the City This Year," *Spectator*, 19 November 1910; "North Enders Make Big Kick," *Herald*, 7 May 1907. On Eastwood, see S. Patricia Filer, "Eastwood, John Morrison," in *DHB*, 3:45. For indications of what was in some of the fill, see "Full Mill Rate," *Spectator*, 9 December 1921; "To Stop Garbage Dumping," *Herald*, 11 May 1933. Recalling Coal Oil Inlet, John Halcrow, a Hamilton old-timer, remarked that "the smell was terrible. It swarmed with big snakes six feet long," yet it also "had its good points, and there grew the most beautiful white water lilies in the whole district." John James Halcrow, "Burlington Bay as I Remember It," *Wentworth Bygones* 9 (1971): 61.

64 The name has sometimes even been applied to a completely different inlet at Wellington Street, an error that we perpetuated in our "Blighted Areas and Obnoxious Industries: Constructing Environmental Inequality on an Industrial Waterfront, Hamilton, Ontario, 1890–1960," *Environmental History* 9, 3 (July 2004): 464–96.

65 BOHM, 4 January 1895, 266–67.

66 James Roberts, "Coal Oil Inlet," *ARBH*, 1906–07, 30. For the Coal Oil Inlet controversy, see "Coal Oil Inlet Must Be Cleaned," *Spectator*, 22 August 1906; "Four Nuisances Found at Inlet," *Spectator*, 31 May 1907; "Coal Oil Inlet," *Spectator*, 3 March 1908; "Hamilton Harbor as It Was and Is," *Herald*, 2 June 1922; Charles Sheard and Charles A. Hodgetts, "Special Report re: 'Coal Oil Inlet' Nuisance," 20 May 1907, *OSP*, 1908, no. 36, 55–56.

67 "Are Anxious to Have Inlet Filled," *Spectator*, 31 August 1915; "Coal Oil Inlet: Town Planning Commission Discusses the Situation," *Spectator*, 23 August 1916; "Expect Jutten to Head Polls: Has Done Valuable But Quiet Work for City, Responsible for Filling In of Coal Oil Inlet," *Spectator*, 29 December 1916; BOCR, 31 August 1915, in HCCM, 1915, 609–10; BOCR, 31 October 1916, in HCCM, 1916, 631; HCCM, 1916, Bylaw, 28 November 1916, 755–56; BOCR, 29 May 1917, in HCCM, 1917, 370; BOCR, 28 January 1919, in HCCM, 1919, 33; HCCM, 1919, Bylaw 2231, 24 June 1919, 535; BOHM, 27 May 1923, 20; BOCR, on Lottridge's Inlet, 11 November 1930, in HCCM, 1930, 875–76.

68 Our interpretation of Roberts's role in the Coal Oil Inlet problem is somewhat at odds with that of Rosemary Gagan: in our view, she too readily assumes that Roberts handled the inlet issue with the vigorous and sometimes controversial approach that he applied to the cleaning of filtering basins and reservoirs. Gagan, "Disease, Mortality, and Public Health."

69 Quoted in Gagan, "Mortality Patterns," 163.

70 HCCM, 1910, Bylaw 1060, "Respecting Public Health," 673–84.

71 *An Act Respecting Public Health*, Statutes of Ontario, 1912, 2 Geo. V, c. 58, s. 96(1).

72 Michael J. Doucet and John C. Weaver, *Housing the North American City* (Montreal and Kingston: McGill-Queen's University Press, 1991), 107, 442–43; Weaver, *Hamilton*, 104; "Report of Chief Sanitary Inspector," *ARBH*, 1921–22, 48–49. Doucet and Weaver note that 77 percent of households in annexed areas had access to the sewer system, a lower percentage than in 1916, the result of another eastern annexation in 1920. See also Elizabeth Bloomfield, Gerald Bloomfield, and Peter McCaskell, *Urban Growth and Local Services* (Guelph: Department of Geography, University of Guelph, 1983), 104–5.

73 "Report of Chief Sanitary Inspector, *ARBH*, 1921–22," 48–49; W.J. Deadman, "Report of Director of City Laboratories," *ARBH*, 1921–22, 15–16, 21.

74 "Some Untreated Sewage Finds Its Way into Bay," *Spectator*, 7 June 1921; "Guarding against Pollution of Bay," *Spectator*, 24 June 1921; "Pollution of Bay Water May Cause Disease," *Spectator*, 5 July 1921; "Report on City's Sewage Problems," *Spectator*, 17 January 1922. Roberts reportedly held firm to his view that the bay pollution would have no effect on drinking water. "Pollution of Bay Waters Is Some Problem," *Spectator*, 7 July 1921.

75 Gore, Nasmith and Storrie, *Report on Sewage Disposal*, 11. The firm is a predecessor of today's CH2M Hill, Canada's largest environmental engineering consulting firm.

76 Gore, Nasmith and Storrie, *Report on Sewage Disposal*, 8–12, 15.

77 Ibid., 14–26.

78 "Health Officer Would Abandon the Old Basins," *Spectator*, 19 March 1923. Although the consultants had not officially released their report when Roberts made this statement, their general conclusions were already known. "Engineers Warn against Impure Supply of Water," *Spectator*, 16 March 1923.

79 "Take No Risks with the City Water Supply," and "City's Drinking Water," editorial, *Spectator*, 29 March 1924.

80 "Waterworks Found to Be Inadequate," *Spectator*, 3 June 1926.

81 "Vigorous Dispute upon Water Report: Dr Roberts Clashes with Toronto Experts," *Spectator*, 26 June 1926. Roberts's position had not changed at all. He wrote, "Sand strip offers natural protection from millions of gallons of sewage annually deposited in the bay. Expertise and concern is about typhoid, and way to prevent is through chlorination, to be done without delay." James Roberts, *ARBH*, 1924–25, 16–17.

82 "Filtration Plant Now Recommended," *Spectator*, 27 January 1930; "Filtration Plant Is Only Solution," *Spectator*, 4 February 1930; "Filtration of City Water Is before Council," *Spectator*, 12 February 1930; "Three Great Feats," *Herald*, 18 December 1931; "Civic Betterment Come from Three Engineering Projects," *Herald*, 19 December 1931; "Filtration Plant Now in Operation," *Spectator*, 20 March 1933; "Filtration Plant Is Formally Opened by Ministry of Health," *Herald*, 9 June 1933; McFaul, "City Growth."

83 Frank Seecombe, "City Sewage in Plant Is Heavily Strained," *Spectator*, 20 February 1946; "Parts of Bay Mere Pools of Rotting Waste," *Spectator*, 20 August 1934. The final two sentences of this paragraph are, of course, a paraphrase of Roberts on Coal Oil Inlet.

84 "One of the Many," letter to editor, "Clean Up," *Spectator,* 28 April 1923.
85 Roberts, *ARBH,* 1923–24, 22.
86 Roberts sometimes spoke in favour of keeping the bay cleaner so that it could be used for swimming and fishing, but he saw pollution as a long-standing problem and not one that really concerned his office. "Pollution of Bay Waters Is Some Problem," *Spectator,* 7 July 1921.
87 In 1919, the factory became part of International Harvester's industrial complex in Hamilton.
88 These sources, which must be approached with some caution, have been used in combination with other primary sources containing demographic information. City directories, published annually, are a good source for the names of neighbourhood residents. However, they typically report only household heads, helping little to identify young, unestablished, or transient people. Since not all manuscript censuses are available, their aggregate published versions have also been used. However, they have a number of drawbacks: they were held only at ten-year intervals, did not record individuals who came and went between the censuses, and tend to under-record unskilled workers and people who did not own property.
89 Paul Palango, "Brightside: Old Survey Levelled but It Still Won't Die," *Spectator,* 12 July 1975; Property Surveys, W.D. Flatt, *Brightside, 1910,* Lloyd Reeds Map Collection, McMaster University.
90 John B. Nicholson, *Greater Hamilton: Comprising the Township of Bardon: All Present Subdivisions and Proposed Layouts by the City Corporation and Parts of the Townships of Saltfleet, Binbrook, Glanford, Ancaster, West Flamboro, East Flamboro* (Hamilton: Ramsay Thomas, 1913), 1:2,000 ft., Lloyd Reeds Map Collection, McMaster University.
91 "Brightside," 4 March 1911, *Times* Advertisement Scrapbook, 18, LH&A, HPL.
92 Ontario, Divisional Court of High Court of Justice, *Susan Stipes versus City of Hamilton,* 29 January 1912, reprinted in HCCM, 1919, 2 May 1919, 106–10; BOCR, on Stipes land purchase and sewage disposal plans, HCCM, 15 October 1919, 370–73.
93 Lister, *Hamilton Canada: Its History,* 63. Lister mentions only fishing and boating, but his book clearly depicts bathing. Hamilton Commissioner of Industries, *Hamilton, Canada: The City of Opportunity, 1928,* 11, refers to both bathing and boating.

Chapter 4: Organizing Nature

1 "Swimming Program Opens with Bang," "O-O-Oh Boy," "Swarm Away for Good Old Lake Ontario," *Hamilton Herald* (hereafter *Herald*), 15 July 1924; "Crowd Cars for Daily Dip," *Herald,* 16 July 1924; "Oh, Skinnay – Let's Go," *Herald,* 24 July 1924; "Inasmuch as Ye Have Done It unto One of the Least of These," *Herald,* 29 July 1924. Organizers also set aside a special day for girls, during which boys were not allowed to use the free streetcars. "When It's Girls Day at the Beach," *Herald,* 29 July 1924.
2 "Crowd Cars for Daily Dip" (emphasis in original).
3 Herbert Lister, *Hamilton Canada: Its History, Commerce, Industries and Resources* (Hamilton: Spectator Printing, 1913), 63. Lister writes, "Yachting, boating and fishing are pastimes within the reach of the most humble"; other examples can be found in *Hamilton: The Birmingham of Canada* (Hamilton: Times Printing, 1892); and Commissioner of Industries and Publicity, *Hamilton, Canada: The City of Opportunity: 500 Diversified Industries* (Hamilton: Commissioner of Industries, 1928).
4 We focus, then, on reformers who leaned toward what Paul Boyer would term positive environmentalism, who sought to create "the kind of physical environment that would

gently but irresistibly mold a population of cultivated, moral and socially responsible city dwellers." Paul S. Boyer, *Urban Masses and Moral Order in America, 1820–1920* (Cambridge, MA: Harvard University Press, 1978), 190; the focus on order and organization as a theme of the early twentieth century found its first full expression in Robert Wiebe's *The Search for Order, 1877–1920* (New York: Hill and Wang, 1977).

5 See, for example, the description of various events in the summer of 1909: "Aquatic Carnival," *Hamilton Spectator* (hereafter *Spectator*), 3 June 1909; "Swimming Is Again Coming into Favour," *Spectator*, 12 June 1909; "Swimming Tests at Victoria Yacht Club on August 2," *Spectator*, 21 July 1909; "Lieut.-Governor to Attend Championships," *Spectator*, 30 July 1909; "At the Swimming Carnival," *Spectator*, 9 August 1909; "William Henry's Aquatic Exhibition," *Spectator*, 30 August 1909.

6 See Nancy B. Bouchier, *For the Love of the Game: Amateur Sport in Small-Town Ontario, 1838–1895* (Montreal and Kingston: McGill-Queen's University Press, 2003); Bruce Kidd, "Muscular Christianity and Value-Centred Sport: The Legacy of Tom Brown in Canada," *International Journal of the History of Sport* 23, 5 (2006): 701–13; Christopher J. Anstead, "Fraternalism in Victorian Ontario: Secret Societies and Cultural Hegemony" (PhD diss., University of Western Ontario, 1992); M.A. Clawson, *Constructing Brotherhood: Class, Gender and Fraternalism* (Princeton: Princeton University Press, 1989); and B. Greenberg, *Worker and Community: Response to Industrialization in a Nineteenth-Century American City, Albany, New York, 1850–1884* (New York: SUNY Press, 1985).

7 "Elsinore Opening," *Spectator*, 12 June 1911. Sir William Sanford – a clothing manufacturer, senator, and philanthropist – and his wife created and built Elsinore initially for Hamilton's sick and destitute children and later for convalescing females who couldn't "afford to pay for an outing for themselves." Two letters of recommendation – one from a medical doctor and one from a clergyman – were needed to gain access to the program. "Fresh Air Camp," *Spectator*, 14 March 1921. On Elsinore, see Dorothy Turcotte, *The Sand Strip: Burlington/Hamilton Beaches* (St. Catharines: Stonehouse, 1987), 29–30; Peter Hanlon, "Sanford, William Eli," *Dictionary of Canadian Biography* online, http://www.biographi.ca/en/bio/sanford_william_eli_12E.html; on Sanford's aunt Lydia Jackson and women's charity in Hamilton generally, see Carmen J. Nielson, *Private Women and the Public Good: Charity and State Formation in Hamilton, Ontario 1846–93* (Vancouver: UBC Press, 2014); Diana Pederson, "Keeping Our Good Girls Good: The YWCA and the 'Girl Problem,' 1870–1930," *Canadian Women's Studies* 7, 4 (1986): 20–24; and Dawn Sebire, *A Woman's Place: The History of the Hamilton Young Women's Christian Association* (Hamilton: YWCA, 1990).

8 "Young Miss Lure of Ole Swimmin Hole," *Herald*, 19 June 1924; Craig Heron, "The Boys and Their Booze: Masculinities and Public Drinking in Working-Class Hamilton, 1890–1946," *Canadian Historical Review* 86, 3 (September 2005): 411–52.

9 "Bathing Beach at Land's Inlet," *Spectator*, 6 July 1915; Board of Control, Report (hereafter BOCR), 8 August 1916, in Hamilton City Council Minutes (hereafter HCCM), 1916, 480, Local History and Archives Department (LH&A), Hamilton Public Library (HPL), Hamilton; BOCR, 10 July 1917, in HCCM 1917, 470.

10 "Where Hamilton Children Swim," *Herald*, 9 July 1924. For recollections of swimming, see Ontario Workers Arts and Heritage Center (hereafter OWAHC), *A Walking Tour: Hamilton's North End* (Hamilton: OWAHC, 1995), n.p., and the volume's accompanying tape recording. OWAHC is now the Workers Arts and Heritage Center.

11 "Bathing Beach in Ward Five Is Finding Favour," *Spectator*, 9 May 1925.

12 "African Golf," *Hamilton Times* (hereafter *Times*), 14 November 1919; "To Inspect Boathouses," *Spectator*, 28 August 1920; "Boathouse Party Broken Up When Police Knocked," *Spectator*, 19 May 1921.

13 "Young Women Indulge in It off North Shore," *Times*, 13 July 1913; "Strict Rules for Bathing Dresses Were Laid Down about 16 Years Ago," *Spectator*, 6 July 1926, 10; "Bathing Costumes: Modesty Will Be Insisted Upon at Wabasso Park," *Spectator*, 1 June 1921.

14 "That Troublesome Beach," *Spectator*, 10 October 1895; "Will Oppose Annexation," *Spectator*, 13 November 1895; "To Defeat Annexation," *Spectator*, 5 February 1896; "Beach Annexation: The City Council Will Discuss the Important Question," *Spectator*, 24 February 1896; "In Favour of Annexation," *Spectator*, 25 February 1896; "Oppose Annexation," *Spectator*, 29 February 1896; "Beach Bill Withdrawn," *Spectator*, 17 March 1896.

15 "The Beach Bill," editorial, *Spectator*, 25 February 1896.

16 "The Beach," *Spectator*, 24 August 1895.

17 "Who Runs the Beach," editorial, *Spectator*, 21 August 1900.

18 Brian Henley, "Beach Residents Opposed Streetcars," *Spectator*, 1 August 1997.

19 "Second of the Radials," *Spectator*, 1 September 1896.

20 Lewis D. McCowell, Joan L. Pikor, and Winsome M. Cain, *Hamilton Beach in Retrospect* (Hamilton: Hamilton Beach Alternate Community and History Project, 1981), 19–22.

21 See, for example, an advertisement for Bennett and Thwaites, which built cottages for as little as $2,500, in "Our Beach," *Spectator*, 25 May 1912; Burlington Beach Commission Minutes (hereafter BBCM), 20 May and 24 July 1911, record the filling in of Beach Strip swampland north of the canal for a Kenmore Park Company survey; within a year, the BBCM note the great number of cottages being built in the area. BBCM, 13 June 1912.

22 The annual financial statements of the Burlington Beach Commission show that the Canada Amusement Company leased the land near the Burlington Canal for $250 a year. For a history of the amusements, see Coaster Enthusiasts of Canada, Closed Canadian Parks, "Burlington Beach," http://cec.chebucto.org/ClosPark/BurlBech.html; see also Stewart Brown, "On the Beach: You Don't Have to Be Foolish to Have Fun – But It Helps," *Spectator*, 16 July 1977, and "Death Knell for Rides on the Beach Strip," *Spectator*, 3 April 1978; Turcotte, *The Sand Strip*, 32; McCowell, Pikor, and Cain, *Hamilton Beach in Retrospect*, 21.

23 "Annexation or Incorporation," *Spectator*, 4 June 1901.

24 For Powis's property, see "Beach House to Rent," *Spectator*, 24 April 1902. Although one reason for this neglect may have been to demonstrate the folly of rejecting City control, it was probably also connected with a jurisdictional dispute between two City agencies. The newly created Board of Parks Management and city council's Harbour Committee both claimed the right to collect and spend the small amount of money derived from the beach leases. See P.D., "Powis, Alfred," in *Dictionary of Hamilton Biography* (hereafter *DHB*), ed. T.M. Bailey (Hamilton: Dictionary of Hamilton Biography, 1992), 3:169–70.

25 "Who Runs the Beach"; "Mean to Go Ahead," *Spectator*, 12 May 1900.

26 BBCM, 10 September 1907; McCowell, Pikor, and Cain, *Hamilton Beach in Retrospect*, 23–24.

27 BBCM, 14 January 1909.

28 Ibid., 13 June 1912.

29 "Beach Plans Were Approved," *Spectator*, 22 August 1910.

30 The amusement park was known at various times as Knapman Beach, the Canal Amusement Park, and simply Hamilton Beach. See Coaster Enthusiasts of Canada, Closed Canadian

Parks, "Burlington Beach"; Turcotte, *The Sand Strip;* Peter Munger, "Decoys of Burlington Bay: Tools for the Art of 'Screening,'" *Decoy Magazine,* May-June 2011, 24.

31 This did not stop elite residents from grumbling, especially regarding activities that occurred on Sunday – one of the few days that working people had any leisure time. In 1905, Fisheries Inspector Charles John Kerr noted that Sunday fishing on the bay was "carried on extensively all the summer in every part of Burlington Bay by the rich and the poor, which looked bad in a Christian land like our beloved Canada." Ontario, *Sessional Papers* (hereafter *OSP*), 1905, no. 31, 33. In June 1912, a beach commissioner complained about beach visitors who played baseball on Sunday. A few years later, Sir John Gibson complained to the Burlington Beach Commission about people who "were in the habit of coming to the beach on Sunday and making themselves objectionable." BBCM, 13 June 1912, 11 August 1915.

32 "Bathing Beach at Land's Inlet"; Ottawa Contractors Ltd. to H.E. Waterman, secretary, Hamilton Harbour Commission, 2 July 1915, and T.J. Stewart to A.R. Dufresne, assistant chief engineer, Department of Public Works, 5 November 1915, Hamilton Harbour Commission Records, file "Bathing Beaches: Operation and Jurisdiction"; BOCR, 8 August 1916, in HCCM, 1916, 480; BOCR, 10 July 1917, in HCCM, 1917, 470. The Hamilton Harbour Commission file contains various plans for the construction of the beach, which give some idea of the design features. Special thanks to the Port Authority for making this file available to us.

33 "Great Plans to Improve City's Harbor," *Herald,* 20 December 1919; E.L. Cousins, "Report on Harbor Front Development," 20 February 1919; HCCM, 1919, 549–56; Mark Sproule-Jones, *Governments at Work: Canadian Parliamentary Federalism and Its Public Policy Effects* (Toronto: University of Toronto Press, 1993), 146–49.

34 "Ready to Buy Oaklands Park," *Spectator,* 19 October 1911; "Buying Parks," *Spectator,* 6 February 1912; "Bathing Beach on North Shore," *Spectator,* 28 May 1920; "Wabasso Docks Are Completed," *Spectator,* 20 October 1920; HCCM, 1921, 31 May 1921, 478; Gary Evans, *The Prints of Aldershot: A Photographic View of Another Era* (Burlington: North Shore, 2000).

35 "Double Drowning Has Aroused Public Feeling," *Spectator,* 14 July 1921; H.E. Waterman to Mayor George C. Coppley, 15 June 1922, George A. Carson, YMCA, "Report of Activities at Landsdowne Park," "Swimming Report Week of July 3–9," in Hamilton Harbour Commission Records, file "Bathing Beaches: Operation and Jurisdiction."

36 "Bay Is Unsafe to Bathe In, States Ald. Dr. Wythe," *Spectator,* 9 July 1924; "Untreated Sewage Is Polluting Bay Water," *Herald,* 15 April 1926.

37 WAHC, Floyd Read, interview by Rob Kristofferson, May 1995.

38 "Swimming Parties: First Crowd of Children Leave for North Shore To-morrow," *Spectator,* 15 July 1925. By 1925, there were increasing problems with the ferry service. See "Wabasso Park," *Spectator,* 7 January 1925; and "Wabasso Park," *Spectator,* 20 May 1925.

39 BOCR, 10 October 1916, in HCCM, 1916, 580; City Engineer E.R. Gray, "Report to Board of Control," 22 December 1916, 845–46; BOCR, 26 December 1916, in HCCM, 1916, 836; BOCR, 12 August 1919, in HCCM, 1919, 600; "Bathing Beach Scheme," *Spectator,* 22 June 1920.

40 BOCR, 12 June 1923, in HCCM, 1923, 484–85; HCCM, 31 March 1925, 151; "Wants a Bathing Beach This Year," *Spectator,* 14 July 1924; "Bathing Beach Plan Too Costly, Board Declares," *Spectator,* 17 March 1925; "Bathing Beach in Ward Five Is Finding Favour," *Spectator,* 9 May 1925; "Four Proposals for Committee," *Spectator,* 7 May 1925; "O'Heir

Making Last Move for Bathing Beach," *Spectator,* 8 June 1925; "Halcrow Disgusted," *Spectator,* 10 June 1925; "Public Baths," *Spectator,* 18 June 1925; "Bathing Beach: Halcrow Will Make Another Effort to Have Matter Settled," *Spectator,* 15 July 1925; "Shelved Proposal for Bathing Beach," *Spectator,* 12 August 1925; Craig Heron, "Halcrow, George," in *DHB,* 3:112–13.

41 "Oil Bath," *Spectator,* 4 June 1925; "Tracing Oil," *Spectator,* 12 June 1925; "Action Needed," *Spectator,* 4 November 1925.

42 For a sample of the debate over water quality, see "Tope Opposed to Using Bay Front," *Spectator,* 23 March 1925; "Halcrow Favours Bathing Beach," *Spectator,* 19 June 1925.

43 HCCM, 1925, "Report of Special Committee on Bathing and Wading Facilities," 11 July 1925, 580–81; HCCM, 1926, 25 May and 31 August 1926, 394–95, 523–24; HCCM, 1927, Bathing Beach Committee Report, 26 July 1927, 382; "Bathing Beach: Halcrow Will Make Another Effort to Have Matter Settled," *Spectator,* 15 July 1925; "Four Proposals for Committee," *Spectator,* 7 May 1925; "Estimated Cost of Bathing Pool Ready for Board," *Spectator,* 24 June 1926; "Criticizes Board: For Holding Up Bathing Beach Recommendations," *Spectator,* 3 July 1926; "Plan for Bathing Beach Is Approved," *Spectator,* 1 September 1926; "Bathing Beach Plans Adopted," *Spectator,* 12 May 1927.

44 Committee to Board of Control, 12 June 1928, in HCCM, 1928, 458; BOCR, 26 June 1928, in HCCM, 1928, 475; Property Sub-Committee Bathing Beach Report to Property and License Committee, 22 April 1929, in HCCM, 1929, 316–17; "Cleared Bay Front," *Spectator,* 5 April 1927.

45 WAHC, Charles Bulmer, interview by Rob Kristofferson, 23 May 1995. Parts of this interview are now available online. In it, Bulmer recalls growing up around the bay in the 1930s and 1940s. See http://workerscity.ca/north-end/recreation-on-the-bay/; Lawrence Murphy and Philip Murphy, *Tales from the North End* (Hamilton: Authors, 1981), 47, 52, 137; WAHC, Ken "Breezy" Withers, interview by Rob Kristofferson, 23 May 1995, who recounted that his brother shot craps behind the bandstand at Eastwood Park and that his godfather raised fighting cocks. The Modjeska House, formerly Harvey's Hotel, then the Burlington House, is now Fisher's Pier 4 Pub and Grub. See also Bill Manson, *Footsteps in Time: Exploring Hamilton's Heritage Neighbourhoods* (Burlington: North Shore, 2006), 2:42.

46 Murphy and Murphy, *Tales from the North End,* 90, 94, 159; Rahima Visram, "Then and Now: Recreation, Lived Experiences and the Polluting of the Bay – Hamilton Harbour" (bachelor's thesis, McMaster University, 1998).

47 T.H. Whillans, "Historic Transformations of Fish Communities in Three Great Lakes Bays," *Journal of Great Lakes Research* 5, 2 (1979): 206; Margaret Beattie Bogue, *Fishing the Great Lakes: An Environmental History, 1783–1933* (Madison: University of Wisconsin Press, 2000), 279–86.

48 "Report of the Ontario Game and Fish Commission," *OSP,* 1912, no. 52, 89. On female anglers generally, see David McMurray, "'The Charm of Being Loose and Free': Nineteenth-Century Fisherwomen in the North American Wilderness," *International Journal of the History of Sport* 30, 8 (April 2013): 826–52.

49 "Report of the Ontario Game and Fish Commission," 50, 75, 90, 114, 119.

50 Bogue, *Fishing the Great Lakes,* 305–7. The jurisdictional bickering between Ottawa and the Province continued to affect enforcement, as Bogue suggests, although after Charles John Kerr was appointed, he was much more vigorous in enforcing regulations.

51 Quoted in "Sportsmen Voice Regret Game Report Is Shielded," *Toronto Star*, 28 February 1930, 3.

52 "Angling Club, "*Spectator*, 17 January 1921; "Local Anglers Swap Yarns at Annual Dinner," *Spectator*, 24 March 1931.

53 The 1901 manuscript census lists Charles J. Kerr as a machinist who lived with his wife and sons in his Mary Street North End home. In 1911, his occupation is given as fish and game warden. Many thanks to Eric Sager, University of Victoria, for access to digitized versions of the manuscript 1901 and 1911 Canada censuses for Hamilton.

54 "Report of the Ontario Game and Fish Commission," 82; the report summarizes the arguments for and against carp, 80–85, which can be found regularly in the fisheries reports. Nine club members who were mentioned in newspaper accounts between 1921 and 1925 have been record-linked to city directories. Their occupations were clerk, tobacco retailer, manager at Dominion Power and Transmission and at the Abrasive Company of Canada, owner of a boat-building firm, and sporting goods salesman. *Vernon's City of Hamilton … Annual Street, Alphabetical, General, Miscellaneous and Classified Business Directory* (Hamilton: H. Vernon and Son, 1922).

55 Fisheries Division, Annual Report, 1906, *OSP*, 1907, no. 33, 34; Game and Fisheries Department, Annual Report, 1912, 82–83; "Net and Rod Fishing," editorial, and "Anglers Object to Seine Nets," *Spectator*, 22 April 1920. Hamilton City Council had already protested the application. HCCM, 1920, 24 February 1920, 117.

56 "Notice to Anglers," *Spectator*, 12 January 1921; "Angling Club," *Spectator*, 17 January 1921; "Angling Club to Utter Protest," *Spectator*, 10 March 1921; "Angling Club: Moving Pictures of Famous Fishing Spots Enjoyed," *Spectator*, 27 January 1925.

57 Fisheries Division, Annual Report, 1906, 34; Game and Fisheries Department, Annual Report, 1908, *OSP*, 1909, no. 32, 33; "Illegal Fishing Will Be Stopped," *Spectator*, 30 April 1931, 7; "Anxious to Net Herring in the Bay," *Spectator*, 7 December 1931; "Fish Poaching Now Curtailed," *Spectator*, 11 January 1932. Kerr's successor continued to go after net fishing. See, for example, "Bay Netting," *Herald*, 28 January 1933.

58 "Fish Spearing: Privilege Will Again Be Permitted This Year," *Spectator*, 29 December 1909; "Fish Spearing," *Spectator*, 10 December 1926.

59 "Report of the Special Committee on the Game Fish Situation in Ontario," *OSP*, 1930, no. 54, 44.

60 "Anglers Would Stop Spearing," *Spectator*, 13 February 1925; "Inspector Kerr Issues Warning to Fishermen," *Spectator*, 21 March 1921; "Spear Fishing," *Spectator*, 19 August 1921; "Winter Fishing," *Spectator*, 18 November 1921; "Fish Spearing," *Spectator*, 7 December 1931; "Pike, Pickerel to Be Protected This Spring," *Herald*, 28 February 1933; "Pike Spearing," *Herald*, 10 January 1934; "Pike Removed from Bay When Most Valuable," *Spectator*, 12 April 1934; "Advise Ban on Spear Fishing," *Spectator*, 10 February 1933.

61 "Report of the Ontario Game and Fish Commission," *OSP*, 1912, no. 52, 72.

62 "Angling Club to Utter Protest"; "Bay Pollution," *Spectator*, 20 January 1925; "Co-operation in Cleaning Up Bay," *Spectator*, 21 January 1925.

63 "Report of the Special Committee," 53–54; "Beach News," *Spectator*, 27 June 1934.

64 "Angling Clubs Competition," *Spectator*, 27 May 1921; "Restocking Bay Waters," *Spectator*, 22 June 1921; "Angling Club," *Spectator*, 24 March 1925; "Bay Stocked," *Spectator*, 8 June 1932, 10; "Report of the Special Committee," 12–14, 24–42, 81–110, and particularly 88–98 on black bass and the history of propagation efforts.

65 "Report of the Special Committee," 14.

66 "Local Anglers Swap Yarns at Annual Dinner."

67 "Ambitious Plan by Angling Club," *Spectator*, 25 November 1931; "Are Working at Fish Hatchery," *Spectator*, 12 April 1932; "Ten Thousand Bass for Bay," *Spectator*, 11 November 1932; "Thousands of Bass for Bay," *Spectator*, 4 April 1933; "Islands in the Bay," *Herald*, 4 April 1933; "Alligator Dies Violent Death," *Spectator*, 28 April 1933; "Hamilton Beach," *Spectator*, 19 May 1933; "Fish Get Away, Anglers Smile," *Spectator*, 18 June 1933; "Will Develop Fish Hatchery," *Spectator*, 20 April 1934; *OSP*, 1933, no. 9, 22.

68 Harry L. Penny, *One Hundred Years and Still Sailing: A History of Hamilton Yachts, Yachtsmen, and Yachting, 1888 to 1988 – Centennial Yearbook* (Hamilton: Royal Hamilton Yacht Club, 1988). For an overview, see Walter G. Peace, "Landscapes of Victorian Hamilton: The Use of Visual Materials in Recreating and Interpreting the Past" (Department of Geography, McMaster University, 1989); *Bird's Eye View of the City of Hamilton: Province of Ontario, 1876* (Madison, WI: J.J. Stoner, 1876); M.F. Fox, "Bird's Eye Views of Canadian Cities: A Review," *Urban History Review* 1, 77 (June 1977): 38–34.

69 *Hamilton Souvenir Calendar, 1907: Royal Hamilton Yacht Club* (Hamilton: Stanley Mills, 1907); *Hamilton: The Birmingham of Canada;* Lister, *Hamilton Canada: Its History,* 63, 67; *Bylaws of the Royal Yacht Club* (Hamilton: Cook and Reid Printers, 1893), Canadian Institute for Historical Microreproduction, 60795. Article 8 of the bylaws stipulates a ten-dollar entrance fee and an annual subscription of five dollars. Penny, *One Hundred Years and Still Sailing,* 4–15; "Revival of Yachting Brings Joy to Sailors and Builders," *Spectator,* 13 October 1934; "RHYC Annual Was Held on Saturday," *Spectator,* 13 March 1911; Ted Smith, "Greening, Harold," *DHB,* ed. T.M. Bailey (Hamilton: Dictionary of Hamilton Biography, 1999), 4:106–7.

70 "Revival of Yachting Brings Joy to Sailors and Builders"; "Regatta at Victoria YC," *Spectator,* 11 July 1910; P.D. "Jutten, Thomas," in *DHB,* 3:99–100; Penny, *One Hundred Years,* 14.

71 "The Oar," *Spectator,* 12 April and 20 May 1901; "Boom in Rowing," *Spectator,* 8 June 1909; "Rowing Club Needs Suitable Quarters," *Spectator,* 12 August 1909; "Oarsmen Suffered," *Spectator,* 17 December 1910; Colin Crozier, "Steele, Robert T.," in *DHB,* 3:152; Robert S. Hunter, *Rowing in Canada since 1848* (Hamilton: Davis-Lisson, 1933); Neil Wigglesworth, *The Social History of English Rowing* (London: Frank Cass, 1992); Mary Keyes, "Sport and Technological Change," in *A Concise History of Sport in Canada,* ed. Don Morrow et al. (Toronto: Oxford University Press, 1989), 260–62; Ian F. Jobling, "Sport in Nineteenth Century Canada: The Effects of Technological Changes on Its Development" (PhD diss., University of Alberta, 1970); Hamilton Tiger Cat Alumni Association, http://www.htcaa.ca/history-Ticats.asp; Robert Sproule, The Ontario Rugby Football Union: 1883–1906, www.cflapedia.com/Documents/sproule/ORFU.pdf.

72 Penny, *One Hundred Years,* 20–34.

73 "Rowing Club to Have Strong Team," *Spectator,* 9 May 1921; "Hamilton Rowing Club Expects Two Eights for Canadian Henley," 23 May 1921; "Leander Club Shows Balance for Season," *Spectator,* 7 February 1930; Hunter, *Rowing in Canada.*

74 For two photographs that depict the christening of the club's new eight-oared shell, called the *City of Hamilton,* see *The Official Program of the British Empire Games, 1930* (Hamilton: Robert Duncan, 1930), n.p.

75 "Revival of Yachting Brings Joy to Sailors and Builders."

76 Ibid.; "Yachts Need Wharf and an Anchorage," *Spectator,* 13 October 1934. For examples of earlier articles that highlighted this "revival," see "Royal Hamilton Yacht Club Adds to

Fleet," *Spectator,* 4 May 1934; "Bay Becoming Popular Spot; Sailing Back," *Spectator,* 30 June 1934.

77 Penny, *One Hundred Years,* 33–34, on the management committee and Ker's involvement in sailing. Penny does not mention the proposal, and it does not appear in any city council minutes or other documentation.

78 "The Boating Season: Something about Our Boat-Houses," *Spectator,* 12 March 1872. People who had money to spend became a substantial market for the work of family-based boat-building firms such as Bastien, Askew, Thompson, and Zealand. Laura Edith Baldwin, *The Boat Builders of Hamilton* (Hamilton: In Harmony Promotions, 1992); J. Brian Henley, "Bastien Hit Gold with His Boats," *Spectator,* 23 September 1987; S. Patricia Filer, "Bastien, Henry Louis," in *DHB,* ed. T.M. Bailey (Hamilton: Dictionary of Hamilton Biography, 1991), 2:11.

79 WAHC, Charles Bulmer, interview by Rob Kristofferson, 23 May 1995.

80 Murphy and Murphy, *Tales from the North End,* 13.

81 Ibid., 156; interview by Nancy Bouchier, 20 April 2000.

82 *The Official Program of the British Empire Games;* British Empire Games, Hamilton, 1930 Scrapbook, LH&A, HPL; Daniel Gorman, "Amateurism, Imperialism, Internationalism and the First British Empire Games," *International Journal of the History of Sport* 27, 4 (March 2010): 611–34; Katharine Moore, "'The Warmth of Comradeship': The First British Empire Games and Imperial Solidarity," *International Journal of the History of Sport* 6, 2 (September 1989): 242–51.

83 Walter McMullen, "The Sport Trail," *Spectator,* 21 August 1930.

84 Lou E. Marsh, "With Pick and Shovel," *Toronto Star,* 20 August 1930; Lou E. Marsh, "Wright Retiring Unless His Race Is Rowed Today," *Toronto Star,* 21 August 1930. Canadian sports reporters awarded Pearce the Lou Marsh Trophy in 1938 for being Canada's top athlete, professional or amateur.

85 Dermot Keogh, "Australian Oarsman Was Never Extended," *Spectator,* 22 August 1930; Lou E. Marsh, "Bobby Pearce Easily Takes Empire Skulling Honors," *Toronto Star,* 22 August 1930; on Pearce, who has been inducted into both the Canadian (in 1975) and Australian Sport Halls of Fame (in 1985), see "Honoured Member Robert Pearce," http://www.sportshall.ca/stories.html?proID=7&catID=all, and Sport Australia, Hall of Fame, "Henry 'Bobby' Pearce – Rowing," http://www.sahof.org.au/hall-of-fame/member-profil e/?memberID=424&memberType=athlete.

86 Lou E. Marsh, "With Pick and Shovel," *Toronto Star,* 21 August 1930; Alexandrine Gibb, "Bobby Pearce Soon to Take Life Partner," *Toronto Star,* 2 December 1930. Pearce eventually became a Canadian citizen. See William Paul Beedling, "Henry Robert 'Bob' Pearce: A Biography" (master's thesis, University of Western Ontario, 1982).

87 "Bay Becoming Popular Spot; Sailing Back."

CHAPTER 5: PLANNING NATURE

1 "Reconnaissance Report on Development of Hamilton," October 1917, 68, Noulan Cauchon Papers, MG 30, vol. 1, file 38, Library and Archives Canada (LAC); "How Hamilton Might Become Beautiful," *Hamilton Herald* (hereafter *Herald*), 4 August 1917; Brian Henley, "Cauchon Had Unique Vision for Hamilton," *Hamilton Spectator* (hereafter *Spectator*), 26 April 1997; David L.A. Gordon, "'Agitating People's Brains': Noulan Cauchon and the City Scientific in Canada's Capital," *Planning Perspectives* 23, 3 (July 2008): 349–79.

2 Nicholas Terpstra, "Local Politics and Local Planning: A Case Study of Hamilton Ontario, 1915–1930," *Urban History Review* 14, 2 (October 1985): 121.

3 "The Ethical Basis of Town Planning," *Spectator,* 11 December 1920; Noulan Cauchon Papers, MG 30, vol. 2, 2–16; vol. 2, 1920, 21, LAC; *Spectator,* 19 June 1920.

4 E.L. Cousins, "Report on Harbor Front Development," 20 February 1919; Hamilton City Council Minutes (hereafter HCCM), 1919, 549–56, Local History and Archives Department (hereafter LH&A), Hamilton Public Library (hereafter HPL), Hamilton. On the 1912 creation of the harbour commission, see Mark Sproule-Jones, *Governments at Work: Canadian Parliamentary Federalism and Its Public Policy Effects* (Toronto: University of Toronto Press, 1993), 135–42.

5 On Parks Board developments during this period, see John C. Best, *Thomas Baker McQuesten: Public Works, Politics and Imagination* (Hamilton: Corinth Press, 1991), especially Chapter 5, "A Bachelor ... Whose Bride Is the City Parks System," 51–68; on modernity, nationalism, and McQuesten's work as Ontario minister of highways, see Joan Coutu, "Vehicles of Nationalism: Defining Canada in the 1930s," *Journal of Canadian Studies* 37, 1 (Spring 2002): 180–203.

6 Best, *Thomas Baker McQuesten,* 1–24.

7 Mary Anderson, *The Life Writings of Mary Baker McQuesten: Victorian Matriarch* (Waterloo: Wilfrid Laurier University Press, 2004), 60. None of the McQuesten children married.

8 Apart from the work of Anderson and Best, McQuesten's views can be teased out of various letters in the Whitehern Museum Archives. For example, on his overseas trip, see Thomas B. McQuesten to Calvin McQuesten, 16 June 1901, W4490, Whitehern Museum Archives, http://www.whitehern.ca/index.php.

9 Terpstra, "Local Politics and Local Planning," 121; see also John C. Best, "McQuesten, Thomas Baker," in *Dictionary of Hamilton Biography* (hereafter *DHB*), ed. T.M. Bailey (Hamilton: Dictionary of Hamilton Biography, 1999), 4:181.

10 "Reconnaissance Report on Development of Hamilton," Noulan Cauchon Papers, MG 30, vol. 1, file 38, 68, LAC; "The Ethical Basis of Town Planning," 11 December 1920, vol. 2, 2–16, and vol. 2, 1920, 21, from *Spectator,* 19 June 1920; "How Hamilton Might Become Beautiful"; Henley, "Cauchon Had Unique Vision for Hamilton." Part of Cauchon's vision involved a memorial to honour the Hamiltonians who fought in the First World War. He proposed having Cootes Paradise lands irrigated and given to war veterans, a measure that would already have been at odds with local nature conservationists.

11 Terpstra, "Local Politics and Local Planning," 115; Best, *Thomas Baker McQuesten,* 51–68. McQuesten would also use this position to help bring McMaster University from Toronto to Hamilton and to establish the Royal Botanical Gardens.

12 Hamilton Naturalists Club Records, 1919–78, MU 1285–9, F797, Archives of Ontario, Toronto. Henry Nunn, a Hamilton businessman and founding member of the society, publicized its work during the 1920s through his company's sponsorship of *Birdland News,* a nature radio program on Station CKOC. By 1937, the new curriculum of the Ontario Department of Education would stress natural science and officially approve the Audubon Junior Club system as a teaching aid in the classroom. Robert Owen Merriman adjudicated the school-based birdhouse competition, and the society awarded sets of Audubon bird cards to the winners. Paul Mercer, "Merriman, Robert Owen," in *DHB,* 4:191–92; H. Williams, "History of Hamilton Bird Protection Society," *Wood Duck* 12, 1 (September 1958): 123–25.

13 Hamilton Naturalists Club Minute Book, 26 June 1920, MU 1285, F797, Archives of Ontario.

14 "Duck Shooters Are Opposed to Bird Sanctuary," *Spectator,* 28 September 1920. The *Spectator* referred to Long as one of the government's hunting and licence inspectors: untitled article, *Spectator,* 4 February 1927. *Vernon's Directory for the City of Hamilton* (Hamilton, 1929) lists him as a clay-pigeon manufacturer.

15 "Lease of Marsh Lands for Bird Preserve Fought," *Spectator,* 21 April 1925. This article re-stated the case originally made in the 1920 petition. Craig Heron discusses pothunting among other household strategies to enhance working-class living standards in *Lunch-Bucket Lives: Remaking the Workers' City* (Toronto: Between the Lines Press, 2015), 112–13, 586.

16 "Duck Shooters Are Opposed to Bird Sanctuary."

17 Ibid.

18 Jack Miner, *Wild Goose Jack* and *Jack Miner and the Birds,* quoted in Tina Loo, *States of Nature: Conserving Canada's Wildlife in the Twentieth Century* (Vancouver: UBC Press, 2006), 81. Miner was involved in the Hamilton case throughout the dispute, and his work at the Kingsville sanctuary was often cited in support of the bird protection society's efforts. For example, see "Coote's [sic] Paradise," *Spectator,* 24 January 1921; "Bird Sanctuary Will Be Created in Dundas Marsh," *Spectator,* 1 May 1925; and "Miner Praises Dundas Marsh," *Spectator,* 30 November 1926. Tina Loo's chapter on Miner, which is a fine analysis of his role as a conservationist, emphasizes the appeal and working-class rural roots of his ideas. To situate the activities of the Hamilton Bird Protection Society within the context of the larger Canadian movement, see also Janet Foster, *Working for Wildlife: The Beginnings of Preservation in Canada* (Toronto: University of Toronto Press, 1978), especially Chapter 6, "Protecting an International Resource," 120–54.

19 Quoted in "Dundas Marsh: Natural Place for Sanctuary: So Jack Miner, Bird Lover Assures Adam Brown," *Spectator,* 30 September 1920.

20 Ibid.

21 Hamilton Naturalists Club Minute Book, 5 April 1923. According to its own records, and apart from its affiliation with the American Audubon Society and Jack Miner, the Hamilton Bird Protection Society had good connections, including Provincial Ornithologist C.W. Nash, the Quebec Society for the Protection of Birds, the McIlwraith Society of London, Ontario, the Ontario Fish and Game Association, the Hamilton and District Angling and Casting Association (which on the occasion of the sanctuary designation sent the society an oak gavel to commemorate the event), and the Hamilton Parks Board. When lobbying the City to enforce its own anti-pollution bylaws, the society appealed to other local organizations for support, including the Trades and Labour Congress, the Chamber of Commerce, the Kiwanis and Rotary Clubs, the Burlington Beach Commission, the Local Council of Women, the Humane Society, the Angling Club, the Gyro Club, and the Parks Board. Minute Book, 1919–32.

22 Ibid., 16 January 1922.

23 Ibid., 29 April 1924.

24 Stewart reportedly approached Minister of Marine and Fisheries P.J.A. Cardin on numer-ous occasions and, in doing so, "actively forwarded Midford's application." See "Certain Marsh Lands Will Be Safeguarded," *Spectator,* 13 May 1925. Another paper stated that he had "written at least two score letters to the department, and had waited upon [the minister]

many times in the interests of Captain Midford." See "T.J. Stewart Has Fought His Last Battle," *Herald,* 8 November 1926.

25 "Revives Plan to Create Haven for Wild Birds: Capt. Midford Explains Sanctuary Proposal," *Spectator,* 20 January 1927; Brian Henley, "Duck Farm Proposal Sparked Local Furore," *Spectator,* 29 March 1997.

26 "Paradise Lands Bird Sanctuary," *Spectator,* 11 February 1925.

27 "Lease of Marsh Lands for Bird Preserve Fought," *Spectator,* 21 April 1925.

28 "Get Assurance: No Permit for Marsh Lands until Board Is Heard From," *Spectator,* 27 April 1925. A Hamilton controller and alderman joined a deputation led by the Parks Board, the harbour commission, and the Angler's Club to the minister of marine and fisheries in Ottawa. HCCM, 1925, 382, and 1926, 144. However, a year would elapse before the sanctuary would finally be designated by the provincial government, and the *Spectator* was premature in reporting on its establishment. See "Bird Sanctuary Will Be Created in Dundas Marsh," *Spectator,* 1 May 1925; "Bird Sanctuary," *Spectator,* 9 May 1925; "Certain Marsh Lands Will Be Safeguarded," *Spectator,* 13 May 1925; "Coote's Paradise," *Spectator,* 26 May 1925. Midford, however, was not about to let the issue die an easy death. According to "Wants Midford to Control the Bird Sanctuary," *Spectator,* 1 April 1926, he tried another tack in presenting his case to the Board of Control. Through his representative, Alex McMullen, Midford requested that he be appointed the head of the new bird sanctuary. By January 1927, when he again tried to resurrect his tourist scheme, the local press was dismissing him as a bit of a pest: "a bonnie fechter who refuses to admit himself licked." "Revives Plan to Create Haven for Wild Birds," *Spectator,* 20 January 1927; "City Determined to Prevent Loss of Marsh Lands," *Spectator,* 10 March 1927; "Coote's Paradise," *Spectator,* 11 March 1927.

29 William Lyle Sommerville, Robert Anderson Pope, and Desmond McDonough, "Report of Survey and Recommendations: McKittrick Properties of Hamilton, Canada" (1 February 1919), 6, Hamilton Real Estate Board Collection, William Ready Division of Archives and Research Collections, McMaster University Library, Hamilton. McKittrick Properties had long been involved in developing waterlots along the south shore of Cootes Paradise. See "Division of Water Lots Agreed Upon," *Spectator,* 24 April 1916; "Coote's Paradise," *Spectator,* 1 December 1921; "May Take Over Bridge Costs," *Spectator,* 28 October 1926; "Application of McKittrick Co., Is Dismissed," *Spectator,* 17 December 1926; "Will Appeal," *Spectator,* 14 January 1927; "McKittrick Lands: Syndicate Has Rights to Coote's Paradise," *Spectator,* 31 January 1927; "McKittrick Deal," *Spectator,* 1 March 1927; and "In Westdale," *Spectator,* 14 October 1927. For an overview, see John C. Weaver, "From Land Assembly to Social Maturity: The Suburban Life of Westdale (Hamilton) Ontario, 1911–1951," in *A History of Ontario: Selected Readings,* ed. Michael J. Piva (Toronto: Copp Clark Pitman, 1988), 219–21; and Best, *Thomas Baker McQuesten,* 56–57.

30 "Bird Sanctuary Law in Force," *Spectator,* 1 March 1927; "Dundas Marsh Is Designated a Crown Game Reserve: Unlawful to Carry Arms on the Property," *Herald,* 12 February 1927. Hunters apparently had to obtain these licences from provincial authorities in Toronto, rather than local authorities as was normally the case.

31 "Dundas Marsh to Be Saved as Bird Sanctuary," *Spectator,* 22 January 1927; "Marsh Sanctuary Given Approval," *Spectator,* 25 January 1927; "Marsh Declared Bird Sanctuary," *Spectator,* 1 February 1927; "Marsh Will Be Sanctuary for Wildflowers," *Spectator,* 3 March 1927; "Government Sanction for Preserve Pleases City," *Herald,* 11 February 1927; "Dundas Marsh Is Designated a Crown Game Reserve: Unlawful to Carry Arms on the Property."

32 The extent of the community is best documented in six aerial photographs taken by Jack V. Elliott Air Services in 1928, now in the Royal Botanical Gardens at Burlington. City records document the expropriation of only 50 of the 120 boathouses pictured on the photos. How many of the remaining 70 homes were occupied by squatters is simply not known.

33 Craig Heron argues that city waterfront areas generally "caused the most consternation in Hamilton's polite society." See Craig Heron, "Working Class Hamilton, 1896–1930" (PhD diss., Dalhousie University, 1981), 61. On working-class waterfront culture in Montreal and Toronto, see Peter Delottinville, "Joe Beef of Montreal: Working Class Culture and Tavern, 1869–1899," *Labour/Le travail* 8–9 (1981–82): 9–40; and Mary Louise Adams, "Almost Anything Can Happen: A Search for Sexual Discourse in the Urban Spaces of 1940s Toronto," *Canadian Journal of Sociology* 19, 2 (1994): 218–32. For fictionalized accounts of Hamilton's boathouse community and its struggle to survive, see Rachael Preston, *The Fishers of Paradise* (Victoria: First Choice Books, 2012); and John Terpstra, "Mr. McQuesten," in John Terpstra, *Falling into Place* (Kentville, NS: Gaspereau Press, 2002), 151–61.

34 On housing in the city and owner-constructed homes, see Michael J. Doucet, "Working Class Housing in a Small Nineteenth Century Canadian City: Hamilton, Ontario, 1852–1881," in *Essays in Canadian Working-Class History,* ed. Gregory S. Kealey and Peter Warrian (Toronto: McClelland and Stewart, 1976), 83–105; Michael J. Doucet and John C. Weaver, *Housing the North American City* (Montreal and Kingston: McGill-Queen's University Press, 1991); and Richard Harris, *Unplanned Suburbs: Toronto's American Tragedy, 1900 to 1950* (Baltimore: Johns Hopkins University Press, 1996).

35 Hamilton Board of Health, Annual Report of the Board of Health, 1911–12, 20; Bryce Stewart, *Report of a Preliminary and General Social Survey of Hamilton* (Hamilton: Department of Temperance and Moral Reform of the Methodist Church and the Board of Social Service and Evangelism of the Presbyterian Church, 1913); "Say Slum Conditions Exist in Hamilton," *Spectator,* 20 May 1913; "Sounds Death-Knell of the Slum Districts," *Spectator,* 23 July 1913; "Social Survey of Hamilton in 1913," *Herald,* 6 January 1914; more generally, see Rosemary Gagan, "Mortality Patterns and Public Health in Hamilton, Canada, 1900–1914," *Urban History Review* 17, 3 (February 1989): 161–75.

36 HCCM, 1931, 413–14, 649. The City of Hamilton took over some tenancies of the boathouse colony previously controlled by the Toronto, Hamilton and Buffalo Railway. See "Would Remove Squatters on Marsh's Edge," *Spectator,* 14 February 1939. The best information about the composition of the boathouse community comes from the list of names that the Hamilton Board of Control used to purchase expropriated properties. HCCM, 1 March 1921, Bylaw 4188, "To Acquire Lands and Boat Houses Necessary for the Establishment and Laying Out of Longwood Road," Schedule A, "Parcels of Land Occupied by Certain Buildings and Boathouses Erected on City Property to the North of Desjardins canal and West of York Street," 31 March 1931; Board of Control, Report (hereafter BOCR), 10 and 31 March 1931, 14 and 28 April 1931, in HCCM, 1931. No manuscript census records between 1851 and 1901 specify any people as marsh dwellers. Whether they were squatters or tenants of leaseholders is unknown. There is an indication that subleasing went on, as in the case of a home that burnt in a 1931 fire. See "War on Squatters," *Spectator,* 17 March 1926.

37 "Would Remove Squatters on Marsh's Edge." An argument about the rights of one squatter was presented by defence attorney A.L. Shaver, KC, on behalf of his client, Herbert Matthews, a cable man who lived in boathouse No. 7, in the case of *The City v. Herbert Matthews.*

38 Interview by Bouchier, 20 April 2000.

39 Ibid.

40 J. Brian Henley, "Hamilton History: When the Livin' Was Easy in Cootes Paradise," *Hamilton Magazine*, May 1979, 11.

41 Interview by Bouchier, 20 April 2000. Perhaps these games were played across the water near Easterbrook's, where, according to historians of the North End, men would "indulge themselves in their usual feast, including a keg or two of beer, and generally enjoy themselves." Lawrence Murphy and Philip Murphy, *Tales from the North End* (Hamilton, 1981), 14.

42 Interview by Bouchier, 20 April 2000; Jeff Mahoney, "Requiem for Cootes Paradise 'Canal Rats,'" *Spectator*, 9 January 2013; see also Terpstra, "Mr. McQuesten," 156.

43 "A Glimpse of Hamilton's Picturesque Old Marshland: Weatherbeaten Shacks Form Beautiful Scene at Head," *Herald*, 2 August 1924. Apparently, the bridge-diving tradition carried on for decades. See "Sad Drowning at High Level Bridge," *Spectator*, 25 June 1910; "Dangerous Sport," *Spectator*, 8 September 1953.

44 "The Fox and Hounds," *Spectator*, 9 August 1924; interview by Bouchier, 20 April 2000. The newspaper article describes a piece "written so long ago that [Harry Barnard, an old-time sportsman] would only make a guess at the date [the 1850s or 1860s]." Another area man, "old man Skuce," the proprietor of the Fox and Hounds, was a prominent figure in local sporting culture. He apparently was one of the best shots around, which is amazing since he reportedly had just one arm. As one resident recalled of his youth, Skuce was not at all hindered by his disability. In the day's early light, he easily took down braces of ducks with a few shots. His surname is also recorded as Skues or Skuce; the Fox and Hounds is also given as the Foxhounds Inn. See "The Fox and Hounds," *Spectator*, 23 June 1923; "The Fox and Hounds," 9 August 1924. See also Edward Roper, *Herald*, 13 February 1907, republished in Brian Henley, *1846 Hamilton: From a Frontier Town to the Ambitious City* (Burlington: North Shore, 1995), 59–63.

45 "Immorality Practiced in Boathouses: This Spreads Venereal Disease, Says Inspector Thornley," *Herald*, 12 August 1920.

46 Interview by Bouchier, 20 April 2000; also transcript of interview by Andrew Stevenson, Niagara College, for documentary film *No Trespassing: Stories from Hamilton's Waterfront*, sound rolls 18/19, 2000. See also "Citizen Recalls Tramps of the Depression," *Spectator*, 26 March 2001; and "Animals Can Still Find High Level Home: Art Portraying Plants and Creatures Is Perfect for Highway Gateway to City," *Spectator*, 2 September 2000. "Animals Can Still Find" suggests that the empty spaces on the high-level bridge pylons should be used as a "tribute to the hoboes who came to town on the tracks below that bridge and took up residence in small caves around it."

47 "Hoboes Like Poor: They Are Always Present and Flock to the Cities," *Hamilton Times* (hereafter *Times*), 12 January 1911; "Tramps Imposing on the Citizens: Police Trying to Break Up a Plan of Professional Hoboes," *Herald*, 25 November 1909.

48 Interview by Rob Kristofferson, Workers Arts and Heritage Center, April 1995. Many thanks to Rob and the Workers Arts and Heritage Center for access to these data; interview by Rob Krisofferson, November 1999; interview by Bouchier, 20 April 2000.

49 Interview by Bouchier, 20 April 2000.

50 "Ferdinand Morrison: Death Claims One of the City's Oldest Residents," *Spectator*, 28 December 1920; "The Fox and Hounds."

51 On drinking in Hamilton generally, see Craig Heron, "The Boys and Their Booze: Masculinities and Public Drinking in Working-Class Hamilton, 1890–1946," *Canadian Historical Review* 86, 3 (September 2005): 411–52.

52 Cockpit Island, which lies off the south shore of the marsh, just west of Princess Point, is not so named on the *Surtees Map of the County of Wentworth, 1859*. It is listed, however, on maps by the turn of the century. See Department of Militia and Defence, Geographical Section, General Staff, No. 2197, Topographic Map, Hamilton, Ontario, Sheet 33, 1907–09, 1:63360.

53 Interview by Bouchier, 20 April 2000; "To Inspect Boathouses," *Spectator*, 28 August 1920; "Boathouse Party Broken Up When Police Knocked," *Spectator*, 4 May 1920; "Harbour Board Is After Offenders," *Spectator*, 22 June 1921.

54 Murphy and Murphy, *Tales from the North End*, 177–78; see also "African Golf: Big Game Broken Up When Patrol Appeared," *Spectator*, 10 November 1919; Robert Kristofferson, *The Workers' City: Hamilton's North End* (Hamilton: OWAHC, n.d.). The Worker's City series' rich collection of tours, interviews, maps, photographs, and other resources is now available online as well as through a downloadable app for mobile devices at http://workerscity.ca/

55 Interview by Bouchier, 20 April 2000.

56 "A Glimpse of Hamilton's Picturesque Old Marshland." This article appeared on the heels of a series of public-interest pieces in the *Herald*, which focused on water-quality problems in the bay and the need for recreational space and programs for children.

57 See, for example, "Clean Waterfront Ainslie's Order," *Times*, 11 July 1924; "War on Squatters: Harbour Board to Clean Up 'Boathouses' on the Bay," *Spectator*, 17 March 1926.

58 Leslie Laking, "Royal Botanical Gardens – A Historical View – Early Days at RBG," *Pappus* 11, 1 (1992): 9–11; Leslie Laking, "A History of Royal Botanical Gardens (Part 2)," *Pappus* 11, 1 (1992): 9–11; Best, *Thomas Baker McQuesten*, 59–60. This competition was the subject of an Art Gallery of Hamilton exhibit presented by the Architectural Conservancy of Ontario Hamilton Region Branch, titled *Hamilton, the City Beautiful: Visions of Civic Beauty in the 1920s*, which ran from 5 to 31 October 1999. See also Doug Foley, "Hamilton the Beautiful," *Spectator*, 16 October 1999; Karen Mills, "Gallery Design Reflects Hamilton's Earliest Visionaries," *Spectator*, 9 December 1999.

59 Geoffrey Hunt, *John M. Lyle: Toward a Canadian Architecture* (Kingston: Agnes Etherington Art Centre, Queen's University, 1982); D. Hamilton, "Lyle, John," in *DHB*, 4:161–62.

60 Best, *Thomas Baker McQuesten*, 60.

61 R.C. Reade, "Hamilton Shows Toronto How," *Toronto Star Weekly*, 16 November 1929.

62 Ibid.

63 "War on Squatters."

64 Thomas B. McQuesten High Level Bridge Scrapbook, vol. 1, LH&A, HPL. The bridge was not named after McQuesten during his lifetime; he was much too modest and, as he put it, interested in achieving development "by stealth."

65 A search of the local newspapers uncovered no Trades and Labour Council discussion of the matter. The same is true for the Hamilton and District Labour Council papers in the William Ready Division of Archives and Research Collections, McMaster University Library.

66 "Beautification of Marsh Is Proposed," and "Champion of the Boathouses in the Field: Alderman Sherring Prepared to Tilt for Owners," *Spectator*, 21 June 1932.

67 "Eviction of Squatters Will Throw Many on Relief," *Spectator,* 14 May 1936; Nora-Frances
    Henderson Scrapbook of Clippings, 1924, LH&A, HPL; on her picket-line crossing, see
    Molly Pulver Ungar, "Henderson, Nora-Frances," in *DHB,* 4:127.

68 Russell Geddes, "Hamilton: A Case Study in Local Relief and Public Welfare during the
    Depression" (essay, 1982), LH&A, HPL; "Champion of the Boathouses in the Field"; "Where
    Little Colony Has Grown," *Spectator,* 4 April 1934; "Settlers on Bay Front to Be Dispos-
    sessed," *Spectator,* 3 November 1934; "Eviction of Squatters Will Throw Many on Relief."

69 "Fire Destroys Six Boathouses," *Spectator,* 9 January 1931.

70 "Coroner's Jury Urges Removal of Boathouses: Either This or Fire Protection Jurors
    Say," *Spectator,* 10 March 1931. Unfortunately, neither the records of this jury nor the fire
    marshal's report have been located in the LH&A, HPL, or in the Archives of Ontario.

71 For an example of a previous fire, see "Boathouse Fire Was Spectacular," *Spectator,* 13
    December 1921. The boathouses of North End boatbuilders were equally at risk of fire.
    See "Boathouse Blaze Does $1000 Damage," *Spectator,* 13 November 1924. When asked
    about the boathouses on the southeast portion of the Burlington Heights, one inter-
    viewee responded, "Quite a few bad things happened on this side, because a lot of the
    houses burnt with children in them." He was a young lad of six or seven when the 1931
    fire occurred, and it is unclear whether he was remembering that event, referring to another
    fire, or simply voicing a commonly held perception of the general area.

72 HCCM, 1 March 1921, Bylaw 4188, Schedule A, 31 March 1931; BOCR, 10 and 31 March
    1931, 14 and 28 April 1931, in HCCM, 1931. There is a discrepancy between Jack Elliott's
    1928 air survey of the Desjardins Canal area, which showed about 120 buildings, and the
    1931 Hamilton City Council minutes, which recorded 107. After a considerable search in
    City Hall, the LH&A, HPL, and the Lloyd Reeds Map Collection at McMaster Univer-
    sity, no map showing these boathouse numbers was found to correspond with the city
    list. Whether the list recorded all buildings (such as sheds and outhouses), or solely the
    boathouses in which people lived is not known.

73 "Aldershot," *Spectator,* 28 February 1935; "Last of Squatters Hurled from Land Boathouses,"
    and "Made to Move, Say Squatters Not Gone Far," *Spectator,* 27 May 1936; "Harbour
    Board Plans Ejecting Shore Dwellers," *Spectator,* 12 June 1936. For similar battles in Van-
    couver, see Jill Wade, "Home or Homelessness? Marginal Housing in Vancouver, 1886–1950,"
    Urban History Review 25, 2 (March 1997): 19–29.

74 "Marsh Dwellers Taking Legal Action to Retain Homes," *Spectator,* 19 May 1936; "City
    May Be Restrained from Evicting Family," *Spectator,* 19 May 1936; "Would Remove
    Squatters on Marsh's Edge."

75 "Final Notices Are Served on Dundas Marsh Dwellers," *Spectator,* 16 June 1936; "Would
    Remove Squatters on Marsh's Edge."

76 "Marsh Dwellers to Vacate Homes, Move into City," *Spectator,* 21 May 1936.

77 "Made to Move, Say Squatters Not Gone Far." The City contemplated reusing this
    tactic some years later, although whether it did is unknown. "Board Taking Means to
    Oust Shack Dwellers: Parks Officials May Put Up Fences to Stop Access to Marsh Homes,"
    Spectator, 7 May 1940.

78 "Marsh Tenants Told to Vacate Property," *Spectator,* 11 May 1936.

79 *An Archeological Assessment of Part of the East Shoreline of Coote's Paradise, Hamilton Ontario*
    (Hamilton, 1994), 94–99. Evidently, two shacks remained almost to the early 1960s, when
    Highway 403 was built along the water's edge in Cootes Paradise, over the old Longwood

Street path. Whether they were boathouse homes is unknown. See Brian Henley, "Cootes Paradise 'Shacktown' Lasted Almost 100 Years," *Spectator*, 13 August 1994.

80 "A Boathouse Dweller," letter to editor, and "Boathouse Dwellers," *Spectator*, 11 May 1940.

81 "Board Taking Means to Oust Dwellers," *Spectator*, 7 May 1940.

82 Quoted in Best, *Thomas Baker McQuesten*, 64–65.

83 Best, *Thomas Baker McQuesten*, 93–137.

84 Ibid., 158–60; *An Act respecting the Royal Botanical Gardens*, 9 April 1941, 5 Geo. VI, c. 75, *OSP*.

85 Best, *Thomas Baker McQuesten*, 184; Leslie Laking, "Early Days at RBG," *Pappus* 10, 4 (1991): 3–9; Laking, "A History."

86 *Programme: Her Royal Highness the Princess Margaret, Countess of Snowdon Officially names the Thomas B. McQuesten High Level Bridge and Unveils the Ontario Historical Plaque* (Hamilton, 11 July 1988).

CHAPTER 6: CONFINING NATURE

1 Trevor Lautens, "Place for Everyone – Objective for Hamilton Harbour," *Hamilton Spectator* (hereafter *Spectator*), 12 November 1960. On Lautens, see Trevor Lautens, "About Me," http://www.trevorlautens.ca/about.html. His older brother Gary, whom he joined at the newspaper in 1953, is perhaps better known for his years as a *Toronto Star* columnist and for his popular books.

2 Lautens, "Place for Everyone."

3 Quoted in D.H. Matheson, *A Consolidated Report on Burlington Bay* (Hamilton: Department of Municipal Laboratories, 1958).

4 "To Deepen Harbour," *Spectator*, 24 July 1931; "Citizens Proud of Excellent Harbour," and "Tax Free Harbour Plan Is Endorsed," *Spectator*, 30 June 1934; "Deepening Shipping Channels in Harbour," *Spectator*, 20 October 1934. For the history of some of the industrial docks, see Hamilton Harbour Commissioners, *Annual Report* (hereafter *HHCAR*), 1951. On the Fourth Welland Canal, see John N. Jackson, *The Welland Canals and Their Communities: Engineering, Industrial, and Urban Transformation* (Toronto: University of Toronto Press, 1997), 269–300.

5 Pierre Camu, *Le Saint-Laurent et les Grands Lacs au temps de la vapeur: 1850–1950* (Montreal: Hurtubise HMH, 2005), 146; "Citizens Proud of Excellent Harbour," "Tax Free Harbour Plan Is Endorsed." In 1932, 106,000 tons were exported and 1,555,000 tons were imported; coal accounted for 79 percent of imports and iron ore for 8 percent.

6 Various company accounts can be found in the *Spectator* special edition of 12 November 1960. For a historical outline of Hamilton By-Products wastes, see Intera Technologies, "Inventory of Coal Gasification Plant Waste Sites in Ontario," Ontario Ministry of the Environment, 1987, 2:72–73, Appendix B, "Fact Sheet for Survey of Coal Gassification Plant Waste Sites, Hamilton By-Products Coke Oven," 133–35.

7 "Steeltown: A Century of Steel," *Spectator*, 11 February 2012; "Mark of a City's Growth: Steel," *Spectator*, 12 November 1960; "Stelco Begins Extension Near Strathearne Docks," *Spectator*, 26 April 1955.

8 "Dofasco Expansion Breathtaking," and Frank Sherman, "Dofasco Boosts Production 400 Per Cent in 15 Years," *Spectator*, 12 November 1960; "Work Started by Dofasco on Large New Plant," *Spectator*, 2 March 1954.

9   "Scrap Brings More Business," "Coal Tar Produces Bounty," and "Gases Once Burned as 'Waste' Now Captured for Useful Purposes," *Spectator*, 12 November 1960. On the demand for scrap metal by steel companies, see Carl A. Zimring, *Cash for Your Trash: Scrap Recycling in America* (New Brunswick, NJ: Rutgers University Press, 2005), 108–9.

10 "'Waste' Wins New Role Building Roads, Docks," *Spectator*, 12 November 1960; Paul Wilson, "SlagWorld – A Cinder-ella Story?" *Spectator*, 30 September 1993.

11 "Stelco Develops New Processes," *Spectator*, 12 November 1960.

12 Board of Control, Report (hereafter BOCR), 30 May 1933, in Hamilton City Council Minutes (hereafter HCCM), 12 May 1933, 318–19, Local History and Archives Department (hereafter LH&A), Hamilton Public Library (hereafter HPL), Hamilton; "Harbour Dues Would Yield Big Revenue," *Spectator*, 14 June 1934; "Tax Free Harbour Plan Is Endorsed"; "Harbour Dues Will Be Sought by City," *Spectator*, 22 February 1935; "City Is Seeking Harbour Surplus," *Spectator*, 13 June 1935; see also Mark Sproule-Jones, *Governments at Work: Canadian Parliamentary Federalism and Its Public Policy Effects* (Toronto: University of Toronto Press, 1993), 146–50.

13 *HHCAR*, 1951.

14 For Seaway preparations, see *HHCAR*, 1955, 1958; "Port of Hamilton," a series of daily articles, *Spectator*, 27, 28, and 29 May 1957; Argue Martin, "Nearly $60,000,000 Spent on Harbour in Decade," and David J. Walker, "Harbor Shows How Ottawa Helped in City's Growth," *Spectator*, 12 November 1960; "Mark of a City's Growth: Steel"; see also Sproule-Jones, *Governments at Work*, 148–49; Hamilton Port Authority, *Spanning Two Centuries, 1912–2001: Commemorative History, the Hamilton Harbour Commissioners* (Hamilton: Hamilton Port Authority, 2001), n.p. The skyway bridge would later be renamed the Burlington Bay James N. Allan Skyway.

15 John C. Weaver, *Hamilton: An Illustrated History* (Toronto: James Lorimer, 1982), Table 9 (annexations), Table 14 (population), Table 13 (automobile registrations), 199–201; on postwar consumerism, see Joy Parr, *Domestic Goods: The Material, the Moral, and the Economic in the Postwar Years* (Toronto: University of Toronto Press, 1999).

16 "Acids and Oil Find Way to Bay," *Hamilton Herald* (hereafter *Herald*), 13 June 1931; "Provincial Expert Presents Report on Pollution of Bay," *Spectator*, 23 December 1943; HCCM, 28 December 1943. On local reports to city council, see HCCM, 1942, 299–300, "Report Addressed to W.L. McFaul, City Engineer (25 June 1942)"; HCCM, 1943, 29 June and 28 December 1943.

17 "City Receives Prices of Sewage Plant Job," *Spectator*, 19 August 1957.

18 On steel company attempts to improve the situation, see, for example, "Bay Pollution: New Stelco Equipment Cuts Waste," *Spectator*, 19 February 1952; "Dofasco Plant Installs New Dumping Equipment," *Spectator*, 16 December 1953.

19 A study of Stelco emissions for one month in 1963, which included phenols, suggested that the estimate presented in Table 3 is reasonable.

20 Robert Hanley, "Ring of Oil around Bay May Remain All Summer," *Spectator*, 30 June 1953.

21 "Acids and Oil Find Way to Bay"; "Editorial: Pollution of the Bay," *Spectator*, 18 August 1934; "Oil Floating Again on Bay," *Spectator*, 21 April 1932; "Dye Dumping in Bay Must Stop," *Spectator*, 29 November 1932; "Blames Private Sewers," *Herald*, 6 July 1933; "Bay Pollution Remedy Sought," *Herald*, 31 July 1934; "Parts of Bay Mere Pools of Rotting Waste," *Spectator*, 20 August 1934; "Hamilton to Name Cttee to Find Reason Why Bay Is

Polluted," *Spectator*, 13 July 1943; "Pollution of Bay Increased," *Spectator*, 14 July 1943; "Oil on Bay Is Claimed Worst Ever," *Spectator*, 22 June 1953; "Solution of Sewage Problem in Bay May Cost $10,000,000," *Spectator*, 23 June 1953; "Ring of Oil around Bay May Remain All Summer"; "Queen's Park Health Officials Start Probe into Bay Filth," *Spectator*, 3 July 1953; "Stiff Penalty Provided for Polluting Bay," *Spectator*, 20 February 1954.

22 Matheson, *A Consolidated Report*.

23 "Sewage in Bay Not Shown Bad for City Water," *Spectator*, 1 September 1949.

24 "Building Needed Plant Could Cost Millions," *Spectator*, 13 November 1951; "Warns $4,300,000 Needed to Move Disposal Plant," *Spectator*, 20 December 1951; "Disposal Plant Condition May Be Key to Land Sale," *Spectator*, 21 February 1952.

25 "Experts Plan to Spend Millions on Expansions See 500,000 Population," *Spectator*, 5 December 1955; "Expert Urges City Construct Huge Primary Sewage Treatment Plant," *Spectator*, 7 December 1955. For a fine account of the debate over provincial and federal government assistance in Ontario, see Jennifer Read, "Managing Water Quality in the Great Lakes Basin: Sewage Pollution Control, 1951–60," in *Ontario since Confederation: A Reader*, ed. Edgar-Andre Montigny and Lori Chambers (Toronto: University of Toronto Press, 2000), 339–61.

26 Matheson, *A Consolidated Report*; for a thoughtful reflection on changing approaches to water-quality study, see Arn Keeling, "Urban Waste Sinks as a Natural Resource: The Case of the Fraser River," *Urban History Review* 34, 1 (Fall 2005): 58–70.

27 Matheson, *A Consolidated Report*, n.p.

28 Ibid., especially "Introduction" and "Chapter 4: Sanitary Conditions," n.p.

29 "Approve Calling of Tenders on Portion of Sewage Treatment Plant," *Spectator*, 14 October 1959, 11; "OMB Gives City the Green Light on Sewage Plant," *Spectator*, 2 October 1958, 9.

30 "Decision Awaited on Sewerage," editorial, *Spectator*, 12 December 1960. For the debate on the system, see "Costlier Disposal Method Sought for Sewage Plant," *Spectator*, 20 September 1960; and "Approve Disposal System," *Spectator*, 1 March 1961.

31 "$10 M Plant Battles Pollution," *Spectator*, 27 October 1964; Hugh Whittington, "Hamilton Bay a Sewer – OWRC," *Spectator*, 24 May 1969. See D.B. Redfern, "Design of the Hamilton, Ontario, Sewer System and Treatment Works," *Journal* (Water Pollution Control Federation) 34, 10 (1962): 1052–69.

32 "Hamilton Harbour Great Asset," *Spectator*, 17 December 1927.

33 Faludi held a doctorate in architecture from the University of Rome. See "Administrative History/Biographical Sketch," Eugenio Giacomo Faludi fonds, Archives Canada, http://www.archivescanada.ca/english/search/ItemDisplay.asp?sessionKey=999999999_142&l=0&lvl=1&v=0&coll=0&itm=263346&rt=1&bill=1; on modernist urban renewal in Hamilton, see Margaret T. Rockwell, "Modernism and the Functional City: Urban Renewal in Hamilton, Ontario and Buffalo, New York (1949–74)" (PhD diss., McMaster University, 2013).

34 These discussions occurred before planning began, according to Faludi, "to lay the foundation of sound future citizen participation and critical appraisal as the actual planning work is undertaken." E.G. Faludi, "Planning in Three Canadian Cities," *Journal of the American Institute of Planners* 11, 2 (September 1945): 33–34.

35 E.G. Faludi, *A Master Plan for the Development of the City of Hamilton* (Hamilton: City Planning Committee, 1947), 54–60; E.G. Faludi, "Planning Progress in Canada I," *Journal of the American Institute of Planners* 13, 3 (Summer-Fall 1947): 9–13; E.G. Faludi, "Planning

Progress in Canada II," *Journal of the American Institute of Planners* 14, 3 (Winter 1948): 29–34.

36 Faludi, *A Master Plan;* "In the Industrial District," advertisement for the Brightside Development, 1911, 18, *Hamilton Times* Advertisement Scrapbook, LH&A, HPL; Paul Palango, "Brightside: Old Survey Levelled, But It Still Won't Die," *Spectator,* 12 July 1975; Michael Quigley, "Flying High," *Hamilton Cue Magazine,* July 1983, 12; Craig Heron, *Lunch-Bucket Lives: Remaking the Workers' City* (Toronto: Between the Lines Press, 2015), 47–48, 567.

37 Faludi, *A Master Plan.*

38 "Robinson's Close Wednesday at 1 O'Clock," advertisement, *Spectator,* 19 March 1946.

39 Y.P., "City's Zoning and the Master Plan," *Spectator,* 1 April 1946.

40 On the zoning more generally, see David Hulchanski, "The Origins of Land Use Planning in Ontario, 1900–1946" (PhD diss., University of Toronto, 1981), 271–352.

41 Today just six houses remain on Birmingham Street between Burlington Street and Beach Road. Planners understood the consequences of the designation, which is why a 1958 planning study argued against "excessive zoning for commercial and industrial uses," since it would "cause the deterioration of older (and newer) residential areas." Mark David and Hamilton Planning Department, *Urban Renewal Study, 1958* (Hamilton: City of Hamilton, 1959), 28. On the general issue, see Yale Rabin, "Expulsive Zoning," in *Zoning and the American Dream,* ed. Charles M. Haar and Jerold S. Kayden (Chicago: American Planning Association Planners Press, 1990), 100–3. Richard Harris and Doris Forrester found that financial institutions were reluctant to lend money in northeast end Hamilton by the early 1950s. The neighbourhoods they studied were more favourably situated than those in this industrial zone. See their "The Suburban Origins of Redlining: A Canadian Case Study," *Urban Studies* 40, 13 (2003): 2661–86.

42 "Nuclear Power Work Here Seen Assisting All Ontario," *Spectator,* 28 December 1955; "Harbour Site Chosen for New Power Plant," *Spectator,* n.d.; "Will Generate Nuclear Power on Harbor Site," *Spectator,* 23 August 1957; *HHCAR,* 1958, n.p., reports that the harbour commissioners had granted Ontario Hydro a two-year option to explore purchasing two hundred acres of waterlots for a proposed plant, "planned to be one of the largest in the world."

43 For a chronicling of incidents in which pollutants destroyed beach community homes, see Lewis D. McCowell, Joan L. Pikor, and Winsome M. Cain, *Hamilton Beach in Retrospect* (Hamilton: Hamilton Beach Alternate Community and History Project, 1981), 54–57.

44 For photos, stories, and local history, see Hamilton Beach Community Forum, http:// hamiltonbeachcommunity.com/forum/forum.php?s=50c2249ec5661b484c3cb15112 b78c7b.

45 "Beach Cottages," *Spectator,* 19 April 1920; "Beach Cottages Are in Demand," *Spectator,* 8 April 1930; "Great Demand for Beach Cottages," *Spectator,* 26 March 1931.

46 On housing development in Hamilton, see Michael J. Doucet and John C. Weaver, *Housing the North American City* (Montreal and Kingston: McGill-Queen's University Press, 1991).

47 "Winter at Beach," *Spectator,* 23 October 1920; McCowell, Pikor, and Cain, *Hamilton Beach in Retrospect,* 24.

48 "Burlington Beach Honours the Beach Bungalow School," Home and School Association, September 1952.

49 See Robert J. Hanley, "Motor Cars Ended an Era along the Beach," *Spectator*, 24 April 1954; John C. van Nostrand, "The Queen Elizabeth Way: Public Utility versus Private Space," *Urban History Review* 12, 2 (October 1983): 1–23.

50 McCowell, Pikor, and Cain, *Hamilton Beach in Retrospect*, 23–24; Burlington Beach Commission Minutes, 10 September 1907. This appointed commission consisted of no fewer than two and no more than five members.

51 "Ontario Moves to Join Part of Hamilton Beach to City," *Spectator*, 7 December 1955; "Aldermen Voice Doubts of Benefits from Hamilton Beach Annexation," *Spectator*, 8 December 1955; "City Officials Unworried about Beach Annexation," *Spectator*, 17 March 1956.

52 McCowell, Pikor, and Cain, *Hamilton Beach in Retrospect*, 33; Gary Evans, *Memories of the Beach Strip* (Burlington: North Shore, 2011), 41–42, 49–51, 58; "History of Burlington Bay James N. Allan Skyway," prepared as part of a series of text panels for Burlington Beach Anniversary Committee.

53 See Coaster Enthusiasts of Canada, Closed Canadian Parks, "Ontario: Burlington," http://cec.chebucto.org/ClosPark/BurlBech.

54 Informal communication, Beach Strip resident, 2001.

55 "Quarters to Cost $220,000 Will Be Constructed on Site Revetment Wall," *Spectator*, 1 February 1943; "Simple Beauty Impressive; Appropriate Surroundings Swell Pride of Crew," *Spectator*, 30 September 1943.

56 "Nature Gave Love of Water and Bay, No Need for Thompsons to Go Away," *Spectator*, 22 July 1957, 24; informal communication, Thompson family member, 1997.

57 "Citizens' Access to Bayfront Drastically Cut," *Spectator*, 14 October 1947. On boatbuilders, "Keeping Watch on the Waterfront," *Spectator*, 7 July 1954, indicates that Kerr and Askew were occupied by privately owned boats; see also Lawrence Murphy and Philip Murphy, *Tales from the North End* (Hamilton, 1981), 243; and Laura Edith Baldwin, *The Boat Builders of Hamilton* (Hamilton: In Harmony Promotions, 1992).

58 HCCM, Sub-Property Committee on Bay St. Bathing Beach Report, 20 November 1939, 507–8.

59 Ibid. People were expressing the view that water currents prevented the area from being affected by pollution as early as 1919. See "Great Plans to Improve City's Harbour," *Herald*, 20 December 1919; "Ferry Service Out of the Question until the War Ends," *Spectator*, 26 July 1943.

60 Constructed to revitalize the park's swimming potential, the wading pool was fifteen metres long and half a metre deep. See "Move to Popularize LaSalle Park May Include $10,000 Wading Pool," *Spectator*, 16 March 1948; "Water Is Contaminated: New Well Has to Be Dug," *Spectator*, 8 September 1948.

61 "Works Controller Alarmed over Pollution of the Bay," *Spectator*, 13 April 1946; "Parks Board Will Retain Control, Renovate 'Valuable' LaSalle Park," *Spectator*, 21 October 1958; "Examining the Future of LaSalle Park," *Spectator*, 26 January 1961; "Hold On to LaSalle," *Spectator*, 13 April 1962; "Board Blocks Attempt 'to Lock Up Whole Bay,'" *Spectator*, 3 October 1963; "Hamilton's Bayfront Park an Asset – for Burlington," *Spectator*, 8 May 1980. See Nancy Bouchier and Ken Cruikshank, "Abandoning Nature: Swimming Pools and Clean, Healthy Recreation in Hamilton, Ontario, c. 1930s–1950s," *Canadian Bulletin of Medical History* 28, 2 (2011): 315–37.

62 Gerald Killan, *Protected Places: A History of Ontario's Provincial Parks System* (Toronto: Dundurn Press, 1993), 74–119.

63 "Sees Solution to Gang Problem in Recreation," *Spectator*, 25 August 1948.

64 "Name Special Committee to Study Rinks, Pools," *Spectator*, n.d. 1951, Parks Board Scrapbook, 2:168, LH&A, HPL.

65 "Bay Pollution," *Annual Report of the Board of Health* (hereafter *ARBH*), 1946, 18–19.

66 In the early 1920s, trained specialists began to supervise wading pools in newly created playgrounds in city and school parks. HCCM, 1925, 580; Elsie Marie McFarland, *The Development of Public Recreation in Canada* (Ottawa: Canadian Parks/Recreation Association, 1970), 37.

67 HCCM, 1928, 863–64, "By Law 3728, For borrowing $150,000 by the Issue of Debentures, for the Northwestern Highway Entrance Development, York Street, and the Construction of Swimming Pool, With Dressing Rooms, at 'Scott Park.'" Of this amount, $100,000 would go to pool construction. This bylaw had been ratified in the December 1928 municipal election, a step that was required for money bylaws. *The Official Program of the British Empire Games, 1930* (Hamilton: Robert Duncan, 1930).

68 "50th Anniversary: Hamilton Playgrounds," Hamilton Recreation Department, 1958, 20–21. The city had already set into place a Post-War Reconstruction Committee, with Parks Board representation, to relieve unemployment after the war. HCCM, 1940, 448–49; "Permanent Plan for Recreation Aim of Leaders," and "Elect Officers for Recreation Committee Jobs," *Spectator*, 18 June 1943; "First Step in Scheme Taken Last Night by Community Leaders: Committee Selected," *Spectator*, 15 February 1944. For the general context of Canadian concerns regarding wartime fitness and recreation, see *An Act to Establish a National Council for the Purpose of Promoting Physical Fitness*, 24 July 1943, Statutes of Canada, 7 Geo. VI, c. 29; *The School Law Amendment Act*, 20 July 1945, Statutes of Ontario, 1945, c. 8, s. 4.2; Ontario, Department of Education, Report of the Minister, 1945, 89–90; see McFarland, *The Development*, 51–62; Mary E. Keyes, "Government Involvement in Fitness and Amateur Sport," in *A Concise History of Sport in Canada*, ed. Don Morrow et al. (Toronto: Oxford University Press, 1989), 325–43; Lorne W. Sawula, "The National Physical Fitness Act of Canada, 1943–1954" (PhD diss., University of Alberta, 1977); and Thomas J. West, "Physical Fitness, Sport and the Federal Government, 1909 to 1954," *Canadian Journal of History of Sport and Physical Education* 4, 2 (December 1973): 26–42.

69 "War's Impact upon Youth to Be Studied by Officials," *Spectator*, 5 January 1955.

70 "Elect Officers for Recreation Committee Jobs," *Spectator*, 18 June 1943.

71 "City Wide Park Development Is Being Considered," *Spectator*, 25 September 1944; "Parks Board Submits Post-War Development Plans," *Spectator*, 28 September 1944; "Synopses of Proposed By-Laws to Be Submitted to a Vote of the Hamilton Electors Entitled to Vote on a Money By-Law, on Monday December 4, 1944," *Spectator*, 10 November 1944. Langs and McQuesten had adopted this strategy before; the debentures for financing the northwestern entrance had included funds for the indoor municipal swimming pool in 1928.

72 "Give Hamilton's Youth the Swimming Pools They Need!" *Spectator*, 29 November 1944.

73 Advertisements in *Spectator*, 28, 29, and 30 November 1944, 1 December 1944. The ads were sponsored by the members of a newly formed group, the Hamilton Committee for Continued Sound Administration, whom we have been unable to identify. The public debate was so intense that Sydney S. Booth, who collected newspaper clippings for Parks Board Scrapbooks, noted in a margin, "It would have been an immense (and unnecessary) task to mount in this scrapbook all those advertisements and letters which appeared.

Selection was made that seemed to cover in this subject matter all the points presented by both sides." Parks Board Scrapbooks, Sydney S. Booth, 2, LH&A, HPL.

74 "Would Take Vote on War Memorial, Parks Program," *Spectator,* 29 September 1944; "Parks Program," editorial, *Spectator,* 6 October 1944; "Memorial Auditorium," *Spectator,* 7 October 1944; "I Maintain That the Tax Payers Have Been Given No Choice! Controller Nora-Frances Henderson," advertisement, CHML Radio, 28 November 1944. In an editorial cartoon that depicted Henderson as callous to the plight of soldiers' kids, she was called a liar by a Hamilton taxpayer. "These Bylaws Will Cost You Four Million Dollars out of Your Pocket," *Spectator,* 19 November 1944. On Lawrence and Henderson, see Craig Heron, "Lawrence, Samuel," and Molly Pulver Ungar, "Henderson, Nora-Frances," *Dictionary of Hamilton Biography,* ed. T.M. Bailey (Hamilton: Dictionary of Hamilton Biography, 1999) 4:150–55, 123–28.

75 See, for example, "Halcrow Favours Bathing Beach," *Spectator,* 19 June 1925.

76 HCCM, 1945, 655–56, Bylaw 5682, "To Provide for the Establishment of the Hamilton Recreation Council."

77 "Report of the Hamilton Community Recreational Council," HCCM, 1946, 48; "Appointment of S/L Anthony George Ley," *Spectator,* 15 July 1946; HCCM, 1947, 329, Bylaw 5968, "To Appoint Members of the Hamilton Recreation Council."

78 HCCM, 1947, 48; HCCM, 1948, 28, 148, 182; "Sees Solution to Gang Problem in Recreation," *Spectator,* 25 August 1948; "Plan Program of Recreation for Whole City," *Spectator,* 27 March 1947; "Tells Progress in Recreation," *Spectator,* 1 December 1947.

79 "35 Playgrounds for 5 to 12 Set Dot City Scene," *Spectator,* 12 November 1960.

80 "Stewart Obtains Support in Suit for Beach Pool," *Spectator,* 11 January 1947; "Building Swimming Pool at Filtering Basin," *Spectator,* 18 January 1947; "Plans for Swimming Pool Seem Confused," *Spectator,* 21 January 1947.

81 HCCM, 1950, 301, "Report of the Property and License Committee," 11 April 1950; BOCR, 29 August 1950, in HCCM, 1950, 669; "Lakeland Beach Opens June 20," *Spectator,* 17 June 1953. On the pool, see Margaret Houghton, "Lakeland Beach," in Evans, *Memories of the Beach Strip,* 159–61.

82 David and Hamilton Planning Department, *Urban Renewal Study, 1958.*

83 Margaret Rockwell, "Modernist Destruction for the Ambitious City" (master's thesis, Department of History, McMaster University, 2003), 45–48; Beryl Brown, "Attractive Resort on City's Doorstep Possible," *Spectator,* 9 April 1958; "City Files Bid for Cash Help on Beach Area," *Spectator,* 10 February 1960. Our account also benefitted from reading Robert Fick, "The Zero Option" (master's major research paper, Department of History, McMaster University, 2007).

84 Quoted in Rockwell, "Modernist Destruction," 49.

85 "People Still Swim in Filthy Bay," *Spectator,* 17 July 1953.

86 "Our Deceptive Bay," editorial, *Spectator,* 17 August 1946.

87 "Bay Pollution," *ARBH,* 1946, 18.

88 "Want Action on Pollution," *Spectator,* 9 July 1948; "Battle of Hamilton Bay Pollution," *Spectator,* 8 November 1962.

89 Quoted in Rick Hughes, "Bringing Back the Bay; Hamilton Hungers for Its Harbour, Part 1," *Spectator,* 23 November 2002, MO4.

90 T.H. Whillans, "Historic Transformations of Fish Communities in Three Great Lakes Bays," *Journal of Great Lakes Research* 5, 2 (1979): 195–215.

91 "Parks Board Is Asked for $25,000 Clubhouse," *Spectator,* 6 June 1960; Hamilton Angling and Hunting Association, "Your Hamilton Angling and Hunting Association," Association Pamphlet, 1962.

92 "New Quarters for Yacht Club Will Be Built," *Spectator,* 9 February 1938; "People Like Real Marine Atmosphere," *Spectator,* 10 September 1959; Harry L. Penny, *One Hundred Years and Still Sailing: A History of Hamilton Yachts, Yachtsmen, and Yachting, 1888 to 1988: Centennial Yearbook* (Hamilton: Royal Hamilton Yacht Club, 1988), 54.

93 Jim Donnelly, "The Leander Club Story, 1927–1962," *Spectator,* 23 March 1962; "Leander Celebrates 60 Years of Success," *Spectator,* 12 June 1987; "Rowers Open New Home," *Spectator,* 27 April 1962; "Elements Too Much for Rowers," *Spectator,* 30 June 1960; Aubrey Oldham, "Four Score Years of Messing About in Boats: A Social History of the Leander Boat Club, 1927 to Present" (essay, McMaster University, 2006).

94 William Cockman, "Hamilton's Royal Botanical Gardens," *Canadian Geographical Journal* 50, 6 (1955): 228–36; Leslie Laking, "A History of Royal Botanical Gardens (Part 2)," *Pappus* 11, 1 (1992): 9–11.

95 Lautens, "Place for Everyone."

Chapter 7: Unchaining Nature

1 Marjorie Wild, "Her Lifestyle Shaped by Her Love of the Bay," *Spectator,* 2 January 1973; Mary K. Nolan, "The People Who Make a Difference," *Spectator,* 15 December 1999, A10; Carmela Fragomeni, "Gil Worked Tirelessly to Clean Up Waterfront," *Spectator,* 23 August 2010, A02; "Obituary (Nee Hanchard Goodwin) Gillian Simmons," *Toronto Globe and Mail,* 4 August 2010; "They Made a Difference: Gill Simmons," editorial, *Spectator,* 30 December 2010; Jeff Mahoney, "Hamilton's Heroine of the Harbour," *Spectator,* 3 May 2013; Paul Wilson, "Gil Was an S.O.B. and Now She Gets a Plaque," *CBC Hamilton,* 7 May 2013, http://www.cbc.ca/news/canada/hamilton/talk/paul-wilson-gil-was-an-s-o-b-and-now-she-gets-a-plaque-1.1376226.

2 G.P. Harris, D.E.N. Jensen, and K.A. Kershaw, "Pollution as a Road to Nowhere," *Ti Estin,* 28 November 1969, 29–30; "Harbor Fill Talks Urged," *Spectator,* 29 June 1971; Bas Korstanje, "Bay Fill-In beyond OWRC," *Spectator,* 9 July 1971.

3 Tom Coleman, "Man-Made Bay Island Town Planned," *Spectator,* 24 September 1970; Marsha Hewitt, "Hamilton Harbour: Politics, Patronage and Cover-Up," in *Their Town: The Mafia, the Media and the Party Machine,* ed. Bill Freeman and Marsha Hewitt (Toronto: James Lorimer, 1979), 153–54. The development was also referred to as the Bal Harbour project. See "Laxes Want Same Deal," *Spectator,* 7 March 1972; "Lax Scrapped Avro Arrow; Scrap Metal Dealer and Developer Ultimately Responsible for Bayfront Park Dies at 86," *Spectator,* 12 February 2002; and "Hamilton Harbour: What's Good, What's Not so Good," *Spectator,* 23 November 2002. On Habitat 67, see Moshe Safdie, *Beyond Habitat* (Boston: MIT Press, 1973); Adele Weder, "For Everyone a Garden: The Failed Dream of Montreal's Habitat '67," *The Walrus,* January-February 2008, http://thewalrus.ca/for-everyone-a-garden/.

4 Gil Simmons, interview by Rahima Visram, 2 February 1998, Arts and Science Project, McMaster University. See also Rahima Visram, "Then and Now: Recreation, Lived Experiences and the Polluting of the Bay – Hamilton Harbour" (bachelor's thesis, McMaster University, 1998).

5 Mitchell Smyth, "The Battle to Unchain Hamilton Bay," *Spectator*, 25 August 1971; Wilson, "Gil Was an S.O.B."

6 "The Lots That Have Been Sold," *Spectator*, 12 March 1970; Hewitt, "Hamilton Harbour," 153. On the business of Luria Brothers in the late 1950s and early 1960s, see Carl A. Zimring, *Cash for Your Trash: Scrap Recycling in America* (New Brunswick, NJ: Rutgers University Press, 2005), 119–23.

7 "The Lots That Have Been Sold" and "Port of Hamilton," series of daily articles, *Spectator*, 27, 28, and 29 May 1957.

8 "Facilities ... Port of Hamilton," Hamilton Harbour Commissioners, *Annual Report* (hereafter *HHCAR*), 1963, 6, 9; "300 Attend 'Seaway Day' Conference and Centennial Terminal Opening," *Seaway Service via Port of Hamilton* (hereafter *SSPOH*) 8, 2 (July 1965): n.p.; "Centennial Docks Project in Final Stages," *SSPOH* 8, 3 (October 1965): n.p.; "Record-Breaking Ore Shipments Anticipated in 1966," *SSPOH* 9, 1 (May 1966): 2–3; "New Terminal Facilities to Be Built for Canada Steamship Lines," *SSPOH* 9, 2 (Summer 1966): 1–2; "Decade of Expansion Summarized," *SSPOH* 10, 3 (Fall 1967): n.p.; "City Given $80,000, Beach," *Spectator*, 25 April 1968; see also Mark Sproule-Jones, "Commercial Shipping," in Mark Sproule-Jones, *Governments at Work: Canadian Parliamentary Federalism and Its Public Policy Effects* (Toronto: University of Toronto Press, 1993), 153–87.

9 Mark P. David and Hamilton Planning Department, *Urban Renewal Study* (Hamilton: City of Hamilton, 1958); Hamilton Urban Renewal Committee, *North End Renewal Project* (Hamilton: City of Hamilton, 1963); Murray V. Jones Ltd., *North End Urban Renewal Scheme* (Hamilton: Urban Renewal Committee, 1968); Margaret Rockwell, "Modernist Destruction for the Ambitious City" (master's thesis, Department of History, McMaster University, 2003), 61–95; Margaret Rockwell, "Modernism and the Functional City: Urban Renewal in Hamilton, Ontario and Buffalo, New York (1949–74)" (PhD diss., McMaster University, 2013).

10 "Plan Industry Park for Harbor Front over 3 to 5 Years," *Spectator*, 20 August 1965; Coleman, "Man-Made Bay Island Town Planned"; Smyth, "The Battle to Unchain Hamilton Bay," includes an artist's conception of the project.

11 "Harbor Commission Land Bid Rejected," *Spectator*, 2 March 1966; F.K. DeVos, "Summary of Meeting with Hamilton Harbour Commission, 22 January 1970," 23 January 1970, Interdepartmental Group on Harbours – Hamilton Harbour Commission, Department of Transport, RG 12, box 15, file 8103–50–4, Library and Archives Canada; "Mile-Long Western Harbor Project Urged," *Spectator*, 22 June 1970; "A Look into the Future," *HHCAR*, 1970, 2, offers an artist's conception of the docks; McNamara Engineering and Hamilton Harbour Commissioners, *Hamilton Harbour Study: Land Use Plan* (Toronto: McNamara Engineering, 1970), 17–18.

12 Jennifer Read, "Addressing 'a Quiet Horror': The Evolution of Ontario Pollution Control Policy in the International Great Lakes, 1909–1972" (PhD diss., University of Western Ontario, 1999), 147–48, 167–74; William McGucken, *Lake Erie Rehabilitated: Controlling Cultural Eutrophication, 1960s–1990s* (Akron: University of Akron Press, 2000), 28–35; Terence Kehoe, *Cleaning Up the Great Lakes: From Cooperation to Confrontation* (Delkalb: Northern Illinois University Press, 1997), 60–65.

13 Victor A. Forde, *A Historical Study of the Pollution of Burlington Bay* (Hamilton: Department of Engineering, Regional Municipality of Hamilton-Wentworth, 1980), 52.

14 F.R. Phoenix and J.W. Vogt, "Summary Report of the Industrial Waste Loadings Discharged to Hamilton Harbour by the Bayfront Industries" (Industrial Wastes Branch, Ontario

Water Resources Commission, 1964), 33. Within a year, the Port of Hamilton trade journal reported that a civic committee had been struck to "study waterfront pollution as it is affected by sewage disposal, industrial waste and other aspects of pollution aimed at safeguarding future water resources, and the adverse effect of water pollution on the recreational facilities in the harbour and on the lakefront." The committee included the city engineer, an alderman, and representatives from the OWRC, the Canadian Manufacturers Association, the harbour commission, McMaster University Engineering faculty, and the port director. See "Hamilton: A Hamilton Harbour Pollution Abatement Committee Formed," *SSPOH* 8, 3 (October 1965), n.p.; "Battle against Pollution Making Rapid Progress," *SSPOH* 9, 1 (May 1966): 6.

15 Hugh Whittington, "Hamilton Bay a Sewer–OWRC," *Spectator,* 24 May 1969.
16 Ontario Water Resources Commission, *Water Pollution Survey of Sewer Outfalls and Tributary Streams to Hamilton Bay* (Toronto: District Engineers Branch, Division of Sanitary Engineering, Ontario Water Resources Commission, 1967), quotations from Appendix 4.
17 Hugh Whittington, "Our Polluted Bay," *Spectator,* 24 May 1969.
18 Phoenix and Vogt, *Summary Report,* 33.
19 "Hamilton Bay," *Spectator,* 23 July 1970.
20 Jennifer Read, "'Let Us Heed the Voice of Youth': Laundry Detergents, Phosphates and the Emergence of the Environmental Movement in Ontario," *Journal of the Canadian Historical Association* 7, 1 (1996): 227–50; Danielle Robinson, "Modernism at a Crossroad: The Spadina Expressway Controversy in Toronto, Ontario ca. 1960–1971," *Canadian Historical Review* 92, 2 (2011): 295–322; Thomas R. Dunlap, ed., *DDT, Silent Spring, and the Rise of Environmentalism: Classic Texts* (Seattle: University of Washington Press, 2008); Mark Hamilton Lytle, *Gentle Subversive: Rachel Carson, Silent Spring, and the Rise of the Environmental Movement* (New York: Oxford University Press, 2008); Adam Rome, "'Give Earth a Chance': The Environmental Movement and the Sixties," *Journal of American History* 90, 2 (2003): 525–54.
21 "Statements by Saul Alinsky – 19 November 1971: The A.B.C.s of Social Action," Clear Hamilton of Pollution records (hereafter CHOP Papers), originals copied and in possession of authors. Gary Quart of the Victoria Park Community Organization, who had worked and studied in an "Alinski-styled [sic] organization in Chicago," used the term "creative conflict" to describe strategic tactics. Bill Freeman, "Selling Out: The Story of the Victoria Park Community Organization," in Freeman and Hewitt, *Their Town,* 101. See also Saul Alinsky, *Rules for Radicals: A Pragmatic Primer for Realistic Radicals* (New York: Random House, 1971).
22 "About This Issue," *Ti Estin,* June 1970, 2. McMaster students, who had their own chapter of the Ontario Public Interest Research Group, had good connections to the University of Toronto's Pollution Probe group. See, for example, CHOP Minutes, 9 December 1969, 19 February 1970, and 10 March 1970, CHOP Papers.
23 *CHOP Newsletter,* 1970; "CHOP History," March 1970; "Letters Patent Incorporating Clear Hamilton of Pollution," 15 October 1973, all in CHOP Papers. For an insightful first-hand account of the history of environmental legal battles in the province, see D. Paul Emond, "'Are We There Yet?' Reflections on the Success of the Environmental Law Movement in Ontario," *Osgoode Hall Law Journal* 46 (2008): 219–42.
24 Interview by Nancy Bouchier, 22 March 2007. According to this man, the CHOP membership was very diverse: "There was this incredible cross-section ... There would be everything from flower children to, you know, hard-nosed number-crunchers, who were

on about well, fluoride or something." "First Annual Report," March 1971, CHOP Papers; CHOP Minutes, 17 May 1971; *Environmental Protection Act,* R.S.O. 1971, c. 86.

25 Bevis Miles, "A Message from Your President," *CHOP Newsletter* 4, June 1972. The writer also reported that CHOP had attracted 240 members.

26 "First Annual Report," March 1971. See also "A Brief History of Waste Diversion in Ontario: A Background Paper on the Review of the *Waste Diversion Act*" (Canadian Institute for Environmental Law and Policy, November 2008), http://www.cielap.org/pdf/WDA_BriefHistory.pdf.

27 Read, "Addressing 'a Quiet Horror,'" 213–15.

28 Miles, "A Message from your President." In 1974, two summer students wrote a paper for CHOP, critically assessing its role in the broader scheme of things. Lamenting the culture of specialization, they posed the question, "Must we be forced to allow a few select individuals to make all significant social decisions when in fact such decisions involve ethics and morals much more than technology and science? It is an unjust and perilous situation when the average citizen is not allowed to be involved in the decision-making process." CHOP, they argued, gave average citizens the opportunity to express their opinion and be heard. Ann Gordon and Marg Wingfield, "A Critical Assessment of CHOP's Organization," 8 October 1974, 1, CHOP Papers.

29 Harris, Jensen, and Kershaw, "Pollution as a Road to Nowhere," 29–30; Robinson, "Modernism at a Crossroad."

30 Memo, D.S. Caverly to George Kerr, 24 June 1971, OWRC Papers, RG 84–1, box 98, Folder: Hamilton – Pollution in Hamilton Bay, Archives of Ontario (hereafter AO), Toronto; *Ontario Water Resources Commission Act,* S.O. 1957, c. 88; see also J.B. Milner, "The Ontario Water Resources Commission Act, 1956," *University of Toronto Law Journal* 12, 1 (1957): 100–2.

31 "The Bay MUST Be Saved," *Community Forum,* June 1971; "Save Our Bay," *Community Forum,* June 1971, CHOP Papers; "Anti-Filling," *Spectator,* 4 June 1971; "Bid to Halt Land-Filling Strikes a Snag," *Spectator,* 7 June 1971; "Harbor Landfill Answers Elusive," *Spectator,* 22 June 1971; Gil Simmons, "The Things We Did Last Summer," *Spectator,* 18 September 1971; Gil Simmons, interview by Rahima Visram, 7 May 2007; CHOP Minutes, 28 June 1971.

32 David Roe, "Bay + Garbage = Gold … for Some," 1971, CHOP Papers.

33 Transcript of interview by Andrew Stevenson, Niagara College, for documentary film *No Trespassing: Stories from Hamilton's Waterfront,* sound rolls 18/19, 2000; Rockwell, "Modernist Destruction for the Ambitious City."

34 Gil Simmons, letter to editor, "Bay's Beauty Needs Protection," *Spectator,* 7 July 1971.

35 *No Trespassing* interview by Andrew Stevenson, sound rolls 18/19.

36 "Save Our Bay."

37 Mitchell Smyth, "Save Our Bay Aims at Harbour Group," *Spectator,* 25 August 1971.

38 E.D. Hickey, Chairman, Hamilton Harbour Commission, letter to editor, "Closeup Views of Harbor Available to Public," *Spectator,* n.d. June 1971; see also "'Iron Curtain' Hides Harbour," *Spectator,* 1 March 1971.

39 Quoted in "Save Our Bay."

40 OWRC Papers, RG 84–1, box 98, Folder: Hamilton – Pollution in Hamilton Bay, AO.

41 Simmons, interview by Visram, 2 February 1998; "Kerr to Initiate Waterfront Study of Hamilton Bay," "Save Our Bay Meets George Kerr," *Spectator,* 7 August 1971; "Kerr on the Waterfront," editorial, *Spectator,* 12 August 1971; Bas Korstanje, "Waterfront Study Gets

Go-Ahead," *Spectator*, 24 August 1971; "Regional Lakefront Study Given Go-Ahead Signal," "Lakeshore Study Head Appointed," *Spectator*, n.d. September 1971; on Kerr, see "Obituary: 'Honest' George Kerr Made Waves during Political Career," *Spectator*, 24 May 2007.

42 "City Wants Bay Fill Say," *Spectator*, 11 August 1971; "SOB Meets Board of Control," *Spectator*, 20 August 1971.

43 "Harbor Control Study Plan Rejected," *Spectator*, 18 August 1971; "City-Harbor Dispute Likely to Go to Court," *Spectator*, 19 August 1971.

44 "Waterfront Swap Provides Park for Beach Strip," *Spectator*, 11 November 1971; "Hamilton Exchanges Waterfront Properties," *Toronto Globe and Mail*, 12 November 1972. These negotiations had been reported locally as early as July but appear to have been little noticed. "Move Afoot to Swap Lots," *Spectator*, 28 July 1971; "Harbor Expansion Snags Seen," *Spectator*, 10 December 1971; "HHC Notes to Financial Statements for the Year Ending 31 December 1973."

45 "Waterfront Swap"; "Board Wants Harbor Deal Explanation," *Spectator*, 15 November 1971; "Harbor Board Raked on Land Swap Secrecy," *Spectator*, 2 December 1974; "5 Demand Land Deal Rehash," *Spectator*, 4 December 1971; Gil Simmons, letter to editor, "A Judicial Enquiry Might Be Best for the Bay," *Spectator*, 9 December 1971.

46 "Custeau Warns of 'Waterfront Cesspool,'" *Spectator*, 17 November 1971.

47 "Landfill Control Power Granted," *Spectator*, 2 March 1972; "City Makes Bid to Stall HRCA Landfill Control," *Spectator*, 4 March 1972; "City Wants Stelco, Dofasco Free of Landfill Control," *Spectator*, 6 March 1972; "Groups Hit at Freeing Mills from Controls," *Spectator*, 7 March 1972; "No Exception in Harbor Landfill: Auld," *Spectator*, 9 March 1972; "Harbour Fill Control Challenged," *Spectator*, 25 March 1972; "Hamilton Groups Challenge Ontario's Pollution Law," *Toronto Globe and Mail*, 25 March 1972; "Firms Warned to Stop Landfill Operations," *Toronto Globe and Mail*, 30 March 1972; "Ottawa Landfill Warning Defied by Harbor Board," *Spectator*, 13 April 1972; "Minister in About Face over Landfill," *Spectator*, 16 June 1972; "HRC Ready to Prosecute Steel Firms," *Spectator*, 30 June 1972; "Steel Companies to Fight Harbour Landfill Ban," *Spectator*, 24 August 1972; "Steel Firms Resume Landfill," *Spectator*, 25 August 1972; "Ontario Permits Landfill Plan of Steel Firms," *Toronto Globe and Mail*, 14 September 1972; Hewitt, "Hamilton Harbour."

48 "Turkstra Fails to Get Elliott fired," *Spectator*, 30 November 1971; "'Dump-Truck Zoning' Ban Urged," *Spectator*, 28 January 1971; "City Sets Up Harbor Watchdog Committee," *Spectator*, 1 March 1972; "Harbor Complaint Talks Likely Today," *Spectator*, 9 August 1972; "Public Will Hear Report on Elliott," *Spectator*, 25 August 1972; "Obituary: Elliott Was at Centre of Hamilton's 'Harbourgate' Scandal," *Spectator*, 2 September 2009; "Ken Elliott, 1933–2009: Key Role in Harbourgate Scandal," *Spectator*, 3 September 2009; Hewitt, "Hamilton Harbour."

49 "Citizens Will Be Watchdogs on Waterfront Study," and "Housewife Heads Lakeshore Group," *Spectator*, 12 January 1971; "Heads Are Beginning to Clear After Environmental Hangover," *Spectator*, 13 January 1971; Mary Orde, "It Concerns Me," *Spectator*, 13 January 1971.

50 "Auld 'a Tyrant' Copps Explodes," *Spectator*, 9 March 1972.

51 Gil Simmons, "Press Release from Save Our Bay Committee," *CHOP Newsletter* 4, June 1972; "North-West Canvass to Spur Interest for Bay Meeting," *Spectator*, 17 July 1972; SOB, "What to Do about the Bay," leaflet for 20 July 1972 meeting, Hamilton Harbour Scrapbook, vol. 4:123a, Hamilton Public Library; "Developers Protest Bay Planning Delay,"

Spectator, 21 July 1972; Gil Simmons, letter to editor, "The Future of Our Bay Said Election Issue," *Spectator,* 20 September 1972.

52 "City May Buy Harbor-Project Property," *Spectator,* 14 February 1972; "Lax Brothers Don't Want to Sell Their Shoreline Property," *Spectator,* 23 February 1972; "Laxes Warned to Stop Fill," *Spectator,* 2 February 1973; "Morrow Wants Ontario to Buy Lax Property," *Spectator,* 30 May 1973; "Bayfront Park Plan Hailed and Slammed," *Spectator,* 18 August 1973; "Hamilton Bay's 56-Acre Eyesore," *Spectator,* 17 May 1974; "Province Not Interested in Lax Land Deal," *Spectator,* 24 April 1975.

53 Acres Consulting Services Limited, "The Halton-Wentworth Waterfront Study" (Halton Region Conservation Authority et al., 1974), 1:21; "26 More Miles of Public Shoreline Urged for Hamilton," *Toronto Globe and Mail,* 5 July 1974.

54 Acres Consulting Services Limited, "The Halton-Wentworth Waterfront Study," 1:79–80.

55 *Hamilton Harbour Commissioners v. City of Hamilton et al.* (1978), 91 D.L.R. 353–87.

56 See, for example, "Harbor Will Be a People Place, Commission Chairman Vows," *Spectator,* 10 January 1973; "Harbor Board Has Plan for Waterfront Parks," *Spectator,* 23 January 1974; Hamilton Harbour Advisory Committee, *Hamilton Harbour: A Heritage and an Opportunity* (Hamilton: Hamilton Harbour Advisory Committee, 1982); Rita Devgan and David Stickney, *Focus on the Bay: Concepts and Design Approaches for Hamilton Harbour* (Hamilton Harbour Advisory Committee, 1983).

57 Bill Johnston, "Fight Seen on Plan for Harbor Industrial Park," *Spectator,* 18 June 1982; "Notice: Application [from Samuel and Sheridan Lax] to Amend the Hamilton Official Plan," *Spectator,* 6 January 1983; "Citizen Group Welcomes Harbor Decision," *West Hamilton Journal,* 19 January 1983; "Lax Brothers File $4.25m Claim for Compensation," *Spectator,* 6 November 1986; "Committee to Meet Lawyer on Lax Land," *Spectator,* 19 February 1987.

58 CHOP Minutes, 8 May, 18 June, and 4 July 1974; Acres Consulting Services Limited, *The Halton-Wentworth Waterfront Study,* 1:153, 167–69. Primary treatment removes solids from the waste water stream. Secondary treatment uses water-borne bacteria to progressively convert the dissolved biological matter into a solid mass. Tertiary treatment takes the treated water and disinfects it chemically or physically in a lagoon or via a microfiltration process that removes elements such as nitrogen and phosphorous. The final effluent is discharged back into the watershed. A good, basic description of the processes can be found at "Water Treatment," http://www.science.uwaterloo.ca/~cchieh/cact/applychem/watertreatment.html.

59 "New Pollution Control Centre Nearing Completion," *Wentworth Marketplace,* 20 January 1971.

60 "Expansion Plan Hit by Expert," *Spectator,* 22 October 1975.

61 CHOP news release, CHOP papers, n.d. According to this document, two students were hired for thirteen weeks.

62 Simmons was CHOP president from April to December 1974.

63 Cootes Paradise Day, 8 September 1974, Schedule of Events, CHOP Papers. Cootes Paradise Day was repeated on 7 September 1975.

64 City of Hamilton, "Report of the Engineering Services Committee," 28 October 1974. The decision was made at a regional council meeting on 5 November 1974; see also "The Facts on Cootes Paradise," 1974, CHOP Papers; "Answers to Questions about Coote's [sic] Paradise," *CHOP Newsletter,* June 1975.

65 R.H. McNutt, Co-Chairman, Federation of Environmental Groups, to Hamilton-Wentworth Regional Council, 1 November 1974, CHOP Papers. McNutt suggested that

the Engineering Committee should start from scratch and establish an ad hoc environmental advisory group so that the issue would be fully researched and the implications of any decision would be fully understood by the decision makers. He also reminded the regional council that it needed to conduct environmental and impact assessments. Bylaw 15–75, 21 February 1975, authorized the borrowing of funds for the construction of the expanded treatment facility before the assessments had been carried out – an issue that CHOP raised at an environmental hearing later that year. See In the Matter of Section 42(1) of *The Ontario Water Resources Act*, RSO 1970, c. 332; and In the matter of an application by the Regional Municipality of Hamilton-Wentworth for approval of an alteration in existing sewage works; Before the Environmental Hearing Board of Ontario, Brief, Clear Hamilton of Pollution (Incorporated), 21 October 1975, 4, 11 (hereafter CHOP brief, 21 October 1975).

66   Marion S. Shivas, letter to editor, *Spectator,* 11 November 1974, (emphasis in original), CHOP Papers. She derisively termed the attitude of councillors "ecoporn" (from the Greek *oikos,* meaning house, habitat, environment). "The style today," she wrote, "is to speak of 'environmentalists' and 'ecologists' with scorn. On and on the words flow from those in office who would paint us as deterrents of 'progress.'"

67   CHOP Minutes, 23 November 1974.

68   Some 331 people signed a petition from the Federation of Environmental Groups, urging the council to rescind its decision and proposing that Dundas sewage improvements be first passed by the Hamilton Region Conservation Authority and the Royal Botanical Gardens.

69   As noted in *CHOP Newsletter,* February 1975; Regional Municipality of Hamilton-Wentworth, "Public Notice to Citizens Interested in the Pollution Control of Cootes Paradise," November 1975. The public notice outlined the terms of reference for a Cootes Paradise study.

70   "Now Is the Time to ACT, Oct. 21 1975: A Crucial Day in the Life of Cootes Paradise," CHOP Papers. At the hearings, CHOP lawyer Michael Moriarity presented three suggestions: that plant expansion be delayed until Ministry of the Environment ecological studies were complete (forecasted for March 1976); that if expansion were approved, the effluent would not be emptied into the marsh; and that the municipality consider alternatives to the proposed system.

71   CHOP brief, 21 October 1975.

72   CHOP press release, 5 December 1975; McMaster Ontario Public Interest Research Group news release, "Comment on the Report of the Environmental Hearing Board Decision on the Expansion of the Dundas Sewage Treatment Plant"; Ministry of the Environment, R.G. Semkin, A.W. McLarty, and D. Craig, "A Water Quality Study of Cootes Paradise: Ministry of the Environment: Water Resources Assessment" (Ministry of the Environment Technical Support Section, 1976).

73   For example, the Westdale neighbourhood in the west end. See C. John Weaver, "From Land Assembly to Social Maturity: The Suburban Life of Westdale (Hamilton), Ontario, 1911–1951," in *A History of Ontario: Selected Readings,* ed. Michael J. Piva (Toronto: Copp Clark Pitman, 1988), 214–41.

74   Acres Consulting Services Limited, *The Halton-Wentworth Waterfront Study,* 1:147, 170–71.

75   Planning Department, "1969 Official Plan for the Beach Strip, 1971 Edition" (Hamilton, 1971).

76 Lewis D. McCowell, Joan L. Pikor, and Winsome M. Cain, *Hamilton Beach in Retrospect* (Hamilton: Hamilton Beach Alternate Community and History Project, 1981); "Beach Strip's Future in Recreation – Munro," *Spectator*, 12 November 1973; "Future of the Beach," editorial, *Spectator*, 15 November 1973.

77 Hamilton Region Conservation Authority, *Project 36: Hamilton Beach Land Acquisition Program* (Hamilton, 1974).

78 "Strip Proposals Rile Homeowners," *Spectator*, 27 June 1973.

79 Tables 6 and 7 diagram class and ethnicity in the waterfront or old inlet neighbourhoods of Hamilton (from North End to Parkdale to East), the Beach Strip, the North Shore (Burlington), and West Hamilton bordering Cootes Paradise (Princess Point and Westdale).

TABLE 6 Occupational and family earnings profiles, selected census districts, 1971

	Managerial, professional (%)	Service workers (%)	Manual workers (%)	Average family earnings ($)
Total city	22	42	36	10,500
North End	6	20	74	7,600
Wellington to Sherman	4	17	79	8,000
Sherman to Ottawa	4	18	77	7,500
Ottawa to Parkdale	3	22	75	7,900
Parkdale to East	4	20	77	9,300
Beach Strip	2	28	70	9,000
Burlington	64	31	5	13,600
Princess Point	22	41	37	11,100
Westdale	24	57	19	16,200

NOTE: Total *n* = 43,335.
SOURCE: Statistics Canada, Canadian 1971 Census Profile (Census Tract level), Canadian Census Analyzer (Computing in the Humanities and Social Sciences, University of Toronto, 2014).

TABLE 7 Ethnic profiles, selected residential areas, 1971

	"Canadian," British, or western European (%)	Italian (%)	Eastern European (%)	Other (%)
Total city	75	8	10	7
North End	61	22	9	8
Wellington to Sherman	70	15	9	6
Sherman to Ottawa	51	13	21	15
Ottawa to Parkdale	71	5	12	12
Parkdale to East	70	9	3	8
Beach Strip	91	2	6	1
Burlington	87	3	7	3
Princess Point	77	7	12	4
Westdale	74	3	19	4

NOTE: Total *n* = 43,335.
SOURCE: Statistics Canada, Canadian 1971 Census Profile (Census Tract level), Canadian Census Analyzer (Computing in the Humanities and Social Sciences, University of Toronto, 2014).

80 Manon Ames, Joan Pikor, and Robert Mendelson, "Preserving the Residential Character of Hamilton Beach," 1982; Dave Greenberg, "Residents Fear Beach Neighbourhood Marked for Destruction by City Hall," *Toronto Star*, 21 June 1983.

81 Valerie S. Preston, Martin Taylor, and David C. Hodge, "Adjustment to Natural and Technological Hazards," *Environment and Behavior* 15, 2 (1983): 143–64.

82 Simmons, interview by Visram, 2 February 1998.

83 Moore/George Associates, *Hamilton Beach Concept Plan, Final Report* (Hamilton, 1987).

84 As the tables below indicate, though Hamilton's waterfront neighbourhoods (North End to Beach Strip) continued to be more working class than the city as a whole, or than the North Shore (Burlington) or the West Hamilton areas bordering on Cootes Paradise (Princess Point and Westdale), only some had a radically different ethnic composition than the rest of the city.

TABLE 8 Occupational and family earnings profiles, selected census districts, 1991

	Managerial, professional (%)	Service workers (%)	Manual workers (%)	Average family earnings ($)
Total city	30	40	30	56,600
North End	14	41	45	34,300
Wellington to Sherman	15	33	52	32,000
Sherman to Ottawa	5	43	52	34,400
Ottawa to Parkdale	8	36	56	36,900
Parkdale to East	13	40	47	39,000
Beach Strip	25	33	42	39,300
Burlington	35	43	22	63,100
Princess Point	42	39	19	45,600
Westdale	53	32	15	77,300

NOTE: Total n = 37,810.
SOURCE: Statistics Canada, Canadian 1991 Census Profile (Census Tract level), Canadian Census Analyzer (Computing in the Humanities and Social Sciences, University of Toronto, 2014).

TABLE 9 Ethnic profiles, selected residential areas, 1991

	"Canadian," British, or western European (%)	Italian (%)	Eastern European (%)	Other (%)
Total city	78	7	7	8
North End	80	6	3	11
Wellington to Sherman	83	5	2	10
Sherman to Ottawa	81	10	9	0
Ottawa to Parkdale	84	2	12	2
Parkdale to East	87	5	6	2
Beach Strip	94	1	1	4
Burlington	87	3	5	5
Princess Point	77	4	8	11
Westdale	81	3	9	7

NOTE: Total n = 37,810.
SOURCE: Statistics Canada, Canadian 1991 Census Profile (Census Tract level), Canadian Census Analyzer (Computing in the Humanities and Social Sciences, University of Toronto, 2014).

85 Robert Howard, "Buying of Beach Strip Parkland Put on Hold," *Spectator,* 14 April 1983; "Switch on the Beach," *Spectator,* 16 April 1983; Rick Hughes, "Hamilton Launches Beach Strip Sell-Off," *Spectator,* 4 August 2001; Paul Wilson, "Beach Strip Sale of Empty Lots Signals of a Fine Future for the Area," *Spectator,* 22 June 2002.

86 David Harvey, *Justice, Nature and the Geography of Difference* (Cambridge, MA: Blackwell, 1996), 304.

87 Kathy Renwald, at the memorial service for Simmons, quoted in Fragomeni, "Gil Worked Tirelessly to Clean Up Waterfront," A02.

88 Quoted in Wild, "Her Lifestyle Shaped by Her Love of the Bay."

89 Quoted in Rick Hughes, "Bringing Back the Bay: Hamilton Hungers for Its Harbour, Part 1," *Spectator,* 23 November 2002, M04.

CHAPTER 8: REMEDIATING NATURE

1 Rick Hughes, "Bringing Back the Bay: Hamilton Hungers for Its Harbour, Part 1," *Hamilton Spectator* (hereafter *Spectator*), 23 November 2002, M04.

2 Canviro Consultants and Bar Environmental, prepared for City of Hamilton, "Remediation Plan for the Former Lax Property" (Hamilton Council, Parks and Recreation Committee, 1989); Images of what was being removed are neatly captured in a photo essay by Cees van Gemerden, which depicts the hidden world at the Lax lands before remediation. His work provides both an environmental critique and one of our few visual records of the area during a time of neglect by authorities. "Trespassing – More Power Anyone?" (Bay Area) Photographers Show, Burlington Cultural Centre, 24 May–26 July 1992. This exhibit has been reshown a number of times, recently at Hamilton's you me gallery, 11 May–23 June 2007. Also see our photo essay, "Remembering the Struggle for the Environment: Hamilton's Lax Lands/Bayfront Park, 1950s–2008," *Left History* 13, 1 (Spring-Summer 2008): 106–28.

3 William Ashworth, *The Late, Great Lakes: An Environmental History* (Toronto: Collins, 1986), 181–82.

4 Ibid., 181; International Joint Commission and Great Lakes Water Quality Board, *1981 Report on Great Lakes Water Quality: Appendices* (Windsor: Great Lakes Water Quality Board, 1981), Appendix 2, Specific Areas of Concern, 33–34.

5 Ashworth, *The Late, Great Lakes,* 182.

6 In the Great Lakes Water Quality Agreement (GLWQA), the Governments of Canada and the United States agreed "to restore and maintain the chemical, physical, and biological integrity of the waters of the Great Lakes Basin Ecosystem." Cited in Lee Botts and Paul Muldoon, *Evolution of the Great Lakes Water Quality Agreement* (East Lansing: Michigan State University Press, 2005), 260. This book contains the full text of the GLWQA and a history of the agreement. International Joint Commission and Great Lakes Water Quality Board, *Report on Great Lakes Water Quality* (Windsor: International Joint Commission, 1985).

7 See, for example, accounts of the work by winners of the Dr. Victor Cecilioni Award for Environmentalist of the Year, held since 1979 in honour of "individuals and groups who have made a significant contribution to the protection and/or enhancement of the environment in the City of Hamilton." Carmela Fragomeni, "Awards for Eco-Warriors," *Spectator,* 5 June 2007.

8 International Joint Commission, *Great Lakes Water Quality Agreement* (Windsor: International Joint Commission, 1978); International Joint Commission, *Revised Great*

Lakes Water Quality Agreement (Windsor: International Joint Commission, 1987), 159; Richard Cloutie, "From BARC to BAIT," *Spectator,* 11 October 1991.

9 Remedial Action Plan for Hamilton Harbour, http://www.hamiltonharbour.ca/index. php?page=index&p=about_the_rap.

10 John H. Hartig and Michael A. Zarull, eds., *Under RAPs: Toward Grassroots Ecological Democracy in the Great Lakes Basin* (Ann Arbor: University of Michigan Press, 1992); Great Lakes Science Advisory Board and International Joint Commission, *Public Participation and Remedial Action Plans: An Overview of Approaches, Activities and Issues Arising from RAP Coordinator's Forums* (Windsor: International Joint Commission Great Lakes Regional Office, 1990); Kathe Glassner et al., *Making RAPs Happen: Financing and Managing Clean-ups at Great Lakes Areas of Concern* (Chicago: Center for the Great Lakes, 1991); Gail Krantzberg, "The Remedial Action Plan Program, Historical and Contemporary Overview," in *Great Lakes: Lessons in Participatory Governance,* ed. Velma I. Grover and Gail Krantzberg (Boca Raton: CRC Press, 2012), 245–56. For a comparative examination of three RAP sites – Hamilton Harbour, Lower Green Bay and Fox River, and Saginaw Bay – see Susan H. MacKenzie, *Integrated Resource Planning and Management: The Ecosystem Approach in the Great Lakes Basin* (Washington, DC: Island Press, 1996); and Mark Sproule-Jones, *Restoration of the Great Lakes: Promises, Practices, and Performances* (Vancouver: UBC Press, 2002).

11 The Bay Area Restoration Council's website includes varied materials such as reports, annual reports, and newsletters, along with a digital community forum about events and issues related to Hamilton Harbour/Burlington Bay.

12 HHRAP, Land Use Research Associates, Ontario Ministry of the Environment (MOE), Environment Canada (EC), and Hamilton Harbour Stakeholders' Group *Interim Report, Hamilton Harbour's Water Quality: The Stakeholders' Proposals* (Toronto: Land Use Research Associates, September 1986), 25; John Jackson, "The Citizen's Perspective on Public Participation in RAPs: A Paper Presented to the IJC's RAP Coordinators' Forum, November 10, 1987," in Great Lakes Science Advisory Board and International Joint Commission, *Public Participation and Remedial Action Plans,* 9–15.

13 The City has recently pursued brownfields development through the Hamilton ERASE Community Improvement Plan. See "Hamilton ERASE Community Improvement Plan," April 2010. This financial incentive program includes the Hamilton Downtown/West Harbourfront Remediation Loan Program, offering bridge financing for brownfield remediation properties. See L.P. Piccioni, "The 'Erasing' of Brownfields in Hamilton, Ontario, Canada," in *Ecosystems and Sustainable Development IV,* ed. C.A. Brebbia, E. Tiezzi, and J.-L. Uso (Wessex Institute of Technology eLibrary, 2003), 2:779–87; and Christopher A. De Sousa, "Urban Brownfields Redevelopment in Canada: The Role of Local Government," *Canadian Geographer* 50, 3 (2006): 392–407.

14 Steve Arnold, "Savings in Hamilton Part of U.S. Steel Plan," *Spectator,* 1 May 2014; "U.S. Steel," *Spectator,* 1 November 2013; Joan Walters, "Chicago: A Model for Brownfield Land," *Spectator,* 31 October 2013; Meredith Macleod, "U.S. Steel Shutdown," Matthew Van Dongen, "What's Next for U.S. Steel Property?" and "The Company's History in Hamilton," *Spectator,* 30 October 2013; David Premi and Paul Shaker, opinion piece, "Life after Steel," *Spectator,* 7 November 2012 ; Lorne Opler, "Queen City, Steel City," *Spectator,* 6 October 2012; "Steeltown: A Century of Steel," *Spectator,* 11 February 2012; Steve Arnold, "A Slow, Tortured Decline," and "Highlights of Stelco's Long Decline," *Spectator,* 9 October 2010; Trevor Cole, "Save This City: Its Days as Steeltown Are Finished – but Can Hamilton See

Its Future?" *Toronto Globe and Mail Report on Business Magazine,* 28 August 2009; Bill Freeman, *Hamilton: A People's History* (Toronto: James Lorimer, 2001), 176–78; June Corman et al., *Recasting Steel Labour: The Stelco Story* (Halifax: Fernwood, 1993).

15 How that character will be shaped in the future remains to be seen, as the waterfront stands at the precipice of great change with the closing of Stelco, something that the editor of the *Spectator* noted in September 2014, pointing out that "the next phase of Hamilton's waterfront redevelopment poses nearly as many challenges as opportunities." Howard Elliott, editorial, "Pay Heed to All the Waterfront Voices," *Spectator,* 23 September 2014. For the waterfront's future in the postindustrial age, see, for example, Steve Arnold, "Land of Opportunity" and "Prime Contaminated Waterfront," *Spectator,* 24 January 2015; Steve Arnold and Amy Kenny, "Port Authority Interested in US Steel Lands," *Spectator,* 11 March 2015; and Any Kenny's seven-part series exploring the "reinvention of steel cities," which ran daily on the front page of the *Spectator* between 6 and 13 June 2015, with photographs by John Rennison.

16 Hamilton Harbour Commissioners, "Port of Hamilton, Ontario, Canada and Its Economic Impact," Coopers and Lybrand Consulting Group, February 1990; Hamilton Port Authority, *Port of Hamilton Celebrates 100 years, 1912–2012* (Hamilton: Hamilton Port Authority, 2012); "The Port at 100," *Spectator,* 17 March 2012; Steve Arnold, "Firms Await Busy Year at Hamilton Terminal," *Spectator,* 23 March 2012; "Booming Hamilton Port Is a $5.9b Winner," *Spectator,* 4 November 2011; "Lake of Commerce," *Toronto Star,* 24 July 2011. In the mid-1970s, the harbour commission briefly floated the idea of an "outer harbour" that would be located east of the city on Lake Ontario, but the proposal fell flat. Hamilton Harbour Commissioners, *Annual Report,* 1974; "Dream Port Backers Eye Ottawa Warily," *Spectator,* 12 December 1975.

17 The Harbour Commission also changed. Reviewing it before its transformation into what would become today's Port Authority, a task force of representatives from the harbour commission, MOE, the Cities of Hamilton and Burlington, boat clubs, Conserver Society, North End Information Service, and Central Area Plan Implementation Committee recommended that issues of the environment, MOE requirements, the RAP, and the use of the west harbour as public waterfront and open space all be incorporated into its planning process and mandate. See Hamilton Harbour Commission, "Report of the Task Force to Review the Mandate and Structure of the Hamilton Harbour Commissioners," Hamilton Harbour Commission, January 1989, 19–24.

18 For example, the question remains about what to do with the Stuart Street rail yard and the Southern Ontario Railway lease of land from CN, which will run out in 2018. See Matthew Van Dongen, "Urgent Opportunity on the Waterfront," *Spectator,* 31 January 2015; Howard Elliott, editorial, "New Beginnings on Industrial Legacy Land," *Spectator,* 16 August 2012; Emma Reilly, "Grassroots Group Tracks Future of West Harbour Lands," *Spectator,* 11 July 2012; David Premi and Paul Shaker, opinion piece, "We Need to Think outside the (Big) Box," *Spectator,* 4 May 2012; Meredith Macleod, "Do It Right, and Transform Hamilton: Think-Tank Study Outlines Plan for 'Fascinating' City," *Spectator,* 10 February 2010; Eric McGuinness, "Local Railway, Recyclers among Objectors to Harbour Plan," *Spectator,* 16 March 2005; Akram Al-Attar, "Planning for Reuse and Redevelopment of Inner City Blighted Contaminated Industrial Sites" (PhD diss., University of Waterloo, 2011), 257–309.

19 Andrew Dreschel, "Brownfields Akin to Randle Reef on Land," *Spectator,* 22 January 2014.

20 International Reference Group on Great Lakes Pollution from Land Use Activities, *Environmental Management Strategy for the Great Lakes System: Final Report to the IJC* (Windsor: International Joint Commission, July 1978), vii, iii, 5–8. Susan Hill MacKenzie, an American political scientist and expert in resource management across the Great Lakes, argues that the ecosystem approach differed from earlier models employed in the Great Lakes in its desire to "protect the integrity of the natural system," its striving to create a self-sustaining environment, its use of ecological rather than political boundaries, and finally, its acknowledgment that both environmental and economic interests must be accounted for. Ultimately, each RAP sought what MacKenzie calls "an ecologically sustainable socio-physical system." Susan Hill MacKenzie, "Ecosystem Management in the Great Lakes: Some Observations from Three RAP Sites," *Journal of Great Lakes Restoration* 19, 1 (1993): 137. Gail Krantzberg maintains that the ecosystem approach entailed "a flexible pragmatism," something she regards as being "perhaps the most productive feature for addressing Great Lakes environmental problems." Krantzberg, "The Remedial Action Plan Program," 254; see also John H. Hartig and John R. Vallentyne, "Use of an Ecosystem Approach to Restore Degraded Areas of the Great Lakes," *Ambio* 18, 8 (1989): 423–28; and A.J. Willis, "The Ecosystem: An Evolving Concept Viewed Historically," *Functional Ecology* 11, 2 (1997): 268–71.

21 Forty-nine stakeholders formed the group, a number that would fluctuate somewhat through time. See Ministry of the Environment (Ontario), Ministry of Natural Resources (Ontario), Ministry of Agriculture and Food (Canada); Environment Canada, Department of Fisheries and Oceans, and Royal Botanical Gardens, "Hamilton Harbour Remedial Action Plan," October 1992, 3, Appendix G, "Hamilton Harbour RAP Stakeholders Group," 235–39. It used a periodic newsletter, *Dialogue on Hamilton Harbour*, sponsored by Environment Canada and the MOE, to provide community information and updates, and to advertise RAP meetings and upcoming events, for which the first meeting held at the Hamilton Convention Centre reportedly attracted some three hundred people. See Land Use Research Associates, "Community Plan for Harbour Clean-Up Underway," *Dialogue on Hamilton Harbour* 1, January 1987, 1. Land Use Research Associates, *Interim Report, Hamilton Harbour's Water Quality*, 6, claims that this public consultation process was "the first major citizen-based effort to contribute, to both governments, recommendations for specific actions to achieve water quality improvement." Hartig and Vallentyne, "Use of an Ecosystem Approach," 426, call it "precedent-setting." Hall and O'Connor argue that it "may well have been one of the first stakeholder engagement exercises used as a planning approach in the great Lakes." John Hall and Kristin M. O'Connor, "Remedial Action Plan Case Study: Participatory Governance Used in Hamilton Harbour," in Grover and Krantzberg, *Great Lakes*, 271. MacKenzie credits its consensus-based decision-making process as "one of the most successful aspects of the Hamilton Harbour RAP." MacKenzie, *Integrated Resource Planning and Management*, 47. Jackson flags the Hamilton Harbour and Green Bay RAPs as "notable successes" and "positive examples" for their development of effective public participation in the RAP process. Jackson, "The Citizen's Perspective," 9.

22 HHRAP et al., *Interim Report, Hamilton Harbour's Water Quality*, 6; MacKenzie reports that "the atmosphere at the meetings was described [by participants] as convivial." MacKenzie, *Integrated Resource Planning and Management*, 47.

23 Quoted in MacKenzie, *Integrated Resource Planning and Management*, 48.

24 Quoted in Hughes, "Bringing Back the Bay," MO4.

25 Hall and O'Connor argue that this was a strength of the process, and they identify a number of keys to the RAP's success: "get all the stakeholders at the table, good facilitation and well defined roles, science based writing team and task groups, value of senior level representation, good communication, and motivated people." Hall and O'Connor, "Remedial Action Plan Case Study," 285. MacKenzie's interviews identified harbour access, land use, and the role of the harbour commission as sources of conflict. MacKenzie, *Integrated Resource Planning and Management,* 51. HHRAP et al., *Interim Report, Hamilton Harbour's Water Quality,* 6, notes that "stakeholders held a co-operative attitude during debate, and resolution of differences was achieved through broad recommendations, frequently qualified to reflect concerns of specific participants. The single exception where resolution was not achieved was shoreline filling, which requires further deliberation of total group."

26 G. Keith Rodgers summarizes the *Interim Report, Hamilton Harbour's Water Quality,* in his "Hamilton Harbour Remedial Action Planning," in Hartig and Zarull, *Under RAPs,* 65–66, especially Table 4; HHRAP et al., *Interim Report, Hamilton Harbour's Water Quality,* 8–12; "Stakeholders' Report," *Dialogue on Hamilton Harbour* 2, March 1987, 3. The issue of public access had been raised earlier, in 1982, when the Hamilton Harbour Advisory Committee (made up of representatives from the City, the MOE, local boat clubs, the Chamber of Commerce, the Hamilton Region Conservation Authority, and the harbour commission) identified seven key topics that needed to be addressed: water quality, public access, west harbour area, marina expansion, Windermere Basin, southeastern fill area, and skyway bridge (at that time, only one bridge existed). Hamilton Harbour Advisory Committee, *Hamilton Harbour: A Heritage and an Opportunity: The Report of the Hamilton Harbour Advisory Committee* (Hamilton: Hamilton Harbour Advisory Committee, 1982).

27 HHRAP Writing Team, *Interim Report of the Writing Team for Hamilton Harbour Remedial Action Plan* (Toronto: Ontario Agreement Respecting Great Lakes Water Quality, February 1987), 4, 19–25; HHRAP et al., *Interim Report, Hamilton Harbour's Water Quality,* Exhibit 2. Stakeholders included representatives from cities, towns, townships, and regional municipalities in the area, federal and provincial ministries, Hamilton's industrial and environmental sectors, and private interest groups that were invested in or concerned about the state of the harbour. Among them were representatives from citizen, conservation, and environmental groups such as the Bay Residents Association, the Conserver Society of Hamilton (formerly CHOP), Great Lakes United, both the Hamilton and Halton conservation authorities, the Hamilton Naturalists Club, the Ontario Public Interest Research Group, Pollution Probe, the Royal Botanical Gardens, and the West Burlington Citizens Group. Government and research representatives came from the International Joint Commission, Environment Canada, Fisheries and Oceans Canada, the Ministry of Natural Resources, the harbour commission, the MOE, the Ontario Federation of Agriculture, and institutions such as McMaster University and the International Joint Commission's Great Lakes Science Advisory Board. Industrial, business, and labour representatives came from Dofasco, the Chamber of Commerce, J.I. Case, Firestone Canada, Procter and Gamble, Stelco, United Steel Workers of America no. 1005, and Westinghouse. Finally, recreational clubs sent stakeholders who provided input on behalf of the Burlington Golf and Country Club, Burlington Sailing and Boating Club, Golden Horseshoe Outdoors Club, Hamilton Yacht Club, Macassa Boat Club, the Royal Hamilton Yacht Club, and the West Leander Boat Club.

28 HHRAP Writing Team, *Interim Report*, 25–29.
29 "Citizens Respond to Remedial Options Package," *Dialogue on Hamilton Harbour* 3, August 1987, 1; "Bay Action Group Wants to Keep Going," and "Citizen Interest Vital – Expert," *Spectator*, 5 May 1987.
30 HHRAP et al., *Remedial Action Plan for Hamilton Harbour: Environmental Conditions and Problem Definition: Second Edition of the Stage 1 Report* (Burlington: MOE, 1987); HHRAP et al., *Remedial Action Plan for Hamilton Harbour: Stage 1 Report: Environmental Conditions and Problem Definition*, 2nd ed. (Burlington: MOE, October 1992).
31 HHRAP, *Remedial Action Plan for Hamilton Harbour: Goals, Options and Recommendations: Stage 2 Report, Volume 2 – Main Report* (Burlington: November 1992), 1; HHRAP et al., *Remedial Action Plan for Hamilton Harbour: Stage 1 Report*, 1992, 191; and Krantzberg, "The Remedial Action Plan Program," 247–49; "A Great RAP Song," *Spectator*, 15 February 1992. See also RAP, "Reflecting on the Future: Celebrating 10 Years of Implementing the Hamilton Harbour Remedial Action Plan" (Burlington: Summer 1996); "Progress toward Delisting a Great Lakes Area of Concern"; Rodgers, "Hamilton Harbour Remedial Action Planning," 59–72.
32 So wrote Anne Redish, Bay Area Restoration Council president, in her letter of endorsement on behalf of the HHRAP Stakeholder group to the co-chairmen of the Canada–Ontario Agreement Review Board on 14 September 1992. Reproduced in HHRAP, *RAP: Goals, Options, and Recommendations Report*, v; for the List of Recommended Remedial Actions, see 153–59.
33 "Stewardship Program Expands across Hamilton and Halton," *Landowner CONTACT* 6 (Winter 2001): 1–3; Eric McGuinness, "Unmuddying Our Harbour," *Spectator*, 28 November 2000; Anne Redish and Kristin O'Connor, "Partnerships in Action: Hamilton Harbour RAP," *Leading Edge 2004: The Working Biosphere* (Niagara: Niagara Escarpment Commission, 2004), 6.
34 For example, its Adopt a Creek, Mini Marsh, Yellow Fish Road,TM and Stream of DreamsTM programs used in schools. Classroom materials (such as the Mini Marsh program) are designed to fit into the science and technology components of provincial elementary and secondary curricula. Between 23 and 30 November 2002, the *Spectator* published a week-long thirty-six-page seven-part "Bringing Back the Bay" series. In 2003, it was reprinted as a single tabloid, and the *Spectator* worked with the Bay Area Restoration Council to turn the information from the award-winning series into an education package that went to a hundred schools in the Hamilton and Halton districts. "Awards of Excellence Salute Conservation Initiatives," *Spectator*, 11 June 2003; "Wishart Dominates Sales Club Awards; Recognize Excellence in Print, TV, Radio and Video Ad Campaigns: Kudos," *Spectator*, 27 October 2003; Meredith Macleod, "Spec Earns Five Newspaper Awards: Bringing Back the Bay Honoured as Special Project," *Spectator*, 12 May 2003; "CPRS National Awards of Excellence: External Communications: Submission by Quorum Communications: Bringing Back the Bay," http://www.mtroyal.ca/library/inc/cprs/pdfs/19-07-MAR-04%20Martin,%20Jeffrey%20C.pdf; Canadian Public Relations Society, "2003 Awards of Excellence Recipients," http://www.cprs.ca/awards/2003.aspx.
35 Bay Area Restoration Council, "Toward Safe Harbours, 2012, and Toward Safe Harbours, 2012: Report Card Supporting Document" (Hamilton: Bay Area Restoration Council, 2012), http://hamiltonharbour.ca/index.php?page=document_library&category_id=18.
36 The updated report contained 57 recommendations and 159 targets; each had a timeline and was assigned to a group of responsible for carrying out recommended actions. Kristin

M. O'Connor et al., *Remedial Action Plan for Hamilton Harbour: Stage 2 Update, 2002* (Hamilton: HHRAP Office, 2003); HHRAP, "Hamilton Harbour Remedial Action Plan 2012 Stakeholder Forum Membership and Terms of Reference," HHRAP Office, 19 December 2011.

37 Redish, letter of endorsement, reproduced in HHRAP, *RAP: Goals, Options, and Recommendations Report,* v.

38 Kenneth A. Gould, "Money, Management and Manipulation: Environmental Mobilization in the Great Lakes Basin" (PhD diss., Northwestern University, 1991), 221, 223. Regarding Hamilton Harbour, political scientist Mark Sproule-Jones argues that "consensus-based processes and institutions have been designed to involve environmentalists and industrialists, but their legitimacy has been seriously undermined by the willingness of industrialists to bypass these processes when it has suited their interests." Mark Sproule-Jones, "Politics and Pollution on the Great Lakes: The Cleanup of Hamilton Harbour," in *Canadian Water Politics: Conflicts and Institutions,* ed. Mark Sproule-Jones, Carolyn Johns, and B. Timothy Heinmiller (Montreal and Kingston: McGill-Queen's University Press, 2008), 179; Eric McGuinness, "Stelco Called Cleanup Saboteur," *Spectator,* 17 February 2010.

39 Simmons was a member of BARC's board of directors when its process was outlined in HHRAP, *RAP, Stage 2, Vol. 2, Main Report,* November 1992, Appendix J, "By-Law Bay Area Restoration Council of Hamilton Wentworth and Halton Regions, Inc.," 305–15. On other Hamilton environmental organizations, see also Lynda M. Lukasik, *Getting Citizens Involved in the Environment: Lessons Learned and Emerging Opportunities in the Hamilton Area* (Hamilton: Hamilton Community Foundation, 2003).

40 Quoted in John Mentek, "Life on the Harbour," *Spectator,* 10 July 1999.

41 Gil Simmons, letter to editor, "Bay's Beauty Needs Protection," *Spectator,* 7 July 1971.

42 "A Great RAP Song."

43 This would rise to 23 percent in 2000. Office of the Auditor General of Canada, *2001 October Report of the Commissioner of the Environment and Sustainable Development,* Chapter 1: Section 3: "Case Study 1.3.3 – Activities and Improvements in the Hamilton Harbour Area of Concern," http://www.oag-bvg.gc.ca/internet/English/att_c101se3-3_e_11696.html; Acres Consulting Services Limited's 1974 study provides an analysis of shoreline access in Halton-Wentworth by sector, including the Lake Ontario shoreline. See Acres Consulting Services Limited, "The Halton-Wentworth Waterfront Study," Halton Region Conservation Authority et al., 1974, 1:112–13.

44 Wade Acres Consulting Services Limited, *The Halton-Wentworth Waterfront Study,* 1:156; "26 More Miles of Public Shoreline Urged for Hamilton," *Toronto Globe and Mail,* 5 July 1974; AO, Provincial Park Development Proposal Files, RG1-47-1, Box 34, Paula Niece, Recreation Planner, Central Region, "Hamilton Recreation Study," 30 May 1974, 1, 18, 35–37. The study identified three areas – the Lax property, Fifty Mile Point on Lake Ontario, and the Beach Strip – but studied only the first two. It concluded that the Lax land could best serve as a municipal park and suggested that Fifty Mile Point met criteria for development as a provincial park (which never transpired). "Committee for Bayfront Recreational Land Forming," *Spectator,* 26 July 1973; "Bayfront Park Plan Hailed and Slammed," *Spectator,* 18 August 1973.

45 "Province Says 'No' but Lax Park Still Sought," *Spectator,* 29 December 1977; "Province Not Interested in Lax Land Deal," *Spectator,* 24 April 1975.

46 "Province Says 'No' but Lax Park Still Sought." The 1975 provincial election, in which Bill Davis's Conservatives lost twenty-seven seats but remained in power with a minority government, also played a part in the delay.

47 "Lax Cleanup Starts This Week," *Spectator*, 22 October 1986; Steve McNeill, "Lax Land Waste Cleanup to Take 60 Days – or More," *Spectator*, 28 October 1986; "Lax Site Costs Rising as More Contaminated Soil Unearthed," *Spectator*, 12 November 1986; Paul Wilson, "Digging Stops on Lax Land: Aldermen Seek RCMP Probe as Cleanup Cost Soars," *Spectator*, 19 November 1986; "Lax Cleanup Worth It," editorial, *Spectator*, 20 November 1986; Kevin Von Appen, "Provincial Cash Likely for Cleanup," *Spectator*, 20 November 1986; Paul Wilson, "$1m Cleanup Plea Fits Criteria: Bradley," *Spectator*, 24 November 1986; Kevin Von Appen, "Make Source Industries Pay, Says Isaacs," *Spectator*, 1 December 1986; Kevin Von Appen, "Lax Land Dumping Was Legal: Old Law Culprit," *Spectator*, 1 December 1986; Steve McNeill, "We Should Have Had Police Dumping Report: Aldermen," *Spectator*, 3 December 1986; Canviro Consultants and Bar Environmental, "Remediation Plan for the Former Lax Property," 1.

48 P. Wilson, "Lax Land: Paradise Regained," *Spectator*, 15 October 1984; T.P. Nolan, "Taking over Lax Property Is a First Step Back to the Water," *Spectator*, 30 October 1984.

49 Coombes, Kirkland, Berridge, *Hamilton Waterfront Study: Master Plan* (Toronto: Coombes, Kirkland, Berridge, 1985), 7. Also in 1985, the City's Culture and Recreation Master Plan listed design objectives for Hamilton Harbour. Among other things, these included improving water and air quality as well as public viewpoints, lookouts, and access to the water's edge; enhancing fish and wildlife habitats; and developing Bayview Park (a small park that overlooked the harbour at the corner of MacNab and Burlington Streets) and Pier 4 Park to improve shoreline access. Although it noted that the Lax property could be an appropriate recreational site, it recommended nothing specific. John A. Stevenson, Margo Gram, and Du Toit Associates, *City of Hamilton Culture and Recreation Master Plan* (Toronto: Du Toit Associates, 1985), 67–68.

50 Coombes, Kirkland, Berridge, *Hamilton Waterfront Study*, 23.

51 Paul Wilson, "Toledo, Cleveland and Detroit – Like Hamilton – Are Industrial Great Lakes Cities Coping with Life on the Waterfront," *Spectator*, 5 July 1986; Booth Aquatic Research and City of Hamilton, *Application for Exemption under Section 29 of the Environmental Assessment Act for Proposed Hamilton Waterfront Master Plan* (Toronto: Booth Aquatic Research Group, July 1986), Appendix 3, n.p.; "Hamilton Island Plan Wins Favor," *Spectator*, 5 September 1985. Gil Simmons, vice-chair of the Waterfront Advisory Sub-Committee, was reportedly its only member to vote against the elaborate design of the plan. When city council tabled the plan and then reduced its funding for the park to $1.6 million (from $33 million), Simmons argued for something simpler – with rolling hills, grass, clumps of trees, and washrooms. "Build No-Frills Harbor Park Says Simmons," *Spectator*, 4 April 1986.

52 "Harbor on the Backburner: A Lack of Vision," editorial, *Spectator*, 10 October 1985.

53 The park would be hastened along when Bob Rae's New Democratic Party defeated Premier David Peterson's Liberals in a sweeping upset victory in the 1990 provincial election. The new majority government had four Hamilton NDP MPPs, three of whom held Cabinet posts – Robert W. Mackenzie, Brian Charlton, and Richard Allen – to be joined in Cabinet by David Christopherson in 1992. See Emilia Casella, "Province Comes Up with Lax Land Cash," *Spectator*, 11 October 1991; "Waterfront Cleanup May Start Anytime," *Spectator*, 11 January 1992.

54 As geographer Sarah Wakefield argues, this approach "privileged environmental concerns over economic and social ones." Sarah Wakefield, "Great Expectations: Waterfront Redevelopment and the Hamilton Harbour Waterfront Trail," *Cities* 24, 4 (2007): 308.

55 Created in 1990 by the City's Economic Development Department as a tourist event on the waterfront, Aquafest eventually lost its major sponsor, the Royal Bank, and ended in 2005. Peter Van Harten, "'Port Days' Festival Gets Bigger Berth," *Spectator*, 24 February 2005; Paul Morse, "Aquafest Sinking After Bank Pulls Cash," *Spectator*, 22 February 2005; City of Hamilton, Culture and Recreation Division, "Memo: Discontinuation of Aquafest," 9 February 2005, http://www.hamilton.ca/Hamilton.Portal/Inc/PortalPDFs/ClerkPDFs/Community-Services/2005/Feb22/CS05004%20-%20Aquafest.pdf.

56 Rita Devgan and David Stickney, "Focus on the Bay: Concepts and Design Approaches for Hamilton Harbour" (Hamilton Harbour Advisory Committee, 1983); City of Hamilton, "Waterfront Parks: Pier 4 and Bayfront Park," 1997, 6; "It's Now Officially Bayfront Park," *Spectator*, 30 August 1995; Hughes, "Bringing Back the Bay."

57 "Harbor Rescue: Dilapidated Tug Will Gain Second Life as Centrepiece of $2m Bayfront Park," "A Living Harbor: Credit Stakeholders," and James Elliott, "Taking Back the Bayfront: Shovels Dig In as Projects Make Harbor a People Place," *Spectator*, 2 June 1992; Jim Poling, "Workshop Hears of Harbor's Comeback," *Spectator*, 24 November 1992. As soon as Pier 4 Park opened, people began to swim there, although bacterial levels would forever determine the sanctioning of this activity. Rick Hughes, "In the Swim Again: They're Taking the Plunge at Hamilton Harbor," *Spectator*, 28 July 1993; Rick Hughes, "High Bacteria Levels Close New Pier 4 Park Beach to Swimmers," *Spectator*, 5 August 1993; Michael Dawson, "Our Toe Is in the Water Too Quickly at the New Harborfront Park," *Spectator*, 17 August 1993.

58 Russ Doyle, "Waterfront Trail Is Worth Bragging About," *Spectator*, 4 August 2000; Gord McNulty, editorial, "Our Harbour Dreams Are Closer to Reality: Community," *Spectator*, 5 June 2000; Andrew Dreschel, "Waterfront Trail Rights Long-Lasting Fault," *Spectator*, 10 July 2000. Current waterfront attractions include the Hamilton Waterfront Outdoor Rink – Pier 8, the Hamilton Harbour Queen Cruise and Hamiltonian Tour Boats, Williams Fresh Cafe, Hamilton Waterfront Scoops Ice Cream Parlour, and the Waterfront Grill. Hamilton Waterfront Trust, "Waterfront Attractions," http://www.hamiltonwaterfront.com/category/waterfront_attractions/.

59 "Council Needs Volunteers to Plant Trees along Trail," *Spectator*, 22 April 2000; John Mentek, "Park Shines on Earth Day," *Spectator*, 24 April 2000.

60 "Worth Repeating – Hamilton's Waterfront Undergoes Rebirth," *Toronto Star*, 5 July 2000.

61 Don Crowe, letter to editor, "Walk Was Perilous, Smelly: Waterfront Trail," *Spectator*, 4 July 2000.

62 He was referring to a comment made by Gil Simmons about the "absolute horror" of the polluted state of the harbour; Hughes, "Bringing Back the Bay."

63 When engineers anticipated human traffic patterns and designed seaways, canals, and bridges to manage them, such as the Beach Strip's first Skyway that opened in 1958, they did not anticipate the biological traffic they were also facilitating, which further complicated efforts to manage Great Lakes ecosystems. Kathy Trotter, John D. Hall, and Victor Cairns, *Northeastern Shoreline Fact Sheet* (Hamilton: Fish and Wildlife Habitat Restoration Project, 1998); Jeff Alexander, *Pandora's Locks: The Opening of the Great Lakes–St. Lawrence Seaway* (East Lansing: Michigan State University Press, 2009); E.L. Mills et al., "Exotic Species and the Integrity of the Great Lakes," *BioScience* 44, 10 (November 1994): 666–76. Our

analysis of the Cootes Paradise restoration work is informed by Rosalind Pfaff, "By Human Hands: The Story of Cootes Paradise Degradation and Restoration" (bachelor's thesis, McMaster University, 2013).

64 On the boathouse community, see Chapter 5 above, and Nancy B. Bouchier and Ken Cruikshank, "'The War on the Squatters': Hamilton's Boathouse Community and the Re-Creation of Recreation on Burlington Bay, 1920–1940," *Labour/Le travail* 51 (2003): 9–46; Kelly Bowen, "Marsh Vegetation in Cootes Paradise: Vegetation Monitoring and Restoration Techniques at Royal Botanical Gardens, Hamilton, Ontario, Canada," Royal Botanical Gardens, 1998, 7; T.H. Whillans, "Historic and Comparative Perspectives on Rehabilitation of Marshes as Habitat for Fish in the Lower Great Lakes Basin," *Canadian Journal of Fisheries and Aquatic Sciences* 53, Supplement 1 (1996): 58–66.

65 Bowen, *Marsh Vegetation in Cootes Paradise*, 1; Thomas H. Whillans, "Changes in Marsh Area along the Canadian Shore of Lake Ontario," *Journal of Great Lakes Research* 8, 3 (1982): 570–77; D.S. Painter, K.J. McCabe, and W.L. Simser, "Past and Present Limnological Conditions in Cootes Paradise Affecting Aquatic Vegetation," *Royal Botanical Gardens Technical Bulletin* no. 13 (1989); W.L. Simser, "Changes in the Aquatic Biota of Cootes Paradise Marsh," *Royal Botanical Gardens Technical Bulletin* no. 12 (1982).

66 A. Wei and P. Chow-Fraser, "Untangling the Confounding Effects of Urbanization and High Water Level on the Cover of Emergent Vegetation in Cootes Paradise Marsh, a Degraded Coastal Wetland of Lake Ontario," *Hydrobiologia* 544, 1 (2005): 1–9; P. Chow-Fraser, "Ecosystem Response to Changes in Water Level of Lake Ontario Marshes: Lessons from the Restoration of Cootes Paradise Marsh," *Hydrobiologia* 539, 1 (2005): 189–204; P. Chow-Fraser et al., "Long-Term Response of the Biotic Community to Fluctuating Water Levels and Changes in Water Quality in Cootes Paradise Marsh, a Degraded Coastal Wetland of Lake Ontario," *Wetlands Ecology and Management* 6, 1 (January 1998): 19–42; Tỹs Theÿsmeÿer, "Environmental Considerations Lake Ontario Water Regulation as It Pertains to the Coastal Marsh Cootes Paradise," Royal Botanical Gardens Science Department, 2003.

67 H.R. McCrimmon, *Carp in Canada* (Ottawa: Fisheries Research Board of Canada, 1968), 20; Lee Emery and Great Lakes Fishery Commission, "Review of Fish Species Introduced into the Great Lakes, 1819–1974," Great Lakes Fishery Commission Technical Report no. 45, Ann Arbor, 1985.

68 W.J. Lamoureux, "A Strange Project – for a Botanical Garden," *Gardens Bulletin* 13, 3 (1961): 13–16; Kelly Bowen and Tỹs Theÿsmeÿer, "The Cootes Paradise Fishway: Carp Control Techniquest at Royal Botanical Gardens Fact Sheet," Royal Botanical Gardens, 1998, 4; K. Trotter et al., "Cootes Paradise Fact Sheet," Royal Botanical Gardens, 1998.

69 Bowen and Theÿsmeÿer, "The Cootes Paradise Fishway." The replanting in the fenced-off wetland was a component of the Fish and Wildlife Habitat Restoration Project, begun in 1993 as part of the RAP. See Royal Botanical Gardens, "Wetland Restoration," https://www.rbg.ca/projectparadise. On types of fishways, see also Lamoureux, "A Strange Project"; Bowen and Theÿsmeÿer, *The Cootes Paradise Fishway,* 4; and McCrimmon, *Carp in Canada,* 78–79.

70 Eleanor Tait, "RBG Waters Will Become Paradise Found: $4-Million Project Takes Aim at a Humble Fish," *Spectator,* 18 March 1993; Jim Poling, "Fighting the Fish for Paradise: RBG Scheme Will Give Carp the Boot," *Spectator,* 7 July 1993; "The Lowly Carp," *Spectator,* 6 April 1994; Bruce Duncan, "Project Paradise," *Bruce Trail News,* Fall 1994, 16–18; S.J.

Kerr, *Fishways in Ontario* (Peterborough: Fisheries Policy Section, Ontario Ministry of Natural Resources, 2010).

71 Mark McNeil, "Carp to Lose Cootes as Paradise: Barrier Will Keep Fish in Harbor," *Spectator*, 6 April 1994; Mark McNeil, "Carp Beat Canal Fish Barrier Deadline: Project Delayed on Drawing Board as Organizers Want to Make It Right," *Spectator*, 22 March 1995; Lori Fazari, "Paradise Revisited," "Cootes Keeping Carp Out," and "Cootes: Work Continues to Restore the Marsh," in "Bringing Back the Bay," series reprint, *Spectator*, 2003, N1E, 14–16.

72 Royal Botanical Gardens, "The Fishway," https://www.rbg.ca/fishway; Tÿs Theÿsmeÿer, *Coastal Marshes, Natural Fish Hatcheries* (Hamilton: Royal Botanical Gardens, 2001); Eric McGuinness, "Thank the Wind: Carp-Free Cootes Now a Paradise for Marsh Plants," *Spectator*, 6 December 2007.

73 Arthur Kelly, "Paradise Postponed," *Hamilton Magazine*, Winter 1996, 48–53; Eric McGuinness, "Perch, Pickerel, Bass Return to Cootes After Carp Leave," *Spectator*, 18 March 2009; Rob Faulkner, "Fewer Male Pike in Fish Habitat," *Spectator*, 10 December 2008; Eric McGuinness, "Cloud Hangs over Marsh," *Spectator*, 28 May 2008; Eric McGuinness, "Silt from Suburbs Threatens Cootes Paradise," *Spectator*, 25 October 2007; Wade Hemsworth, "Sad to See Wasted Efforts," *Spectator*, 28 July 2007; Howard Elliott, editorial, "Toxic Waste Time Bombs," *Spectator*, 13 October 2010; T. Theÿsmeÿer and D. Galbraith, "July 2007 Biedermann Packaging Fire: Effects on Cootes Paradise Marsh," Royal Botanical Gardens Internal Report, 2007; Eric McGuinness, "Ministry Finds 'Significant Damage to Ecosystem,'" *Spectator*, 28 July 2007; Paul Legall, "Contaminated Run-Off Kills Thousands of Fish," *Spectator*, 27 July 2007.

74 McMaster researchers Sarah Thomasen and Patricia Chow-Fraser conclude that "the recovery of a system as complex, large and degraded as Cootes Paradise cannot be expected to be simple or inexpensive. Cootes Paradise offers a good opportunity to educate the public about unintended harmful actions caused by humans on natural systems, and serves as an important reminder that a degraded ecosystem can be difficult, if not impossible, to restore and may require management actions that are different than those appropriate for its original state." Sarah Thomasen and Patricia Chow-Fraser, "Detecting Changes in Ecosystem Quality Following Long-Term Restoration Efforts in Cootes Paradise Marsh," *Ecological Indicators* 13, 1 (2012): 91.

75 Bags of concrete shipped in for the Cooke Concrete Block plant are pictured there in Gary Evans, *The Prints of Aldershot: A Photographic View of Another Era* (Burlington: North Shore, 2000), 28; on the park and Hamilton's search for clean swimming spaces, see Ken Cruikshank and Nancy B. Bouchier, "Dirty Spaces: Environment, the State and Recreational Swimming in Hamilton Harbour, 1870–1946," *Sport History Review* 29, 1 (1998): 59–76.

76 Leased from the City of Hamilton for a dollar a year, the LaSalle land has been a matter of some issue in recent years. "What Is LaSalle Park Worth?" *Burlington Post*, 2 November 2012; Ken Peters, "City Council Members Want Burlington to Buy LaSalle Park," *Spectator*, 9 May 1992; "Bringing Back the Bay: Hamilton Harbour: What's Good, What's Not so Good, Part 1," *Spectator*, 23 November 2002, M10; "Burlington's Full Season Open Public Marina," http://cms.burlington.ca/AssetFactory.aspx?did=12551.

77 J.N. Bowlby, K. McCormack, and M.G. Heaton, "Hamilton Harbour and Watershed Fisheries Management Plan," Ministry of Natural Resources and Royal Botanical Gardens,

2009, 41.

78 In 1996, the Fish and Wildlife Habitat Restoration Project reported that all the harbour shoreline had been hardened and modified, save for the area from Willow Point to the Grindstone Creek in the far western tip of the bay. Fish and Wildlife Habitat Restoration Project, "Shoreline Protection Ideas for Fish and Wildlife Habitat Enhancement," Fish and Wildlife Habitat Restoration Project, n.d., 1.

79 Mark McNeil, "$150m for Great Lakes Cleanup: Harbor Wildlife Project Gets $1.8m of Federal Money," *Spectator,* 19 April 1994; Brad Honywill, "Bay Projects Win Backing of Committee: More Than $5 Million to Be Spent on Projects on Burlington Side," and "Burlington Bay Plan Clears a Hurdle," *Spectator,* 28 May 1993; Hamilton Fish and Wildlife Restoration Committee, "Fish and Wildlife Habitat Restoration in Hamilton Harbour and Cootes Paradise – Preliminary Scoping and Consultation," Fish and Wildlife Habitat Restoration Project, July 1992.

80 Tony Fitz-Gerald, "A Good Wallow in the Mud," *Spectator,* 24 July 1995.

81 Brenda Axon, "Planning and Implementation of Urban Habitat Restoration in Hamilton Harbour," 22 January 2009, http://www.glfc.org/urbanrestore/4_Axon_Planning_ Implementation_Hamilton_Harbour.pdf.

82 In 2002, in the categories of "Fish and Wildlife Desired Outcomes" and "Public Access and Aesthetics," the RAP received grades of B+ for restoring fish and wildlife habitat and populations, for re-establishing 170 hectares of aquatic vegetation in the harbour, and for improving public access to the shoreline. Bay Area Restoration Council, *Toward Safe Harbours: 2002 Report Card* (Hamilton: Bay Area Restoration Council, 2002); "Toward Safe Harbours," *Spectator,* 30 November 2002; "Bringing Back the Bay: Rebuilt Fish Habitats a Success, Part 2," *Spectator,* 25 November 2002; Paul Legall, "Part of the Waterfront Trail System," *Spectator,* 6 August 1996; Kate Barlow, "Burlington LaSalle Park Trail – the Start of Something Big," *Spectator,* 3 November 1994; Katrina Simmons, "Waterfront Coming Back to Life," *Spectator,* 2 August 2003; "It's Sparkling," *Spectator,* 29 November 1995.

83 Yet though fish have increased in the harbour, MOE guidelines severely limit the species that are deemed edible, especially for women of childbearing age and children under fifteen. Only three harbour species – largemouth bass, yellow perch, and rock bass – are recommended for the general and sensitive populations alike. Consuming as many as eight servings a month is considered safe, but only if the fish are under eight inches (twenty centimetres) in length. This is an improvement over the 2003–04 guideline recommendation. MOE, *Guide to Eating Ontario Sport Fish, 2013–2014* (Toronto: MOE, 2013), 273–74; Royal Botanical Gardens and MOE, "Guide to Eating Sport Fish from Hamilton Harbour, 2003–2004," Royal Botanical Gardens, n.d.; "Bringing Back the Bay: Finding Redemption One Fish at a Time, Part 2," *Spectator,* 25 November 2002, and Mark McNeil, "Promising Signs of Renewal in Harbor," *Spectator,* 13 September 1995.

84 Mark McNeil, "RBG Says It Is 'at Peace with Its Beavers," *Spectator,* 30 April 2014; Wade Hemsworth, "Beavers at Work in Harbour," *Spectator,* 9 January 2007.

85 Currently, the protection of trumpeter swans that winter at LaSalle Park has become the focus of controversy in plans for a new breakwater there. See Mark McNeil, "Marina Says Expansion Won't Harm Resident Swans," *Spectator,* 5 March 2014; "Group Fights for Swans' Burlington Marina Home," *Spectator,* 18 February 2014; Trumpeter Swan Coalition, "Comments on the LaSalle Park Marina Breakwater Class Environmental Assessment Environmental Study Report – July 2013 City of Burlington and LaSalle Park Marina

Association," http://www.trumpeterswancoalition.com/important-read-our-response-to
-the-esr-report.html; John Burman, "No Swan Song for Trumpeter," *Spectator*, 6 March
2007; James Elliott, "Swans Are Something to Trumpet About," *Spectator*, 8 March 2002;
Jim Purnell, "Fragile Trumpeter Swan Inspires Devotion," *Spectator*, 24 October 2000;
"Volunteers Breathe Life Back into Bay," *Spectator*, 1 June 1998.

86   Kathy Trotter, John D. Hall, and Victor Cairns, *LaSalle Park Fact Sheet* (Hamilton: Fish
and Wildlife Habitat Restoration Project, 1998).

87   Kevin Marron, "Despite Pollution, Hamilton Harbor Popular with Birds," *Toronto Globe
and Mail*, 20 July 1988; see also Peter Whelan, "The Odd Weird Moment in Birding,"
Toronto Globe and Mail, 2 June 1990; Peter Whelan, "Migration Ends in Hurrah," *Toronto
Globe and Mail*, 4 June 1986; Peter Whelan, "A Kaleidoscope of Gulls," *Toronto Globe and
Mail*, 21 November 1984; Martin B. Gebauer, Rob Z. Dobos, and D. Vaughn Weseloh,
"Waterbird Surveys at Hamilton Harbour, Lake Ontario, 1985–1988," *Journal of Great Lakes
Research* 18, 3 (1992): 420–39; HHRAP, "Windermere Basin Rehabilitation Project: Remedial
Action Plan Stage 1 Report," 131.

88   The area had been popular with game bird hunters as well: the Hamilton Gun Club had
a clubhouse at the tip of Jones Inlet on land that it purchased in 1906 and sold to Stelco
in 1953. Peter Munger, "Decoys of Burlington Bay: Tools for the Art of 'Screening,'" *Decoy
Magazine*, May-June 2011, 24–31; Dick Tobin, *The Story of the Hamilton Gun Club, 1882–1982*
(Hamilton, 1982); Hamilton Gun Club, "History of the Club," http://www.hamiltongun
club.net/HISTORY.aspx.

89   Since the 1930s, it also received backwash water that entered Red Hill Creek from the
sewage treatment plant. Eric McGuinness, "Windermere Will Wait; While Hamilton
Harbour and Cootes Paradise High-Profile Restoration Projects Remain, Windermere
Basin Demands Attention," *Spectator*, 20 November 2002; Envirosearch Limited and
Hamilton Harbour Commission, "Windermere Basin Rehabilitation Project, Initial
Assessment for the Partial Dredging and Filling of Windermere Basin, 13 July 1988,"
Hamilton Harbour Commission, 1990, 5–6.

90   "Sediment in Hamilton the Worst," *Toronto Globe and Mail*, 26 October 1987.

91   Between 1988 and 1990, the Canadian government worked with the harbour commission
to create a series of basins behind dikes on the perimeter of the former basin. Contaminated
sediments from what remained of the basin were dredged and dumped into them, and
they were gradually capped. "Windermere Basin Rehabilitation Project," advertisement,
Spectator, 28 May 1988; Eric McGuinness, "Windermere Dredging Plan Outlined," *Spectator*,
1 June 1988; Barbara Brown, "Keep Windermere Basin for Wildlife Naturalist Club Tells
Clean-Up Probers," *Spectator*, 8 June 1988.

92   Comment by Cees van Gemerden in his comment form during the Windermere Basin
Rehabilitation Project Environmental Assessment and Review Process public information
session. In Envirosearch Limited, *Windermere Basin Rehabilitation Project* Appendix A, n.p.

93   MOE, *Windermere Basin Study* (Toronto: Queen's Printer, 1982); HHRAP, "Windermere
Basin Rehabilitation Project," 126; "Windermere Basin Proposal – Hamilton Naturalists'
Club Recommendations," in Envirosearch Limited, *Windermere Basin Rehabilitation Project*,
Appendix B, n.p.; Michael Keating, "Hamilton Bay Test Subjects Are Dead Ducks," *Toronto
Globe and Mail*, 17 July 1986.

94   Eric McGuinness, "There's Money in Them Thar Hills," *Spectator*, 2 May 2006; Jon Wells,
"Different Visions of a 'Filthy' Place," *Spectator*, 3 July 1999; Keith Rodgers, "Public Needs

Access to East Harbour," *Spectator,* 6 February 1998; Carolynne Wheeler, "Harbour Revitalization Key to Platform," *Spectator,* 31 October 1997; "The Basin: Beauty or Beast?" *Spectator,* 26 September 1997; Brian McHattie, "We Need a Green Entrance to Hamilton," *Spectator,* 23 September 1997.

95　The federal government's Canada Strategic Infrastructure Fund provided $35 million, the provincial government $15 million, and the City of Hamilton paid the remainder toward the Windermere project, along with upgrades to the Dundas and Woodward Avenue Sewage Treatment Plant in work that amounted to $80 million. Canada, "Major Wastewater Infrastructure Improvements Clean Up Hamilton Harbour," Infrastructure Canada news release, 26 June 2013.

96　Emma Reilly, "City Completes $80m Harbour Cleanup," *Spectator,* 27 June 2013; "Pollution Trap to Be Nursed Back to Wetland," *Spectator,* 9 May 2012; Robert Norman and City of Hamilton Public Works Department, Capital Planning and Implementation Division, "Windermere Basin Natural Park Land Development Report," PW06088, 19 July 2006.

97　Carmen Fragomeni, "Windermere Basin: From Cesspool to Ecosystem," *Spectator,* 27 April 2015; Matthew Van Dongen, "Longtime Pollution Trap to Be Nursed Back to Wetland," *Spectator,* 27 April 2012; "Once an Industrial Wasteland, Windermere Basin Is Slowly Going Green," *Spectator,* 11 September 2012; Stacey Escott, "Bringing Windermere Basin Back to Life," *Spectator,* 25 November 2011.

98　The reef, identifiable on maps, was known in the early 1970s for its heavy-metal sediment concentration; by the early 1980s, it was known as the site of the highest concentrations of polycyclic aromatic hydrocarbons along the industrial shoreline. Ontario, Lake Systems Unit, *Hamilton Harbour Study* (Toronto: Water Resources Branch, MOE, 1974), 10; D.J. Poulton, *Hamilton Harbour Trace Contaminants – 1982–83: Loadings to, and Concentrations in the Harbour* (Toronto: Ontario, MOE, 1986), 13; M.R. Pozza, J.I. Boyce, and W.A. Morris, "Lake-Based Magnetic Mapping of Contaminated Sediment Distribution, Hamilton Harbour, Lake Ontario, Canada," *Journal of Applied Geophysics* 57, 1 (2004): 23–41; M.E. Fox, H. Brouwer, and T.P. Murphy, *Coal Tar Contamination Near Randle Reef, Hamilton Harbour* (Burlington: Lakes Research Branch, National Water Research Institute, 1990).

99　*Randle Reef Sediment Remediation Project, Comprehensive Study Report under the CEAA,* 1996, 29, quoted in Mark Sproule-Jones and Lynda Lukasik, "Petition No. 57: Coal Tar Contamination Near Randle Reef, Hamilton Harbour," 16 October 2002, http://www.oag-bvg.gc.ca/internet/English/pet_057_e_28765.html#background.

100　Hamilton Harbour Remedial Action Plan and Carol Ancheta, *Hamilton Harbour RAP: Randle Reef Sediment Remediation Project* (Hamilton: HHRAP, 1996).

101　For the history of the Sydney Tar Ponds to 2000, see Maude Barlow and Elizabeth May, *Frederick Street: Life and Death on Canada's Love Canal* (Toronto: Harper Collins, 2000); for the state of the ponds in 2012 and 2013, see "Final Plan for Sydney Tar Ponds Clean-Up Announced," CBC News Online, 28 October 2012, http://www.cbc.ca/news/canada/nova-scotia/final-plan-for-sydney-tar-ponds-clean-up-announced-1.1152780; and "Remediated Sydney Tar Ponds Unveiled as Green Space," CBC News Online, 30 August 2013, http://www.cbc.ca/news/canada/nova-scotia/remediated-sydney-tar-ponds-unveiled-as-green-space-1.1304232.

102　This account relies on Mark Sproule-Jones, a participant-observer of the events. Sproule-Jones, "Politics and Pollution," 198; Eric McGuinness, "Randle Reef Cleanup Plan Is Protested: Advisory Group Members Fear Covering Toxic Harbour Sediment Poses a Threat to People," *Spectator,* 19 September 2002.

103 As reported in Sproule-Jones, "Politics and Pollution," 198. The Public Advisory Group formed in 2001 consisted of seventeen interest groups: representatives from BARC, HHRAP Office, Great Lakes United, Clean Air Hamilton, Central North End West Neighbourhood Association, Hamilton Beach Preservation Committee, Hamilton Industrial Environmental Association Citizen Liaison Committee, City of Hamilton, City of Burlington, US Steel (formerly Stelco), Local 1005 (USWA), MOE, Ontario Ministry of Labour, Environment Canada, Department of Fisheries and Oceans, Hamilton Conservation Authority, and Hamilton Port Authority.

104 Sproule-Jones and Lukasik, "Petition No. 57"; Gord McNulty, editorial, "$650m Is a Small Price to Pay for a Clean Bay," *Spectator,* 21 September 2002; Eric McGuinness, "Harbour Action Names Stelco, Port Authority," *Spectator,* 18 September 2002; Linda Lukasik, "Toxic Stakes Too High for Stakeholder Approach," *Spectator,* 4 March 2002; Rick Hughes, "Guarantee Randle Reef Cleanup," *Spectator,* 19 January 1999; and Sproule-Jones, "Politics and Pollution."

105 Phase 1 (projected for 2014 to 2016) involves the construction of the containment facility atop 130,000 cubic metres of the most contaminated sediment. During Phase 2 (projected from 2016 to 2018), half a million cubic metres of PAH-contaminated sediments will be dredged from the area around Randle Reef and pumped into the containment facility. In Phase 3 (roughly 2018 to 2021 or 2022), an environmental cap will be placed over the facility, and contaminated sediments will be isolated from surface water, to be used in future as a port facility and green space. Randle Reef Sediment Remediation Project Technical Task Group, *Randle Reef Sediment Remediation Project: Comprehensive Study Report,* 30 October 2012, http://www.ceaa-acee.gc.ca/050/documents/p80001/84290E.pdf.

106 Of the project's $138.9 million cost, the federal and provincial governments are to pay $46.3 million each, and the City of Hamilton, US Steel Canada, and the Port Authority will pay $14.0 million each. The City of Burlington will pay $2.3 million, and the Halton region will pay $2.0 million. Mark McNeil, "Capturing the Blob at Randle Reef," *Spectator,* 26 February 2014; Mel Hawkrigg and Bruce Wood, "Fixing Randle Reef," *Spectator,* 19 March 2010; Howard Elliott, editorial, "Randle Reef Quagmire," *Spectator,* 18 February 2010; Ontario, "Hamilton Harbour Area of Concern: Status of Beneficial Use Impairments," September 2010, http://hamiltonharbour.ca/resources/documents/StatusofBeneficial UseImpairement,ECandOMOE.pdf.

107 Tenders for the first of the work's three phases were solicited in February 2014, but the submitted bids were millions of dollars over budget, prompting fears in June 2014 that the entire project was at risk. This resulted in modifications to the remediation projected, reducing the size of the facility, eliminating much of the green space, and reducing the contaminated sediments that it will hold. More of those sediments will be contained and capped where they are. A new tender is out, with bids due 16 June 2015. Government of Canada, "Update on Randle Reef Sediment Remediation Project," 13 February 2015, http:// news.gc.ca/web/article-en.do?nid=858109. See also Mark McNeil, "More Cost-Effective Randle Reef Plan in the Works: Scheme Involves Smaller Containment Facility, More 'in Situ' Capping," *Spectator,* 5 March 2015; "Game-Changer Randle Reef Cleanup Plan Moving Ahead; Environment Canada Tweaks Cleanup Mega-Project's Design, Set to Re-tender Contracts in 2015," CBC News online, 13 February 2015; Matthew Van Dongan, "Costs Put Randle Reef Project at Risk," *Spectator,* 18 June 2014; Matthew Van Dongan, "Randle Reef Cleanup Stalled," *Spectator,* 17 June 2014; Scott Koblyk, "The Blob Box Hits a Snag,"

17 June 2014, http://hamiltonharbour.ca/index.php?page=blog&id=27.

108 Murray Charlton, letter to editor, "Need to Stick with Randle Reef Plan," *Spectator*, 25 June 2014; see also Mark Sproule-Jones, letter to editor, "Clean Up Randle Reef Bit by Bit," *Spectator*, 20 June 2014.

CONCLUSION

1 *Valastro v. Hamilton Port Authority*, [2010] F.C. 1021 at paras. 16 and 15; Paul Morse, "Judge Sinks Legal Bid to Save Island: 'No Irreparable Harm' If Cormorant Roost in Harbour Turned into Shoals for Fish," *Hamilton Spectator* (hereafter *Spectator*), 28 October 2010. For Valastro's organization, see Peaceful Parks Coalition, "'Nuisance' Wildlife Campaign," http://www.peacefulparks.org/ppc/action_nuisance_wildlife.htm.

2 Mark McNeil, "Three Bird Sanctuaries Will Save Endangered Species," *Spectator*, 14 June 1995; Kathy Trotter, John D. Hall, and Victor Cairns, *Northeastern Shoreline Fact Sheet* (Hamilton: Fish and Wildlife Habitat Restoration Project, 1998).

3 Christopher M. Somers et al., "The Invasive Round Goby (Neogobius melanostomus) in the Diet of Nestling Double-Crested Cormorants (Phalacrocorax auritus) in Hamilton Harbour, Lake Ontario," *Journal of Great Lakes Research* 29, 3 (2003): 392–99; Christopher M. Somers, Marie N. Lozer, and James S. Quinn, "Interactions between Double-Crested Cormorants and Herring Gulls at a Shared Breeding Site," *Waterbirds* 30, 2 (2007): 241–50; Jeff Alexander, *Pandora's Locks: The Opening of the Great Lakes–St. Lawrence Seaway* (East Lansing: Michigan State University Press, 2009), 153–65.

4 James S. Quinn, "Cormorants Part of the Ecosystem," *Spectator*, 4 October 2010.

5 L.J. Howarth, "Cormorants in the Harbour," *Spectator*, 30 September 2010.

6 John D. Hall, RAP co-ordinator, "Restoring an Ecosystem," *Spectator*, 29 September 2010; Jeanne Tootal, "A Stink Too Farr," *Spectator*, 6 October 2010; Paul Glendenning, "A Bridge Too Farr: Questioning the Campaign against Cormorants," *Raise the Hammer*, 22 September 2010; Ron Albertson, "The Battle for Farr Island," *Spectator*, 23 September 2010.

7 Linda R. Wires, *The Double-Crested Cormorant: Plight of a Feathered Pariah* (New Haven: Yale University Press, 2014). Wires credits organizations such as Valastro's for preventing Ontario from adopting a more lethal management approach to the cormorant.

8 Mark Sproule-Jones, *Governments at Work: Canadian Parliamentary Federalism and Its Public Policy Effects* (Toronto: University of Toronto Press, 1993), 150.

9 Samuel P. Hays, *Beauty, Health and Permanence: Environmental Politics in the United States, 1955–1985* (Cambridge: Cambridge University Press, 1989), is often cited for its emphasis on the importance of consumption and the "the quality of the human experience" as characteristic of postwar environmentalism.

10 Barry Commoner, *The Closing Circle: Nature, Man and Technology* (New York: Alfred A. Knopf, 1971), 16.

Note on Sources

Anyone with an interest in the development of Hamilton has a rich collection of historical sources at hand. Shortly after the Hamilton Public Library opened in 1890, its staff started to collect local materials on the city, and they continue to do so. The Local History and Archives Department holds an extensive collection of municipal records, various pamphlets, and a very remarkable set of almost two thousand newspaper scrapbooks, with copies of clippings dating back into the nineteenth century. The scrapbooks capture most of the major news stories and even some minor ones, and they can be supplemented by consulting the newspapers themselves: almost all issues of the oldest and only surviving local daily paper, the *Hamilton Spectator* (1846–present), are available in some format, and there are good but incomplete runs of the *Hamilton Times* (1859–1920) and the *Hamilton Herald* (1889–1936) on microfilm or in other formats.

The public library holds many of the city's municipal records; some years ago, Carolyn Gray prepared a valuable guide, titled "Historical Records of the City of Hamilton, 1847–1973" (McMaster University, 1986). Although it is not possible to track down some of the records, the guide is still a valuable starting point for sleuthing, and it provides an immensely important administrative history of many departments and boards. Among the municipal records that we found most useful for this book were the Hamilton City Council Minutes, which were published and indexed after 1887, and which include reports from the Board of Control and many committees and subcommittees. The minutes of the Board of Health as well as the *Annual Reports of the Medical Officer of Health,* like many government reports, prove most useful through the early twentieth century and increasingly perfunctory from the 1930s onward. The special commission government for the Beach Strip, the Burlington Beach Commission (1907–56), also kept minutes of its meetings, and these are available on microfilm at the public library.

Other agencies and other governments were involved in the work of the harbour. The records of the Hamilton Harbour Commission are disappointingly slight, as the majority appear to have been lost, but we did appreciate the access we were given to a few surviving files and the large collection of photographs that help document the many changes to the waterfront. Mark Sproule-Jones provides a brief overview of the history of the harbour commission – and the harbour more generally – in the second half of *Governments at Work: Canadian Parliamentary Federalism and Its Public Policy Effects* (Toronto: University of Toronto Press, 1993). The library of the Royal Botanical Gardens, currently accessible only on request, has an impressive collection of books and various journals, magazines, and corporate publications, as well as some interesting archival collections, only a few of which we used for this book. A combined history and memoir was written by the director of the gardens from 1954 to 1981, Leslie Laking, *Love, Sweat and Soil: A History of the Royal Botanical Gardens from 1930 to 1981* (Hamilton: Royal Botanical Gardens, 2006).

The Library and Archives Canada holdings for national departments that dealt with fisheries, navigation, public works, transport, and justice proved moderately interesting for our purposes. The same might be said of the provincial records at the Archives of Ontario that deal with fish and game, and water resources and quality. The annual reports of the departments (variously named) responsible for federal and provincial fisheries – published in the *Sessional Papers* of those governments – proved very helpful for the nineteenth and early twentieth centuries. On the changing nature of fish populations, John A. Holmes, "Potential for Fisheries Rehabilitation in the Hamilton Harbour–Cootes Paradise Ecosystem of Lake Ontario," *Journal of Great Lakes Research* 14, 2 (1988): 131–41, summarizes and cites the previous work of Holmes himself and T.H. Whillans; Holmes and Whillans both make use of the observations of John William Kerr.

Indeed, the most remarkable source on the nineteenth-century harbour remains the diary of Fishery Inspector John Kerr, which was continued for a few years by one of his sons, Fred. The Hamilton Public Library has a microfilm of the original Kerr Fonds, once held at the Royal Ontario Museum, now held at Queen's University Archives in Kingston, Ontario. It also has a copy of Ivan S. Brookes, *Hamilton Harbour, 1826–1901* (Halton Hills: Maritime History of the Great Lakes, 2001), an encyclopedic history of shipping in the harbour that is also available at http://www.maritimehistoryofthegreatlakes.ca/documents/brookes/default.asp. The diaries of Captain George Thompson, the lighthouse keeper at the Beach Canal (1854–86), contain a number of interesting observations about Beach Strip society – sometimes leaning toward gossip – and are available at the Brant Museum in Burlington. Thomas McQuesten's family home in Hamilton, Whitehern, is now a museum with an archives that holds electronic copies of four thousand letters, documents, and photographs related to the elite McQuesten family. Its handy search engine is at Whitehern Museum Archives, http://www.whitehern.ca/index.php. Readers can start with the fine political biography by the broadcast journalist John C. Best, *Thomas Baker McQuesten: Public Works, Politics and Imagination* (Hamilton: Corinth Press, 1991).

Our endnotes reference various studies of water quality and the harbour environment over the years. Readers might find interesting if somewhat technical several efforts to reconstruct the non-human aquatic history of Hamilton Harbour, including J.O. Nriagu, H.K.T. Wong, and W.J. Snodgrass, "Historical Records of Metal Pollution in Sediments of Toronto and Hamilton Harbours," *Journal of Great Lakes Research* 9, 3 (1983): 365–73; J.R. Yang, H.C. Duthie, and L.D. Delorme, "Reconstruction of the Recent Environmental History of Hamilton Harbour from Quantitative Analysis of Siliceous Microfossils," *Journal of Great Lakes Research* 19, 1 (1993): 55–71; and B.B. Wolfe, T.W.D. Edwards, and H.C. Duthie, "6000-Year Record of Interaction between Hamilton Harbour and Lake Ontario," *Aquatic Ecosystem Health and Management* 3 (2000): 47–54. The last of these articles suggests the significance of the opening of the canal in the 1820s to the evolution of the harbour. For the best attempt to reconstruct the history of Cootes Paradise, at least in the twentieth century, see P. Chow-Fraser et al., "Long-Term Response of the Biotic Community to Fluctuating Water Levels and Changes in Water Quality in Cootes Paradise Marsh, a Degraded Coastal Wetland of Lake Ontario," *Wetlands Ecology and Management* 6, 1 (January 1998): 19–42.

You can learn a lot about the social geography of Hamilton – where people lived, their occupations, where businesses and industries were located, the physical layout and nature of businesses and homes – by using city directories (various publishers, pretty continuous run from 1853 onward, at the McMaster University and Hamilton Public Libraries), Censuses of Canada (detailed manuscript censuses for 1871, 1881, 1891, 1911; census district-level details 1961, 1971, 1981, 1991, available at many Canadian libraries), and particularly valuable for environmental historians, fire insurance maps (the very fine map library at McMaster University holds 1878, 1898, 1911 with revisions to 1916, 1927 with revisions to 1947, 1960 with revisions to 1964, and has even put two online – 1898 and 1911–16). Early-twentieth-century social directories – specifically the *Blue Books* – offer further information on the location and habits of the elite. Michael J. Doucet and John C. Weaver tell us much about that social geography of Hamilton, in *Housing the North American City* (Montreal and Kingston: McGill-Queen's University Press, 1991).

Perhaps because the local sources are so rich, Hamilton has attracted some very talented academic historians and is also home to a vibrant community of local historical enthusiasts. Many of them contributed entries to the four-volume *Dictionary of Hamilton Biography* (1980–99), which was edited and spearheaded by the late Reverend Thomas Melville Bailey (1912–2005); to our knowledge, no other Canadian city has such a rich biographical resource. For two excellent general overviews of local history, readers need look no farther than the work of two McMaster University historians, Charles Johnston, *The Head of the Lake, a History of Wentworth County* (Hamilton: Wentworth County Council, 1958), and John C. Weaver, *Hamilton: An Illustrated History* (Toronto: James Lorimer, 1982). William Kilbourn's *The Elements Combined: A History of the Steel Company of Canada* (Toronto: Clarke, Irwin, 1960) documents, and celebrates, the history of one of Hamilton's most visible industries. Hamilton hosts an "Industrial Trail," a project spearheaded by the Workers Arts and Heritage Centre; its trail guidebooks and other materials can be found at "Industrial Hamilton: A Trail to the Future," http://epe.lac-bac.gc.ca/100/205/301/ic/cdc/industrial/default.htm. WAHC also produced *The Workers' City*, a series of walking tour guides and audiotapes that add detail on industrial and waterfront history that goes well beyond steel; this series includes a catalogue from our 1997 exhibit, *The People and the Bay*. WAHC has since created an enhanced online version of the series, complete with tours, interviews, maps, photographs, and other resources that are also available through a downloadable app for mobile devices. See http://workerscity.ca/

Hamilton society was the subject of an early, classic quantitative social history, Michael B. Katz, *The People of Hamilton, Canada West: Family and Class in a Mid-19th Century City* (Cambridge, MA: Harvard University Press, 1975), and a pioneering Canadian labour history, Bryan D. Palmer, *A Culture in Conflict: Skilled Workers and Industrial Capitalism in Hamilton, Ontario, 1860–1914* (Montreal and Kingston: McGill-Queen's University Press, 1979). Written shortly thereafter, two doctoral dissertations are well worth reading: Robert Storey's "Workers, Unions and Steel: The Shaping of the Hamilton Working Class, 1935–1948" (PhD diss., University of Toronto, 1981) and Craig Heron's "Working-Class Hamilton, 1895–1930" (PhD diss., Dalhousie University, 1981), which is the basis of his recently published *Lunch-Bucket Lives: Remaking the Workers' City* (Toronto: Between the Lines Press, 2015). Both historians went on to write significant scholarly articles on Hamilton labour and working-class history. Robert B. Kristofferson, *Craft Capitalism: Craftworkers and Early Industrialization in Hamilton* (Toronto: University of Toronto Press, 2007), recently revisited some of the same ground as Palmer, albeit with a slightly different orientation, seeing craftsworkers as both employers and employees. Geographers examine the natural and urban environment, in M.J. Dear, J.J. Drake, and L.G. Reeds, eds., *Steel City: Hamilton and Region* (Toronto: University of Toronto Press, 1987). Sociologists Meg Luxton and June Corman studied the impact of the 1980s and 1990s restructuring on Hamilton working-class families, in *Getting By in Hard Times: Gendered Labour at Home and on the Job* (Toronto: University of Toronto Press, 2001).

There are so many popular histories of the area that it is difficult to include them all. We will no doubt leave out numerous good works in mentioning Brian Henley's many books, including *Hamilton: Our Lives and Times* (Hamilton: Hamilton Spectator, 1994); Bill Freeman, *Hamilton: A People's History* (Toronto: James Lorimer, 2001); Claire Emory Machan, *From Pathway to Skyway Revisited: The Story of Burlington* (Burlington: Burlington Historical Society, 1997); Cheryl Macdonald, ed., *Memories of Van Wagner's Beach and Parkview Survey* (Hamilton: Parkview Survey and Van Wagner's Beach Heritage Association, 1995); Lawrence Murphy and Philip Murphy, *Tales from the North End* (Hamilton: Authors, 1981); Gary Evans's many picture books, including *Memories of the Beach Strip* (Burlington: North Shore, 2011); Dorothy Turcotte's books, including *The Sand Strip: Burlington/Hamilton Beaches* (St. Catharines: Stonehouse, 1987); Bill Manson's *Footsteps in Time: Exploring Hamilton's Heritage Neighbourhoods,* 2 vols. (Burlington: North Shore, 2003 and 2006) and other works; Margaret Houghton's various edited collections, including the Vanished Hamilton series (Burlington: North Shore Publishing, 2005, 2006, 2007, and 2012); and Bill Freeman and Marsha Hewitt, eds., *Their Town: The Mafia, the Media and the Party Machine* (Toronto: James Lorimer, 1979), which offers a fascinating glimpse into 1970s politics, activism, and journalism, including the scandal that engulfed the harbour commission. John Terpstra's poetic *Falling into Place* (Kentville, NS: Gaspereau Press, 2002) is in a class of its own, as Graeme Wynn points out in his foreword to this volume, with its gentle stories of discovery related to one geological feature, the Iroquois Bar, which includes the Burlington Heights.

There is one last popular treatment that we wish to mention: *The People and the Bay: The Story of Hamilton Harbour* (Hamilton: Department of History, McMaster University, 2007), a documentary film by Zach Melnick and Yvonne Drebert that takes viewers on a historical tour round the bay, which we co-wrote and co-hosted for distribution to schools and other educational institutions.

Index

Note: Figures and tables are indicated by italics.

Aboriginal peoples, xiv, 7, 8, 13
access. *See* public access
alcohol, 28, 129, 264*n*41
Aldershot, 96, 111. *See also* LaSalle Park
algal blooms, 175–76
Alinsky, Saul, 178, 276*n*21
amateurism, 28, 113. *See also* recreation
American Cyanamid Company, 143
amusement parks, 29, 34, 93, 95, 96, *158*, 159, 254*n*22, 254*n*30
Ancaster Creek, 19, 20
Anderson, Mary, 117
angling, 42–43, *43–44*, 102. *See also* sport fishing
annexation, 63, 91, 93, 146, 151, 158
Anstead, Christopher, 40
Aquafest, 208, 291*n*55
ArcelorMittal, 200. *See also* Dofasco (Dominion Foundries)
Armstrong, Christopher, 5
Ashworth, William: *The Late, Great Lakes*, 197–98, 218
automobiles, 116, 146, 157, *158*, 162. *See also* roads

Bal Harbour project, 274*n*3. *See also* Lax property
Balfour, St. Clair, Jr., 32
Barker, Samuel, 66
Barnes, Thomas H., 103
Barney, Robert, 36, 238*n*1
Barton Township, 63
Bartrip, Peter, 42
Bastien's boat works, 27, 111
Bay Area Restoration Council, 203–4, 288*n*34
Bay Front Improvement Committee, 246*n*31
Bay Street Beach, *100*, 101, 160–61, 163
Bayfront Park, 208, *209*. *See also* Lax property
Bayshore Village, 172, 174. *See also* Lax property
Bayview Park, 290*n*49
Bayview resort, 29
Beach Community Council, 193–94. *See also* Beach Strip
Beach Girls Friendly Society Holiday Home, 88

Beach Preservation Committee, 194
Beach Strip: Alfred Powis on, 93; amusement park at, 93, 95, *158*, 159, 254*n22*, 254*n30*; annexation of, 91–92, 158; attempted remediation of, 191–95; and automobiles, 157; Beach Community Council, 193–94; and Burlington Bay Skyway, 158–59, *159*; Burlington Beach Commission, 93–95, 157–58, 271*n50*; camping at, 31–32, 237*nn55*–56; changing social nature of, 92–93, 160; cottages built at, 92, 254*n21*; early history of, 13; in E.L. Cousins' plan, 115–16; elites' establishment in, 32, 33–34, 91–92, 95; end of recreation at, 156–57, 159–60; ethnic profiles, 281*n79*, 282*n84*; and fishery, 37–38, 47, 103, 105, 239*nn11*–12; Hamilton's control and involvement in, 30, 31, 32, 33, 34–35, 91, 93, 254*n24*; lack of urban services at, 91; occupational profiles, 281*n79*, 282*n84*; permanent population at, 157, 195; pollution near, 150; railway to, 30–31; as resort area, 28–29, 29–30, 32–33, *93*, 95; and Stelco/ Dofasco land swap, 184; streetcars to, 92; Sunday visitors to, 255*n31*
Beach Strip Fresh Air Camp, 88
beaches. *See* public beaches
Beasley, Henrietta and Richard, xi–xii
Beatty, Samuel, 108
Beckett, Thomas, 180, 185
beer. *See* alcohol
Bell, Patrick, 45
Bethune, Kenneth, 108
birding, 118, 119–22, 187, 216, 217, 260*n12*
Blackmar, Elizabeth, 6
boathouse community, *124*, *125*, 263*n32*; and Burlington Heights development plans, *132*, 133; children in, 126–28; city planners on, 123, 128, 130, 265*n65*; community life of, 125–26, 264*n41*; continuation of after eviction, 135, 266*n79*; development of, 123–24; eviction of, 133–35; fire risk in, 133, 266*n71*; and hoboes, 128–29; number of buildings in, 263*n32*, 266*n72*; residents of, 124–25, 263*n32*, 263*n36*; rough side to, 129

boathouses, North End, 89, 100, 101, 111, 128, 160, 182, 266*n71*
boating: boatbuilders, 24, 111, 160, 259*n78*, 266*n71*; British Empire Games, 111–12; and cormorants, 223; rowing, 26–28, 108–9, 112–13, 169, 170; sailing, 26, 107–8, 109, 110, 169, 170, 235*n35*; social standing of, 109–10; and working class, 27, 110–11. *See also* Burlington Bay Boat Club; Royal Hamilton Yacht Club
Bocking, Stephen, 232*n6*
Bogue, Margaret Beattie, 256*n50*
booze. *See* alcohol
Borgstrom, Carl, 130, 137
Boyer, Paul, 252*n4*
Brightside neighbourhood: development of, 82; ethnic profiles, 82, *84*, *155*; and Faludi's Master Plan, 153; map of, *83*; occupational profiles, *81*, *154*; and pollution cleanup, 84, 153; zoning changes to, 155–56
British Empire Games, 110, 112, 113, 131, 160, 163
Bulmer, Charles, 256*n45*
Burlington (city), 162, 185, 195, 214, 297*n106*. *See also* Aldershot
Burlington Bay. *See* Hamilton Harbour
Burlington Bay Boat Club, 27, 235*n36*
Burlington Bay Skyway, xii, 145, 158–59, *159*
Burlington bayfront neighbourhood: ethnic profiles, 281*n79*, 282*n84*; occupational profiles, 281*n79*, 282*n84*
Burlington Beach. *See* Beach Strip
Burlington Beach Commission, 93–95, 157–58, 271*n50*. *See also* Beach Strip
Burlington Beach Garden Pleasure Grounds, 30
Burlington Canal, 15, 34, 64–65, 66, 140, 145, 156, 157
Burlington Gazette (newspaper), 31
Burlington Heights, 13, 16, *17*, 128–29, 130–32, 132–35, 135–36. *See also* boathouse community
Burlington Steel Company, 246*n22*

Cahill, James, 3, 4, 232*n1*
"Camo": ode to Hamilton, 11–12

Campbell, Thomas, 31
Canada Centre for Inland Waters, *144*, 203
Canada Steel Company, 63, 246*n*22
Canadian Association of Amateur
 Oarsmen, 27
Canadian Industries Ltd., 140, 143, 200.
 See also Graselli Chemical Company
Canadian National Railway, 201, 285*n*18
Canadian Pacific Railway, 60, 244*n*8
canals: Burlington Canal, 15, 64–65, 140,
 156; Desjardins Canal, 15, 16, 123, *124*,
 169, 213, 264*n*43; St. Lawrence Seaway,
 145, 200; Welland Canal, 57, 61, 64, 65,
 139, 140
carp, 38, 101, 104, 168–69, 212–14, 218,
 257*n*54
Carroll's Point, 29, *126*, 127, 239*n*9
Cataract Power Company, 61
Cauchon, Noulan, 114, *115*, 117–18, 260*n*10
Centennial Docks project, 173
Charlton, Ben, 48
children: in boathouse community, 126–
 28; Elsinore built for, 253*n*7; in Junior
 Bird Club, 118; swimming in North
 End, 89, *90*, *99*, *100*; swimming pools
 campaign for, 163, 164, *165*; swimming
 programs for inner-city, 86–87, 88,
 252*n*1
CHOP (Clear Hamilton of Pollution):
 approach of, 178, *179*; and Cootes
 Paradise, 188–91, *189*, 279*n*61; creation
 of, 178; on Dundas treatment plant,
 279*n*65, 280*n*70; and land swap deal,
 184; membership of, 276*n*24, 277*n*25;
 social significance of, 277*n*28
Chow-Fraser, Patricia, 293*n*74
City Beautiful movement, 114, 117
civic boosterism: approach to, xviii, 8–9;
 for attracting industry, *56*, *59*, 60, 62–
 63, 67–68; challenges to, 84–85, 87; on
 drinking water, 58, 78; frontispiece for,
 59; goals of, 57, 68; *Hamilton, Canada:
 The City of Opportunity*, 68; *Hamilton:
 The Birmingham of Canada*, 55–57, *93*;
 and Hamilton's natural environment,
 57–59; and hydroelectric project, 61;
 and public health, 68–69; and sewage

disposal, 72, 79; and William Mullis,
 63, 68
Clarke, L.E., 167, 168
Clear Hamilton of Pollution. *See* CHOP
 (Clear Hamilton of Pollution)
Coal Oil Inlet, 73–74, 79, 82, 249*n*57,
 250*nn*63–64, 251*n*68. *See also* Sherman
 Inlet
cockfighting, 88, 101, 111
Cockpit Island, 129, 265*n*52
Commoner, Barry, 226
Confederation Park, 166–67, 191
conservation. *See* conservation authorities;
 environmental activism; environmental
 remediation; Hamilton Region Con-
 servation Authority. *See also under*
 Cootes Paradise (Dundas Marsh);
 Hamilton, plans for; *Hamilton
 Spectator*; Kerr, John William
conservation authorities, 180. *See also*
 Hamilton Region Conservation
 Authority
Conserver Society. *See* CHOP (Clear
 Hamilton of Pollution)
Consolidated Report on Burlington Bay
 (Matheson), 149–50
Cootes Paradise (Dundas Marsh): bird
 sanctuary at, 118–21, 122–23, 262*n*28;
 campaign against pollution, 188–91;
 cleaning up, *189*, *190*; Desjardins Canal
 through, 15, 16; early recreation in,
 44; environmental degradation of, 50,
 72, 76, 169, 212–13; fishing restrictions
 for, 39–40; John Kerr on conservation
 of, 42; jurisdiction over, 121; lessons
 learned from, 199, 293*n*74; and
 Midford's private duck farm, 121–22,
 261*n*24, 262*n*28; preservation of for
 recreation, 136, 169–70; restoration
 of, 212, 213–14, 292*n*69; transportation
 through, 13. *See also* boathouse
 community
Copps, Victor, 184
cormorants, 221–23, *223*–24, 298*n*7
Coronation Park, 166
cottages, 92, *93*, 156–57, 166, 192, 254*n*21
Cousins, E.L., 115–16

creeks: Ancaster, 19, 20; Grindstone, 294n78; Red Hill, 153, 198, 216, *217*, 295n89; Spencer (through Dundas), 50–51, 214, 243n72

Culture and Recreation Master Plan, 290n49

Dagenais, Michèle, 5

Davey, J.E., 161, 162, 167

Deering Harvesting Company, 63. *See also* International Harvester

"Denial" (Sokoloff), xix–xx, xxi

Desjardins Canal, 15, 16, 123, *124*, 264n43

disease: and city planning, 18, 19, 32; germ theory of, 71; and miasmic concerns, 18, 19, 69, 71; and swimming pools, 99; venereal, 128; water testing and, 69; and waterfront, 123. *See also* pollution; public health; sewage and sanitation system; water, drinking

Dofasco (Dominion Foundries): growth of, 142–43, 145, 147, 173; and Hamilton Region Conservation Authority, 185; and land swap, 184; and National Steel Car, 200; recent history of, 200; and sinking of Farr Island, 223

Dominion Tar and Chemical Company, 143

donkey baseball, 126, 264n41

Dr. Victor Cecilioni Award for Environmentalist of the Year, 283n7

Dundas (town), 50–51, 121, 188, 190. See also sewage and sanitation; Dundas treatment plant campaign.

Dundas Marsh. *See* boathouse community; Cootes Paradise

Dundurn Park, 97–98

Durand neighbourhood, 171

Dynes Hotel, 95

Eastwood, John Morrison, 72–73

Eastwood Park, 72–73, 101, 160, *161*, 163, 166

ecological politics, 195–96. *See also* environmental activism

ecoporn, 280n66

ecosystem approach, 201, 202, 286n20

electric street railway, 55, 92, 157

electricity generation, 61

elites, in Hamilton: on Beach Strip, 32, 33–34, 91–92, 95; and boating, 26, 108, 109; and fishery, 37, 51–52; homes of, 18, 56; importance of in shaping city, 28, 87, 227; and swimming, 87–88. *See also* working class

Elsinore, 253n7

entertainment. *See also* alcohol; donkey baseball; recreation

environment. *See* environmental activism; environmental remediation; Hamilton, and environment; pollution

Environment and Behavior (journal), 194

environmental activism: introduction to, xviii, 9; and 1974 conservation authorities' study, 186–87, 188; beginnings of, 178; Cootes Paradise campaign, 188–91; early advocating for, 79; educational programming, 203–4, 288n34; Hamilton groups for, 178–79; Lakeshore Citizens Council, 185–86; and Lax property, *175*, 179–80, 182–86, 188; and public access to harbour, 204–6, 209–11; reasons for, 195–96; Save Our Bay committee (SOB), 172, 180, 182, 186; *Ti Estin* (student newspaper), 178, *179*, 180, *181*. *See also* CHOP (Clear Hamilton of Pollution); environmental remediation; pollution; Simmons, Gillian

Environmental Protection Act (1971), 189–90

environmental remediation: introduction to, 10; artificial islands for, 209, *211*, 221, 222; challenges facing, 220, 289n38; Cootes Paradise, 213–14, 292n69; Hamilton ERASE Community Improvement Plan, 284n13; Hamilton Harbour Remedial Action Plan (HHRAP), 199–200, 202–4, *205*, 286n21, 287n25, 287n27, 294n82; LaSalle Park, 214–15; Lax property, 206–9; and public access, 210–12, 287n26; Randle Reef, 218–20, 297nn105–7; remedial action plans (RAPs), 198–200, 202, 204, 286n20; Waterfront Trail, 209–10, *210*,

211; Windermere Basin, 216–18, *217*, 296*n*95. *See also* environmental activism
environmentalism, postwar, 298*n*9
ethnic profiles, *84*, *155*, *281n79*, *282n84*
Evans, Kelly, 102–3, 105
Evenden, Matthew, 5
excursions, 29, 111

Falling into Place (Terpstra), xi–xvii, xx–xxi, 231*n*27
Faludi, Eugenio G., 152–54, 160, 269*nn*33–34
Farr Island, 221, 223–24
Federation of Anti-Pollution Groups, 178
Ferguson Avenue outlet, 23, 71, 72–73
Ferguson's Inlet, 23
Ferguson/Wellington neighbourhood: ethnic profile, *84*; occupational profile, *81*, 82
ferries, 24, 29, 97, 139, 173
Fifty Mile Point, 289*n*44
fire insurance maps, 67
Firestone Rubber and Tire Company, 67, 141, 200
First Nations. *See* Aboriginal peoples
Fisheries Act, 39, 41, 50, 242*n*56
fishery: introduction to, 8, 35; at Beach Strip, 37–38, 47, 103, 105, 239*nn*11–12; and carp, 38, 101, 104, 168–69, 212–14, 257*n*54; conflict over, 3–4, 37, 45–46, 51–53, 54, 102–5, 242*n*53, 242*n*59; and cormorants, 223; decline of, 36–37, 39, 53, 101; early history of, 37–38; enforcement of regulations, 256*n*50; and environmental and development changes, 38, 39, 101; legislation for, 39–40, 41, 106, 240*n*16, 242*n*56; and overfishing, 39; and pollution, 48–51, 54, 101, 105–6, 168–69; regulatory authority over, 102–3; "Report of the Ontario Game and Fish Commission," 242*n*50, 257*n*54; restocking of, 54, 106–7, 243*n*85; restoration of, 212–15, 294*n*83; and sinking of Farr Island, 223, 224; Sunday fishing, 3, 36, 255*n*31; winter fishing, 40, 242*n*49. *See also* fishing; Kerr, John William; spear fishing; sport fishing

fishing: angling, 42–43, 43–44, 102; by nets, 42, 47–48, 102, 104. *See also* spear fishing; sport fishing
fishing stations, 38
Flatt, W.D., 82, 84

Gagan, Rosemary, 251*n*68
Gage neighbourhood: ethnic profile, *155*; Faludi on, 153; occupational profile, *154*; zoning changes to, 155–56
Gage's Inlet, *62*, 76
gambling, 24, 26, 28, 43, 88, 89, 123, 129. *See also* cockfighting
garbage, 73, 74, 79, *177*, *190*. *See also* infilling; Lax property; pollution; sewage and sanitation system
Gibson, John, 255*n*31
Gordon, Ann, 277*n*28
Gore, Nasmith and Storrie: *Report on Sewage Disposal*, 75–77, 84, 251*n*78
Gould, Kenneth, 204
Grand Trunk Railway, 64, 97–98
Graselli Chemical Company, *62*, 67, *83*. *See also* Canadian Industries Ltd.
Great Depression, 78, 105, 109, 132–33, 140–41, 163
Great Lakes Water Quality Agreement, 198, 201, 283*n*6
Great Lakes Water Quality Board, 198
Great Western Railway, 16, 18, 26, 27, *43*, 66
Greening, Harold, 108
Grindstone Creek, 294*n*78

Halcrow, George, 98, 99
Halcrow, John, 250*n*63
Hall, John, 202, 223, 287*n*25
Hamilton: beginnings of, 7–8, 12–13, 15–16, 18–19; ethnic profiles, *84*, *155*, *281n79*, *282n84*; expansion of boundaries, 62, 63, 146, 151, 158; historical overview, xii–xiii; literature on, 5; maps of, *17*, *58*, *80*; occupational profiles, *81*, *154*, *281n79*, *282n84*; population growth, 15, 16, 18, 63–64, 146; as Steeltown, xiii, 142. *See also* civic boosterism; Hamilton, and environment; Hamilton, plans for;

Hamilton Board of Health; Hamilton Harbour; Parks Board

Hamilton, and environment: approach to, xvi–xix, xx–xxi, 5–7, 10, 228–29, 252n4; mid-Victorian era, xvii, 3–5, 8, 12–13, 35, 37, 225; early twentieth century, xvii, 8–9, 57–59, 87, 113, 225; 1930s to 1960s, xvii–xviii, 9, 116, 137, 139, 225–26; and environmental movement, xviii, 9–10, 172, 199–200, 226; challenges managing nature, 226–27. *See also* environmental activism; environmental remediation; industrialization, of Hamilton Harbour; pollution; recreation; sewage and sanitation system; water, drinking

Hamilton, Canada: The City of Opportunity (brochure), 68

Hamilton, George, xii

Hamilton, plans for: 1974 conservation authorities' study, 186–87, 188, 192–93; Burlington Heights plans, 130–32; Cootes Paradise as bird sanctuary, 118–19, 122–23; Culture and Recreation Master Plan, 290n49; E.L. Cousins', 115–16; Eugenio Faludi's Master Plan, 152–54, 154–56, 160, 269n34; Hamilton ERASE Community Improvement Plan, 284n13; Hamilton Harbour Remedial Action Plan, 202–4, 205, 286n21, 287n25, 287n27, 294n82; Noulan Cauchon's, 114, 115, 117–18, 153, 260n10; Sally Leppard consultation, 201–2, 286n21; for sewage, 71–72, 76–77, 151

Hamilton and Northwestern Railway, 30, 31

Hamilton and Toronto Radial Electric Railway, 55, 92, 157

Hamilton Angling and Casting Club, 103–4, 104–5, 105–7, 169, 257n54, 261n21

Hamilton Beach. *See* Beach Strip

Hamilton Bird Protection Society, 118, 261n21. *See also* Hamilton Naturalists Club

Hamilton Blast Furnace Company, 56, 60

Hamilton Board of Health, 23, 73, 74, 78, 123. *See also* public health; Roberts,

James; sewage and sanitation system; water, drinking

Hamilton By-Products Company, 62, 67, 140, 141, 147

Hamilton Committee for Continued Sound Administration, 164, 165, 272n73

Hamilton Gun Club, 118–20, 295n88

Hamilton Harbour (Burlington Bay): area of, 5, 232n2; constitutional status of, 247n33; current attractions, 291n58; early transportation in, 13, 15–16; economic activity through, 140–41, 145, 200, 267n5; on maps, 14, 58, 233n5; naming of, 57, 66, 247n34. *See also* Hamilton; Hamilton, and environment; Hamilton Harbour Commission; Hamilton Port Authority; industrialization, of Hamilton Harbour; pollution

Hamilton Harbour Advisory Committee, 287n26

Hamilton Harbour Commission: advertisements for harbour, 140, 141; and boathouse community, 130; conflict over waterfront redevelopment, 174; creation of, 66; and development of harbour, 66, 143, 145, 173; funding of, 143–44; and Hamilton Region Conservation Authority, 185; Harbourgate, 185; land swap arranged by, 184; and Lax property controversy, 182–83, 184; lost legitimacy of, 187; mandate of, 68, 115; "outer harbour" proposal, 285n16; and public beaches, 95–96, 166; recommendations for, 285n17. *See also* Hamilton Port Authority

Hamilton Harbour Remedial Action Plan (HHRAP), 199–200, 202–4, 205, 286n21, 287n25, 287n27, 294n82

Hamilton Herald (newspaper): on Beach Strip, 31; on boathouse community, 127, 128, 129–30; on Burlington Heights bridge, 135–36; on children swimming, 86, 89, 90; on spear fishing, 54; on William Mullis, 68

Hamilton Naturalists Club, 118, 189–90, 260n12

Hamilton Port Authority, 221. *See also* Hamilton Harbour Commission

Hamilton Region Conservation Authority, 180, 185, 186–87, 191, 192, 193, 194–95

Hamilton Rowing Club, 108–9

Hamilton Spearman's Association, 52–53

Hamilton Spectator (newspaper): on bird conservation, 222; on boathouse evictions, 134–35; on Cataract's DeCew Plant, 61; and drinking water development, 20; on failed Beach Strip annexation, 91–92; on fishing, 43–44; on garbage cleanup, 79; on Hamilton as Steeltown, xiii; on Hamilton Rowing Club, 109; on Lax property remediation, 206, 208; on Midford controversy, 122; on pollution, 151, 167, 168, 176, *177*; on sailing, 110; special issue on Hamilton, 138–39, 167; on summer recreation, 28; on swimming for children, *165*

Hamilton Steel and Iron Company, *56*, 60, 64, 65. *See also* Stelco (Steel Company of Canada)

Hamilton: The Birmingham of Canada, 55–57, *93*

Hamilton Times (newspaper), 63, 91

Hamilton Waterworks, 20, *21*, *22*, 22

Hanlan, Ned, 27

Harbourgate, 185

Hardy, Stephen, 6

Harvey, David, 195

Hays, Samuel P., 298*n*9

health, public, 68–69. *See also* Roberts, James; sewage and sanitation system; water, drinking

helicopters, 154

Henderson, Nora-Frances, 133, 164, 273*n*74

Heron, Craig, 261*n*15, 263*n*33, 273*n*74

HHRAP (Hamilton Harbour Remedial Action Plan), 199–200, 202–4, *205*, 286*n*21, 287*n*25, 287*n*27, 294*n*82

highways. *See* roads

HMCS *Star*, *161*. *See also* naval docks

hoboes, 128–29, 264*n*46

Hodgins, William, 19, 20, 23

holidays, 26, 30, 88, 92

Hornborg, Alf, 7

horse racing, 12, 24–26, *25*

housing, 18–19, 123, 130, 156–57, 192. *See also* boathouse community; cottages; Hamilton, plans for; zoning changes

hunting: in boathouse community, *120*, 128, 264*n*44; class connotations of, 42–43; and Cootes Paradise bird sanctuary, 118–20, 122–23; legislation for, 39, 123, 262*n*30; and working class, *120*

Hurley, Andrew, 6

Hutchinson, Leonard, *99*

hydroelectricity, 61

immigration, 63–64, 82

Inch Park, 166

industrialization, of Hamilton Harbour: approach to, 9; attracting industry, 60, 61–63, 68; changes to shoreline, 66, 101, 143, *144*, 285*n*15, 294*n*78; development of, 15–16, 18, 66–67, 139–41, 145, *146*, 173, 246*n*31; and Hamilton Harbour Commission, 66; and immigration, 63–64; loss of public space to, 88–89, 101; pollution from, 48–51, 78, 147–48; recent history of, 200–201; and St. Lawrence Seaway, 145, 173, 200; steel industry, *56*, 60–61, 142–43, 173, 200; transportation problems, 64–65; zoning changes for, 154–56. *See also* canals; Hamilton Harbour; infilling; railways

inequality, 18–19, 23, 79, 81–82, 84, 132–35, 153–56

infilling: environmental damage from, 101; and Hamilton Region Conservation Authority, 185; for industrial development, 66, 74, 145, *146*; Lax property, *175*, 180, 182–84, 188; material for, 234*n*11; new method for, 143; and pollution, 176–77, 180, *181*, 187, 197. *See also* industrialization, of Hamilton Harbour

inlets: Coal Oil, 73–74, 79, 82, 249*n*57, 250*nn*63–64, 251*n*68; Ferguson's, 23; Gage's, 76; Lottridge's, 74, *83*; Ogg's,

67; Sherman, *49*, 50, 219; Stipes, *62*, 78, *83*. *See also* infilling
International Harvester, 63, 64, 65, 66, 67, 74, 200
International Joint Commission, 179, 198–99, 201, 202
iron and steel industry, *56*, 60–61, *142*, 143, 173, 200. *See also* Dofasco; Stelco
Iroquois Bar, xi–xii, xiv–xv

Jockey Club, 68
Johnson, George Washington, xiii
Jolly Good Fellows Club, 111
Junior Bird Club, 118, 260*n*12
Jutten, Thomas, 77, 95, 108

Katz, Michael, 231*n*22, 232*n*4
Keefer, Thomas C., 20, 22
Ker, Frederick, 110, 259*n*77
Kerr, Charles John, 103–4, 105, 255*n*31, 256*n*50, 257*n*53
Kerr, Frederick, 52
Kerr, George, 183–84
Kerr, John William: approach to, 8; and angling, 41–42, 43, 44, 51–52; background of, 41; diaries of, 239*n*11; and fish restocking, 243*n*85; on fishery conservation, 4, 36, 54, 241*n*46; as fishery inspector, 37, 41–42, 44–45, 45–46, 242*n*53; and fishery restoration, 212; and John Smoke, 3, 221; and net fishing, 42, 47–48; and pollution, 48–51, 148; and remedial action plan, 199–200; and spear fishing, 36, 37, 44–45, 46–47; and Wentworth Society, 40
Kheraj, Sean, 6
Killan, Gerald, 162
Kirkpatrick, C.W., 247*n*34
Klingle, Matthew, 232*n*7
Krantzberg, Gail, 286*n*20
Kuichling, Emil, 71–72

LaFarge, 216. *See also* National Slag Company
Lake Yacht Racing Association, 108
Lakeland Pool, 166, 173
Lakeshore Citizens Council, 185–86

Landsdowne Park, 89
Landsdowne Park beach, 95–96, 97
Langs, Cecil Vanroy, 118, 130–31, 163, 272*n*71
LaSalle Park, *96*, 97, 110, 150, 161–62, 214–15, 271*n*60, 293*n*76
Late, Great Lakes (Ashworth), 197–98, 218
Laurier, Wilfrid, 59–60
Lautens, Gary, 267*n*1
Lautens, Trevor, 138–39, 167
Lawrence, Sam, 164
Lax property: Bayshore Village project, 172, 174, 274*n*3; Cees van Gemerden photos of, *207*, 283*n*2; cleanup costs, 197; contamination of, 197, 206, *207*; controversy over development, 174–75, *175*, 179–80, 186, 188; park for, 206–9, 289*n*44, 290*n*49, 290*n*51, 290*n*53; purchase of by city, 188, 197, 206; purchase of by Lax brothers, 172–73
Leander Rowing Club, 109, 110, 169, 170
Leander Rowing Club (original), 27, 28, 108
Leppard, Sally, 201–2, 286*n*21
Ley, A.G., 165
Lister, Herbert, 57–58
Local Council of Women, 88, 89–90
Long, Nelson, 119, 122, 261*n*14
Lottridge's Inlet, 74
Luria Brothers Company, 172–73, 174
Lyle, John, 130, 133

MacEachern, Alan, 5
MacKenzie, Susan Hill, 286*n*20
MacNab, Allan, 40
Malcolmson, Robert, 233*n*5
Marina Towers, 174
masculinity, 111, 121. *See also* alcohol; gambling
Matheson, D.H.: *Consolidated Report on Burlington Bay*, 149–50
McCann, Larry, 237*n*61
McDonald, Robert A.J., 6
McIlwraith, Thomas, 234*n*11
McKittrick Properties Company, 122
McMaster University, 162, 188, 260*n*11, 276*n*22. See also *Ti Estin* (student newspaper)

McNutt, R.H., 279*n*65
McQuesten, Calvin, 116, *119*
McQuesten, Mary Baker, 116–17
McQuesten, Thomas Baker: introduction
    to, 9, 113; background of, 116–17; and
    Burlington Heights development plan,
    130–31; and Cootes Paradise bird sanc-
    tuary, 122–23; financing strategy, 272*n*71;
    and Gillian Simmons, 204–5; involve-
    ment in city planning, 117–18, 137,
    260*n*11; involvement in provincial plan-
    ning, 136–37; personality of, 265*n*64;
    and remedial action plan, 199; vision of
    for city, 116, 136; and Waterfront Trail
    strategy, 211–12
memorial arena proposal, 163–64, 272*n*73
Merriman, Robert Owen, 118, 260*n*12
middle class, the: and angling, 41; and
    boathouse community, 129; and frater-
    nal organizations, 40; and recreation,
    24, 27, 28; and swimming, 87–88
Midford, George, 121–22, 261*n*24, 262*n*28
mills, cotton and textile, 39, 50, 51, 141
Milne, John, 60
Miner, Jack, *119*, 120–21, 261*n*18
Modjeska House Hotel, 101, 256*n*45
morality: and beautiful surroundings, 117;
    and boathouse community, 100, 128,
    130, 135; class-based nature of, 43; and
    recreation, 100, 120; and Sunday fishing,
    4. *See also* middle class; respectability
Moriarity, Michael, 280*n*70
Mullis, William, 63, 68
Municipal Swimming Baths, 110, 163,
    272*n*71
Murphy, "Pud," 100–1

National Slag Company, 143. *See also*
    LaFarge
National Steel Car, *67*, 145, 200
nature. *See* environmental activism;
    environmental remediation; Hamilton,
    and environment; pollution
Nautilus Club, 27–28, 108
naval docks, 138, 160, *161*
Neighbourhood Recreation Councils,
    165–66

Nelles, H.V., 5
net fishing, 42, 47–48, 102, 104
New Democratic Party (ON), 290*n*53
Niagara Escarpment: and Ancaster Creek,
    19; development of, 114, 136, 153, 171–
    72, 180; elite homes at foot of, 56;
    and hydroelectricity, 61; map of, *21*;
    and mill sites, 13; railway to, 55; and
    sewage system, 23, 57–58; and water-
    works, 20; Terpstra on, xiv
Niagara Parks System, 136
North End Improvement Society, 73
North End neighbourhood: Bayshore
    Village, 172, 174; establishment of,
    18; ethnic profiles, *84*, 281*n*79, 282*n*84;
    in Faludi's Master Plan, 153, 160; occu-
    pational profiles, *81*, 281*n*79, 282*n*84;
    pollution near, 72–73; renewal of,
    173–74; swimming at, 89, 97
Nunn, Henry, 260*n*12

Oaklands, 28, 29. *See also* LaSalle
    Park
occupational profiles, *81*, *154*, 281*n*79,
    282n84
Ocean House, 33, 91, 237*n*66
O'Connor, Kristin, 202, 287*n*25
Ogg, Charles, 249*n*57
Ogg's Inlet, *67*
oil refineries, 48–50, 51
Oliver Chilled Plow Company, 66, 67,
    74, 252*n*87
Oliver neighbourhood: ethnic profiles,
    84, *155*; occupational profiles, *81*, *154*;
    zoning changes to, 155–56
Ontario Federation of Anglers, 105
Ontario Hydro, 156, 270*n*42
Ontario Municipal Board, 151
Ontario Public Interest Research Group,
    276*n*22
Ontario Rolling Mills, *56*, 60
Ontario Water Resources Commission
    (OWRC), 151, 175, 176–77
Otis-Fenson Elevator Company, 89, 95
overfishing, 39
OWRC (Ontario Water Resources
    Commission), 151, 175, 176–77

Parkdale neighbourhood, 166
parks. *See* Parks Board; public parks;
   amusement parks.
Parks Board: introduction to, 118; and
   Burlington Heights development, 130–
   32; and Cootes Paradise bird sanctuary,
   122, 123; memorial arena proposal, 163–
   64, 272*n*73; and waterfront recreation,
   156
Peaceful Parks Coalition, 221
Pearce, Bobby, 112–13, 259*n*84, 259*n*86
Penny, Harry, 107, 259*n*77
picnicking, 29, 87, 88, 96, 111, 126, 169
Pier 4 Park, 208–9, 290*n*49, 291*n*57
Pier 4 Pub and Grub, 256*n*45
planning. *See* Hamilton, plans for;
   McQuesten, Thomas Baker; Parks
   Board
Platt, Harold, 232*n*7
police, 90, 111, 129
pollution: acceptance of, 139, 151–52; and
   algal blooms, 175–76; bacteria counts,
   148, 150; and drinking water, 75, 78,
   148–49, 251*n*74; editorials on, 167–68,
   176, *177*; and fishery, 48–51, 54, 101,
   105–6, 168–69; and Great Lakes Water
   Quality Agreement, 201; Hamilton's
   approach to, 151, 198, 275*n*14; and infilling, 176–77, 180, *181*, 187, 197; James
   Roberts on, 252*n*86; *The Late, Great
   Lakes* (Ashworth), 197–98; neighbourhoods impacted of, 81–82; sources of,
   78, 99, 147–48; from Stelco, *148*; studies
   on, 176, 187; and swimming, 99; and
   water currents, 72, 271*n*59. *See also*
   environmental activism; environmental
   remediation; sewage and sanitation
   system
population growth, 15, 16, 18, 63–64, 146
positive environmentalism, 252*n*4
postwar environmentalism, 298*n*9
Post-War Recreation Department, 272*n*68
Powell, William, 185
Powis, Alfred, 93
Princess Point neighbourhood: ethnic
   profiles, *281n79*, *282n84*; occupational
   profiles, *281n79*, *282n84*

Procter and Gamble, 64, 141, 200
Provincial Board of Health, 73–74, 78
public access, 204–6, 209–11, 287*n*26,
   289*n*43
public beaches, 89–91, 95–98, 99–101,
   160–62, 166
public health, 68–69. *See also* Roberts,
   James; sewage and sanitation system;
   water, drinking
public parks: approach to, 6; Bayfront
   Park, 208; Bayview Park, 290*n*49;
   Confederation Park, 166–67, 191;
   Cootes Paradise bird sanctuary, 118–21,
   122–23, 262*n*28; Coronation Park, 166;
   Dundurn Park, 97–98; Eastwood Park,
   160, *161*, 163, 166; Inch Park, 166;
   Landsdowne Park, 89; Landsdowne
   Park beach, 95–96, 97; LaSalle Park,
   96–97, 110, 150, 161–62, 214–15, 271*n*60,
   293*n*76; Pier 4 Park, 208–9, 290*n*49,
   291*n*57; post-WWII, 162; and settlement displacements, 228. *See also* Beach
   Strip; Parks Board; public beaches

Quart, Gary, 276*n*21
Queen Elizabeth Way, xii, 136

rail yards, 16, *43*, 72, 97–98, 209, 285*n*18
railways: and Beach Strip, 30–31;
   Canadian National Railway, 201,
   285*n*18; Canadian Pacific Railway, 60,
   244*n*8; development of, 16, 18; Grand
   Trunk Railway, 64, 97–98; Great
   Western Railway, 16, 18, 26, 27, *43*, 66;
   Hamilton and Northwestern Railway,
   30, 31; Hamilton and Toronto Radial
   Electric Railway, 55, 92, 157
Randle Reef, 218–20, 296*n*98, 297*nn*105–7
RAP Forum, 204, 288*n*36
RAPs (remedial action plans), 198–200,
   202, 204, 286*n*20. *See also* environmental
   remediation; HHRAP (Hamilton
   Harbour Remedial Action Plan)
Rawson, Michael, 232*n*7
Reade, R.C., 131, *132*
recreation: approach to, xviii, 6, 9, 227;
   class tensions over, 25–26, 28; and

competition from industry, 89, 156;
Culture and Recreation Master Plan,
290n49; in development plans, 23–24,
114–16; in Hamilton Harbour Remedial
Action Plan, 203; memorial arena proposed, 163–64, 272n73; motivation
for, 24, 87, 101, 107; Neighbourhood
Recreation Councils, 165–66; permanent recreation council, 164–66; Post-
War Recreation Department, 272n68;
private resorts for, 28–29, 30; Wartime
Recreation Council, 163–64. *See also*
amateurism; amusement parks; angling;
Beach Strip; boating; British Empire
Games; children; gambling; horse
racing; hunting; picnicing; public
beaches; public parks; sport fishing;
swimming; swimming pools
Red Hill Creek, 198, *217*, 295n89
reform. *See* environmental activism;
morality; positive environmentalism;
recreation; sewage and sanitation
system; water, drinking
Regional Municipality of Hamilton-
Wentworth, 189–90
remedial action plans (RAPs), 198–200,
202, 204, 286n20. *See also* environmental
remediation; Hamilton Harbour
Remedial Action Plan
"Report of the Ontario Game and Fish
Commission," 102, 242n50, 257n54
Report on Sewage Disposal (Gore, Nasmith
and Storrie), 76–77, 84, 251n78
resorts, private, 28–29, 30, 33
respectability, 8, 24, 25, 39, 43–44, 88
retrospective method, xv
RHYC. *See* Royal Hamilton Yacht Club
roads: and Beach Strip, *58*, 157, *159*;
Burlington Bay Skyway, xii, 145, 158–59,
159; oil and gas runoff from, 75, 99, 101,
147–48; Queen Elizabeth Way, xii, 136.
See also automobiles
Roberts, James: appointment as medical
officer of health, 69; on Bay Street Beach
water quality, 160–61; and Coal Oil
Inlet pollution, 72, 73, 251n68; on pollution, 77, 251n74, 251n81, 252n86; and

sewage system, 70–71, 74–75, 79, 81;
and water system, 69–70, 77, 79, 251n74
Rock Bay resort, 29
Rosenzweig, Roy, 6
round gobies, 222–23
rowing, 26–28, 108–9, 112–13, 169, 170
Royal Botanical Gardens, 133, 137, 169–70,
203, 212–13, 260n11
Royal Hamilton Yacht Club (RHYC): in
1950s, 169, 170; club house, 33–34, 93,
94, 109, 169; founding of, 26; and harbour's industrialization, 169; LaSalle
Park proposal, 110; membership, 107–8,
169; membership fees, 258n69; "royal"
in name of, 238n68; and swimming, 88;
during WWI and Depression, 109

Sabbath, 3, 36, 46
Safdie, Moshe, 172
sailing, 26, 107–8, 109, 110, 169, 170,
235n35. *See also* Royal Hamilton Yacht
Club
Saltfleet Township, 30, 91
Sanford, William, 253n7
sanitation. *See* sewage and sanitation
system
Save Our Bay (SOB) committee, 172, 180,
182, 186. *See also* Simmons, Gillian
sequent occupance, xv
sewage and sanitation system: introduction
to, xviii, 226; access to, 74–75, 251n72;
and civic boosterism, 79; Coal Oil Inlet
issue, 73–74, 79; *Consolidated Report on
Burlington Bay* (Matheson), 149–50;
Dundas treatment plant campaign,
188–91, 279n65, 280n68, 280n70; early
development of, 19, 22–23, 35; Emil
Kuichling's plan for, 71; Ferguson
Avenue issue, 72–73; and Great Lakes
Water Quality Agreement, 201; Hamilton's response to, 70–72, 78–79, 84,
151–52, 162; levels of treatment, 279n58;
Report on Sewage Disposal (Gore,
Nasmith and Storrie), 75–77, 84, 251n78;
Stelco study on, 149; *Water Pollution
Survey* (OWRC), 176–77. *See also* pol-
lution; Roberts, James

Sherman, Frank, 143

Sherman Inlet, *49*, 50, 219. *See also* Coal Oil Inlet

Sherman (Coal Oil) Inlet neighbourhood: ethnic profiles, *84*, *155*; occupational profiles, *81*, *154*; zoning changes to, 155–56

Sherring (alderman), 133

shipping and navigation: in civic booster-ism, 64; development of, 15, 60, 65, 140, 142–43, 156; and dispute over waterfront use, 87; and Hamilton Harbour Commission, 173; on map, *115*; and St. Lawrence Seaway, 145. *See also* canals; industrialization, of Hamilton Harbour

Shivas, Marion S., 280n66

Short, Martin, 205

Simcoe, Elizabeth, xi–xii, 37

Simcoe, John Graves, xi–xii

Simmons, Gillian: introduction to, 9; and Beach Strip redevelopment, 194; and Cootes Paradise campaign, 188–89; and Lakeshore Citizens Council, 185; and Lax property, 184, 290n51; on pollution, 291n62; and public access, *183*, 204–6; reason for living in North End, 171; reasons for activism, 171–72, 195–96; and remedial action plans, 199, 204; and Save Our Bay committee, 180, 182. *See also* environmental activism; en-vironmental remediation; Lax property; Save Our Bay (SOB) committee

Simmons, Robert, 171

slag, 84, 106, 143, 200, 216

Smoke, John, 3–4, 6, 7, 221

Snider, Judith A., 221–22, 223

SOB (Save Our Bay) committee, 172, 180, 182, 186. *See also* Simmons, Gillian

Social Gospel movement, 117

Sokoloff, Carol Ann: "Denial," xix–xx, xxi

Southam, Willie, 32

spear fishing: conflict over, 3–4, 45–46, 52, *53*, 54, 102, 104–5, 242n59; John Kerr on, 4, 37, 46–47; legality of, 36, 39, 46; origins of, 7, 45; technique, 45

spectatorship, 24, 26, 28

Spencer Creek, 214, 243n72

sport fishing, 43–44, 52, 101–2, 103, 104. *See also* angling

sports. *See* recreation

Sproule-Jones, Mark, 202, 224, 247n33, 289n38

St. Lawrence Seaway, 145, 173, 200

steel and iron industry, *56*, 60–61, *142*, 143, 173, 200. *See also* Dofasco; Stelco

Steel Company of Canada. *See* Stelco

Steele, Robert T., 108

Stelco (Steel Company of Canada): and Brightside, *83*, 153; expansion of, *142*, 143, 173; formation of, *56*, 60–61; and Hamilton Region Conservation Authority, 185; infilling by, 74, 145, 153; and land swap, 184; pollution from, 147, *148*; and Randle Reef, 219; recent history of, 200, 285n15; report by on sewage, 149; and slag, 106, 143

Stewart, Thomas J., 66, 121, 122, 261n24

Stilgoe, John R., 32, 237n61

Stipes Inlet, *62*, 78, *83*

streetcars. *See* electric street railway

Sunday. *See* Sabbath

swans, trumpeter, 215, 294n85

swimming, 26, 86–87, *87*–89, 98–99, 113, 167. *See also* public beaches

swimming pools, 98, 99, 110, 162–64, 166, 272nn66–67

Syme, J.J., 163

tariff revisions, 60

Taylor, John, 232n1

Taylor, Joseph, 39

Terpstra, John: *Falling into Place*, xi, xii, xiii–xvi, xvii, xx–xxi, 231n27

textile mills, 39, 50, 51, 141

thermonuclear plant, 156, 270n42

Thomasen, Sarah, 293n74

Thompson, George, 30

Ti Estin (student newspaper), 178, *179*, 180, *181*

Tilden, John, 60

Toronto, xix

Toronto Star Weekly (newspaper), 131, *132*
town planning, xviii, 9. *See also* Hamilton,
  plans for; McQuesten, Thomas Baker;
  Parks Board
Town Planning Consultants, 152. *See also*
  Faludi, Eugenio G.
Trades and Labour Council, 99–100, 121,
  133, 168
transportation, 13, *58*, 291*n*63. *See also*
  automobiles; canals; electric street
  railway; helicopters; roads; railways
Trudeau, Pierre Elliott, 179
trumpeter swans, 294*n*85
Turkstra, Herman, 185
Tye, William, 117

unions, 29, 146, 152
urban boosterism. *See* civic boosterism
urban parks. *See* public parks
urban planning, xviii, 9. *See also* Hamilton,
  plans for; McQuesten, Thomas Baker;
  Parks Board
US Steel Canada, *56*, 200. *See also* Stelco
  (Steel Company of Canada)

Valastro, AnnaMaria, 221, 223–24
van Gemerden, Cees, *207*, 283*n*2
vehicles. *See* automobiles
Victoria (steamer), 30
Victoria Park Community Organization,
  180
Victoria Yacht Club, 108, 109
voluntary associations, 29, 40, 88

Wabasso Park, 96–97. *See also* LaSalle
  Park
Wagner, Phil, xvi
Wakefield, Sarah, 291*n*54
Wamsley, Kevin, 39
Wartime Recreation Council, 163
Wasaga Beach, 162
water, drinking: approach to, 226–27;
  civic boosters on, *58*, 78; development
  of, 19–20, *21*, 22, 69–70, 77, 78; and
  pollution, 75, 78, 148–49, 251*n*74
Water Pollution Survey (OWRC), 176–77
Waterfront Trail, 209, *210*, *211*

waterlots, 16, 60, 64, 66, 142–43, 145, 153,
  171–75, 177, 182, 184, 234*n*11, 262*n*29,
  270*n*77
Weaver, John, 67, 251*n*72
Welland Canal, 57, 61, 64, 65, 139, 140
Wentworth Fish and Game Protection
  Society, 51–52, 243*n*78
Wentworth Society for the Protection of
  Game and Fish, 40–41, 46, 240*n*25
Westdale Kiwanis Club, 169
Westdale neighbourhood: ethnic profiles,
  281n79, *282n84*; occupational profiles,
  281n79, *282n84*
Westinghouse Company, 63, 64
Whittlesey, Derwent, xv
Williams, James, 30, 49–50
Wilmot, Samuel, 53, 54, 243*n*85
Windermere Basin, 215–18, *217*, 295*n*91,
  295*nn*88–89, 296*n*95
Wingfield, Marg, 277*n*28
Wires, Linda R., 298*n*7
Withers, Ken "Breezy," 256*n*45
women's organizations, 88, 89–90, 99
Wood, Andrew Trew, 60
working-class, the: in Beach Strip, 160,
  193–95; and boating, 27, 110-11and carp,
  212; and Cootes Paradise controversy,
  122; and effects of pollution, 23, 82,
  227–28; and LaSalle Park, 97; and recreation, 28, 43; and sewage system, 74,
  79; and spear fishing, 46, 105; swimming for children, 86–87, 89, *90*, 98;
  zoning changes effect on, 155–56. *See
  also* boathouse community; elites, in
  Hamilton; inequality
Worster, Donald, 5
Wright, "Boss" Alf, 98

yachting. *See* Royal Hamilton Yacht Club;
  sailing
YMCA (Young Men's Christian
  Association), 89, 97
YWCA (Young Women's Christian
  Association), 88

Zealand, Edward, 26
zoning changes, 154–56, 160, 270*n*41

NATURE | HISTORY | SOCIETY
GENERAL EDITOR: GRAEME WYNN

Claire Elizabeth Campbell, *Shaped by the West Wind: Nature and History in Georgian Bay*

Tina Loo, *States of Nature: Conserving Canada's Wildlife in the Twentieth Century*

Jamie Benidickson, *The Culture of Flushing: A Social and Legal History of Sewage*

William J. Turkel, *The Archive of Place: Unearthing the Pasts of the Chilcotin Plateau*

John Sandlos, *Hunters at the Margin: Native People and Wildlife Conservation in the Northwest Territories*

James Murton, *Creating a Modern Countryside: Liberalism and Land Resettlement in British Columbia*

Greg Gillespie, *Hunting for Empire: Narratives of Sport in Rupert's Land, 1840–70*

Stephen J. Pyne, *Awful Splendour: A Fire History of Canada*

Hans M. Carlson, *Home Is the Hunter: The James Bay Cree and Their Land*

Liza Piper, *The Industrial Transformation of Subarctic Canada*

Sharon Wall, *The Nurture of Nature: Childhood, Antimodernism, and Ontario Summer Camps, 1920–55*

Joy Parr, *Sensing Changes: Technologies, Environments, and the Everyday, 1953–2003*

Jamie Linton, *What Is Water? The History of a Modern Abstraction*

Dean Bavington, *Managed Annihilation: An Unnatural History of the Newfoundland Cod Collapse*

Shannon Stunden Bower, *Wet Prairie: People, Land, and Water in Agricultural Manitoba*

J. Keri Cronin, *Manufacturing National Park Nature: Photography, Ecology, and the Wilderness Industry of Jasper*

Jocelyn Thorpe, *Temagami's Tangled Wild: Race, Gender, and the Making of Canadian Nature*

Darcy Ingram, *Wildlife, Conservation, and Conflict in Quebec, 1840–1914*

Caroline Desbiens, *Power from the North: Territory, Identity, and the Culture of Hydroelectricity in Quebec*

Sean Kheraj, *Inventing Stanley Park: An Environmental History*

Justin Page, *Tracking the Great Bear: How Environmentalists Recreated British Columbia's Coastal Rainforest*

Daniel Macfarlane, *Negotiating a River: Canada, the US, and the Creation of the St. Lawrence Seaway*

Ryan O'Connor, *The First Green Wave: Pollution Probe and the Origins of Environmental Activism in Ontario*

John Thistle, *Resettling the Range: Animals, Ecologies, and Human Communities in British Columbia*

Carly A. Dokis, *Where the Rivers Meet: Pipelines, Participatory Resource Management, and Aboriginal-State Relations in the Northwest Territories*

Printed and bound in Canada by Friesens

Set in Garamond by Artegraphica Design Co. Ltd.

Copy editor: Deborah Kerr

Indexer: Stephen Ullstrom

Cartographer: Rajiv Rawat